The Renaissance

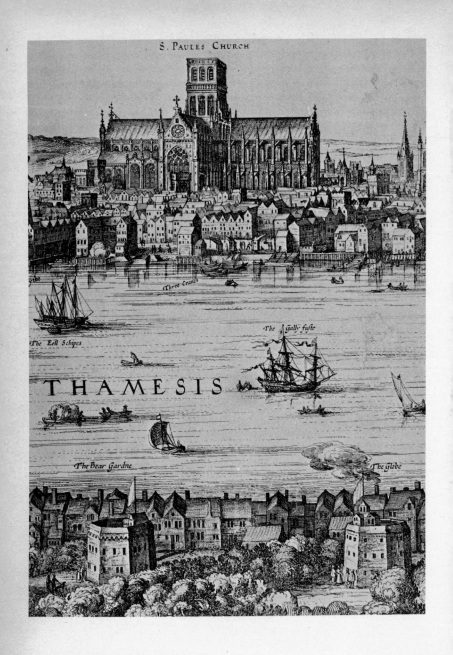

The Globe and the Bear Garden on Bankside, London.
From the engraving by J. C. Visscher, *c.*1616.
Guildhall Library, London

MASTERWORKS OF WORLD DRAMA

THE
RENAISSANCE

Anthony Caputi

CORNELL UNIVERSITY

D. C. HEATH AND COMPANY

Acknowledgments

FUENTE OVEJUNA by Lope Felix de Vega Carpio and translated by
Roy Campbell. Reprinted from Eric Bentley's *The Classic Theatre*,
Volume Three, Doubleday Anchor Books. Copyright © 1959 by
Eric Bentley. Printed by permission of Eric Bentley.

LIFE IS A DREAM by Pedro Calderon de la Barca and translated by
D. F. MacCarthy. From *The Chief European Dramatists* edited by
Brander Matthews, by permission of Houghton Mifflin Company.

THE MANDRAKE by Niccolo Machiavelli. Reprinted from Eric Bentley's *The Classic Theatre*, Volume One, Doubleday Anchor Books
copyright © 1958 by Frederick May and Eric Bentley.

*Grateful acknowledgment is made for indispensable help in obtaining
illustrations.*
—to MISS HELEN D. WILLARD, *Curator of the Harvard Theatre Collection, and her staff.*
—to PROFESSOR A. M. NAGLER *of Yale University, who made available pictures from his own collection and from his book,* A Source Book
in Theatrical History.

The drawings on pages 36, 49, and 350–351 are by PETER KAHN,
Cornell University.

Copyright © 1968 by Raytheon Education Company

Library of Congress Catalog Card number 68-15400

CONTENTS

THE DRAMA OF *the Renaissance*   ix
   introductory essay

Niccolo Machiavelli
   THE MANDRAKE   3
   translated by Frederick May and Eric Bentley

Angelo Beolco
   BILORA   38
   translated by Anthony Caputi

Anonymous
   THE SCENARIO OF THE IMPOSTER PRINCE   50
   translated by Anthony Caputi

Christopher Marlowe
   THE TRAGICAL HISTORY OF DOCTOR FAUSTUS 58

Ben Jonson
   VOLPONE   97

John Webster
   THE TRAGEDY OF THE DUCHESS OF MALFI   199

Francis Beaumont and John Fletcher
    THE KNIGHT OF THE BURNING PESTLE   283

Lope Felix de Vega Carpio
    FUENTE OVEJUNA   352
       translated by Roy Campbell

The Renaissance

Pantalone, the Magnifico of the *commedia dell'arte,* fleeing from
a Pulcinella. Probably a 16th-century drawing. *Photo Giraudon*

THE DRAMA OF
the Renaissance

RENAISSANCE DRAMA IN ITALY   In Italy the ferment of forces that produced the Renaissance also produced a drama of great importance and merit, though unfortunately one inferior to Italy's accomplishment in painting and sculpture. Confused and complex even in its early stages, the story of Italian Renaissance drama traces to a wide variety of sources. Like other European countries, Italy too had seen the birth of a new drama in the Church. Moreover, Italy had a rich popular tradition that, even though dim for want of records from the Middle Ages, was clearly vigorous enough in the Renaissance to have provided the major focus for dramatic activity, including, very frequently, the occasions on which religious plays were produced.

Religious drama in Italy had developed in the medieval church much as it had in other countries: over a considerable period liturgical playlets were written for the principal religious feasts and performed in the churches by clergymen. In Italy, however, these playlets were never worked into cycles of plays, and they remained the property of religious communities, even though some laymen are known to have performed in certain elaborate ones. Perhaps because the liturgical tropes remained essentially learned works, a second form of religious play called the *Lauda* was developed by the laity. The *Laude* were the work of secular confraternities of penitents, who performed them on religious holidays as one of their religious exercises. In the vernacular, they dramatized episodes from the Bible in a form distinctly allegorical and lyrical, and they were produced in the church and on platforms at fixed stations under the same conditions used for liturgical tropes. Best known in Perugia, Orvieto, and Florence, they were sufficiently numerous in the second half of the thirteenth and the early fourteenth centuries to have been compiled in anthologies and circulated, and sufficiently successful from a literary point of view for non-dramatic writers to have adopted the form. From the *Laude* the *Sacre Rappresentazioni* then evolved to flourish in the fourteenth and fifteenth centuries in central Italy. The *Sacra Rappresentazione* was actually a rather loose name for all the religious plays that followed the *Laude;* essentially a more complex *Lauda* both dramatically and musically, it reached its highest development in Florence in the second half of the fifteenth century, particularly in the hands of Feo Belcari (1410–1484), whose *Abraham and Isaac* was often performed and reprinted. Though the *Sacre Rappresentazioni* were nominally religious plays, their piety was generally overshadowed by their technical and literary interest, and, in fact, they were as often performed at carnival and private celebrations as on religious occasions. Certain especially lavish productions of these plays provided the first examples of the new art of scene-design in which Italy was soon to show the way.

This mixed and rather learned religious tradition persisted to the end of the sixteenth century in Italy, when it finally yielded to the secular tradition that had vied with it throughout its history and that had preceded it by many centuries. Popular drama in Italy, like that in other European countries, is in large part lost in a profusion of activities and performers of which we have too little precise evidence. We know something of the minstrel-like performers called *guillari* and of the mimes, *contrasti*, and partially dramatic dances with which they filled out their repertories, but we do not know enough to hazard more than a speculation that they kept certain features of Roman dramatic entertainments alive and spread the knowledge of certain native popular forms. Far more evidence exists of the vigorous carnival tradition that flourished in Italy and that clearly provided the impetus and materials for much of the dramatic activity during the Middle Ages and the Renaissance. The traditional carnival tradition was a kind of seasonal celebration with ritual stories and activities that was early adapted, if only partially, to Christian occasions at the New Year, May Day, and especially at Lent. These festivities provided the principal focus for folk plays and local farces, as well as for the expensive triumphs and processions supported by noble families. It is among these forms that many of the materials and characters of later Italian comedy are first to be met, and the occasion of carnival persisted through the entire Renaissance as the chief occasion for the production of plays in Italy.

Despite its vitality and the depth of its traditions, perhaps the most remarkable fact about Italian drama during this period is that it did not produce a structured professional theater, except for the *commedia dell'arte,* which will be taken up presently; instead, it continued to be an adventitious institution throughout the Renaissance. Many plays were written—sometimes merely to be read, sometimes to be produced; but no public theaters were founded, and plays were produced only at the instigation of individuals or special groups. Yet altogether there was a great deal of activity. Plays were frequently performed at weddings, private feasts, and carnival celebrations; private dramatic societies like the Company of the Rozzi in Siena were to be found in most major cities; and certain noble houses became famous for the sumptuousness of their dramatic presentations. Gradually, a considerable dramatic literature accumulated, if always against the background of an insubstantial theatrical world.

Part of the explanation for this situation lies in the fact that most playwrights in Italy were amateurs—dilettantes or scholars, men of learning who, having proved themselves in other forms, turned to the drama for no better reason than that it had been a major genre in antiquity. The writers of comedies in Latin, for example, were far more interested in scholarly work in classical languages and literature than in the theatrical world in Renaissance Italy. Spurred by the interest in classical manuscripts and by such events as the Aldine editions of Sophocles in 1502, Euripides in 1503, and Aeschylus in 1518, they quite understandably attempted imitations, particularly of Plautus and Terence in comedy and of Seneca in tragedy. Petrarch had written a Terentian comedy entitled *Philologia* and destroyed it, but others were more content with their efforts: to name a few, Pier Paulo Vergilio wrote a very early comedy on student life in Bologna called *Paulus* (*c.*1390); Enea Silvio Piccolomini (Pope Pius II) wrote a verse comedy in 1444 entitled *Chrysis;* and Thomas Medius, who was perhaps the best of the playwrights in Latin, wrote his *Epirota* by 1483. Historically, these plays are very important because, though they owed much to the Romans, they unmistakably reflect a blend of classical features with those of religious and popular drama. These playwrights seemed entirely aware that they were doing something new, as evidenced by their many references to the "new manner" and the *"nova comoedia."* It was but a short step from this work to the so-called Learned Comedy in the vernacular that began to appear in great quantity in the first quarter of the sixteenth century.

The writing of tragedy traces much the same pattern. Albertino Mussato (1261–1329) had written his Latin tragedy *L'Ecerinis* in about 1315, modelled on Seneca but loose and medieval in structure. In the early sixteenth century he was followed by Giorgio Trissino (1478–1550), who self-consciously wrote his *Sofonisba* (*c.*1515) as a classical tragedy in Italian, holding fairly faithfully to the Aristotelian "unities" of time and action, if not of place. Stiff and cold though Trissino's work appears now, it was highly esteemed in its time, often reprinted, and often imitated. Giovanni Rucellai (1475–1525) produced his *Rosamunda* in about 1515, and about 1520, *Orestes,* which has been called a "sugary paraphrase" of Euripides' *Iphigenia in Taurus.* Shortly afterward, Lodovico Martelli (1503–*c.*1531) drew particulars from a number of Greek plays for his *Tullia* (*c.*1530). After Trissino, however, perhaps the most important writer of tragedy was Lodovico Dolce (1508–1568), who, in addition to adapting a number of Greek tragedies in Italian versions, wrote a number of original tragedies in the "classical" style, as well as numerous comedies. But the writing of tragedy in Renaissance Italy seems to have been largely a literary tradition. Although we do have some notices of the productions of tragedies, like the presentation of Dolce's *Mariana* in the ducal palace in Ferrara in 1565, the writing of tragedy certainly was less oriented to production than was the writing of comedy.

The story of what has come to be known as Learned Comedy is considerably different: Learned Comedies were far more numerous than tragedies, and many more of them were written to be performed. Although most of the writers of comedy in the vernacular followed the lead of the humanist writers of comedy in Latin by borrowing from Plautus and Terence, they also derived much of their material from popular comedy and from sources like the short stories and short novels loosely called *novelle*–so much so that these highly vivacious, highly contemporary comedies seem to have very little in common with the word "Learned," except to distinguish this vein of comic writing superficially from popular farce. Yet these playwrights, too, were largely men of learning, men who, having distinguished themselves in some other field, turned to drama as to a cultural diversion. Bernardo Dovizi (1470–1520), the Cardinal Bibbiena, wrote one of the earliest and most successful in his *La Calandria,* which was produced at carnival in 1513 at the Court of Urbino on a sumptuous stage designed by Girolamo Genga. He was followed by such litterateurs as Ludovico Ariosto (1474–1532), who wrote five comedies, most of which were performed at the ducal palace in Ferrara, and Pietro Aretino (1492–1554), who wrote six plays, including a tragedy. Niccolò Machiavelli (1469–1527), meantime, took time off from his political writings to complete *The Mandrake* (*c.*1515) and the *Clizia* (*c.*1524). *The Mandrake* is probably the most famous play of the period and certainly one of the most successful. By mid-century work was appearing on all sides; among the most effective writers were Annibale Caro (1507–1566), Giovanni Maria Cecchi (1518–1587), and Giambattista Della Porta (1535–1615), all of whom continued to work lively variations on Plautine plots of deception and mistaken identity, filled out with elements from popular farce and the contemporary scene.

Italy's accomplishment in Learned Comedy undoubtedly constitutes its main contribution in the Renaissance to western dramatic literature, though it does not exhaust the list of important and influential forms cultivated during this period. Closely related to Learned Comedy was that unwieldy group of comedies known as popular farce. Much of this work was rather primitive and written in dialect, but some of it attained a high decree of artistic achievement that persists even today in certain dialect traditions in Italy. The most successful writer in this vein was Angelo Beolco (1502–1542), known as Ruzzante after his most famous character. Writing for the most part in the Padovan dialect, Beolco produced and himself performed a series of short, pungent farces of remarkable originality, including *Ruzzante Returns From the Wars* and *Bilora* (both *c.*1528).

Meanwhile, other dramatic activity in the late sixteenth century was exerting considerable influence on the development of the theater and on international Renaissance literature. Related to the sentimental variations on Learned Comedy that began to appear in the second half of the century was the pastoral drama that culminated in Torquato Tasso's *Aminta* (1573) and Battista Guarini's *The Faithful Shepherd* (1585). Finally, somewhat apart from drama proper, the first experiments in opera were being developed in Florence by the Society of the Camerata.

In addition to developing this wide variety of dramatic forms, Italy was at the same time cultivating the art of scene-design; in that field it unquestionably provided the lead that other countries were soon to follow for some centuries. The degree of lavishness, the high order of sophistication in the use of colors, textures, and shapes, and the great mechanical ingenuity achieved in Italian scene-design during the Renaissance can best be explained, perhaps, by two circumstances: that it was always closely allied to the plastic arts there and that it was supported by wealthy families which could afford far more than the professional theatrical troupes of other countries. Historically, the transition from medieval stations inside the church or on the town square to constructed sets took place in the fourteenth and fifteenth centuries as the *Sacre Rappresentazioni* became more elaborate and as their productions were taken over by wealthy families which began more ambitiously to mount triumphs, carnivals, and wedding celebrations at which plays of one kind or another were given. The first theaters were typically the temporary ones constructed in ducal halls, usually by architects, painters, and sculptors hired for the occasion and interested in solving problems of perspective in theatrical terms. People like Filippo Brunelleschi (1377–1446), the architect, and Baldassare Peruzzi (1481–1537) looked first, perhaps, to Vitruvius (*fl.* 50 B.C.) and his famous book *De Architectura,* which was discovered in 1414 and printed in 1486 and which long served as the authority for the Renaissance on classical theater construction. Ultimately, of course, Italian theorists themselves produced books, like Sebastiano Serlio's *Archittetura* (1544) and Nicolò Sabbatini's *Manual For Constructing Scenes and Machines in the Theater* (1638), and then finally a number of permanent theaters were built.

In general, the Italian stage during this period consisted of an ingenious translation of the Roman stage as the Renaissance, looking to Vitruvius, understood it, a translation that provided a single closed space like that found on a shallow proscenium stage. Artfully constructed and gorgeously painted and decorated, this space was typically divided into five lateral planes, the first four of which were plastic while the fifth and most remote was a flat painted surface. All were contrived to give the space a sense of depth and ambience, usually the illusion of a city street with houses and streets going off into the distance. It was, in other words, a unitarian stage as contrasted with the multi-stage plan seen in the Middle Ages and in other countries at this time, and it was invariably quite magnificent. Among the earliest permanent theaters, one of the most important was the Teatro Olimpico, which still survives. Commissioned by the Olympic Academy of Vicenza, its original plan was designed by Andrea Palladio (1508–1580) and, when he died, was carried out by his son and Vicenzo Scamozzi (1552–1616); it marked the fullest development of a perspective stage, with skillfully arranged surfaces and passages within the stage space. After its inauguration in 1585, it became an important model for subsequent theater architects, both in and outside Italy. Slightly later came the Sabbionetta, a smaller theater built by Scamozzi and also extant, and the Teatro Farnese in Parma, which was seriously damaged in the Second World War. Altogether, the achievements of Renaissance Italy in the arts of theater construction and scene-design conditioned later conceptions in these fields everywhere in Europe. They influenced practice most immediately and profoundly by the indirect route of the staging used for Italian opera and pastoral drama, which they provided models for and which in turn influenced architects and designers elsewhere. These spectacular performances, calling for many scene changes, gave impetus to the development of mobile scenery, moveable wings, back curtains, and borders in the late sixteenth and seventeenth centuries. The wings were painted flat surfaces placed parallel to the front of the stage along its sides and diminishing in size toward the rear to give a sense of depth; they were mounted so that they could be drawn to meet and in this way create a new background picture. The back curtains and borders were painted and either raised or rolled as they were needed to frame a new stage picture. With its obvious possibilities for scene-changing, this modified version of the unitarian stage was soon to furnish the basic design for stages and, by extension, for indoor theaters all over Europe.

An even more immediate influence on theatrical art elsewhere in Europe was exerted by another field of activity in Renaissance Italy, the immensely popular and widely travelled troupes of professional performers who made up the *com-*

media dell'arte. These players are to be sharply distinguished from the amateurs who acted in productions of tragedies and Learned Comedies by their professionalism—they were actors of the profession, or *dell'arte;* and although many of them are known to have taken part in occasional productions in noble houses in the company of amateurs, typically they worked in small troupes, travelling about and giving performances wherever they received hospitality. Such troupes began to appear and flourish in the last half of the sixteenth century, but their origins are obscure. They may have owed something to the elusive mime tradition that lingered among popular entertainers; perhaps they also derived something from Atellan farce as it may have survived in popular comedy; certainly they owed something to the specific performers who are known to have developed the characters that became a permanent part of their material. But the antecedent activity that explains most about them is the carnival celebrations that, with King Carnival and his array of servants and assistants, most clearly anticipate the characters and farce-actions exploited by the *commedia* actors in infinite variations.

The most singular fact about the *commedia* troupes is that they rarely performed a written text. The actors, each of whom had specialized in a single character for a considerable time, followed a general plot outline, improvising as they went and feeding into the performance in impromptu fashion speeches and comic turns that they had gradually made part of their personal repertories and painstakingly polished. The characters to be found in the separate troupes varied to some extent, but they usually included certain standard types. There was generally a Pantalone, the Magnifico from Venice who in his loose slippers, red tights, long black gown, and tight skull cap sometimes played a father, sometimes an aging lover, but always a lean, suspicious, avaricious old man. There were always young lovers, Flavios and Columbinas (though they went by many names), desperately trying to outwit their parents. Frequently there was a Gratiano, the doctor of law from Bologna who in his heavy black gown and large black hat could be either a father or an aging lover, but who was always a pretender to learning and a magniloquent framer of specious arguments. Usually there was a Capitano, a roaring braggart soldier often played as a Spaniard, whose claims to heroism were only matched by his fictitious conquests in love. And then there were also the many servants, both clever and stupid, the Zannis in their wide trousers, loose blouses, and black masks, the Arlecchinos in their parti-colored suits, and the Pulcinellas with their hooked noses and stuffed stomachs. The typical *commedia* performer cultivated one of these roles and perfected it throughout his professional life. Among the most famous were Francesco Andreini's Capitano del Vall'Inferno, Tiberio Fiorillo's Scaramuccia, an offshoot of the Capitano figure, Tristano Martinelli's Arlecchino, and such ingenues as Vittoria Piissimi. Women seem always to have had a place in both professional and amateur performances in Renaissance Italy.

As business units, the *commedia* troupes were organized as cooperatives. Led by a manager-actor, the group typically owned in common a supply of costumes, a few properties, and the materials for a stage, when they needed one, and they divided the profits among the members after expenses had been paid. With this equipment they travelled from town to town, or from noble house to noble house, to perform their farces and occasionally a pastoral play or tragedy on either a booth stage or on a stage erected in a hall. Among the many companies of which records survive, the most famous were the Gelosi, the Uniti, and the Confidenti, all of which were active in the last quarter of the sixteenth century, and the Accesi, the Fedeli, and Flaminio Scala's Confidenti, which were the best known troupes in the first half of the seventeenth century. In these troupes, apparently, a standard of performance was achieved that has rarely been matched anywhere; the best of them were not only favorites in aristocratic circles in Italy but the rage wherever they travelled, particularly in France and Spain. Unfortunately, all that remains of this remarkable tradition are a few contemporary accounts of performances, some drawings and paintings, and some 700 of the plot outlines or scenarios. Yet we know enough to be assured that the *commedia dell'arte* permanently and profoundly influenced both western comedy and acting as an art.

RENAISSANCE DRAMA IN ENGLAND: THE ELIZABETHAN TRADITION EMERGES

By the first quarter of the sixteenth century English drama, too, offered a rather confused picture of several distinct theatrical currents, each maintaining a certain autonomy, but each also feeding into the broader stream that at the end of the century we know as the Elizabethan tradition. The miracle play was in slow but steady decline. The morality, by now largely in the hands of humanists and propagandists, was variously modified as new purposes were brought to it or as it was blended with other forms. The folk play continued relatively unchanged, and unmistakably contributed to other forms something of its loose epic sweep and its popular character types. To these currents we must now add the academic drama and the hybrid popular drama that by this time was the established fare of the small troupes of professional players circulating in the kingdom.

The growth of interest in classical drama in England revealed itself first at the universities, at court, or in such learned academies as the law schools of the Inns of Court; and the techniques and conventions of classical drama made their way into the English tradition largely by way of plays produced under these auspices. For the most part the classical models followed were Plautus and Terence for comedy and Seneca for tragedy; Greek drama, though known, was almost negligible in its influence except as it was filtered through Roman example. English schoolboys had long read and acted in Roman plays as part of their study of Latin. Now, as new stimulus was provided by editions of classical texts and by reports of the work of men like Trissino and Dolce in Italy and of Jodelle and Buchanan in France, it was natural that certain learned men in England should try their hand at writing plays in imitation of classical models. Their efforts produced a wide range of plays intended for performance by the highly disciplined children's choirs at court, by university students, and by the dilettantes residing at the Inns of Court.

The legacy of Plautus and Terence is perhaps most evident in plays like Nicholas Udall's *Ralph Roister Doister* (*c*.1550) and a certain Master S.'s *Gammer Gurton's Needle* (*c*.1563), both of which were written for university performance. Although neither play imitates Roman models slavishly, both derived techniques and standards of structural tightness, as well as certain characters and conven-

xvi THE DRAMA OF THE RENAISSANCE

The popular farce in France, played
on a platform booth-stage, as in
this Renaissance print, developed
along lines similar to the farce
and *commedia* theater of Italy.
Photo Historical Pictures Service—Chicago

tions, from Roman precedents. In tragedy the appropriation of Roman practice is even clearer. The profound dependence of sixteenth-century tragic writers on Senecan dramaturgy served not only to import many of Seneca's practices into the English tradition, but also to imbue English tragedy with Senecan horror and luridness for the next hundred years. The English debt to Seneca is perhaps best exemplified by the famous production of Thomas Sackville's and Thomas Norton's *Gorboduc* before the Queen in 1562. Altogether, such efforts succeeded in grafting onto English dramatic practice an awareness of the famous Aristotelian unities of time, place, and action, a predisposition to divide a dramatic action into five parts, a number of stock characters such as the braggart soldier and the cunning servant, and a wide selection of such other features as the ghost, the chorus, the stage messenger, and dumb shows. The impact of these practices on the native English tradition was tremendous. Yet like the other contributory traditions in the inheritance that was soon to be Marlowe's and Shakespeare's, the Roman tradition too was assimilated rather than accepted as exclusive model. Even in the most learned of academic plays we find Roman practice modified and conditioned by native practices in a way that implies the gradual, elusive, but unmistakable emergence of a peculiarly English way of constructing plays.

The slow and confused process by which a number of distinct dramatic strains met and mysteriously coalesced to make up the legacy available at the end of the century is best summed up, perhaps, by yet another type of drama, the hybrid popular drama performed for the most part by the small professional troupes that were increasingly in evidence. Professional players in England are known to have travelled in small groups as early as the first quarter of the fifteenth century, though they were not widely known until the beginning of the sixteenth century, by which time they had achieved the distinctive pattern of organization that was to prove important for subsequent dramatic companies. These groups modelled themselves initially on the troupes of household minstrels that entertained their noble masters in the winter and travelled in the summer. Typically there were four men and a boy who toured under the name of their patron (they frequently wore his livery), putting on plays in the halls of noble houses, inn yards, town squares, or wherever they could obtain hospitality. Since economy was essential to their survival, they became skillful at adapting themselves to a variety of conditions: they doubled in multiple parts; they made few costumes serve for many occasions; they mastered a style of staging which enabled them to do a variety of plays in essentially any location providing them with an open space. Frequently they performed on a kind of booth stage that consisted of a platform erected on barrels with a curtained enclosure at the back. Characteristically, they derived their income from collections made in the audience, which, after their expenses were paid, they divided among the group's members.

These players were often called "Interluders," apparently for no other reason than that their "Interlude" plays were often performed in the interval between the courses of a banquet. The plays covered a considerable range and drew fairly freely from all the separate streams of dramatic activity in evidence in the sixteenth century. If many of them, like *The Four P's* (*c.* 1520), were short, relatively straight-forward farces deriving from a popular tradition now largely lost, some, like *Lusty Juventus* (*c.* 1550), were fairly long and allegorical in structure;

others, like *Horestes* (*c.* 1567), derived conspicuously from the academic tradition, while still others, like *Clyomon and Clamydes* (*c.* 1570), were taken from folk drama and romance. Provisioned with such mixed repertories, the professional players performed throughout the century, gradually strengthening their position and perfecting their craft. In their hands more than in any others, the diverse traditions embraced by English drama in the sixteenth century fused to become the many-veined tradition of the Age of Elizabeth. It was their example that recommended to James Burbage (*c.* 1530–1597) that he construct in London a permanent theater building in which plays could be performed for profit.

THE ACHIEVEMENT OF THE AGE OF SHAKESPEARE With the establishment of the first public theater in 1576, the English theater quickly assumed the status of a fairly well defined craft practised by a limited number of craftsmen in whose hands English Renaissance drama achieved what was to be its prevailing character for some sixty years. The initial work of clarifying still further the guiding principles of this drama—of reconciling, adapting, and fusing its various resources and of proving its conventions and techniques—was largely the accomplishment of a group of playwrights in the 1580's and early 1590's known as the University Wits, all educated men and accordingly inclined to academic and classical precedent. But their tastes were by no means narrow; if they valued classical example, they also drew freely from the other traditions making up their heritage. Thomas Kyd (1558–1594) gave a prominence to Senecan conventions and techniques in his *Spanish Tragedy* (*c.*1587) that probably had a considerable effect on tragic writers for the next six decades, but he derived his narrative technique and panoramic scope from native drama. John Lyly (*c.*1554–1606), George Peele (*c.*1557–1596), and Robert Greene (1558–1592) also reveal an awareness of classical precedent, but do so in plays that succeed in defining a new, peculiarly English dramatic style. To these men, and especially to the greatest of them, Christopher Marlowe (1564–1593), fell the important task of working out some of the basic tendencies in handling subject matter and dramatic construction that were to constitute the tradition during the age of Shakespeare and beyond.

The ingrained vivacity and solidity of that tradition reveal themselves first in the subject matter to which its playwrights typically turned. Although they occasionally treated invented and legendary stories, for the most part they selected their materials from history or quasi-history, and especially from the recent chronicles of England and Italy. Here, taking their lead from the morality play, they typically looked for material illustrative of great truths, very often moral commonplaces, and found them in the lives of men and women bearing the color and odor of the real world. This tendency accounts for the large number of history plays produced, particularly from 1580 to 1610, as well as the large proportion of tragedies and comedies throughout the period that treat historical or quasi-historical material. The impulse to look to history, moreover, was consistent with the tendency to favor materials abundant in incident. During this age English drama revealed a decided preference for action over talk; high adventure, crime, passion, tales of success and failure, these the playwrights found in the populous flux of chronicles, biographies, romances, short stories, and novels.

In the hands of Marlowe and his contemporaries the characteristic treatment of such materials made for a panoramic, multilinear drama that typically ran to many characters, many locales, and several strands of intrigue, all caught in a loosely orchestrated, inclusive dramatic action. The Elizabethan dramatists were typically disposed to treat their subject matter with great freedom—to alter history so as to tell the story with the greatest effect, to change a character's age so as to point a contrast, to offer new conclusions to old stories in the interests of poetic justice. Like their medieval predecessors, they had little regard for inconsistencies in time and place, and even less for the celebrated unities; their aim was to put as much of the story as would interest their audience on the stage, and to do this while giving as much attention as possible to spectacle, highlights, and meaning.

This predisposition for spectacle goes all the way back to the processional drama of the miracle plays and before, but among the Elizabethans it included not only lavish costumes, intricate ceremonies, and tableau-scenes, but also a tendency to adhere as far as possible to a fully developed narrative line. The Elizabethan playwrights began as close to the beginning of the story as they could, even when doing so involved gaps of several years, and they introduced into represented scenes as much of the story's exciting matter as they could, including battle scenes and mob scenes in most ages thought too difficult to stage. In fact, they exhibited an amazing ingenuity at staging almost anything. Given this fully developed narrative line, they proceeded to write by episodes, that is, to construct plays as a series of highly colored, highly dramatic scenes with relatively little connective tissue, building loosely, but steadily and impressively, to a many-faceted picture of a particular dramatic world.

Fundamental to this dramaturgy was that the tone or mood of these many scenes was rarely the same from moment to moment. In keeping with the example of their non-classical predecessors, the Elizabethans revealed a marked preference for a mixture of scenes in various keys—comic, pathetic, tragic, and satiric. In the hands of the best of the playwrights, this tendency to mix decorums, blending comic and solemn, kingly and base in a single action, became a principal way of emphasizing the many-sided character of the reality being represented. Yet in a more general way it was also the function of this way of writing plays to do precisely this. Perhaps nothing is more fundamental to the dramaturgy of this period than that the actions were designed to embrace not only diverse tones, many episodes, and many characters, but several strands of action or multiple plots. This feature of structure enforces the sense of reality seen simultaneously on many levels and in many rhythms and brings to these plays great richness and complexity. The kind of unity achieved when such multiplicity coalesces to generate a single thrust is perhaps the chief esthetic achievement of English Renaissance theater.

As such practices concerning subject matter and play construction were becoming standard, a progressive clarification of the particular kinds of play that were to be important in the dawning age was also taking place. In the work of Kyd, Marlowe, Lyly, Greene, and Shakespeare the English Renaissance concepts of tragedy and comedy were worked out; and early in the period they were supplemented by the history play, and later by tragicomedy. Yet though these proved to be the important dramatic types in the age, they were so loosely defined and they came to embrace such a variety of plays that the names themselves do little to suggest the range of drama comprehended by them.

Even tragedy came gradually to include a diversity unknown to previous traditions. Like all English Renaissance drama, it tended to an amplitude in scope and detail unknown earlier—to a breadth of canvas and a profusion of characters represented in considerable detail. Important parts of this amplitude were the many associative, analogical, and symbolic devices used to clarify and extend the meaning of the action, such devices as mirror scenes and analogies in action and character that serve to suggest that all humanity is somehow involved in the particular action at issue. Part of this amplitude, too, came from the tendency to heighten and magnify everywhere, to deal with emotions in their full dimensions, to strive for fullness rather than economy. This predisposition to amplitude, at any rate, made for some of the variety within the dramatic type.

But an even more fundamental cause of the diversity within tragedy was the profound change in outlook that with the advent of the Renaissance prompted writers—and most significantly tragic writers since their purpose, as always, was to confront the most distressing facts of human experience—to base their work on sectarian, sometimes private systems of value. Whereas in medieval drama the underlying system of values was invariably the orthodox Christian one supported by the Church, as the western world passed from the Middle Ages to the Renaissance, its fundamental values remained Christian but became less and less orthodox in the sense that they related less and less frequently to a single, unalterable system and depended more and more on the playwright's individual view of Christianity. Hell as it exists in Marlowe's *Doctor Faustus* is a Christian concept, but a Christian concept as it has been partly reinterpreted by Marlowe. In other words, Renaissance playwrights, especially in England, began to abandon the view of the human condition fixed fairly rigidly by medieval Christian thought for a private vision, and with this impulse we again find a searching for justice and equity in this world, an attempt to discover a coherence in earthly life that would enable men to assert that, however painful and insecure, human experience has its grandeur. To this individualistic impulse we can trace many of the differences between separate tragedies and between individual tragic writers, something of the new inwardness of English tragedy, and much of its tendency to affirm human life as it is rather than to see it as a brief moment in an eternal drama.

The quickened sense of search, discovery, and self-importance that we find in tragedy carries over clearly to the history play, a dramatic type that for the most part exalts English destiny by discovering a sovereign wisdom in the events of English history. Ranging all the way from loose chronicle plays through serious studies of power politics to historical tragedies of the sort that we meet in *Richard II,* the history play had great popularity in the first twenty-five years of the period, when, under Elizabeth, national enthusiasm ran high, and then declined markedly toward the end of the period. More usefully identified by its subject matter than by its purpose, it lent itself to sunny, epic hymns to English greatness at one extreme and to representations of the blackest tragic pessimism at the other. Yet despite its apparent amorphousness, it yielded some of the greatest plays of the period and in some ways best sums up the high confidence and adventurousness both of the drama and of the age.

It is in English Renaissance comedy, however, that we find the clearest proofs of the fertility and creativity of this tradition and its practitioners. Within a period of thirty years a range of comedies appeared that it would be impossible to describe briefly, extending, as it does, from the airy joyousness of *A Midsummer Night's Dream* on the one extreme to the bitterness of Ben Jonson's *Volpone* on the other. Of the principal types to emerge, what is usually called Romantic Comedy includes a fair proportion of the important work produced. This type of comedy typically uses a lovers-in-distress action as its structural frame, and the lovers are usually characters of sufficient complexity so that we can feel strongly about them and can derive an authoritative satisfaction from their victory. But its other materials are too miscellaneous to define. Practically every known type of comic element found a place in the form, including farce, slapstick, repartee, burlesque, and parody, and other literary types, notably satire, the pastoral, and lyric, were readily assimilated to it. What is constant, unifying, and highly important is that all these features dovetail into a kind of omnibus structure that intensifies an exuberant sense of rejoicing—a celebration of the sort most fully realized in Shakespeare's *As You Like It* or *Twelfth Night*. The other comic form that comprehends enough of the accomplishment of the period to deserve mention is the satiric or critical comedy perfected after the turn of the century by Ben Jonson. Satiric comedy was more limited in its scope than Romantic comedy; though it contained elements of farce and slapstick, it dealt typically with a spectacle of villains or fools being outwitted, often by greater villains.

Closely related to the comic forms produced during this age but sufficiently different to deserve separate mention is that elusive form usually known as tragicomedy. Because of its frequent seriousness and its lack of the hilarity so often found in comedy, Renaissance playwrights and later critics have tended to set it off by itself; yet tragicomedy clearly shares with comedy the purpose to present the status quo hopefully. Typically representing an action in which the protagonist is led from one distress to another, it often entails moments of great pathos and even great pain; but it always ends happily, and at its best, in plays like Shakespeare's *The Winter's Tale,* it expresses a wistful, mellow acceptance of the world.

These are the chief dramatic types to be met in English Renaissance drama, and from 1580 to 1640 they were used by an exceedingly productive and versatile group of playwrights. Among the University Wits, Marlowe's accomplishment is the most remarkable; in the first decade of this amazing dramatic development he clarified the rich possibilities of his inheritance. Shakespeare's work, which followed hard upon Marlowe's in the 1590's and 1600's, not only realized those possibilities but clarified still richer ones. Then, to complete this trinity of giants, Ben Jonson began to write for the stage at about the turn of the century and in the first decade produced much of his best work. In all, the period from 1580 to 1610 brought forth a development in the art of drama in England as electrifying in its speed as it was staggering in its quality. Yet these playwrights were scarcely alone. Among their contemporaries and successors were many who also wrote well and sometimes brilliantly. Thomas Dekker (*c.*1572–*c.*1632) and Thomas Heywood (*c.*1570–1641) were respectable journeyman playwrights, who, if they never wrote a great play, at least wrote one important play apiece. Among the generation of later playwrights known as the Jacobeans, John Marston (1576–1634) and John Ford (1586–1639) are memorable, while John Webster (?–1634) produced two minor masterpieces in *The White Devil* and *The Duchess of Malfi* and Thomas Middleton (*c.*1570–1627) a full half dozen satirical comedies only slightly inferior to those of Ben Jonson at his best. By the end of the period the tradition had begun to play itself out for reasons to be touched on presently, but not so completely that its last important exponents, James Shirley (1596–1666) and Philip Massinger (1583–1640) did not produce a few plays of great value.

THE ENGLISH PLAYHOUSE IN THE RENAISSANCE The origins of the physical theater in which this tradition evolved and achieved its victories are confused almost to the point of obscurity. It has long been thought, and probably justly, that the basic plan of the building owed something to the typical physical conditions encountered by small professional companies when they performed on makeshift platforms in innyards. The apparent arrangement used in innyards—consisting of a platform with an open space before it for standing spectators, and second-story windows, or galleries, on three sides—gives us the essential plan of the Elizabethan theater. But now it is also clear that the building probably owed something to the booth stage in wide use in England and on the continent in the sixteenth century. The structure of the booth stage, with its platform, its shallow curtained area at the rear from which the actors entered, its possibility for actors to play from "above" when they stood on a ladder behind the curtain, and its trapdoor for special effects, suggests a number of well-known features of the later theater, as well as many of the staging techniques practised by Elizabethan troupes. Yet it is also probable that something, if only the need for a large playing area, was derived from the productions presented in the halls of great houses or even on open terrain in town squares. The question of origins is confused, probably because so many basic questions about the Elizabethan theater building itself have never been answered.

With these physical conditions as precedents the Elizabethan theater literally sprang into existence when in 1576 James Burbage constructed in London the first of the series of theaters to rise and fall during the period, aptly named the "Theatre." The Theatre was followed by the Curtain and later by such famous houses as the Rose, the Swan, the Globe, which housed Shakespeare's company, the Fortune, the Red Bull, and others. Of the structure of these buildings we know a good deal from contemporary descriptions, drawings, building contracts, and the plays themselves, though not enough to be perfectly secure about all the details. It is clear that they were quite large buildings for the period, three stories in height and as much as eighty by eighty feet along the outer walls. Square, polygonal, or round, they consisted chiefly of covered galleries around the perimeter, a large central area open to the sky, and at one end of the perimeter a building facing into the open yard, called the 'tiring house (i.e. attiring or dressing quarters). Spectators could obtain seats in the variously priced galleries or could stand for the basic price of admission in the uncovered area known as the pit; the actors' domain was the 'tiring house and its related areas.

For the production of plays the most important part of the playhouse was the 'tiring house and its system of stages or playing areas. Although there is still much controversy about the composition and use of these stages, enough is known to reconstruct a general, if in some respects tentative, plan. Most important was

A modern, conjectural reconstruction of the Swan Theater
by C. Walter Hodges, based on Johannes de Witt's drawing
of 1596. (Inset at right, *photo Historical Pictures Service–Chicago*)

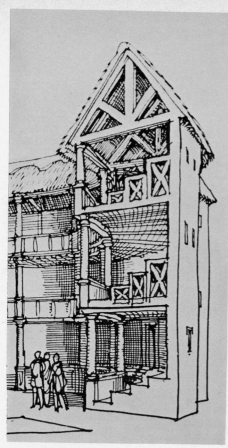

the large platform, perhaps forty feet wide by twenty-five feet deep, that jutted out into the uncovered yard almost to the halfway point. Nearly seven feet high and fenced by a low railing, this was the principal playing area, and about half of it or something more was sheltered from the sky by a canopy projecting from the 'tiring house and supported by two large pillars based on the platform. At the rear of this platform were two doors on either side of the stage that gave access to and from the 'tiring house, and in the center between the doors a room that was normally concealed from view by a traverse curtain. Above this so-called "inner room" on the next level of the 'tiring house was another room or gallery with a railing or balcony, while to either side of this gallery there may have been windows above the stage doors. On the level above the gallery was yet another room for the musicians, and above that was probably a cupola from which the trumpet was blown and the flag was raised to announce a play.

Altogether, this structure was superbly suited for the multi-scened drama of Shakespeare's age. Even if we eliminate the stage windows as possible playing areas, since there is much question about them, and severely curtail the use made of the inner room and the gallery above, we are left with a highly flexible, efficient stage complex. Most of the action took place on the main platform, but by convention it was an unlocalized place unless a throne were pushed out from the inner room to establish a king's court or a few prop-trees were brought out to establish a forest setting. Actors entering through the stage doors could in one scene be in France, while the next to appear could indicate they were in Scotland. The very size of the platform, moreover, made a great many things possible: one group could conceal itself from another, considerable numbers of actors could appear, and athletic events, like sword fights and battles, could be presented with relative ease. Add to these advantages the possibility of occasionally locating scenes in the inner room, which could easily become a study or a bedroom, or in the gallery above, which could easily become a balcony or the parapet of a castle, the possibility of entrances and exits through a trapdoor in the main platform, and the possibility of flights by means of a crane operated from the canopy and the inherent adaptability of the Elizabethan theater is clear.

Closely related to these physical conditions were the conventions of production which governed their use. The Elizabethan theater was fundamentally a flamboyant and rhetorical institution; it put great emphasis on the imagery of actors in action and on the beauty of the spoken word, and relatively little on the creation of illusions. Properties were used—thrones to suggest a court, a bed to indicate a bedroom, tables, chairs, prop-trees, and stones—but for the most part they were limited to the few stools, ladders, and benches which were absolutely indispensable to the play. It was usual, therefore, to see magnificently dressed actors declaiming speeches never intended to sound like actual conversation on an otherwise naked stage. These actors commanded all attention, and they were aided in holding it by, among other things, costumes on which little expense was spared. The costumes were for the most part contemporary: kings, soldiers, paupers, shopkeepers' wives—all were usually dressed like their sixteenth century counterparts. Only occasionally were attempts made to suggest particular places and particular historical periods, as in, for example, the plays laid in Rome, and only certain characters such as ghosts always had a specialized dress. But other conventions, too, imply the essentially non-illusionistic character of this theater. The plays themselves make clear that soliloquies and asides were commonplace, that disguise, however transparent to the audience, was understood never to be penetrated by the characters, and that time could be drastically speeded up or slowed down according to the needs of the playwright. The prevailing acting style, moreover, seems to have been based on relatively heightened, stylized conventions of gesticulation, movement, and delivery, which, if not exaggerated to the point of being severely formal, at least imply a type of acting remote from the cinematic style of our time. Like dramatic composition and other aspects of dramatic production, acting, too, apparently underwent between 1580 and 1600 a dazzling development and refinement; in men like Richard Burbage, Will Kemp, and Will Alleyn, Shakespeare and his fellow-writers had actors who were masters of their craft.

The training of actors and production personnel as well as, indirectly, of playwrights, fell almost entirely to the separate theatrical companies, which, as the basic business units, also lent to the theater world of the English Renaissance its prevailing structure. Taking their lead from the small professional companies that long had been nourished in noble houses, such companies first obtained the nominal patronage of some person of position and then tended to all but ignore it by organizing themselves on familiar business principles. Such companies functioned much like corporate firms. Including usually from twenty to thirty people, they consisted of clearly distinguishable classes or groups, each with its responsibilities and each with its rewards. At the top of the organization were the sharers, those men who owned stock in the company and shared the profits after expenses were paid; by and large they were also the principal actors. In the famous Globe company there were usually twelve, and they included Shakespeare and Richard Burbage. Next were the apprentices, the boys who from ages ten to thirteen were apprenticed to the sharers to learn how to act and who, since actresses were unknown in the English theater at this time, played all the female and children's roles. When they grew up, they either became sharers themselves or they left the profession, but at any one time in the Globe company there were usually at least five. Then there was a miscellaneous group of persons called the hired men. These were the salaried people hired to do odd work around the theater: supervise the properties (the stagekeeper), care for the costumes (the tireman), hold the book (the prompter), or take any of a variety of small acting parts as messengers, soldiers, members of a mob, etc. In the Globe company there were usually about eight in this group. Finally, in addition to these three groups, there was sometimes a fourth called the housekeepers because they owned stock, not in the company, but in the theater building. Frequently, these men were also sharers, as, in fact, Shakespeare and several of his colleagues were.

In any case, it was against this generalized picture of sharers, apprentices, and hired men working together that dramatic production in England at this time must be imagined. Such companies provided their own capital and facilities, they trained their personnel, they sustained repertories of staggering dimensions when performing in London, they went on tour in the provinces and abroad when conditions in London required it, they contracted for and purchased their plays, and even arranged for their publication when that appeared profitable. A playwright might be a member of such a company, as Shakespeare was, or a free agent in the style of Ben Jonson; in either event he typically sold his play outright to the company, and the theatrical company saw to its production and printing and realized any further profit that the work might produce. Normally plays were published in small, wretchedly printed books called quartos. Because the playwright often had no stock in the operation by this time, the texts reproduced were frequently bad, and sometimes horrendously inaccurate, as when they were published illegally by a class of play-thieves known as pirates. Because plays were at the time so little respectable as literary works, moreover, only rarely was the total output of an author collected and published in a large, so-called folio version. These editions, by contrast, were produced with some care: Ben Jonson oversaw the publication of his *Works* in 1616, and Shakespeare's colleagues published his plays after his death in the First Folio of 1623.

THE GREAT AGE PASSES The decline of English Renaissance theater after 1610 was probably as much the result of the passing of time, of a rare coincidence between great men and great opportunities, as it was the result of identifiable historical causes. It is clear that the nation underwent a profound change after the death of Elizabeth in 1603, when something of its confidence and ebullience went out of it. It is probable, moreover, that by 1620 the tradition itself had begun to show signs of exhaustion; so much great work had already been accomplished during the period that there appeared to remain little that could be done. Certainly, whatever the causes, the drama underwent a number of clear changes that mark, for this tradition at least, a progressive enfeeblement and decay.

Although the story is complex, it is clear that much of it can be explained by the gradual shift in the English theater from the broad, general public of Shakespeare's day to a progressively more limited audience. The theater of Shakespeare's age spread throughout the kingdom and appealed to farmer and courtier alike; yet even in Shakespeare's great decade, from 1598 to 1608, a beginning was made by the so-called private playhouses that were to lead to a theater of a quite different kind. In 1600, roughly, a number of entrepreneurs organized two companies of boy actors who in the special surroundings of small, covered, lighted playhouses offered to the London public a rather different bill of dramatic fare from that found in the public playhouses. The boy actors were well trained and drew on a long tradition of acting cultivated in royal choirs. They consciously catered to the intelligentsia with witty satirical comedies and philosophical tragedies for which some minimal academic preparation was necessary and they favored a polite audience by charging high admission prices. For a few years they achieved a success which, if it did not sustain them, left a lasting mark on the English theater, and in 1608, when Shakespeare's company took over Blackfriars' Theater, one of the private playhouses, a decisive step had been taken. Although Shakespeare's company was to continue for a few years more to use both the Globe and Blackfriars, the one in the summer and the other in the winter, they and their brother companies continued thereafter to move in the direction of the small, limited theater designed to please the few rather than the many.

By the 1620's the tastes of these few were already imprinted on the plays being produced. The aristocratic standards that had been in some measure imported from France by the new queen Henrietta-Maria had taken hold to the extent that some plays, like Philip Massinger's, can scarcely be understood today unless an aristocratic code of values is assumed. The old history play that had so well summed up the spirit of Elizabethan England had all but been replaced by increasingly more exotic tragicomedies. Moreover, some of the best dramatic talent had been drawn off to produce airy poetical entertainments of little dramatic value for the court and noble families. The kind of drama that would appeal to everyone and that would be understood by everyone made fewer and fewer appearances. By 1642, when a law was passed suspending dramatic activity because of the Civil War, a split had developed between the drama and the nation at large: the nation was no longer behind it in the sense that it was no longer participating in it. Although it fell to the Puritans, traditionally foes of the theater, to close it in 1642, what they closed was more the theater of a coterie than the theater as it had been in Shakespeare's age.

Yet even these decades of decline were not without significant accomplishments. From such playwrights as John Webster and John Ford came several black tragedies that stand as tortured monuments to human anguish; from Thomas Middleton and the collaboration of Francis Beaumont (c.1584–1616) and John Fletcher (1579–1629) came a series of satirical comedies and tragicomedies of great value. Moreover, Ben Jonson continued to produce important work, though much of it is in that courtly form of musical drama known as the masque. Perhaps even more important than Jonson's accomplishment in the masques was that of his collaborator, the architect Inigo Jones (1573–1652). Jones' knowledge of Italian scene-design was applied to the construction of elaborate stages, scenery, and machines with such success that his work exerted a profound influence on the stage-designers of the next age.

RENAISSANCE DRAMA IN SPAIN   Although the development of theater in medieval Spain seems to have been somewhat retarded—perhaps because of the Moorish domination, perhaps because of resistance from the Church—our scanty records for the early period indicate that it apparently followed the general pattern found elsewhere in Europe. The earliest known Spanish liturgical play exists in the form of a fragment in Spanish from the twelfth century; certainly its treatment of the coming of the three kings suggests the normal evolution from the Latin trope. In any event, such plays were known as *autos sacramentales,* a phrase in which the word *"autos"* means "actions" or "acts." Through most of their early history they were short, self-contained dramatizations of some biblical episode and were presented under the auspices and with the full participation of the clergy. In Spain these liturgical plays never developed into cycles of plays, and for a considerable time they retained a distinctive simplicity of structure and purpose. Gradually, however, the term *auto* came to embrace almost any religious or moral play, including dramatic treatments of saints' lives and even romantic fables of Moors and pirates allegorized to illustrate Christian doctrine. Finally, in the hands of the professional playwrights who began to write them as early as the fifteenth century and who continued to produce them until well into the eighteenth, the *auto* became a sophisticated literary form, as intricate in structure as it was elaborate in the dramatic means that it frequently required in production. All of Spain's important playwrights in the sixteenth and seventeenth centuries wrote numerous *autos.*

But even in the early period the production of *autos* differed in significant ways from the production of liturgical plays elsewhere in Europe. To begin with, they were never presented alone, and even when presented in the church (in Spain they continued to be given in the churches later than elsewhere), they were typically accompanied by farces and dances. A normal production in thirteenth century Spain might begin with Mass at the high altar, proceed then to a short farce, then to the *auto,* and finally to singing and dancing. We have an interesting document from about 1260 in which Alfonso the Learned forbids the clergy to act in or see the farces, which apparently enjoyed a vigorous popularity at this time. As the production of the *autos* passed from churchmen to the craft guilds, the city fathers assumed responsibility for the productions and fixed them on the Feast of Corpus Christi. In this later phase an initial presentation of the plays would take place in or near the city's main church, and then the players and their properties would be mounted on wagons and taken in procession to pre-determined points in the city where the arms of the City Council had been hung. Here the wagons, or *carros,* would be backed up to a platform, and on the combined system of platform and wagons the plays would be presented, always in company with interludes of singing, dancing, and farcical skits. The occasion came to be known as *La Fiesta de los Carros.* By the fifteenth century it was in some communities sufficiently ambitious to justify the hiring of professional directors and actors and, occasionally, the awarding of prizes to participating dramatic companies. Other methods of presentation were also known in Spain—sometimes quite elaborate wagons or floats serving as the stages were used, and the station system that was more famous in France was not unknown. The method using *carros,* however, was the most widespread. By the early seventeenth century *autos* were frequently presented in public theaters. They continued to be seen until their suppression in 1765, when, after a long history of opposition from the Church, they were at last prohibited by a decree from Charles III.

The vigor and vitality of the liturgical drama in Spain is symptomatic of the tremendous energy to be met everywhere in Renaissance Spanish theater. The drama of the Age of Gold, as the period from 1550 to 1650 is called, emerged from much the same religious and popular origins found elsewhere; but once it had crystallized into the tradition sustained by the professional theatrical companies, it generated a quantity of dramatic activity matched by no other nation.

The growth of this tradition is perhaps most easily traced in the work of its founding fathers and in the formation of the professional companies. In Spain, as elsewhere, a background of interest in classical drama was evident in university plays and translations of Greek and Latin works. But even such early aristocratic writers as Juan del Encina (1468–1534) and Bartolomé de Torres Naharro (*c.*1480–*c.*1530) largely ignored classical example by working with a loose narrative structure emphasizing incident. Torres Naharro is usually credited with establishing the manner of writing that became standard in the Age of Gold; he also invented the *loa,* a form of introduction that ranged from a monologue to a brief skit, and developed the *gracioso,* a comic character that became very popular.

Later, Juan de la Cueva (*c*.1550–1610), though also aristocratic in inclination, consolidated the tendency to incident by basing his plays on the highly episodic materials of the romances and national history, and he improved on the form with advances in characterization, versification, and plot construction.

It was, however, with Lope de Rueda (*c*.1515–1565) that the emerging tradition achieved a firm footing. Rueda worked exclusively for the public theater. As a young man he had been so deeply impressed by touring *commedia dell'arte* performers that he had left his trade as a goldbeater to form a strolling company of players of the sort that embodied the national tradition in Spain down to about 1575. Known as an *autor de comedias,* a rather miscellaneous term which then designated an actor-playwright-manager (only later did it mean simply a manager), he concerned himself with all aspects of theater art and ultimately assembled one of the most famous companies of his time. As a playwright he composed plays in both verse and prose and invented the *pasos,* a comic sketch in prose performed between the acts of a regular play. Although Miguel de Cervantes (1547–1610), remembering Rueda fifty years after having seen him, recalled only simple, rather primitive performances on a crude booth stage in innyards, it was this work that prepared the way for the staggering accomplishment of the age of Lope de Vega.

Through most of the Age of Gold the theater in Spain was dominated by the towering figure of Lope de Vega (1562–1635). "A monster of nature," as someone once called him, he produced more than a thousand plays, perhaps more than 1500, and packed into one lifetime adventure and romance sufficient for ten men. But the prodigious energy of Lope was really only a flagrant extreme in a period of dramatic activity itself remarkably outsized. By this time every substantial city in Spain had a public theater, many had several, and practically every provincial city was visited regularly by travelling companies.

The plan for the physical theater serving this tradition was first devised in the makeshift theaters used by travelling companies. In the south these companies typically appropriated an innyard, or *patio,* and constructed at one end of it a temporary booth stage consisting of a platform with a shallow curtained area at the back. In the north, where *patios* were unknown, they typically used a *corral,* a rectangular courtyard created by the backs of four adjoining buildings where refuse was usually thrown but where conditions otherwise were roughly those found in a *patio.* Such temporary theaters were soon known everywhere in Spain as *corrales,* the term which designated a theater building in Spain down to the eighteenth century; here spectators either stood in the open area in front of the stage or watched from the overlooking windows. These simple conditions were gradually improved upon when public theaters with some degree of permanence were established, as they were as early as 1520 in Malaga and throughout the sixteenth century in cities like Seville, Valladolid, and Barcelona. Larger stages were built, seats and special seating areas were introduced, and backstage facilties were enlarged. But the essential *corral* plan was retained, even in the later permanent theaters.

The history of these early public theaters in Spain was closely tied to certain hospitals which by law were allowed to sustain them so that they might derive revenue from them. The association was mutually beneficial—the hospitals shared in the profits from one of the most popular of national pastimes, while the theaters continually used the hospitals to fend off attacks from the Church and legislative attempts to close them. On the initiative of two such hospitals the first permanent theaters were built in Madrid: the Corral de la Cruz in 1579 and the Corral del Principe in 1582; soon cities all over the kingdom had permanent *corrales*. Still rectangular in shape, these theaters differed from their prototype only in point of refinement. Galleries were built along the inner walls, and the overlooking windows now became a series of boxes. Against the far wall facing the stage a special section of seats for women was located, indecorously called the "stewpan," and sometimes seats were introduced into the open area, though for the most part it served for standing spectators. Since plays were always given in the afternoon, the stage and portions of the audience were frequently sheltered from the sun by awnings. Of the numbers of spectators accommodated in these buildings we have no certain knowledge, but the typical figure ranged well over a thousand, and the largest, the Coliseo of Seville, supposedly housed from four to five thousand. On days when plays were given the *corrales* were scenes of near-riot. Bullies and bravoes argued and frequently fought to obtain what was apparently the distinction of not paying the entrance fee; gallants quarrelled as they jostled for favor with the women in the "stewpan"; vendors circulated selling fruit and drinks. The actors lived in terror of the rowdy "musketeers," as the standing spectators were called, for, notoriously difficult to please, they were given to hurling fruit as well as insults.

The stage facilities in these theaters were spacious but simple. A large bare platform, broader than it was deep, extended across the entire width of the *corral* at one end. It had a trapdoor, but no front curtain, though curtains were hung at the sides behind which actors frequently hid. In the rear wall there was a stage door on each side, serving for normal entrances and exits, and a third opening in the center that may have been a door or perhaps a curtained recess; above the stage doors a gallery that served as a secondary playing area ran across the rear wall. In these circumstances plays were produced with the scantest attention to scenic and spectacular effects. Some few properties of painted canvas were used, and occasionally the platform became a simultaneous set representing several locales at once. But for the most part the main stage was unlocalized, or only generally localized by the actors' speeches, and a new scene was understood to begin every time the stage was cleared. Musicians apparently sat on the stage and accompanied the action with guitars and sometimes viols and then sang or accompanied dancers during the intervals. Almost the only concession to spectacle was the extravagant costumes of the actors. They were easily the most expensive items owned by the theatrical troupes, and like their counterparts in other countries, they were contemporary in style, with attempts at accuracy made only in plays dealing with Spanish history. Even the *autos,* which were frequently given lavish productions with spectacular mechanical effects under private circumstances, were presented modestly in the public theaters.

The presentations themselves, however, were anything but modest, for in keeping with the tradition established earlier in the production of *autos* the public theaters held firmly to the practice of garnishing the *comedia* of the day with numerous supporting entertainments. A normal performance opened with a *loa* and then proceeded to the play, which it periodically interrupted with songs, dancing, or any of the interludes called *entremeses*. *Entremeses,* from a French term meaning "side dish," were short farces that the playwrights produced in great numbers; usually two (though sometimes more) accompanied a play at the principal intervals. When the play was concluded, the performance was typically rounded off with a *baile,* or dance.

The plays themselves, moreover, were far from simple entertainments. Characteristically quite long and running to many characters and scenes, they epitomized the bustling, adventurous, romantic spirit of the age. Generically, they were known as *comedias,* though again the term is not very helpful since it designated any of the many kinds of three-act plays of the period. The most popular of them was known as the *comedia de capa y espada,* or the cloak and sword play, a title drawn from the customary dress of persons of rank. This species of *comedia* was distinguished from other types by its use of events from ordinary life rather than events from history, mythology, or saints' lives; yet it too was a highly miscellaneous category, easily embracing tragedy, comedy, and melodrama, as these terms are normally understood. Usually written in a mixture of verse forms, some of them highly intricate, these plays typically stressed flamboyant action at the expense of characterization and depth. Although we find exceptions to this statement in the works of the best playwrights, the Spanish drama that flourished during the Age of Gold centered for the most part on colorful tales of heroism, adventure, and romance, treated with as much attention as possible to lyricism and narrative excitement. In them problems of love, honor, and justice were often treated, but they were more frequently occasions for action and melodramatic suspense than subjects to be revealed in any complexity.

Theatrical companies during the period ranged from the single player, who, travelling alone, mounted a bench and gave recitations in small towns, to the full-sized troupe comprising as many as thirty people. Normally, however, the larger companies ran from sixteen to twenty members who worked either for a salary paid by the *autor de comedias* or on a system of shares. Such a company included thirteen or fourteen actors, the *autor,* a person in charge of costumes and equipment, and a musician or two. Theatrical companies took up relatively permanent residence in public theaters; often they travelled, and occasionally they were commissioned by noblemen or communities to give special performances. Typically, the *autor* hired playwrights to supply the company with plays or bought plays from freelance writers. Once the *autor* had ceased being a play-wright and actor to become solely a business manager, there was rarely, if ever, a place for the playwright as a member of a theatrical troupe. In such troupes, how-ever, there were always two or three women; though in Spain, as elsewhere, boys were initially used in women's roles, the prominence of dancing in the Spanish theater, even in the medieval period of *autos,* early secured a function for women in theatrical activities which they filled with vivacity and frequently with distinc-tion. All in all, the players of the Age of Gold seem to have been as accomplished as the writers who supplied them with material. The records single out such names as Damian Arias de Peñafiel, apparently the greatest actor of the day, Cosme Perez, a famous comic actor, and Jusepa Vaca, an actress for whom Lope de Vega wrote a great deal. We may guess something about the great skill and accomplishments of these actors from the demands they met. They kept something like fifty *comedias* in repertory in a full season. Most of them sang and danced as well as acted, and all of them were held to the most exacting standards by the audiences, both popular and aristocratic. Certainly the players were numerous—the fact that more than 2000 of their names are known is itself testimony to the vitality of Renaissance theater in Spain.

Whatever else might be praised or blamed in Spanish theater in the Age of Gold, its most striking feature was its magnitude. In 1681, the year of the death of Calderón de la Barca (1600-1681), the last of the great playwrights, Madrid alone had forty theaters. Someone once estimated that during the period as a whole something more than 30,000 plays were written and produced. Lope de Vega led the way, of course, with effective plays in every known type; perhaps his best known and most highly valued are *The Dog in the Manger,* a comedy, the "honor" play, *Punishment Without Vengeance,* a tragedy, and such social plays as *Fuente Ovejuna* and *The Best Magistrate, The King.* Somewhat later than Lope de Vega, Calderón, too, produced a large number of important plays, including *The Prodigious Magician* and *Life is a Dream.* But in addition to the monumental output of Lope and Calderón, the age also brought forth such distinguished playwrights as Cervantes, Tirso de Molina (*c.*1584-1648), and Juan Ruiz de Alarcón (1580-1639). A clergyman, Tirso de Molina wrote roughly 200 plays, including *The Condemned For Lack of Faith,* sometimes called the greatest of all religious plays, and *The Trickster of Seville,* the first important treatment of the Don Juan story. Alarcón, a more painstaking writer than most of his contemporaries, produced no more than twenty plays, but among them number some of the best comedies of the period, including *Truth Itself Suspected.* All in all, the theatrical energy of the period was unparalleled. Even as the political star of Renaissance Spain waned, the public theaters continued to increase in popularity—romantic, flamboyant, exuberant to the last, perhaps the most luxuriant expression of the spirit of Renaissance Spain.

Bibliography

Drama and Theater in Renaissance Italy:

Duchartre, Pierre Louis, *Italian Comedy,* trans. R. T. Weaver, London, 1929.

Fletcher, Jefferson B., *Literature of the Italian Renaissance,* New York, 1934.

Herrick, Marvin T., *Comic Theory in the Sixteenth Century,* Urbana, Ill., 1950.

——, *Italian Comedy in the Renaissance,* Urbana, Ill., 1960.

——, *Italian Tragedy in the Renaissance,* Urbana, Ill., 1965.

Kennard, Joseph Spencer, *The Italian Theater,* Vol. I, New York, 1932.

Lea, K. M., *Italian Popular Comedy: A Study of the Commedia dell'Arte, 1560-1620,* 2 vols., Oxford, 1934.

McDowell, J. H., "Some Pictorial Aspects of Early *Commedia dell'Arte* Acting," *Studies in Philology,* XXXIX (1942), 47–64.

Nagler, A. M., *Theatre Festivals of the Medici,* New Haven, Conn., 1964.

Nicoll, Allardyce, *Masks, Mimes, and Miracles,* London, 1931.

Sanctis, Francesco de, *History of Italian Literature,* trans. Joan Redfern, 2 vols., London, 1932.

Smith, Winifred, *Italian Actors of the Renaissance,* New York, 1930.

———, *The Commedia dell'Arte: A Study in Popular Italian Comedy,* New York, 1912.

Drama and Theater in Renaissance England:

Bentley, G. E., *The Jacobean and Caroline Stage,* 5 vols., Oxford, 1941–56.

Boas, F. S., *An Introduction to Stuart Drama,* Oxford, 1946.

Bowers, Fredson T., *Elizabethan Revenge Tragedy, 1587–1642,* Princeton, N.J., 1940.

Bradbrook, Muriel C., *Themes and Conventions of Elizabethan Tragedy,* Cambridge, 1935.

———, *The Growth and Structure of Elizabethan Comedy,* London, 1955.

Campbell, Lily B., *Scenes and Machines on the English Stage during the Renaissance,* Cambridge, 1923.

Chambers, E. K., *The Elizabethan Stage,* 4 vols., Oxford, 1923.

Doran, Madeleine, *Endeavors of Art: A Study of Form in Elizabethan Drama,* Madison, Wisc., 1954.

Ellis-Fermor, U. M., *The Jacobean Drama, An Interpretation,* London, 1936.

Farnham, Willard, *The Medieval Heritage of Elizabethan Tragedy,* Berkeley, Calif., 1936.

Hodges, C. W., *The Globe Restored, A Study of the Elizabethan Theatre,* London, 1953.

Prior, Moody E., *The Language of Tragedy,* New York, 1947.

Reynolds, G. F., *The Staging of Elizabethan Plays at the Red Bull Theater 1605–1625,* New York, 1940.

Spencer, Theodore, *Death and Elizabethan Tragedy, A Study of Convention and Opinion in the Elizabethan Drama,* Cambridge, Mass., 1936.

Wilson, F. P., *Elizabethan and Jacobean,* Oxford, 1945.

Drama and Theater in Renaissance Spain:

Benavente, Jacinto, "Some Characteristics of the Spanish Theatre of the Golden Age," in *Four Plays by Lope de Vega,* trans. John G. Underhill, New York, 1936.

Chandler, Richard E. and Kessel Schwartz, *A New History of Spanish Literature,* Baton Rouge, 1961.

Crawford, J. P. W., *Spanish Drama Before Lope de Vega,* Philadelphia, 1922.

———, *The Spanish Pastoral Drama,* Philadelphia, 1938.

Fitzmaurice-Kelly, James, *Lope de Vega and the Spanish Drama,* Glasgow, 1902.

Gillet, Joseph E., *Torres Naharro,* Vol. IV: *Torres Naharro and the Drama of the Renaissance,* ed. Otis H. Greene, Philadelphia, 1961.

Lewes, George Henry, *The Spanish Drama, Lope de Vega and Calderón,* London, 1846.

Matulka, B., *The Feminist Theme in the Drama of the Siglo d'Oro,* New York, 1936.

Parker, A. A., *The Approach to the Spanish Drama of the Golden Age,* London, 1957.

Rennert, H. A., *The Spanish Stage in the Time of Lope de Vega,* New York, 1909.

Shoemaker, William H., *The Multiple Stage in Spain during the 15th and 16th Centuries,* Princeton, N.J., 1935.

Niccolò Machiavelli

Niccolò Machiavelli (1469–1527) *is best known as a political theorist and historian. His studies of* realpolitik, *including* THE PRINCE *and* THE DISCOURSES UPON LIVY, *laid the foundation for an objective, unsentimental approach to statecraft and diplomacy. In the Renaissance, indeed, his honesty and pessimism earned him a reputation as an amoral tactician and associated his name with diabolism. But Machiavelli was also a humanist of great learning and varied talents. In addition to his better known works, he translated Terence and, apparently as relief from his political and historical projects, wrote two comedies of the type known as Learned Comedies (to distinguish them from popular entertainments):* THE MANDRAKE *and* CLIZIA.

Chronology

1469 Born in Florence, the second son of a modestly wealthy lawyer.

1494 Flight of the Medici from Florence; establishment of the Republic.

1498 Began his political career as secretary to the Florentine Chancery. He served in government until 1512.

1500–12 Travelled in France, Germany, and Italy on diplomatic missions.

1504 Wrote humorous dramatic sketches called *Masks* in imitation of Aristophanes.

1512 Return of the Medici to Florence; Machiavelli suspected of having taken part in the plot against them, and forced to retire to a villa near Florence.

1513–17 Wrote *The Discourses Upon Livy* and *The Prince.*

1513–20 Translated Terence's *Woman of Andros* and wrote *The Mandrake.*

1520 Wrote *The Life of Castruccio Castracani.*

1520–25 Wrote *Clizia,* a second comedy, and *The History of Florence.*

1527 Died in Florence.

Selected Bibliography

Chabod, Frederico, *Machiavelli and the Renaissance,* trans. by David Moore, London, 1958.

Hale, John Rigby, *Machiavelli and Renaissance Italy,* London, 1961.

Ridolfi, Roberto, *The Life of Niccolò Machiavelli,* trans. by Cecil Grayson, London, 1963.

Design for the comic scene in Vitruvius, *Architecture*, 1547.
The Metropolitan Museum of Art, Rogers Fund, 1922.
Photo Charles Phelps Cushing

THE MANDRAKE

by Niccolò Machiavelli

English Version by Frederick May and Eric Bentley

Characters
CALLIMACO, *a young man*
SIRO, *a servant*
MESSER NICIA CALFUCCI, LL.D.
LIGURIO, *a parasite*
SOSTRATA, *a mother*
TIMOTEO, *a friar*
A WOMAN
LUCREZIA, *wife of Messer Nicia, daughter of Sostrata*

Florence in the early sixteenth century

Prologue

Ladies and gentlemen, God bless you!
May Fate and Fortune long caress you!
(I thought I'd make a little fuss
Of you, so you'll be nice to *us*.)
Just sit quite still, don't make a sound,   5
And you will like us, I'll be bound.
The story's good we'll tell to you.
It happened here. What's more: it's true.
Florence we'll show you now, your home;
Tomorrow, maybe, Pisa, Rome,   10
The nicest towns you ever saw.
(Don't laugh so hard; you'll break your jaw.)
This right-hand door—can you all see?—
Belongs to a learnèd LL.D.
His erudition's vast: I'm told   15
He has Boethius* down cold.
That dingy street is Lovers' Lane:
Those who fall there don't rise again.
If you don't leave us in the lurch
You'll see emerging from that church   20
A well-known friar (though I would not

---

[16] Anicius Manlius Severinus Boethius (*c.*480–*c.*524 A.D.) was a Roman philosopher and statesman who was best known in the Middle Ages and early Renaissance for his *Consolation of Philosophy*. Also influential were his Latin translations of Aristotle's treatises on logic and his own books on logic.

Presume to say well known for what).
Next, you are all to get to know
A young man called Callimaco
Who lives in this next house by chance.   25
He is just back from Paris, France.
Callimaco is such a dandy
One look at him makes women randy.
This fellow loved unto perdition
A certain girl of good position   30
And played a little trick on her.
And who are we that should demur,
Good people, since on this our earth,
Of trickery there is no dearth?
(When you are tricked, fair ladies, see   35
That you are tricked as pleasantly.)
The mandrake of our title is
A plant with certain properties:
When women eat the root, their fate . . .
But this is to anticipate.   40
Our author's called . . . alas, his name
As yet is not well known to Fame.
If you should find his tale confusing,
The whole show somewhat unamusing,
He's quite a decent chap, I think,   45
And may well stand you to a drink.
He offers, though, for your delight
Well, what? An evil parasite . . .
A scholar who is not too bright . . .
A lover who is full of fight . . .   50
A friar whose moral sense is slight . . .
Is that sufficient for one night?
True, true, such antic jollity
Is nothing but frivolity.
This comedy is not profound.   55
I'm not so sure it's even sound.
Our author sends you his excuses.
He says life's hard, the world obtuse is,
And he most gladly would display
His gifts in any other way,   60
The only question is: who'd pay?
Attribute then to lack of money
His condescending to be funny.
Can he expect a warm reception?
If so, he'll be a rare exception.   65
This age to sour contempt is quicker,
To twisted smile, malignant snicker.
The virtues that did thrive of yore,

D'you think we'll see them any more?
Men won't devote their nights and days   70
To toil without their meed of praise:
Who on a plant would spend his powers
Knowing that all his lovely flowers
Would by a tempest then be tossed
Or in a fog concealed and lost?   75
Moreover, if you have concluded
Our man's your victim, you're deluded.
No matter for what sort you take him
You cannot nudge him, push him, shake him,
And, as for malice, he can do   80
Far better at the trade than you
For in the whole of Italy
Wherever reigns, not *yes,* but *sì,*
There's not a soul he would kowtow to.
The only man he'd make a bow to   85
Is the only V.I.P. he knows:
A man in more expensive clothes.
Backbite him if you please, but we
Must get on with his comedy
If you are to be home by three.   90
Don't take the play too much to heart.
If you see a monster, do not start:
Just look right through him, and he'll go.
But, wait, here comes Callimaco,
Siro his servant at his side.   95
These two, between them, will confide
The plot to you. Pay close attention!
The play will now unfold without my intervention.

Act One

(*Enter* CALLIMACO *and* SIRO)

CALLIMACO Don't go, Siro, I want to talk to you.

SIRO I'm not going.

CALLIMACO You must have been quite surprised by my sudden departure from
   Paris, and now very likely you're surprised that, having been here a month,
   I still haven't done anything.   5

SIRO I don't deny it.

CALLIMACO If I haven't told you already what I'm about to tell you, it's not
   because I don't trust you, but because it seemed best not to talk of confi-
   dential matters unless one was forced to. But now, since I shall need your
   help, I am going to tell you everything.   10

SIRO I am your servant, and servants must never question their masters, nor
   pry into their affairs. But when the master volunteers information, the servant

must serve him faithfully. Which is what I've done, and what I propose to do.

CALLIMACO   I know. I think you've heard me say a thousand times—but it won't hurt you to hear it the thousand and first—that when I was ten years old, my father and mother being dead, I was sent by my guardians to live in Paris, where I've been these twenty years. After ten years the Italian Wars began—as a result of King Charles's invasion of Italy, which laid waste this country—so I decided to settle in Paris and never go back to my native land. I thought I should be safer than in Italy.

SIRO   Very true.

CALLIMACO   Having sent instructions that all my possessions here, with the exception of my house, should be sold, I settled down in Paris. And I have passed the last ten years in great happiness . . .

SIRO   I know.

CALLIMACO   . . . devoting part of my time to study, part to pleasure, and part to business, and so arranging things that the three never got in each other's way. In consequence, as you know, I lived quietly, helping whoever I could, trying to injure nobody, so that, it seems to me, I came to be well thought of by everyone, be he gentleman or merchant, foreign or native, rich or poor.

SIRO   That's true, too.

CALLIMACO   But Fortune, deeming that I was *too* happy, sent to Paris a certain Cammillo Calfucci.

SIRO   I begin to guess what your trouble is.

CALLIMACO   Like the other Florentines, he was frequently invited to dine at my house, and one day, when we were gathered together, an argument started as to where the more beautiful women were to be found—Italy or France. I could have no opinion concerning Italian women—I was so little when I left the country—so Cammillo Calfucci took up the cudgels for the Italians and another Florentine defended the French. After a great deal of arguments back and forth, Cammillo, in something of a temper, said that, even if Italian women in general were monsters, he had a kinswoman who could redeem her country's reputation all by herself.

SIRO   I see what you're after.

CALLIMACO   And he named Madonna Lucrezia, wife of Messer Nicia Calfucci, and so praised her beauty and sweetness of manner that he left us all amazed and aroused in me such a desire to see her that I set out for Florence, putting aside all other considerations and not bothering whether there was a war on or not. Having arrived here, I found that Madonna Lucrezia's reputation fell far short of the truth; which is quite a rare phenomenon. And I'm burning with such desire to make her mine, I hardly know what to do with myself.

SIRO   If you'd told me this when we were in Paris, I'd have known how to advise you. Now, I don't know what to say.

CALLIMACO   I'm not telling you this with a view to advice, but to get it out of my system. And so you can be ready to help when the need arises.

SIRO   I couldn't be readier. What hopes have you got?

CALLIMACO   Alas, none. Or very few. Let me explain. First, her nature is hostile to my desires. She's the quintessence of chastity. The thought of love affairs is alien to her. Then, her husband's very rich, lets himself be ruled by 60 her in everything, and, if he's not exactly young, he's not antique either, that's clear. Again, there are no relatives or neighbors whose homes she frequents at wakes and holidays and the other pleasant occasions that young women delight in. No tradesman sets foot in her house, and she hasn't a single servant or retainer who doesn't go in fear of her. Bribery and cor- 65 ruption are therefore excluded.

SIRO   What are you thinking of doing, then?

CALLIMACO   No situation is so desperate that one may not continue to hope. Even if one's hopes are feeble and vain, the determination to see a thing through causes them to seem far otherwise. 70

SIRO   So what makes you go on hoping?

CALLIMACO   Two things. First, the simple-mindedness of Messer Nicia, who, though he holds an LL.D. from the university, is the most thickheaded and foolish man in Florence. Second, his desire, and hers, to have children. Having been married for six years without getting any, and being very rich, they're 75 dying of their desire for a family. There's a third factor: her mother. She was a bit of a baggage when she was young; but she's rich now, and I've no idea how to deal with her.

SIRO   Since that's how matters stand, have you tried anything?

CALLIMACO   Yes. In a small way. 80

SIRO   Tell me.

CALLIMACO   You know Ligurio, who's always coming to eat at my house? He used to be a professional matchmaker. Now he goes around cadging dinners and suppers. Being a pleasant sort of chap, he's had no trouble becoming intimate with Messer Nicia, and leading him a dance. The old boy 85 wouldn't invite him to dinner, it's true, but he's been lending him money from time to time. As for me, I've struck up a friendship with this Ligurio, told him of my love for Madonna Lucrezia, and he's promised to help me with all he's got.

SIRO   Take care he doesn't deceive you. These parasites don't make a habit 90 of fidelity.

CALLIMACO   True. Nonetheless, when you place yourself in someone's hands, you place yourself in someone's hands. I've promised him a large sum of money if he succeeds, and, if he fails, a dinner and a supper. I'd never eat alone in any case. 95

SIRO   So what has he promised to do?

CALLIMACO   He's promised to persuade Messer Nicia to take his wife to the Baths—this May.

SIRO   What good would that do you?

CALLIMACO   What good would it do me? The place may well make a different 100 woman out of her. In haunts like that, they do nothing but throw parties and such. And I'd be taking with me all the plausible arguments I could think up, omitting no tittle of pomp and circumstance. I'd become the bosom pal of both parties, wife and husband. Who can say what will happen? One thing leads to another. Time rules all. 105

SIRO   I'm quite impressed.

CALLIMACO Ligurio left me this morning saying that he'd take this matter up with Messer Nicia and would let me know the answer.

SIRO Here they come—together.

CALLIMACO I'll step to one side—to be on hand for a word with Ligurio 110 when he takes leave of the old boy. Meanwhile you go home and get on with your work. If I want you for anything I'll let you know.

SIRO Right. (SIRO *goes*; CALLIMACO *stands aside*)

(*Enter* MESSER NICIA *and* LIGURIO)

MESSER NICIA I think your advice is good, and I talked the matter over last 115 night with my wife. She said she'd give me her answer today. But, to tell the truth, I'm not over-keen.

LIGURIO Why not?

MESSER NICIA Because I'm in a rut and I'd like to stay in it. What's more, to have to transport wife, servants, household goods, it doesn't appeal to 120 me. Besides, I was talking yesterday evening to some doctors. One of them said I should go to San Filippo; another said Porretta; another, Villa. What a bunch of quacks! If you ask me, the medical profession doesn't know its business.

LIGURIO What you mentioned first must be what troubles you most: you're 125 not accustomed to lose sight of the Cupola.*

MESSER NICIA You're mistaken. When I was younger I was a victim of Wander-lust. They never held a fair at Prato* but I was there. There's not a castle in the neighborhood that I haven't visited. Better yet: I've been to Pisa and Livorno. What do you think of that? 130

LIGURIO Then you must have seen the Sliding Tower of Pisa?

MESSER NICIA You mean the Leaning Tower.

LIGURIO The Leaning Tower, of course. And at Livorno, did you see the sea?

MESSER NICIA You know very well I did.

LIGURIO How much bigger is it than the Arno?* 135

MESSER NICIA Arno! Pooh! It's four times bigger, no, more than six; you'll make me say more than seven times in a minute. Nothing but water, water, water!

LIGURIO Well then, I'm amazed that you, who—as the saying is—have pissed your way through so much snow, should make such a fuss about going 140 to the Baths!

MESSER NICIA Your mother's milk is still on your lips, my child. Do you think it's a small matter to transplant an entire household? Yet my desire for children is so strong I'm ready to do anything. But have a word or two with those M.D.s. See where *they* advise me to go. Meanwhile I'll join 145 my wife at home. I'll see you there later.

LIGURIO Good idea. (MESSER NICIA *goes*)

LIGURIO Can there be a bigger fool in the whole wide world? And how Fortune has favored him! He's rich, and his beautiful wife is well bred, virtuous, and fit to rule a kingdom. It seems to me that the proverb about marriage 150

126 The cupola of the cathedral of Florence.
128 Prato is about eight miles from Florence.
135 The river that runs through Florence to the sea.

seldom proves true—the one that runs: "God makes men, but they find their mates for themselves." For in general we see a man of parts paired off with a shrew while a prudent woman gets a half-wit for a husband. But that fellow's half-wittedness has this much to be said for it: it gives Callimaco reason to hope. (CALLIMACO *comes forward*) And here he is. Hey, Callimaco—lying 155 in wait for someone?

CALLIMACO   I'd seen you with our learnèd friend, and I was waiting for you to part company with him, so I could hear what you'd done.

LIGURIO   He's a fellow of small prudence and less spirit, as you know. He doesn't want to leave Florence. However, I worked on his feelings for a while, 160 and he told me he'd do just as I said. I believe we'll be able to move him in the right direction. Whether we can complete our project is, of course, another story.

CALLIMACO   How so?

LIGURIO   Well, as you know, all sorts of people go to these Baths, and it 165 might be that a man would come along who'd find Madonna Lucrezia as attractive as you do. He might be richer than you. He might be more charming. So there's the danger of going to all this trouble for someone else's benefit. It is also possible that, with so many competitors for her favor, she might become the harder to attain. Or that, having got used to the idea 170 of yielding, she might yield, not to you, but to another.

CALLIMACO   You have a point. But what am I to do? Which way am I to turn? I must try something. Something tremendous or something dangerous, something harmful or something infamous, I don't care. Better to die than to live like this! If I could sleep at night, if I could eat, if I could engage in 175 conversation, if I could find pleasure in anything at all, I should be able to await Time's verdict more patiently. Here and now I can see no remedy. If hope is not kept alive within me by some course of action, I shall assuredly die. Faced with this prospect of Death, I am resolved to fear nothing, but adopt a course of action that is bestial, cruel, and nefarious. 180

LIGURIO   You mustn't talk like that! You must curb such excess of passion!

CALLIMACO   Actually, by feeding my imagination on thoughts like this, I keep myself in check—as you can see. However, it is necessary for us either to proceed with our plan for sending him to the Baths or to try some other avenue, if only that I may have a little hope to feed on. And if it can't be 185 true hope, then let it be false, so long as it provides me with thoughts that lighten my burden of troubles!

LIGURIO   You're right. I'm for doing as you say.

CALLIMACO   Though I know that men of your sort live by cheating others, I believe you. I don't propose to fear your cheating me because, if I saw 190 you try to, I should proceed to take advantage of the fact. And you would forfeit your right to come and go in my house, and all hope of receiving what I have promised you.

LIGURIO   Don't doubt my fidelity. Even if I had no sense of my own interests, and did not hope what I hope, well, you and I are so congenial, I'm almost 195 as desirous as you are that you should get what you want. But enough. Messer Nicia has commissioned me to find a doctor who can say which of the Baths it would be best for him to go to. Let yourself be advised by me. Tell him you've studied medicine and been practicing for some time in Paris. Simpleminded as he is, he'll believe you, and, since you're an educated man, 200 you'll be able to treat him to a little Latin.

CALLIMACO What good will that do us?

LIGURIO It will enable us to send him to whichever Baths we wish, and put into operation another plan I've thought of—one that's more likely to succeed and takes less time. 205

CALLIMACO What did you say?

LIGURIO I say you're to take heart: if you put your trust in me, I'll have the whole thing finished by this time tomorrow. Even if he investigates your claim to be a doctor—and he won't—the short time at his disposal and the nature of the case will stop him getting anywhere. By the time he figured 210 anything out—if he did—it'd be too late for him to frustrate our plan.

CALLIMACO You fill me with new life. Oh, this is too fair a promise! You feed me with too much hope! How will you do it?

LIGURIO You'll find out at the proper moment. Right now there's little enough time for action, let alone talk. Go home and wait for me. I'll hunt up our 215 learnèd friend. And if I bring him along, take your cue from me, and make everything you say fit in.

CALLIMACO I'll do as you say, though the hopes you raise within me may, I fear, go up in smoke. (*They go out*)

Act Two

(*Enter* LIGURIO *and* MESSER NICIA)

LIGURIO As I say, I believe God expressly sent us this man that you might have your desire. His practice in Paris was extensive and successful, and you needn't be surprised that he hasn't practiced here in Florence. The reasons are, first, that he's rich, and second, that he has to return to Paris at once.

MESSER NICIA Well, now, brother, there's an important point: I shouldn't like 5 him to get me into an awkward situation and then leave me in it.

LIGURIO The only thing you have to worry about is that he might not be willing to undertake your cure. If he does take you on, he won't leave you till he's seen it through.

MESSER NICIA That part I'll leave to you, but, as for science, once I've talked 10 with him, *I'll* tell *you* whether he knows his stuff or not. He won't sell *me* any pig in a poke!

LIGURIO Because you're the man I know you to be, I *want* you to talk with him. And if he doesn't impress you, for presence, learning, and Latin, as someone you can trust like your dear old sainted mother, my name's not 15 Ligurio.

MESSER NICIA Well then, by the Holy Angel, so be it! And let's get going! Where does he live?

LIGURIO On this square. That's his door right opposite.

MESSER NICIA Good Fortune attend us! 20

LIGURIO (*Knocks at the door*) Here goes!

SIRO (*From within*) Who is it?

LIGURIO Is Callimaco at home?

SIRO Yes, he is.

MESSER NICIA Why don't you call him *Master* Callimaco? 25

LIGURIO Oh, he doesn't care about such trifles.

MESSER NICIA Tsk, tsk, tsk. You must pay him the respect due to his profession: if he takes it amiss, so much the worse for him.

(*Enter* CALLIMACO, *dressed as a doctor*)

CALLIMACO Who is it that wants me? 30

MESSER NICIA *Bona dies, domine magister.**

CALLIMACO *Et vobis bona, domine doctor.**

LIGURIO What do you think?

MESSER NICIA By the Holy Gospel, he's good!

LIGURIO If you want me to stay, you must talk a language I understand. If not, 35 let's part company.

CALLIMACO What fair business brings you here?

MESSER NICIA I wonder. I want two things that another man might run a mile to avoid. *Primo,* to give myself a lot of trouble. *Secundo,* to inflict it on someone else. I have no children, I'd like some, and, to get myself into this 40 trouble, I've come to importune you.

CALLIMACO It will never be less than a joy to me to give pleasure to you and to all other men of merit and virtue, nor have I practiced these many years in Paris but for the privilege of serving such as you.

MESSER NICIA I appreciate that, and should you ever need my own professional 45 services, I would be happy to oblige. But to return *ad rem nostram.** Have you thought which of the Baths is most likely to get my wife pregnant? I know, you see, that Ligurio here has told you—what he has told you.

CALLIMACO Very true. But, that we may enable you to have your desire, we must know the cause of your wife's sterility. For there can be various causes. 50 *Nam causae sterilitatis sunt: aut in semine, aut in matrice, aut in strumentis seminariis, aut in virga, aut in causa extrinseca.**

MESSER NICIA This is the most worthy man one could hope to find!

CALLIMACO Alternatively, the sterility might be caused by impotence in you. If that should be the case, there would be no remedy. 55

MESSER NICIA Impotent? Me? Hoho! Don't make me laugh! I don't believe there's a more vigorous, virile man than me in Florence.

CALLIMACO Well, if that's not it, you may rest assured we'll find a remedy.

MESSER NICIA Would there be any remedy other than the Baths? Because *I* don't want to go to all the inconvenience, and my wife would be unwilling to 60 leave Florence.

LIGURIO Let me answer your question in the affirmative. Callimaco, being

---

[31] "Good day, sir teacher."

[32] "And a good one to you, sir doctor."

[46] "To our affair."

[52] "For the causes of sterility are as follows: either in the semen, or in the matrix, or in the seminal materials of the flux, or in the staff, or in an extrinsic cause."

circumspect, sometimes carries circumspection to excess. Didn't you tell me you knew how to prepare certain potions that will make a woman pregnant quite infallibly? 65

CALLIMACO   I did. But it has not been my habit to communicate that fact to strangers. They might regard me as a charlatan.

MESSER NICIA   Don't worry about me. I'm amazed at your abilities. There's nothing I couldn't believe you capable of. There's nothing I wouldn't do for you! 70

LIGURIO   I think you ought to see a specimen of her water.

CALLIMACO   Undoubtedly. One could get nowhere without it.

LIGURIO   Call Siro, tell him to go home with Messer Nicia, pick up the specimen, and then come back. We'll wait for him indoors. (CALLIMACO *fetches* SIRO)

CALLIMACO   Siro, go with him. And if you agree, messere, you come back too, 75 and we'll think of a way out.

MESSER NICIA   If I agree? I shall be back like a shot. I place more confidence in you than Hungarians do in swords! (CALLIMACO *and* LIGURIO *go off*)

MESSER NICIA   That master of yours is a very distinguished man.

SIRO   Better than that, even. 80

MESSER NICIA   The King of France holds him in great esteem?

SIRO   Very great.

MESSER NICIA   And for that reason, I take it, he is glad to stay in France?

SIRO   That's my belief.

MESSER NICIA   He's quite right. The people of this city are dirty dogs. No 85 appreciation of merit. If he were to stay, no one would trouble to look at him twice. I speak from experience. I've given it everything, learning my *hics, haecs,* and *hocs,** and, if I hadn't got a private income, I'd be having a thin time of it, I can tell you.

SIRO   Do you make a hundred ducats a year? 90

MESSER NICIA   Go on. I don't make a hundred *lire*. Or a hundred groats. The fact is, if you don't spend your time keeping up with the neighbors—such is Florence—you won't find a dog to bark you a civil greeting. The rest of us are good for nothing but funerals and wedding breakfasts and loafing all day on the square. But they don't bother me. I have no need of anybody. There 95 are plenty who'd be glad to change places with me. But I shouldn't like what I've just said to get around, or someone might slap a fine on me or slug me in a dark alley.

SIRO   Don't worry, messere.

MESSER NICIA   This is my house. Wait for me here. I'll be right back. 100

SIRO   Go ahead. (MESSER NICIA *goes in*)

SIRO   If all men of learning were like that one, the rest of us would have straw in our hair. (*Gesture indicating insanity*) I'm quite sure that the wicked Ligurio and my mad master are leading him to his downfall. And, to tell the truth, I'd enjoy his downfall, if only we could be sure of getting away with it. 105 Otherwise I'm risking my neck and my master is risking both his neck and his property. He's already turned himself into a doctor. I just don't know

---

88 That is, my Latin grammar.

what their little plan is, or where they're heading with all this deception. But here's Messer Nicia again, specimen in hand. You can't help laughing at him, the old cuckoo. 110

(*Enter* MESSER NICIA)

MESSER NICIA (*To someone in the house, evidently* LUCREZIA) Up till now I've always done everything your way. In this matter I want you to do things *my* way. If I'd thought that you and I weren't going to have children, I'd rather have married a peasant girl. Siro! Follow me. The trouble I had getting My 115 Lady Fool to give me this specimen! That's not to say, of course, that she wants children less than I do. On the contrary! But the moment I suggest anything practical, oh, what a song and dance!

SIRO Be patient: soft words make women do what other people want.

MESSER NICIA Soft words! She raised the roof! Go, this instant: tell your 120 master and Ligurio I'm here.

SIRO Look, they're just coming out of the house.

(*Enter* LIGURIO *and* CALLIMACO)

LIGURIO (*Aside to* CALLIMACO) Messer Nicia will be easy to persuade. The problem will be his wife. But we shall find a way to bring her round. 125

CALLIMACO Have you got the specimen?

MESSER NICIA Siro has it under his cloak.

CALLIMACO Give it to me. Aha! Weak kidneys!

MESSER NICIA Yes, it does look a bit turbid. Yet she only just did it.

CALLIMACO Oh, don't let that surprise you. *Nam mulieris urinae sunt semper* 130 *maiioris glossitiei et albedinis et minoris pulchritudinis quam virorum. Huius autem in caetera, causa est amplitudo canalium, mixtio eorum quae ex matrice exeunt cum urina.**

MESSER NICIA Whores of Heaven! This man gets better all the time! He thinks of everything! 135

CALLIMACO I'm afraid this woman is not properly covered at night. For that reason her urine is not of the finest quality.

MESSER NICIA She has a good quilt over her. But she spends four hours on her knees before she gets into bed, stringing off paternosters. She's as strong as a horse when it comes to standing the cold. 140

CALLIMACO Well, to cut a long story short, Messer Nicia, either you trust me or you don't. Either I am to expound a sure remedy to you or I am not. For myself, I'd let you have the remedy. Only put your trust in me, and you shall have it. And if, one year from now, your wife is not holding a child in her arms, a child of her own, I will gladly pay you two thousand ducats. 145

MESSER NICIA Pray tell me what this remedy is. My only wish is to honor you in everything, and to trust you more than my father-confessor.

CALLIMACO This, then, you must know. Nothing more surely makes a woman pregnant than getting her to drink a potion made from the root of the mandrake. This is something I have tested several times. Every time, it 150

---

133 "For the urines of women are always of greater glossiness and whiteness and of lesser beauty than those of men. However, the cause of this generally is the amplitude of the canals, the mixture of those things which come out with the urine."

worked. Were that not so, the Queen of France would be childless, not to mention countless other princesses of that land.

MESSER NICIA   Is it possible?

CALLIMACO   It is exactly as I say. And Fortune must love you dearly, for she has caused me to bring to Florence all the ingredients of that potion. You could have it at once. 155

MESSER NICIA   When would she have to take it?

CALLIMACO   This evening after supper. The moon is well disposed. There could not be a more propitious moment.

MESSER NICIA   Well, that won't be hard to arrange. Make it up in any case. 160 I'll see that she takes it.

CALLIMACO   There's a further consideration. The first man who has to do with her after she's taken this potion will die within the week. Nothing in this world can save him.

MESSER NICIA   Blood and guts! I won't touch the filthy stuff! You can't make 165 me run my neck into *that* kind of noose!

CALLIMACO   Be calm. There is a remedy.

MESSER NICIA   What is it?

CALLIMACO   Arrange for someone else to sleep with her. Immediately. So that, spending the night with her, he may draw upon himself all the infection 170 of the mandrake. After which you can lie with her without danger.

MESSER NICIA   I won't do it.

CALLIMACO   Why not?

MESSER NICIA   I don't want to make my wife a whore and myself a cuckold, that's why not. 175

CALLIMACO   What did you say, Messer Nicia? Is this our wise Doctor of Laws? You are not prepared to do what the King of France has done, and great lords at his court without number?

MESSER NICIA   Who on earth do you expect me to find? Who would do such a thing? If I tell him about it, he won't want to do it. If I don't tell him, 180 I shall be guilty of treachery—which is a felony in Florence. And I don't want to get into hot water!

CALLIMACO   If that's your only trouble, I believe I can take care of it.

MESSER NICIA   How?

CALLIMACO   I'll tell you. I'll give you the potion this evening after supper. 185 Have her drink it, then put her straight to bed. It'll be about ten o'clock. Then we'll disguise ourselves—you, Ligurio, Siro, and I—and go search the New Market, the Old Market, every street and alley. The first idle young lout that we come upon, we gag him, and, to the tune of a sound drubbing, take him into your house—and into your bedroom—in the dark. Then we put him 190 in the bed and tell him what to do. I don't think there'll be any problem. In the morning you send the fellow packing before daybreak. Then get your wife washed and you can take your pleasure of her without the slightest risk.

MESSER NICIA   I'll go along—since you tell me that a king and princes and lords have used this method. One request, though: let's keep this secret—on 195 account of the felony!

CALLIMACO   Who d'you think would blab?

MESSER NICIA There's another obstacle. A tricky one, too.

CALLIMACO What?

MESSER NICIA We must get my wife to agree. And I don't think she ever 200 will.

CALLIMACO An excellent point. Personally, I would never marry in the first place unless I knew I could get the lady to see things my way.

LIGURIO I have it!

MESSER NICIA What? 205

LIGURIO The remedy. We make use of her father-confessor.

CALLIMACO And who'll persuade the father-confessor?

LIGURIO You, me, and money. Our own wickedness and that of the priests.

MESSER NICIA I'm afraid she'll refuse to talk with her father-confessor, if only to contradict her husband. 210

LIGURIO There's a remedy for that too.

CALLIMACO Tell me.

LIGURIO Get her mother to take her to him.

MESSER NICIA True. She trusts her mother.

LIGURIO And I happen to know that her mother is of our way of thinking. 215 Well, now, time's running on, and it'll soon be evening. Callimaco, go and take a little stroll, and be sure that you're at home to receive us at eight o'clock with the potion all ready. We'll go see the mother, then call on the friar, then report back to you.

CALLIMACO (*Aside to* LIGURIO) Hey! Don't leave me alone! 220

LIGURIO You look as if your goose were cooked.

CALLIMACO Where am *I* supposed to put myself?

LIGURIO Here, there, everywhere. Up this street and down the next. Florence is such a big city.

CALLIMACO I'm dead. (*They go off*) 225

Act Three

Scene 1

(*Enter* SOSTRATA, MESSER NICIA, *and* LIGURIO)

SOSTRATA I have always heard it said that it is the part of the prudent man to choose the lesser of two evils. If this is the only way you can have children, you must take it—provided it in no way offends against conscience.

MESSER NICIA That's right.

LIGURIO You will go and see your daughter, and Messer Nicia and I will call 5 on her confessor, Friar Timoteo. We'll tell him how things stand, so that you won't have to. Then you'll hear what *he* has to say.

SOSTRATA Very good. You take that street there. I'll go see Lucrezia and, come what may, I'll take her to talk with Friar Timoteo. (SOSTRATA *goes*)

MESSER NICIA You're probably surprised, Ligurio, that we have to go all 10 round the world to persuade my wife? You wouldn't be—if you knew the whole story.

LIGURIO I imagine it's because all women are suspicious.

MESSER NICIA   It's not that. She used to be the sweetest person in the world, and the easiest to manage. But one of her neighbors told her that, if she made a vow to attend first Mass at the Chapel of the Servites for forty mornings in a row, she would become pregnant. She made the vow and went to the chapel about twenty times. Well, you know how it is, one of those frisky friars started pestering her. Naturally, she refused to go back. It's a sad state of affairs when the very people who ought to be setting a good example turn out like that. Am I right?

LIGURIO   Right, by Satan!

MESSER NICIA   From that day to this she's gone around with her ears pricked like a hare. Suggest anything at all, and she kicks up a fuss.

LIGURIO   My surprise is gone. But that vow—how did she go about fulfilling it?

MESSER NICIA   She got a dispensation.

LIGURIO   Good. Now let me have twenty-five ducats if you have them. Affairs of this kind cost money. One must make friends with the friar and give him hopes of better things to come.

MESSER NICIA   Here you are, then. I'm not worried. I'll get it back in other ways.

LIGURIO   These friars are smart. Shrewd. Which stands to reason, since they know both their own sins and everyone else's. If you're not wise to their ways, you can easily get gypped, and not know how to make them do what you want. So don't spoil everything by talking to him. A man like you, who spends the whole day in his study, knows all about his books, but can't cope with mundane matters. (*Aside*) This fellow is such a fool, I'm afraid he'll spoil everything.

MESSER NICIA   Tell me what you want me to do.

LIGURIO   Leave the talking to me. Don't say a word unless I give the signal.

MESSER NICIA   I'm happy to do as you say. What signal will you give?

LIGURIO   I shall wink—and bite my lip. No, no. Let's try something else. How long it is since you last spoke with Friar Timoteo?

MESSER NICIA   Over ten years.

LIGURIO   Good. I'll tell him that you've gone deaf and can't answer him: you needn't say a word unless we shout.

MESSER NICIA   I'll do that.

LIGURIO   And don't be upset if I say something that doesn't seem to fit. Everything contributes to the final result.

MESSER NICIA   When the time comes! (*They go*)

Scene 2

(*Enter* TIMOTEO *and* A WOMAN)

TIMOTEO   If you wish to make confession, I shall accede to your wish.

THE WOMAN   Not today. Someone's expecting me. It's enough if I worked some of it out of my system just standing here. Have you said those masses to Our Lady?

TIMOTEO   Yes, madonna.

THE WOMAN   Here, take this florin. Every Monday for the next two months

I want you to say the Mass for the Dead for my husband's soul. He was a terrible man, but then there's the call of the flesh. I get a bit of the old feeling whenever I think of him. Do you think he's in Purgatory?

TIMOTEO Undoubtedly.

THE WOMAN I'm not so sure. You know what he did to me—and not just once either. I used to complain about it to you. I got as far over in bed as I could, but he was so importunate. Ugh, Lord Above!

TIMOTEO Don't worry. God's clemency is great. If a man lack not the will, he shall not lack the time for repentance.

THE WOMAN Do you think the Turks will invade Italy this year?

TIMOTEO If you don't say your prayers, yes.

THE WOMAN Glory be! Lord preserve us from the Turks and all their deviltries! All that impaling they go in for—it scares the life out of me! But there's a woman with a piece of linen for me—in the church yonder. I must let her know I'm here. Good day.

TIMOTEO God be with you. (*She goes*)

(*Enter* MESSER NICIA *and* LIGURIO)

TIMOTEO Women are the most charitable creatures, and the most trying. The man who shuns them avoids the trials, but also goes without their services; while the man who accepts them gets both the services and the trials. Well, it's the old truth, you can't have honey without flies. What are you about, my worthy friends? Can that be Messer Nicia?

LIGURIO You'll have to shout. He's got so deaf, he can't hear a word.

TIMOTEO You're welcome, messere.

LIGURIO Louder!

TIMOTEO Welcome!!

MESSER NICIA Pleased to see you, Father!

TIMOTEO What are you about?

MESSER NICIA Oh, nicely, thanks.

LIGURIO You'd better talk to me, Father. If you want *him* to hear, you'll have to shout till the whole square resounds with it.

TIMOTEO What do you want with me?

LIGURIO Messer Nicia here and another worthy man—I'll tell you about *him* later—are charged with the distribution of several hundred ducats as alms.

MESSER NICIA Blood and guts!

LIGURIO (*Aside*) Hold your tongue, damn you. We shan't need that much. (*Aloud*) Don't be surprised at anything he might say, Father, he can't hear a thing. Every now and again he *thinks* he hears something and replies with an irrelevant remark.

TIMOTEO Pray continue. Let him say what he likes.

LIGURIO I've got some of the money with me now. They've chosen you as the person to distribute it.

TIMOTEO I'll be very glad to.

LIGURIO But first, you must help us. A strange thing has happened to Messer Nicia. Only you *can* help us. It concerns the honor of his house.

TIMOTEO What is it?

LIGURIO   I don't know if you've met Messer Nicia's nephew, Cammillo Calfucci?

TIMOTEO   Yes, I have.

LIGURIO   Well, a year ago, he went to Paris on business, and, as his wife was dead, he left his daughter, who was of marriageable age, in the care of a convent which shall be nameless.   110

TIMOTEO   What happened?

LIGURIO   What happened? Just this. As a result of the nuns' carelessness or her own featherheadedness, she now finds herself four months pregnant. If things can't very discreetly be put to rights, Messer Nicia, the nuns, the girl, Cammillo, and the house of Calfucci will all be dishonored together. Now   115 Messer Nicia values his honor so highly and is so sensitive to scandal that—if the whole thing can be prevented from leaking out—he will give three hundred ducats for the love of God.

MESSER NICIA   There's a story for you!

LIGURIO   (*Aside*) Quiet! (*Aloud*) And he wants to put the matter in your   120 hands. Only you and the mother superior can set things to rights.

TIMOTEO   How?

LIGURIO   You can persuade the mother superior to give the girl a potion. To make her miscarry.

TIMOTEO   This is something that requires a little thinking over.   125

LIGURIO   Think over all the good that will result. You'll be preserving the honor of the convent, the girl, and all her relatives. You'll be restoring a daughter to her father. You'll be giving satisfaction to Messer Nicia here and all *his* relatives. And you'll be able to distribute alms to the tune of three hundred ducats. While, on the other hand, the only harm you do is to a piece of   130 unborn flesh that knows neither sense nor sensation and might miscarry anyhow in any number of ways. I believe in the greatest good of the greatest number. Always do what benefits the greatest number!

TIMOTEO   So be it, in God's name! You shall have your way! May all be done for the good Lord's sake and in Holy Charity's name! Give me the name   135 of the convent, give me the potion, and, if you agree, the money you mentioned, that we may start to do good!

LIGURIO   There's a man of God for you! Just what I expected. Here's the first installment. (*Gives him money*) The convent is called . . . Oh, but wait. There's a woman in the church signaling to me. I'll be right back. Don't leave,   140 Messer Nicia. I've a couple of things to say to this woman. (LIGURIO *leaves*)

TIMOTEO   How many months gone is she?

MESSER NICIA   I'm amazed!

TIMOTEO   I said: How many months gone is she?

MESSER NICIA   God blast him where he stands!   145

TIMOTEO   Why?

MESSER NICIA   So that he'll get hurt, that's why!

TIMOTEO   I seem to have landed in mud right up to my neck. Of these fellows I've got to deal with, one is crazy, and the other's deaf as a post. One runs away and the other hears nothing. But if they're trying to put one over   150 on me, I'll beat them at that game any day of the week. But look, Ligurio is back.

(*Enter* LIGURIO)

LIGURIO Keep quiet, messere! Oh, Father, I have wonderful news!

TIMOTEO What is it? 155

LIGURIO That woman I just spoke to told me the girl has had a miscarriage.

TIMOTEO Good! This money will go into the general fund.

LIGURIO What did you say?

TIMOTEO I said you've more reason than ever to distribute alms.

LIGURIO The alms are yours for the asking. But now you'll have to do some- 160
thing else for Messer Nicia.

TIMOTEO Such as what?

LIGURIO Something less burdensome, less scandalous, more acceptable to us,
more profitable to you.

TIMOTEO What is it? I'm with you all the way. We've been growing so 165
intimate, there's nothing I wouldn't do for you.

LIGURIO I'll tell you all about it in church. Just the two of us. Messer Nicia
will be so kind as to wait for us. We'll be back in a trice.

MESSER NICIA As the hangman said to his victim.

TIMOTEO Let us go. (LIGURIO *and* TIMOTEO *go off*) 170

MESSER NICIA Is it day or night? Do I wake or dream? Am I drunk? I haven't
touched a drop all day and I can't make head or tail of these carryings-on.
We've got something to tell Friar Timoteo, so he tells him something else.
Then he wanted me to pretend to be deaf. I'd have had to stop my ears up
as if there were Sirens* around if I wasn't to hear the mad things he was 175
saying. God only knows what he had in mind. I find myself twenty-five ducats
the poorer, not a word has been said about my affair, and now they leave me
looking like a stuffed dummy. But look, they're back. If they haven't been
talking of *my* affair, they're going to catch it.

(*Enter* TIMOTEO *and* LIGURIO) 180

TIMOTEO Get your womenfolk to come and see me. I know what I have to do.
And if only my authority prevail we shall conclude this alliance tonight.

LIGURIO Messer Nicia, Friar Timoteo is ready to do everything we ask. It's for
you to see that the ladies come and see him.

MESSER NICIA You make a new man of me. Will it be a boy? 185

LIGURIO A boy.

MESSER NICIA I weep for sheer tenderness!

TIMOTEO Go into the church. I'll wait for the ladies here. Keep to one side,
so they don't see you. As soon as they're gone, I'll tell you what they said.

(MESSER NICIA *and* LIGURIO *go*) 190

TIMOTEO I wish I knew who's being taken in by whom. This scoundrel Ligurio
came with that first story just to try me out. If I hadn't consented to do what
he asked, he wouldn't have told me what he's now let out and revealed their
plot for nothing. That first story was neither here nor there. So I myself have
been taken in! And yet the cheat is not against my interests. Messer Nicia 195
and Callimaco are rich, and both of them, for different reasons, will have
to spend some of their riches. It is fitting that the affair should be kept secret:

---

[175] Sea nymphs who lured sailors to their death by singing. In the *Odyssey* Odysseus stops up his sailors'
ears with wax and has himself tied to the mast so that they can elude the sirens.

that's as important to them as it is to me. Whatever happens, I have no regrets. It's true there are going to be difficulties. Madonna Lucrezia is a good woman and nobody's fool. But I'll get at her through her goodness. 200 Women are pretty brainless, anyhow. A woman need only put one word after another, and she's considered a genius. In the kingdom of the blind, the one-eyed man is King. Here she comes with her mother, a real shrew who will help me make the daughter do as I want. (*He stands aside*)

(*Enter* SOSTRATA *and* LUCREZIA) 205

SOSTRATA I believe you believe me, daughter, when I tell you that no one in the world holds your honor more dear than I, and that I would never advise you to do anything that wasn't right. As I've told you over and again, if Friar Timoteo says that something shouldn't weigh on your conscience, don't give it a thought—go ahead and do it. 210

LUCREZIA I've always feared that Messer Nicia's desire to have children might cause him to make some blunder. That's why, when he talked to me about anything, I always felt suspicious and doubtful, particularly since that business at the Chapel of the Servites. But of all the things he's tried, this seems the strangest. To have to submit my body to such an outrage! To be the cause 215 of a man's death by such an outrage! If I were the only woman left alive, and the world depended on me for the continuance of the human race, even then I don't see how I could agree to it.

SOSTRATA There's not much *I* can say to you, daughter. You'll be talking with the friar: see what he says, and then do as he tells you. As I tell you. As 220 everyone that loves you tells you.

LUCREZIA This is torture. I'm breaking out in a sweat.

(TIMOTEO *comes forward*)

TIMOTEO Welcome, ladies. I know what you want to hear about: Messer Nicia has already talked to me. As a matter of fact I've been poring over my 225 books two hours and more, studying up on the subject. My researches have yielded many things, both general and particular, that support our case.

LUCREZIA Are you serious? You're not laughing at me?

TIMOTEO Ah, Madonna Lucrezia, this is no laughing matter! Don't you know me better than that? 230

LUCREZIA I know you, Father. But this seems to me the strangest thing ever.

TIMOTEO I believe you, madonna: but I would not have you continue to talk so. There are many things which, at a distance, seem terrible, unbearable, strange, but which, when you come close, are found to be human, bearable, familiar. That's why they say that fear can be greater than the thing feared. This 235 is a case in point.

LUCREZIA I pray God it is!

TIMOTEO To return to what I was saying before. As far as conscience is concerned, you must pay attention to this general truth: when it is a question of a certain good and a doubtful evil, one must never forego the good 240 from fear of the evil. Here we have a certain good—that you will become pregnant—that you will win a soul for the Lord God. The uncertain evil is that whoever lies with you after you've taken the potion will die. In some cases the man does not die. But, since there's an element of doubt, it is best that Messer Nicia should not run the risk. As to the act itself, to call it 245 a sin is mere moonshine, for it is not the body that sins, it is the will. The real sin would be to act contrary to your husband's wishes, and you will be acting in accordance with them. It would be a sin to take pleasure in the act, but you *won't* be taking pleasure in it. Besides, what one should always think of is the end in view. What are your proper aims? To fill a seat in Paradise 250 and to make your husband happy. Now the Bible says that the daughters of Lot, believing that they were the only surviving women in the world, consorted with their father. Their intention being good, they were not sinning.

LUCREZIA   What are you persuading me to do, Father?

SOSTRATA   Let yourself *be* persuaded, daughter. Can't you see that a childless 255 woman has no home? Her husband dies, and she's no better than a lost dog. Everyone abandons her.

TIMOTEO   Madonna, I swear to you, by this consecrated breast, that to yield to your husband's wishes in this matter need weigh on your conscience no more than eating meat on Fridays. A little holy water will wash the sin away. 260

LUCREZIA   Where are you leading me, Father?

TIMOTEO   To such things as will ever cause you to pray to God on my behalf, and will bring you greater joy next year than this.

SOSTRATA   She'll do what you want. I'll put her to bed tonight myself. What are you frightened of, crybaby? I know fifty women in this city who'd 265 thank God for the opportunity.

LUCREZIA   I consent. But I do not believe that I shall live to see tomorrow.

TIMOTEO   Have no fear, my daughter. I shall pray to God for you. I shall call upon the Archangel Raphael to be with you. Go then, make haste. Prepare yourself for this mystery. Evening is upon us. 270

SOSTRATA   Peace be with you, Father.

LUCREZIA   God and Our Lady help me, and keep me from harm! (LUCREZIA *and* SOSTRATA *go*)

(*Enter* LIGURIO *and* MESSER NICIA)

TIMOTEO   Oh, Ligurio, come out here!

LIGURIO   How is it going? 275

TIMOTEO   Well. They've gone home, prepared to do everything. There'll be no hitch: her mother's going to stay with her. She'll put her to bed herself.

MESSER NICIA   Is that the truth?

TIMOTEO   Oh! So you've been cured of your deafness? 280

LIGURIO   St. Clement has granted him that boon.

TIMOTEO   Then you must set an *ex voto** on the altar to publicize the event and enable me to share in the proceeds.

MESSER NICIA   We're getting off the subject. Will my wife make a fuss about doing what I want? 285

TIMOTEO   No, I tell you.

MESSER NICIA   I'm the happiest man alive.

TIMOTEO   I can well believe it. You'll soon be the father of a fine boy. Let childless men go hang!

---

282 Votive offerings; usually candles are lit when a contribution is made.

LIGURIO   Then go to your prayers, Father. If we need anything else, we'll come for you. You, messere, go to her and keep her steadfast in this resolve. I'll go see Master Callimaco and have him send you the potion. Arrange things so that I can see you at seven o'clock and settle what's to be done at ten. 290

MESSER NICIA   Well said. Good-by! 295

TIMOTEO   God be with you. (*They go out*)

Act Four

(*Enter* CALLIMACO)

CALLIMACO   I'd very much like to know what those fellows have done. Shall I ever see Ligurio again? It's the eleventh hour, after all, maybe even the twelfth. What anguish I've had to suffer! What anguish I'm still suffering! It's very true that Nature and Fortune keep man's account in balance: there's nothing good befalls but that it's made up for by something bad. The more my hopes have grown, the more my fears have grown. Unhappy that I am! Can I go on living amid such afflictions? Tormented by hopes and fears like these? I am a ship rocked by opposing winds, and the nearer she gets to the harbor, the more she has to fear. Messer Nicia's simple-mindedness gives me grounds for hope; the foresight and resolution of Lucrezia give me cause for fear. No respite, no peace anywhere! From time to time I try to regain my self-control. I take myself to task for my raging passion. I say to myself: "What are you doing? Are you mad? If you possess her, what then? You'll see what a mistake you've made. You'll repent all the trouble and thought that you lavished on the affair. Don't you know how little good a man discovers in the things that he desires, compared with what he thought he would discover? Look at it another way. The worst that can befall you is that you will die and go to hell. Many a man has died before you, a large number of worthy men have gone to hell, are *you* ashamed to go there? Look Fate in the face. Fly from evil—or, if you cannot fly from it, bear it like a man, don't grovel and prostrate yourself before it like a woman!" That is how I cheer myself up! But it doesn't last very long. The desire to be with her at least once comes at me from all points of the compass. It shoots through me from top to toe and changes my whole being. My legs tremble, my bowels melt, my heart is pounding fit to burst, my arms hang limp, my tongue falls mute, my eyes are dazed, my head swims. If I could only find Ligurio I'd have someone to pour out my woes to. Here he comes now —in a hurry, too. The news he brings will either grant me a few more moments of life or kill me. 5 10 15 20 25

(*Enter* LIGURIO) 30

LIGURIO   I've never been more eager to find Callimaco, and I've never found it harder to find him. If it had been bad news that I was bringing, I'd have found him right away. I've been to his house, out into the square, down to the market, along the Pancone degli Spini, up to the Tornaquinci Loggia,

and not found him. These young lovers have quicksilver under their feet, ³⁵
they can't stand still. (LIGURIO *is wandering all over the place*)

CALLIMACO   Why do I hold back? Why not give him a shout? He looks rather
pleased with himself. Ligurio! Ligurio!

LIGURIO   Callimaco! Where have you been?

CALLIMACO   What's the news?   ⁴⁰

LIGURIO   Good.

CALLIMACO   Really good?

LIGURIO   The best.

CALLIMACO   Lucrezia is willing?

LIGURIO   Yes.   ⁴⁵

CALLIMACO   Friar Timoteo did the necessary?

LIGURIO   He did.

CALLIMACO   Blessèd Friar Timoteo! I shall pray for him all the rest of my life!

LIGURIO   That's a good one! As if God's Grace were for evil as well as good!
The friar will need more than prayers.   ⁵⁰

CALLIMACO   Such as what?

LIGURIO   Money.

CALLIMACO   We'll give him some. How much have you promised him?

LIGURIO   Three hundred ducats.

CALLIMACO   Excellent.   ⁵⁵

LIGURIO   And Messer Nicia came up with twenty-five.

CALLIMACO   Why on . . . ?

LIGURIO   Suffice it that he did.

CALLIMACO   And what did Lucrezia's mother do?

LIGURIO   Almost everything. The moment she knew her daughter was going ⁶⁰
to have such a pleasant night—and without sin—she went to work on
Lucrezia, pleading, commanding, reassuring, everything. She got her over to
Friar Timoteo's place, continuing the good work till she gave her consent.

CALLIMACO   God, what have I done to deserve such a boon? I could die for joy!

LIGURIO   What sort of man *is* this? Whether for joy or sorrow, he's deter- ⁶⁵
mined to die! Did you get the potion ready?

CALLIMACO   Yes, I did.

LIGURIO   What'll you send him?

CALLIMACO   A glass of hippocras.* Just the thing to settle the stomach and cheer
the brain. Oh dear, oh dear, oh dear! I am undone!   ⁷⁰

LIGURIO   What's the matter? What can it be?

CALLIMACO   There's no remedy now.

LIGURIO   What the devil's the matter with you?

CALLIMACO   We're getting nowhere! I'm locked in a fiery furnace!

LIGURIO   Why? Why won't you tell me? What's the matter? Take your hands ⁷⁵
from your face!

CALLIMACO   Don't you remember I told Messer Nicia that you, he, Siro, and I
would catch somebody to put in bed with his wife?

---

⁶⁹ Wine highly flavored with spices.

LIGURIO   What of it?

CALLIMACO   What of it? If I'm with you, I can't be the man that's caught! And 80 if I'm not with you, he'll see through the deception!

LIGURIO   True. But can't we find a remedy?

CALLIMACO   I don't see how.

LIGURIO   Yes, we can.

CALLIMACO   What?   85

LIGURIO   Let me think it over for a moment.

CALLIMACO   So that's it! If you're still at the thinking stage, my goose *is* cooked.

LIGURIO   I have it!

CALLIMACO   What?

LIGURIO   The friar. He's brought us this far. He can bring us the whole way.   90

CALLIMACO   How?

LIGURIO   We must all wear disguises. I'll have the friar wear a disguise, then get him to change his voice, his features, his clothes, and then tell Messer Nicia that he's you. He'll believe me.

CALLIMACO   I like that. But where do I come in?   95

LIGURIO   I'm counting on you to put a tattered old cloak on, then to come round the corner of his house, lute in hand, singing a little song.

CALLIMACO   With my face showing?

LIGURIO   Yes. If *you* wore a mask he'd smell a rat.

CALLIMACO   He'll recognize me.   100

LIGURIO   No, he won't. I want you to grimace, twist your face up, open your mouth, grind your teeth together. Close one eye. Go on, try it!

CALLIMACO   Like this?

LIGURIO   No.

CALLIMACO   Like *this?*   105

LIGURIO   Not enough.

CALLIMACO   This way?

LIGURIO   Yes, yes, keep that. And I have a false nose at home. I'd like you to stick that on.

CALLIMACO   All right. Then what?   110

LIGURIO   As soon as you appear at the corner, we'll be there. We'll snatch the lute from you, grab hold of you, twirl you round and round, take you into the house, put you into the bed. The rest you'll have to do for yourself.

CALLIMACO   The thing is to get there.

LIGURIO   You'll get there. But as to how you're to get there again, *you* must 115 solve that one.

CALLIMACO   How?

LIGURIO   Possess her tonight, and, before you leave, let her know how things stand, reveal the deception. Let her see how much love you bear her, tell her you adore her. Tell her she can be your friend without loss of reputation or 120 your foe *with* loss of reputation. It's inconceivable that she wouldn't want to co-operate. On the contrary, she won't want this night to be the only one.

CALLIMACO   Do you believe that?

LIGURIO   I'm certain of it. But don't let's waste any more time. It's eight o'clock

already. Call Siro and send the potion to Messer Nicia. Then wait for me   125
at home. I'll collect Friar Timoteo, see that he gets into disguise, and bring
him back here. Then we'll dig out Messer Nicia, then do what's left to do.

CALLIMACO   That sounds good. Get going. (LIGURIO *goes*)

CALLIMACO   Hey, Siro!

(*Enter* SIRO)   130

SIRO   Sir?

CALLIMACO   Come here.

SIRO   Here I am.

CALLIMACO   Get the silver goblet from my bedroom closet. Cover it with a cloth.
Bring it here. And be sure you don't spill the stuff on the way over.   135

SIRO   (*Going*) I'll do that.

CALLIMACO   That fellow's been with me ten years now, and he's always served
me faithfully. I believe I can trust him even in this affair. And, although I've
not said a word to him about this deception, he's guessed what's afoot, for he's
quite a rascal, and he's falling in, I see, with my plans.   140

SIRO   (*Returning*) Here it is.

CALLIMACO   Good. Now go to Messer Nicia's house, and tell him this is the
medicine that his wife is to take right after supper. And the sooner supper is,
the better it'll work. Tell him that we'll be at the corner, in due order, at the
time he's to meet us there. And hurry.   145

SIRO   Right.

CALLIMACO   One moment. Listen. If he wants you to wait for him, wait, and
come back here with him. If he *doesn't* want you to wait, come right back as
soon as you've given him this—and the message.

SIRO   Yes, sir. (SIRO *goes*)

CALLIMACO   Here I stand, waiting for Ligurio to come back with Friar Timoteo.   150
And the man who said that waiting is the hardest part spoke true. I'm wasting
away at the rate of ten pounds an hour, thinking where I am now and where
I may be two hours hence and fearing lest something should happen to upset
my plan. For, if anything did, this would be my last night on earth. I   155
should either throw myself in the Arno, or hang myself, or fling myself out of
the window, or stab myself on her doorstep. But isn't that Ligurio? And
there's someone with him with a hunchback and a limp. That'll be the friar
in disguise, I'll swear. These friars! Know one, and you know the lot! Who's
the fellow that's joined them? It looks like Siro. He must have finished his   160
errand at Messer Nicia's. It's him all right. I'll wait here for them. Then— to
business!

(*Enter* SIRO, LIGURIO, *and* TIMOTEO, *in disguise*)

SIRO   Who's that you've got with you, Ligurio?

LIGURIO   A very worthy man.

SIRO   Is he lame, or shamming?   165

LIGURIO   Mind your own business.

SIRO   Oh, he looks like a regular scoundrel.

LIGURIO   For God's sake, be quiet, you'll spoil everything! Where's Callimaco?

CALLIMACO   Here. Welcome!   170

LIGURIO   Oh, Callimaco, give a word of warning to this lunatic Siro. He's said a thousand crazy things already.

CALLIMACO   Listen, Siro. This evening you must do everything Ligurio says. When he tells you to do something, it is I who am telling you to do it. And everything you see, feel, hear, and smell you're to keep strictly to yourself. 175 That's if you value my honor, my wealth, my life, and your own best interests.

SIRO   I'll do as you say.

CALLIMACO   Did you give the goblet to Messer Nicia?

SIRO   Yes, sir.

CALLIMACO   What did he say?   180

SIRO   That everything was now in order, and that he'd go ahead.

TIMOTEO   Is this Callimaco?

CALLIMACO   At your service. Let's agree on the terms of the transaction: you may dispose of me and mine as of yourself.

TIMOTEO   So I have heard and, believing every word of it, I have agreed to do 185 what I should never have done for any other man in the world.

CALLIMACO   Your labor shall not be in vain.

TIMOTEO   It will be enough to possess your favor.

LIGURIO   An end to all this hanky-panky! We'll get into our disguises, Siro. Callimaco, you come with us, and make your preparations. Friar Timoteo 190 will wait for us here. We'll be right back and then dig out Messer Nicia.

CALLIMACO   Good idea. Let's go.

TIMOTEO   I'll wait for you. (LIGURIO, CALLIMACO, and SIRO go)

TIMOTEO   It's true what they say: "Bad company will lead a man to the gallows." And a man often comes to grief by being too easygoing and goodhearted, 195 not by being too wicked. God knows, I never thought of doing anybody any harm. I stayed in my cell, said my office, tended my flock, until that devil Ligurio turned up, and made me dip my finger in this transgression. I then had to follow with my arm, and finally it was total immersion. I still have no idea where I'll end up. I comfort myself with this thought: when some- 200 thing involves a large number of people, a large number of people have to be extremely careful. But here's Ligurio with that servant.

(Enter LIGURIO and SIRO)

TIMOTEO   Welcome back!

LIGURIO   Do we look all right?   205

TIMOTEO   More than all right.

LIGURIO   Only Messer Nicia is missing. Let's walk toward his house. It's after nine. Let's go.

SIRO   Who is that opening his door? Is it his servant?

(Enter MESSER NICIA)   210

LIGURIO   No, it's the man himself. Ha! Ha! Ha!

SIRO   You find it funny?

LIGURIO   Who wouldn't? Just look at him—wearing some kind of jerkin that doesn't even cover his arse. And what the devil has he got on his head? It looks like one of those silly hoods that canons wear. And—lower down— 215 a smallsword! Ha! Ha! Ha! And he's muttering God knows what under his breath. Let's stand to one side and hear his tale of woe about his wife and what she's been doing to him. (*They stand aside*)

MESSER NICIA   The way that loony wife of mine has been carrying on! She sent the maidservant to her mother's house and the manservant to our country 220 house. I applaud her for that—but not for making such a fuss before she'd get into the bed. "I don't want to!" "What is it I'm to do?" "What are you making me do?" "Woe is me!" "Mother, Mother!" And if "Mother, Mother" hadn't given her a tongue-lashing, she'd never have got into that bed. I hope she catches a fever that goes from bad to worse! I like my women finicky, 225 it's true. But not that finicky! She's made my head swim, the bird brain! Oh, these women! They drive you crazy, you tell 'em so, and they come back at you with: "What have I done now? What's eating you this time?" Oh, well. Soon—very soon now—we shall be seeing a little action around here. And I intend to see it with both hands, so to speak. I'm doing all right, aren't I? 230 Look at me now: taller, younger, slimmer. . . . At this rate I could get me a woman without even paying for the privilege. But where have the others got to?

(LIGURIO, TIMOTEO, *and* SIRO *come forward*)

LIGURIO   Good evening, messere.   235

MESSER NICIA   Oooh! Hey! Oooh!

LIGURIO   Don't be afraid, it's only us.

MESSER NICIA   Oh! You're all here! If I hadn't recognized you, I'd have run you through with this sword! You're Ligurio, aren't you? And you're Siro! Hm? And the other one's your master. Eh?   240

LIGURIO   Yes, messere.

MESSER NICIA   Let me have a look! Oh, he's well disguised! His own mother wouldn't know him!

LIGURIO   I had him put a couple of nuts in his mouth, so nobody can recognize his voice.   245

MESSER NICIA   You're stupid.

LIGURIO   Why?

MESSER NICIA   Why didn't you tell me sooner? Then *I* could have put nuts in my mouth. You know how important it is that nobody should recognize our voices!   250

LIGURIO   Here you are then. Put this in your mouth!

MESSER NICIA   What is it?

LIGURIO   A ball of wax.

MESSER NICIA   Give it here. . . . Ca, pu, ca, coo, co, cu, cu, spu . . . A pox take you, you murdering hound!   255

LIGURIO   Oh, forgive me! I must have got them mixed up.

MESSER NICIA   Ca, ca, pu, pu . . . What, what was it?

LIGURIO   Bitter aloes.

MESSER NICIA   Damn you, Ligurio! Master Callimaco, do you stand by and say nothing?   260

TIMOTEO   I'm very angry with Ligurio.

MESSER NICIA   You *have* disguised your voice! That's *good!*

LIGURIO   Don't let's waste any more time here. I'll take over the duties of captain and give the army the order of the day. Callimaco will take the right horn of the crescent; I'll take the left. Messer Nicia will be in between us. Siro 265 will bring up the rear and back up any of our forces that yield ground. The password shall be St. Cuckoo.*

MESSER NICIA   Who's St. Cuckoo?

LIGURIO   He's the most venerated saint in all France. Let's go. Let's prepare our ambush at this corner. Listen! I hear a lute.   270

MESSER NICIA   That's our man. What shall we do?

LIGURIO   We'll send a scout forward to find out who he is. On hearing his report, we decide what action to take.

MESSER NICIA   Who'll go?

LIGURIO   You go, Siro! You know what to do. Observe, study the situation, 275 return at the double, report.

SIRO   Right.

MESSER NICIA   I hope we don't make some terrible mistake. Suppose it's a cripple or a sickly old man, we'd have to repeat the performance tomorrow night!   280

LIGURIO   Don't worry: Siro's a reliable fellow. And here he comes. What have you found, Siro?

SIRO   The loveliest piece of man you ever saw and still on the right side of twenty-five! He's alone—walking along in a tattered old cloak playing a lute.

MESSER NICIA   It's a stroke of luck, if what you say is true, but be sure of what 285 you say, it'll be your fault if anything goes wrong.

SIRO   He's just like I said.

LIGURIO   Let's wait for him to turn this corner, then pounce!

MESSER NICIA   Come over here, Master Callimaco. You *are* quiet this evening. Here he comes.   290

(*Enter* CALLIMACO, *disguised and singing*)

CALLIMACO   (*Singing*) Since Fortune keeps me from thy bed
   Mayst thou find the Devil there instead!

LIGURIO   Hold him! Tightly now! Hand over that lute!

CALLIMACO   Help! What have I done?   295

MESSER NICIA   You'll soon see! Put something over his head. Gag him.

LIGURIO   Twirl him around!

MESSER NICIA   Give him another twirl! And another! Now pop him into the house.

TIMOTEO   Messer Nicia, I'm going to take a rest. I've got a splitting headache. 300 I won't come back in the morning unless you need me.

MESSER NICIA   No, of course, Master Callimaco, don't bother. We can take care of this. (LIGURIO, SIRO, *and* MESSER NICIA *bustle* CALLIMACO *into the house*)

TIMOTEO   Now they're safely in the house, I'll be off to the monastery. And you, spectators, don't be impatient with us, for none of us will take time out to 305 sleep tonight—so the action of the play won't be interrupted. I'll be saying my office. Ligurio and Siro will be having supper, since they haven't eaten all

267 Ligurio's patron saint of cuckolds.

day. Messer Nicia will be pacing the floor like a cat on hot bricks till the suspense is over. And, as for Callimaco and Madonna Lucrezia, if I were he and you were she, do you think we'd sleep tonight? (*He goes out*) 310

Act Five

Scene 1

(*Enter* TIMOTEO)

TIMOTEO   I've not been able to shut my eyes all night, so great was my desire to know how Callimaco and the others were getting on. While waiting I've been killing time in various ways: I said Matins,* read a life of one of the Holy Fathers, went into church and relit a lamp that had gone out, changed the veil on a Madonna that works miracles. How many times have I told those 5 friars to keep her clean! And then they're surprised that people aren't devout any more! I can remember the time when there were five hundred *ex votos*. Today there aren't twenty. It's our own fault. We haven't known how to keep up her reputation. Every evening after Compline* we used to have a procession in there. We used to sing Lauds* there every Saturday. We were 10 always making vows, so there were always fresh *ex votos* on the altar. We used to comfort our confessees and get *them* to make offerings to her. Now none of this is done, and they're surprised that the life's gone out of it all! Oh, the dim-wittedness of my brothers in Christ! But I hear a rumpus in Messer Nicia's house. By my faith, there they are! They're shoving their 15 prisoner out of the house. I'm just in time. They certainly took ages getting him out. It's daybreak already. I'll stay and listen without letting them see me. (*He stands aside*)

(*Enter* MESSER NICIA, CALLIMACO *disguised*, LIGURIO, *and* SIRO)

MESSER NICIA   You take this side, and I'll take the other. Siro, you take him by 20 his cloak from behind.

CALLIMACO   Don't hurt me!

LIGURIO   Don't worry! Just get moving!

MESSER NICIA   Don't let's go any further!

LIGURIO   You're right. Let's let him go. Let's give him a couple of turns, so 25 that he won't know which house he came out of. Round with him, Siro!

SIRO   Here we go!

MESSER NICIA   One more!

SIRO   There you are!

CALLIMACO   My lute! 30

LIGURIO   Be off, you scoundrel! And if I ever hear you breathe a word about this, I'll slit your windpipe for you!

MESSER NICIA   He's gone. Now let's go and get these disguises off. And we must all be seen out of doors bright and early so that it shan't appear that we've been up all night. 35

LIGURIO   Correct.

<hr>

3 Prescribed prayers, properly recited at midnight, but often at daybreak.

9 The last service of the day.

10 Hymns of praise.

MESSER NICIA You and Siro, go find Master Callimaco and tell him all went well.

LIGURIO But what can we tell him? We don't know a thing. As you know, when we got into the house we went straight down to the cellar and started drinking. You and your mother-in-law were still at grips with him when we left you. We didn't see you again till just now when you brought us to throw him out.

MESSER NICIA That's true. Oh, I've got some fine things to tell you. My wife was in bed in the dark. Sostrata was waiting for me by the fire. I got up there with the said young fellow and, to leave nothing to chance, I took him into a small room off the big room, where the lamp casts a very faint light—he could hardly see my face.

LIGURIO Wisely done.

MESSER NICIA I made him undress. When he boggled, I turned on him and showed him my teeth like a dog. He couldn't get out of his clothes fast enough. Finally he was naked. He'd got quite an ugly mug. His nose was tremendous. His mouth was sort of twisted. But you never saw such fine skin. White, soft, smooth. As for the rest, don't ask.

LIGURIO No good *talking* of that sort of stuff. You had to see it.

MESSER NICIA You're not making fun of me? Well, since I had my hands in the dough, so to speak, I decided to go through with it, and find out if the fellow was hale and hearty. For if he had the pox, where would I be then, hm?

LIGURIO Oh, you're right.

MESSER NICIA As soon as I saw he was healthy I dragged him to the bedroom, put him into bed, and, before I left, stuck in both hands to feel how things were going. I'm not a man to take a firefly for a lantern.

LIGURIO How prudently you've managed this affair!

MESSER NICIA Having made this checkup, I left the room, bolted the door, and went to join my mother-in-law by the fire—where we spent the whole night talking.

LIGURIO What about?

MESSER NICIA About how foolish Lucrezia had been, and about how much better it would have been if she'd given in without shilly-shallying. Then we talked about the baby. I felt as if I held him in my arms already, dear little chap! Then I heard it striking seven and, fearing that day might be breaking any minute, back I went to the bedroom. Now what would you say if I told you that I just couldn't wake the scoundrel up?

LIGURIO I can well believe it.

MESSER NICIA He'd enjoyed his anointing. Finally I got him up, called you, and we whisked him out of the house.

LIGURIO Things *have* gone well.

MESSER NICIA Now what will you say if I tell you I'm sorry?

LIGURIO About what?

MESSER NICIA About that young man. To have to die so soon! That this night should cost him so dear!

LIGURIO That's *his* problem. Don't you have your own worries?

MESSER NICIA You're right. But it will seem a thousand years before I see Master Callimaco and share my joy with him.

LIGURIO He'll be out and about within the hour. But it's broad daylight now. We'll go and get these things off. What will you do? 85

MESSER NICIA I'll go home too and put on my best clothes. I'll have them get my wife up and washed. Then I'll see that she goes to church to receive a blessing on this night's work. I'd like you and Callimaco to be there. And we should talk to the friar and thank and reward him for his good offices.

LIGURIO An excellent notion. Let's do that. (*They go off*) 90

(TIMOTEO *comes forward*)

TIMOTEO I heard what they were saying, and liked it. What a stupid fellow this Messer Nicia is! It was the conclusion they came to that pleased me most. And since they'll be coming to see me, I won't stay here, I'll wait for them in church, where my merchandise will have a greater value. But who's 95 coming out of that house? It looks like Ligurio, and the man with him must be Callimaco. I don't want them to find me here, for the reason I just gave. After all, if they don't come and see me, there's always time for me to go and see them. (*He goes*)

(*Enter* CALLIMACO *and* LIGURIO) 100

CALLIMACO As I've already told you, my dear Ligurio, I didn't begin to be happy till past three o'clock this morning, because, though I *had* had a lot of pleasure, I hadn't really enjoyed it. But then I revealed to her who I was, and made her appreciate the love I bore her, and went on to tell her how easily—because of her husband's simplemindedness—we should be able 105 to live together in happiness without the slightest scandal. I finished by promising her that whenever it pleased God to translate her husband I should take her as my wife. She thought this over and having, among other things, tasted the difference between my performance and Nicia's, between, that is, the kisses of a young lover and those of an old husband, she said to me, 110 after heaving several sighs:

"Since your guile, my husband's folly, the simple-mindedness of my mother, and the wickedness of my father-confessor have led me to do what I should never have done of my own free will, I must judge it to be Heaven that willed it so, and I cannot find it in myself to refuse what Heaven wishes 115 me to accept. In consequence, I take you for my lord, my master, and my guide. You are my father, my defender, my love and sovereign good, and what my husband wanted on *one* night I want him to have forever. So make friends with him, and go to church this morning, and then come and have dinner with us. You shall come and go as you please, 120 and we shall be able to meet at any time without arousing the least suspicion."

When I heard these words I was ravished by their sweetness. I couldn't tell her more than a fraction of what I wished to say in reply. I'm the happiest and most contented man that ever walked this earth, and if neither Death 125 nor Time take my happiness from me, the saints themselves shall call me blessèd!

LIGURIO I am delighted to hear of all your good fortune. Everything's worked out just as I said it would. But where do we go from here?

CALLIMACO We walk in the direction of the church, because I promised her 130

I'd be there. She'll be coming with her mother and Messer Nicia.

LIGURIO   I can hear their door opening. Yes, it's the ladies, and the learnèd doctor's bringing up the rear.

CALLIMACO   Let's go into the church and wait for them there. (*They go*)

Scene 2

(*Enter* MESSER NICIA, LUCREZIA, *and* SOSTRATA) 135

MESSER NICIA   Lucrezia, it is my belief that we should do things in a God-fearing manner, not foolishly.

LUCREZIA   Why, what is there to do now?

MESSER NICIA   There! The answer she gives me! She's getting quite cocky!

SOSTRATA   You mustn't be so surprised: she's a little bit changed.   140

LUCREZIA   What are you getting at?

MESSER NICIA   I meant that it would be best for me to go on ahead and have a word with Friar Timoteo. I want to tell him to meet us at the church door, so he can confer the blessing on you. Why, this morning, it's as if you'd been reborn!   145

LUCREZIA   Then why don't you get moving?

MESSER NICIA   You're saucy this morning! Last night you seemed half dead!

LUCREZIA   I have you to thank, haven't I?

SOSTRATA   Go and find Friar Timoteo. But there's no need: he's just coming out of church.   150

MESSER NICIA   So he is.

(*Enter* TIMOTEO; CALLIMACO, *and* LIGURIO *at a distance*)

TIMOTEO   Callimaco and Ligurio told me that Messer Nicia and the ladies are on the way to church, so I've come out.

MESSER NICIA   *Bona dies,* Father!   155

TIMOTEO   Welcome! And Heaven's blessing upon you, madonna! May God give you a fine baby boy!

LUCREZIA   May God so will it!

TIMOTEO   You may rely on that: He *will* so will it!

MESSER NICIA   Is it Ligurio and Master Callimaco that I see there in church?   160

TIMOTEO   Yes, messere.

MESSER NICIA   Invite them over.

TIMOTEO   Come, sirs!

CALLIMACO   God save you!

MESSER NICIA   Master Callimaco, give my wife here your hand.   165

CALLIMACO   Willingly.

MESSER NICIA   Lucrezia, when we have a staff to support our old age, we shall owe it to this man.

LUCREZIA   I hold him dear. May he be a good friend of the family!

MESSER NICIA   Heaven bless you! I should like him and Ligurio to come and   170 dine with us this morning.

LUCREZIA   By all means.

MESSER NICIA   And I should like to give them the key to the downstairs room off the loggia, so that they can come and go when they like. For they have no women at home. They must live like beasts.   175

CALLIMACO   I accept, and I'll use it whenever the occasion arises.

TIMOTEO   Am I to have the money for the almsgiving?

MESSER NICIA   You are, *domine:* I shall be sending you some today.

LIGURIO   Does no one remember poor old Siro?

MESSER NICIA   He only has to ask, I'm at his service. Lucrezia, how much 180
shall I give the friar for his blessing?

LUCREZIA   Give him ten groats.

MESSER NICIA   God Almighty! (*He nearly chokes*)

TIMOTEO   Madonna Sostrata, you seem to have taken on a new lease of life!

SOSTRATA   Who wouldn't be happy today?   185

TIMOTEO   Let us enter the church and say the customary prayers. After the service,
go dine at your leisure. As for you, spectators, don't wait for us to come out
again. The service is long, and I shall stay in church, and they'll go off home
through the side door. Farewell!

The Teatro Olympico, Vicenza, showing
the scenic façade (1580) by Palladio,
with perspective vistas (1585) by Scamózzi.
Probably a 17th-century engraving.
Harvard Theatre Collection

Captain Babeo, a braggart soldier of the *commedia dell' arte,*
after a 16th-century drawing.

Angelo Beolco

Angelo Beolco (*c.1502–1542*), *known as Ruzzante after his most famous character, was an actor, playwright, and director of a troupe of actors in Padua, Venice, and Ferrara. After entering the lively theatrical world of these communities in about 1520— a world that contained such famous actors, carnival entertainers, and writers as Zan Polo* (fl. *1500–1532*) *and Cimador* (fl. *1510– 1535*), *as well as the first public theaters in Renaissance Europe— Beolco appeared almost yearly in the journals and histories of the day as a writer and an actor. In addition to his farces, he made adaptations of plays by Plautus and wrote a number of Learned Comedies, perhaps the best known of which is* THE GIRL FROM ANCONA.

Chronology

*c.*1502 Born in Padua, the natural son of a doctor, of a family of well-to-do wool merchants.

1520 Probable year of his debut in the theater, in a production of one of his own plays, after a banquet in the Foscari palace in Venice.

1521 Production of another of his plays, probably the *Pastoral,* at the Pesaro palace in Venice.

1523 Gave a recitation of his *First Oration* in Padua to celebrate the triumphal entry of Cardinal Marco Cornaro. Later he presented another of his farces at the Ducal palace in Venice.

1524 Probable year of his farce *Betia.*

*c.*1524 Death of his father; Beolco received a modest inheritance and the guardianship of the family property. Thereafter he realized a steady, if modest, living as a landlord of farms.

1524–42 Notices of productions by his company or recitations by himself almost every year in Venice, Padua, or Ferrara.

1528 Probable year of *Ruzzante Returns from the Wars* and *Bilora.*

1529–30 Probable years of *The Flirt, Fiorina,* and *The Girl from Ancona,* the last his first known Learned Comedy.

1532–33 Probable years of Beolco's *Piovana* and *Vaccaria,* the first adapted from Plautus' *Rudens,* the second from his *Asinaria.*

1542 Died in Padua.

BILORA

by Angelo Beolco

Translated by Anthony Caputi

Characters
BILORA, *a peasant*
DINA, *his wife*
PITARO, *his friend, a Venetian*
MESSER ANDRONICO, *a wealthy old Venetian merchant*
ZANE, *his servant*

Venice, late in the afternoon of a summer's day in the early 16th century

(*Enter* BILORA)

BILORA Ye gods! A lover will go anywhere—he'll stick his nose in places you wouldn't shoot a cannonball into. Damn love anyway! Who'd have thought it'd drag me around so ferociously, among people I never saw before, and so far from home? Because the fact is I don't know where I am! They say love is weak and doesn't know how to do anything, but I know now it can 5 do whatever it wants. Take me, for example (for once I want to talk about myself): if it hadn't been for love—love that dragged me to come and see if I couldn't find my woman—I wouldn't have been slogging through woods and fields and berry bushes all of yesterday and last night and today. I'm so torn to pieces I can hardly stand up. Let's get it straight once and for all: 10 love pulls at a lover harder than three teams of oxen. Dammit, it's a real pain, a nasty sickness, love. And then there are some who say it attacks only the young, that it drives only the young crazy. Not me. It drives plenty of old ones that way too. I bet if this old guy didn't have that fancy thorn in his rear, he would never have tried to pull it out by taking my woman away. 15 I hope he eats his heart out, the soft-headed fool. I hope worms eat him alive, the money-lending crook—him and whoever took him to our district. I hope he gets no fun out of his money, just as he won't let me get any out of my wife. Yet, dammit to hell, there's no misery that somehow doesn't do him good. While I worked day and night hauling my grain, he came and took 20 my wife out of my own house. Now, Lord knows if I'll ever see her again. I'd have done better to work around the house; now I wouldn't have to worry about her. Dammit but I'm well organized! Here I am dying of hunger and I've got no bread and no money to buy any. If I only knew where she was, I could at least bum a piece of bread from her. 25

(*Enter* PITARO)

PITARO Well for cripes sakes, what are you doing here?
BILORA Good old Pitaro, you're exactly what I wanted. Look here.

PITARO   Well, what is it?

BILORA   Didn't you hear about that business the other day? Do you know 30 about it?

PITARO   Lord help me, no—not unless you tell me about it.

BILORA   For God's sake, you mean you don't know anything about it. You know, that business about . . . about (dammit, how can I say it) about Messer Androtene* . . . who took my wife . . . that old guy, that foreign gentle- 35 man.

PITARO   Oh yes, that's right. But be careful, you dope; you'd better speak softly here or they'll hear you. Who brought you here?

BILORA   Nobody brought me; I came by myself. Ah, you mean he's here? But where? Is this his door?

40

PITARO   Yes, this one here. All right, now what do you want to do? Do you hope he'll give her back? What do you want to do?

BILORA   Well, here's the truth. I don't really want to go to court, you know, and instead of fighting I'd be happy to accept that what's past is past—if only he'll give me my wife and some money. Understand? This is probably not 45 the place for me to be tough. If we were somewhere else I'd do it differently, but here I don't know a soul. He could probably have me drowned in one of these canals. That way I'd have nothing for my trouble.

PITARO   That's very sensible of you. He's a nuisance of a man. Dammit, around here, in fact, you'd better play up to him with a little "Messer bello" here 50 and "Messer caro"* there.

BILORA   What? Is that his name, "Messer bello"? I was told his name was Ardochene.* What a strange name that is!

PITARO   No, you don't understand. His real name is the one you were told, but I'm not talking about that. I'm saying you should play up to him; here 55 he has things his own way. When you speak to him, say "Your excellency" or praise his famous family. Say, "I throw myself at your feet, dear sir. Please give her back to me." Understand? But don't brag and carry on.

BILORA   Ah, good, good. I get it, goddammit. So he's hard to handle. But does he just bark, or does he bite too?

60

PITARO   He bites, goddammit. Be careful, he'll flatten you without an invitation.

BILORA   Well, this is a nasty mess then. You mean he'd flatten you—the way they flatten a wall, is that it? I mean: he'd do that to a man? That old manure pile! His mother must've been a whore. I'd like to smash him like a glob of spit. So he bites, eh. I hope he has a stroke, that's what he deserves. But 65 tell me now, how can I get around him, so that we don't end by fighting it out? Do you know if he's at home? Has he come back from the piazza?

PITARO   No, he's not come back yet. But listen; let me suggest an idea.

BILORA   But go right ahead, then I'll take over.

PITARO   Listen, then! Go and knock at the door, because now Dina's alone 70 in the house. And don't show that you're angry with her. Call her down and make as if the whole thing hardly concerned you.

---

[35] This mistaken version of Andronico's name has the distant sense of "go away" or "go off" about it.
[51] "Fine Sir" and "dear sir," respectively.
[53] Has the distant sense of "burn."

BILORA   All right, all right. Let me handle it.

PITARO   And say to her, "What do you say, sweetie, do you want to come home now? You did leave me in a lurch, you know." Something like that. But you'll know what to do. 75

BILORA   Sure, Sure. This is a good line, though. But where should I talk to her: here in the doorway, or should I go in?

PITARO   No, in the doorway, here outside, dammit. What if he caught you in the house? He'd have you jumping through hoops. 80

BILORA   But what do you think? Do you think she'll come home with me?

PITARO   I don't know. It's hard to tell. I've got to admit that with him she has a pretty good time of it. No more worries, no work, good food and drink, plenty of service.

BILORA   As for service—Lord help me—nobody serves her better than I do. 85 He, he's not up to it.

PITARO   No, I mean they have a servant, dammit, who serves both of them.

BILORA   Well, I just want that understood. But maybe it'd be better if you didn't go. I'll get something from them before he comes back. Are you sure that's the way it is, that nobody's at home except Dina? 90

PITARO   No, there's no one. Look, stupid, you can believe what I'm telling you. Go on now; I want to go down to the end of the street on an errand. When I come back, I'll pass by here to see what luck you've had. Now don't stand around; go on. (PITARO *goes out*)

BILORA   Go on, go on. I'll be waiting for you, don't worry. Goddammit all, 95 only God knows how this'll end; let's hope it goes as he wishes. Meanwhile, I've got to knock, even if I think I'm going to be chopped into mouthfuls, like a radish. Yes, and what if I knock and they throw a cover over my head? But then there's the chance of getting something, even though I've not got it coming. To hell with it; let it happen as it will. I can feel love waking 100 up in me again—and with it my heart and my bowels and my lungs that have slipped down into my belly. And they're making a noise like a blacksmith banging away at a ploughshare. It's clear, I'm lost if I don't knock. (*He knocks*) Ho! Hey in there. Nobody home? Is anybody home?

(DINA *appears at a window*) 105

DINA   Who's knocking? A beggar? Get lost with my blessing.

BILORA   Even if I am a beggar, you'd never get me to go away like that. But I'm a friend. Open up, it's me.

DINA   Who are you? What friend? The master of the house isn't here. Be good, now, and go away. 110

BILORA   Oh, Dina, come on and open up. It's me (damn you to hell). Don't you know me, is that it, you crazy woman?

DINA   Get out of here, I tell you; I don't know you and the master of the house isn't here. If you don't want trouble, go on about your own business.

BILORA   For God's sake, don't get mad! Listen, come on down so I can talk 115 to you in private. Be a little kind. It's me, Dina. Bilora. I'm your husband.

DINA   Oh, poor me! Did you hear that? What are you doing here?

BILORA   Eh? What are you saying? Come on down so I can see you.

DINA   All right, I'm coming. (*She withdraws from the window*)

BILORA   Now watch me wangle something out of her—some nice trinket, or 120
maybe even some money. Maybe this'll be the making of me. And to think
I was broken up about it.

DINA (*From within*)   Will you beat me if I open?

BILORA   Why should I beat you? For going off one time—unwillingly? Come
on out. You're as dear and as precious to me as ever.   125

(DINA *enters*)

DINA   Hello. But how do you happen to be here? How are you? Are you all
right?

BILORA   Me? I'm fine. And you? You certainly look very well.

DINA   With the help of God, let me tell you, because I don't feel terribly 130
well, if you want the truth. I'm already pretty tired of this old man.

BILORA   I can believe it. It holds you down, doesn't it? And then young people
and old people never get on. We get on better, you and me.

DINA   Good Lord, he's always sick with something or other. All night long he
coughs like a dying sheep. He never sleeps. He's always on top of me, 135
smothering me with kisses because for some reason he thinks I like to be
kissed. Lord help me, I wish I didn't have to see him again; I can't stand
him.

BILORA   And I'll bet his breath stinks worse than a dunghill. And you can smell
his carcass for a thousand miles. And he's so constipated, it's got to go 140
out his side. Isn't that so?

DINA   Damn you, anyway, you're always talking some nastiness.

BILORA   All right, then. But what do you say now, do you want to come home?
Or maybe you mean to abandon me and stay with the old man.

DINA   I'd like to go home, but he won't let me. All he wants, in fact, is to be with 145
me. If you saw the way he caresses me—good heavens!—you couldn't stand it.
Goodness, but he wants me! And I do have a pretty good time with him.

BILORA   But why pay any attention to him? And why say "He doesn't want it"?
Dammit, what if he doesn't like it? If he doesn't want it, neither do you.
Do you want to make me curse? Come on, now, what do you say?   150

DINA   Honest, I don't know. I want to and I don't want to.

BILORA   God help me now! Will he be back soon or not for a while?

DINA   He should be coming along in a little while. Good Lord, I don't want
him to find you here talking to me. Go away now, dearie, and come back
later when he's here so we can work things out.   155

BILORA   Yeah, we'll work things out, like hell. But you'd better hope we work
things out, because by God if I get my back up I can be worse than a Turk.
And don't think I don't appreciate how you're wiggling your rear in all this.
Take care; don't let me catch you doing it with anyone else—damn you to
hell anyway.   160

DINA   Ah, you see; that's what I get from you. (*Aside*) Now he's furious. Listen,
I cross my heart, I'm not joking. Come back in a little while and knock and
say you want to speak to the master of the house. And then say you want
me to come home and we'll see what he says to you. If he agrees, it'll be better
this way; if he doesn't, I'll do what you want anyway.   165

BILORA   Will you really come, even if he doesn't want it?

DINA Yes, I'm telling you I will, cross my heart and hope to die. Now you go away so he doesn't find you here.

BILORA But wait a minute. Can't you give me a piece of bread? Honest, I'm dying of hunger. I haven't eaten since last evening, when I left home. 170

DINA To tell the truth, I'd rather give you some money, then you could go up to the tavern at the end of the street and eat and drink as you please. You see, I wouldn't want him to come and see me giving you stuff.

BILORA That's even better. Give it to me. Where's this tavern? Is it far?

DINA No, no, up there at the end. When you're at the end turn to the left. 175

BILORA (*Looking where she has directed him*) Oh, good gracious, how can I miss it? (DINA *goes into the house*) All right, as I was saying . . . Dammit, she's closed the door. And I'm so hungry I forgot to ask her how long I should wait before coming back. Well, now I want to go eat, whatever happens. I suppose he'll be back even before I've finished. But let's see: what did she 180 give me? Dammit all, what's this? What have I got here? Oh, all right, dammit, all right. Yes, this is a two-franc piece. I didn't recognize it. I haven't seen a piece like this since I first fell in love. And this one's a *moraiuola*,* and this one, the slut, is big and fat, fancier than the others. For cripes sakes, it's worth quite a bit, this one, and I can't remember what it's 185 called . . . Oh yes, a *cornacchione*. And that's about it, I think. But now I want to go eat. Now let's see, this is the door, so that I can find it again. Meantime, let me look at this money again. This is a two-franc piece, and a *moraiuola*, which makes four, and a *cornacchione*, which makes five, and one that I want to keep for myself—that's six—and one to spend later—that's 190 seven. That means I only need nineteen more *marchetti* to have a *tron*. (*He goes out*)

(*Enter* ANDRONICO)

ANDRONICO Therefore, it's as clear as day: if one does not amuse himself as a youth, he must do so as an old man. I can remember from my youth how 195 such splendid men as Messer Nicoletto degli Alleghi and Messer Pantaliseo da Bucintoro, both wealthy, esteemed men, used to say to me, "Andronico, why are you always so preoccupied and listless? Why in the devil's name don't you find yourself a girl and have some fun? When do you expect to have fun, when you're too old to be able to? I don't know how it is, but 200 you always seem to be under some sort of spell. Be careful, and remember what I say, as an old man you'll commit some foolishness for love." And that is exactly what's happened! Yet I would almost be happier to be an old lover than a young one, if it weren't for one fault that spoils the whole picture, that "*non respondent ultima primis.*"* The devil take it, it's a consider- 205 able nuisance to grow old. Lord knows, I have more than sufficient spirit . . . But that's enough of that. The truth is I may be old but I'm not decrepit. Love performs great things. Look how I made off with this doll, simply took her from her husband. In fact, I'm risking my life in having her, especially since I've grown so doting and want her so desperately. But the truth is, 210 *breviter concludendo*,* she's so sweet, such a cherub; she has a little mouth that

---

[184] This and the following are terms for old Venetian coins.
[205] "The old do not reciprocate the young."   [211] "To conclude briefly."

creates an appetite for kisses. *In summa summario,** the only thing I fear is this, and from it I may get some trouble: that one of her relatives will come and ask for her. Let me tell you, he'll be unwelcome and unwelcomed. I'm determined to keep her for myself. I will not lose her now. And just as she does 215 her duty by me, I'll do at least a part of mine by her—perhaps even enough to make her happy. Of course I'm not at all speaking of small duties, but by and large. Up to now she's had a nice kind of security for what she does. She takes care of me as she pleases; she can spend what she likes and indulge herself both at home and outside as she pleases—I don't say a word. More- 220 over, she doesn't have to give an accounting to anyone. Don't think it isn't a nice thing to be a lady and be called "Madonna." She goes up and down, giving orders; in fact, her only work is opening her mouth. Let me tell you, if she's happy she'll know how to treat me. But, ah, I'd pay almost anything if she'd just listen to me a little and learn something about the inner me. 225 Now enough of this. Now I want to go up and see her for a moment. She makes me feel so young and cocky that I'm always getting excited, and if I don't go and fondle her a little bit every now and then, I'll lose control and ruin my business. And don't think I'm not up to it! I feel as if I could dance four sets of the *zoioso,* and even do the fancy steps, and I could do the same 230 with the *rosina,* and do it with all the elaborate flower figures too, which is no mean feat. Ah, yes, this girl does wonders for me. To begin with, she takes care of me whenever I'm a little sickish or come down with the catarrh. Then of course I always have someone to amuse myself with and talk things over with. (*He knocks*) Hey, open up quick. I wonder if the servant has come 235 back with the boat?

ZANE   (*From within*) Who's knocking?

ANDRONICO   Open up, darling. No, open up, you scoundrel. 'Devil take it, I thought it was her. Don't you hear me?

ZANE   (*Opening the door*) What do you want?   240

ANDRONICO   What do you mean, "What do I want?" Have you lit the fire in the study? (*He goes in*)

(*Enter* BILORA *and* PITARO)

BILORA   What in hell do you know about that? Here we are arriving at the same time.   245

PITARO   Well, how was the food? They have a good wine here, don't they?

BILORA   Oh Pitaro, you can say that again. Damn, but it's good. I'm so full you could hone a scythe on my stomach.

PITARO   Fine. Now what do you want to do? Shall we speak to the old man to see what his intentions are? In this way we'll settle it one way or another. 250 Since you said the girl will come with you even if he doesn't want her to . . .

BILORA   That's what she said, if she hasn't changed her mind by now. She's also a little queer, you know, in the head.

PITARO   I understand perfectly. But the sooner we dispose of this mess the better for us. How do you want to speak to him? Shall I speak for you, or would 255 you rather that we speak to him together?

212 "In sum."

BILORA   No, you go ahead and speak to him. You know how to speak better. And listen, if you see he's being difficult, tell him she's got a husband who's a mean one. Say, "If you don't give her back, he might even kill you." And tell him I used to be a soldier. That might scare him.   260

PITARO   All right. Leave it to me.

BILORA   No, but listen. Tell him I'm a tough guy, and swear, and don't forget to say I was a soldier once.

PITARO   Come on now. You stand aside so he doesn't see you when I knock at the door. Leave it to me. I'll present him an argument he'll understand.   265

BILORA   What the hell do we care anyway. If he gives her to me, so much the better. If he doesn't, by the blood of the Virgin of Malgatera, I'll make him crap arrows. Yessir, I'll make the crap run down his legs right into his stockings.

PITARO   That's enough, now, don't stand there cursing. You stand aside and   270 let me knock. What did you say his name was?

BILORA   Well dammit all, I don't know what he's called. I thought his name was Ardochene, but I'm not sure. Messer Ardo . . . Ardoche. Yes, that's it.

PITARO   All right, All right. (BILORA *stands aside.* PITARO *knocks*) Hey, anybody home?   275

(DINA *appears at the window*)

DINA   Who's knocking?

PITARO   A friend. Young woman, tell your master that I'd like a word with him.

DINA   Who are you?

PITARO   Tell him it's me and that I want to speak to him. He'll understand.   280

DINA   He's coming down right away.

BILORA   Listen. Tell him I've murdered I don't know how many men, and that I'm wanted by the police. Understand?

PITARO   Come on now, be quiet and keep to one side. You're driving me crazy.

(*Enter* ANDRONICO *at the door.* BILORA *stands aside again*)   285

ANDRONICO   Who are you and what do you want?

PITARO   Good evening to you, your excellency.

ANDRONICO   Oh, Pitaro. Welcome. Well, what do you want?

PITARO   I'd like to speak ten words with you in private, Messere, very privately. If you'll step this way, please.   290

ANDRONICO   Well, what do you want? Come on, quickly.

PITARO   Now I'll tell you, Messere. Since I'm here, there's no point in trying to hide in a cut field. You know that the other day you absconded with that girl, the wife of that poor boy Bilora, who's half crazy with grief. Now, what I have to say is this: I want to beseech you, your excellency, to give her   295 back out of your own generosity. Why? Think about it, my dear sir; put yourself in his place. To have your wife taken away from you is really a rather nasty thing. In any case, you've probably satisfied your desire and appetite for her; perhaps you're even tired of her. And then finally—if you want the advice of a friend, Messere—she's not the dish for your spoon. You're old,   300 she's young. You'll pardon me, I hope, if I speak frankly, Messere.

ANDRONICO   Do you want me to speak frankly in return? I don't want to do anything about it because frankly I wouldn't be able to give her up. Do you understand me? I've decided to live with her. What the devil! And you'd advise me to let her go back to the country so that she could struggle along with that good-for-nothing of a Bilora, who gives her more beatings than bread? And I should give her up? No, no, never! I'm much too fond of her ever to let that happen. My conscience would hurt me if I let such a delicacy fall into the mouth of a pig. Do you really think I would have made off with her like that if I intended to give her up so soon? Why, I've been wearing armor plates and a mail coat for the whole summer—armed like a Saint George! I'm on the alert night and day. I've gone into training to keep her, to be ready for the day when I might be attacked. So you see, my dear friend, you'd better tell Bilora to take care of his affairs in some other way.

PITARO But Messere, in this way he's sure to make a mess of everything. It would appear that you don't want him to take care of his affairs too well.

ANDRONICO I don't care one iota what he does. I'm prepared to spend half of all I own and to be banished from this land.

PITARO But good heavens, what do you want him to do? Do you want him to despair?

ANDRONICO I don't want him to despair at all. If he's in despair, tell him to run himself onto a roasting spit. But what the hell kind of story is this? He'll be in despair? And what do you want me to do about that? Now you're beginning to annoy me. Soon I'll get angry. Get the hell out of here! Go on, get going, before I lose my temper.

PITARO No, no, Messere, don't get angry. Listen, let's do this: we'll call the girl down and see what she says. If she wants to go home, let her go. If she doesn't want to, take her and do what you wish. What do you say?

ANDRONICO So far so good. But be careful that you don't repent this, because I'm certain you're going to be disappointed. Frankly, this is the case: she just now told me that she wouldn't leave me for all the men in the world. Now we'll see if she's changed her mind so quickly. I want to do you this favor because I wouldn't be happy if you didn't see how this has to finish. Now we'll see if she's really as fond of me as she says. Hey, do you hear me? Don't you hear me? Answer me, darling, did you hear?

(DINA *appears at the window*)

DINA Did you call me, Messere?

ANDRONICO Yes, child, come down here for a minute. (*Aside:* I must say that women have very few brains—at least most of them have few. And if this one has changed her mind so quickly . . .)

(*Enter* DINA)

PITARO Here she is, Messere; she's come.

ANDRONICO Well, you lovely child, what do you say?

DINA About what, Messere? I don't know; I don't say anything.

ANDRONICO Well, listen. This good man has come to ask for you on behalf of your husband, and we've made a pact: that you go, if you want to go, and stay, if you want to stay. You know, of course, what you have here with me, that I'll never let you want for anything. Now do as you wish and as you please. I won't say another word.

DINA I should go with my husband? But what do you want to become of me?

I'll be beaten every day. No, honest to God, I don't want to go. God knows, I wish I'd never known him. He's a dyed-in-the-wool loafer, like no other loafer in the world. My God, honest, no, Messere, no! I don't want to go. When I see him, it's like seeing a wolf.

ANDRONICO All right. That's enough, enough. Well, did you hear? Are you 355 satisfied? When I said she didn't want to go, you didn't believe me.

PITARO Listen to me, Messere. This makes me furious. Only a half hour ago this dissolute creature told Bilora that she'd go with him, even if you didn't want her to.

DINA What? I said I wanted to go? I said—oh, you almost made me say it. 360 I said, as that good woman said, nothing! He must have dreamed it, and of course he can dream what he wants.

ANDRONICO Go inside now and let's not argue further. Enough. Go in peace now. Well, what do you think now? I would have sworn that she wouldn't go. Do you need any more? 365

PITARO No, Messere. What do you want me to say? I can only sum up by saying that Bilora is a nasty type and could do you harm. You'd do better to give her up.

ANDRONICO Well, what does all this mean? I've had about enough. What are you trying to do, threaten me? Don't make me really angry. Let me tell 370 you straight: I can be a lot more unreasonable than I've been. To tell the unpleasant truth, briefly, you seem to me a scoundrel. Now get out of here, and quickly. This is all you're going to get from me. Do you hear me? When I come out again, don't let me find you here, or I swear . . . But enough. No more. Get going. We don't want to see you again. (ANDRONICO *and* 375 DINA *go into the house*)

(BILORA *comes forward. It's getting dark*)

BILORA For cripes sake, you sure know how to talk! You didn't shout, you didn't say I was an outlaw, you didn't curse, nothing. My God and what the hell, what kind of fish are you? If you'd cursed or said I was an outlaw, I'm sure 380 he'd have given her to me, because when you said I was a nasty type and said I wasn't the kind to go soft, his chin began to shiver. He couldn't wait to get into the house.

PITARO So! Then you ought to try it yourself, if you're so good at it! How dare you find fault with me! 385

BILORA I'm not finding fault with you at all. But I must say I've got damn little to be grateful for.

PITARO Then I'm right: you are finding fault. Come on now, do you want to try it?

BILORA Me? No. I'm grateful, I say. I can even say you've done me a favor. 390 Sure, you go on now. (PITARO *goes*) Goddammit to hell, everything is coming down around my ears. Now . . . what can I do? I've got to get back at him, turn him upside down—shoes in the air—make him crap all over himself from laughing, scare him out of his clothes. But how shall I do it? I'm ruined, I haven't anything. The best thing would be to get him outside 395 and settle it here. Feeling like this, though, I couldn't take another bust. Let's see, now, what was I thinking a moment ago. When he comes out,

I'll smash him with one blow. This'll stagger him and he'll fall like a dead tree. Then on top of him and I'll beat the hell out of him. He'll be lucky if he still has his eyes and soul when I'm finished. Yessir! Oh boy. He'll 400 be terrified if I do it like this. Then I'll talk like a Spanish soldier—he'll think he's hearing eight. Let's see, I ought to practice a little how I'm going to do it. By God, first I'll pull out my knife. Let's see if it shines. Dammit, not much. He won't be very scared by that. But let's try it: for example, let's say he's that wall, and I'm me, Bilora, who's an expert at roughing some- 405 body up when he wants to. So now I begin to curse and call down every saint in Padua. And the Holy Mother. And the Holy Cross. Damn the whore that begot him by a Jew, the cursed old whoremonger, may she shiver in hell. You watch me: I'll get rid of this itch in his tail. Now he comes on, and I give it to him—just so I don't kill him. And then I'll take his gown off, 410 even take it from him; in fact I'll undress him from top to bottom . . . And then away I go. And I'll leave him like this, deserted like a great pile of cow dung. Then I'll sell his cloak and buy myself a horse and become a soldier and go off to war. There's not much reason to stay at home. But now I'll set myself here. (*He stands apart*) Oh, I hope he comes out, I hope he isn't 415 long. Quiet, is he coming? Has he come out yet? Yes. Oh, may the plague consume you, you old cripple. Damn it all, where is he? Hasn't he come out yet? This is a nice mess. Maybe he isn't coming. But quiet; by God I think I hear him coming. Yes, he's coming. He won't get away this time. I'd better be careful not to jump on him until he's locked the door. 420

(*Enter* ANDRONICO)

ANDRONICO Who in hell is this scoundrel who's knocking about here at this hour? Some drunk? Damn him, anyway, I hope he rots in hell. God, it makes my blood boil. I'd pay I don't know what to be a night patrolman; then I could give him what he's got coming. Do you hear anything, Zane? 425

(ZANE *comes to the door*)

ZANE I'm here.

ANDRONICO Don't come out. Stay in the house and keep Dina company. Come to get me later, at four, and bring a light. Understand?

ZANE I'll be as quick as I can. Don't worry about it. 430

ANDRONICO It'll be better if I go this way because I can take the ferry down here and be there in a moment. Zane, close the door! (ZANE *withdraws and closes the door*)

(BILORA *comes forward*)

BILORA And you take that, you old cripple. There. There. (*He beats* ANDRO- 435 NICO)

ANDRONICO Oh, young man, young man. Oh. Oh my God. Fire, fire, fire. I'm dead. Oh, you scoundrel. Fire, fire, fire. Oh my God, I'm dying, I'm dead.

BILORA Fire, fire. I just pulled it out of your tail, your fire. Now give me my wife! You should have let her be. Hey, I think he is dead. He's not moving 440 at all. He *is* dead. Well, hail and farewell. He's crapped out his bowels. Didn't I tell you?

The Commedia dell'Arte

The Scenario of the Imposter Prince (c.1630) *is one of the 48* scenari *contained in the* Second Casanatense Miscellany (*Codex 4186*) *in the Casanatense Library in Rome. This group of plays has been associated with the* Commedia *troupe known as the second* Confidenti, *a troupe earlier led by the famous manager, actor, and anthologist Flaminio Scala. This troupe enjoyed great popularity throughout Europe, but especially in Paris, where for a time it played on alternate nights with Molière's troupe at the Petit-Bourbon. Consisting of about eight men and five women, such a company would use the scenario as the outline to be followed as the actors improvised their speeches and stage-business.*

Selected Bibliography

Lea, K. M., *Italian Popular Comedy: A Study of the Commedia dell' Arte, 1560–1620,* 2 vols., Oxford, 1934.

McDowell, J. H., "Some Pictorial Aspects of Early *Commedia dell' Arte* Acting," *Studies in Philology,* XXXIX (1942), 47–64.

Nicoll, Allardyce, *Masks, Mimes, and Miracles,* London, 1931.

Smith, Winifred, *Italian Actors of the Renaissance,* New York, 1930.

————, *The Commedia dell' Arte: A Study in Popular Italian Comedy,* New York, 1912.

Harlequin, of the *commedia dell' arte,* as presented by the
Ballet du Roy, Paris. After a 16th-century drawing.

THE SCENARIO OF THE IMPOSTOR PRINCE

Translated by Anthony Caputi

Characters

PRINCE
VITTORIA, *his sister*
ANGELICA, *his wife*
TRIVELLINO
DIAMANTINA, *his wife*
SPINETTA, *his daughter*
PANTALONE, *the Magnifico* *counsellors*
DOTTORE
CORTE, *a court official*
BRUNETTO, *a slave, unknown brother to Angelica*
GABINETTO, *a jailer*
MESSENGER
MAGICIAN
Policemen, Women of the Court, and spirits
Properties and Scenery: A palace with a wood on one side and a prison on the other; a Magician's costume; a cloak, a hat, and a mirror; a bunch of keys; two slavic cloaks; three small red caps for convicts; two chains; three chairs; small tables; a bell; paper and an inkstand

Act One

(*Enter* PANTALONE *and the* DOTTORE)

PANTALONE AND THE DOTTORE They come out of the palace talking about the Prince, who is away taking part in a joust to win the hand of Angelica. Then the Dottore goes into the palace, while Pantalone remains to soliloquize on his passion for Diamantina.

(*Enter* DIAMANTINA)   5

PANTALONE AND DIAMANTINA Pantalone reveals his love for her, but she refuses him. (*Enter* TRIVELLINO) Diamantina runs to embrace Trivellino. Jealous, Pantalone calls Corte (*Enter* CORTE) and orders him to place Trivellino under arrest as a malefactor and to guard him well. Corte leads Trivellino away as Trivellino takes an elaborate farewell of Diamantina, protesting 10 his love for her as he goes. (CORTE *and* TRIVELLINO *go to the prison*) Diamantina remains, weeping, then goes into the palace to see what help she can find. (*Exit* DIAMANTINA. PANTALONE *follows her into the palace, then returns*)

PANTALONE   He prepares to proclaim Trivellino a public malefactor and calls Gabinetto, the jailer. (*Enter* GABINETTO) Gabinetto calls to the prison for 15 a chair and a table and then goes into the prison and returns with policemen and Trivellino, tied up.

PANTALONE, GABINETTO, TRIVELLINO, AND POLICEMEN   Pantalone and Gabinetto examine Trivellino. When they have finished, Pantalone banishes him. (*They all go off, leaving* TRIVELLINO) Alone, Trivellino laments his mis- 20 fortune.

(*Enter* BRUNETTO)

TRIVELLINO AND BRUNETTO   Together they play their scene of condolences, then Brunetto gives some money to Trivellino. (TRIVELLINO *goes to the woods*)

(*Enter* VITTORIA, *the princess*)   25

BRUNETTO AND VITTORIA   Vittoria, through her actions and speech, reveals that she has been Brunetto's mistress, but he now rejects her. Furious, she calls Pantalone. (*Enter* PANTALONE) Vittoria denounces Brunetto and orders Pantalone to put him in prison. Despite Brunetto's display of passion, Pantalone calls Gabinetto (*Enter* GABINETTO) and orders him in turn to imprison 30 Brunetto on the authority of the princess. Gabinetto calls Corte (*Enter* CORTE) and they take Brunetto to the prison. Pantalone and Vittoria go into the palace.

(*Enter* TRIVELLINO *from the woods, followed by a* MAGICIAN)

TRIVELLINO AND THE MAGICIAN   The Magician performs his *lazzo** of magic, 35 then calls on spirits. (*Enter spirits carrying a hat, a cloak, and a mirror*) The Magician directs them, says the magic words, and transforms Trivellino into the Prince. (*They go out. Enter the real* PRINCE, ANGELICA, *and* CORTE *from the woods*)

THE PRINCE, ANGELICA, AND CORTE   The Prince gives orders to prepare for 40 their reception by his court and vassals. (*They retire to a house in the woods*)

(*Enter* TRIVELLINO *before the palace*)

TRIVELLINO   Alone, he performs his *lazzo* of the prince. (*Enter* PANTALONE *and the* DOTTORE) Seeing Trivellino, they believe him to be the Prince and perform their *lazzi* of welcome and obeisance. (*Enter* VITTORIA) Vittoria, 45 also believing Trivellino to be the Prince, ceremoniously pays her respects and compliments to him. (*They all go into the palace*)

Act Two

(*Enter* PANTALONE *and the* DOTTORE)

PANTALONE AND THE DOTTORE   They discuss the extravagance of the Prince. (*Enter* TRIVELLINO) Trivellino reads various petitions to him as Prince and performs *lazzi* as he answers them. (*Enter* DIAMANTINA) Diamantina, 50

---

[35] A comic turn or routine. Every *commedia dell' arte* actor had a repertory of carefully cultivated and highly polished *lazzi* appropriate to the actor's special character.

believing Trivellino to be the Prince, begs justice of him for her husband, Trivellino. Pantalone argues that Trivellino is a scoundrel and a bandit. Trivellino performs his *lazzi,* then sends Diamantina home. (*She goes out*) Pantalone tells him how Brunetto came to be in prison. (PANTALONE *and the* DOTTORE *go out*) ⁵⁵

(Enter GABINETTO)

TRIVELLINO AND GABINETTO Trivellino orders Gabinetto to bring Brunetto to him. (GABINETTO *goes out and returns with* BRUNETTO) Trivellino then sends Gabinetto away (*He goes*) and releases Brunetto. Brunetto thanks him. (BRUNETTO *goes out*) ⁶⁰

(Enter DIAMANTINA. TRIVELLINO stands aside)

TRIVELLINO AND DIAMANTINA Diamantina expresses her sorrow for the plight of her husband. (*Enter* PANTALONE) Pantalone makes his suit to her again. Just as he is about to take her in his arms, Trivellino moves between them and Pantalone embraces him. Trivellino dresses him down and calls ⁶⁵ Gabinetto and Corte. (*Enter* GABINETTO *and* CORTE) He instructs them to take Pantalone to prison. They carry him off as he calls for help. (*They all go out*)

(Enter the DOTTORE)

THE DOTTORE He reflects on the affairs of court and how different they are ⁷⁰ now from previously. (*Enter* BRUNETTO) Brunetto talks of his gratitude that his innocence has been recognized. The Dottore, with great haughtiness, demands to learn who released him and derides his innocence. When he learns that the Prince has done it, he says the Prince was not well informed.

(Enter TRIVELLINO) ⁷⁵

THE DOTTORE, BRUNETTO, AND TRIVELLINO When the Dottore tries to inform Trivellino that he has been mistaken about Brunetto, Trivellino berates him and calls Gabinetto and Corte. (*Enter* GABINETTO *and* CORTE) He then directs them to conduct the Dottore to prison. (GABINETTO, CORTE, *and the* DOTTORE *go out*) Next he orders Brunetto to go into the kitchen to prepare a *polenta** ⁸⁰ for him. (*Exit* TRIVELLINO *and* BRUNETTO)

(Enter the PRINCE and ANGELICA before the palace)

THE PRINCE AND ANGELICA They marvel that no one has come to meet them. (*Enter* VITTORIA) Vittoria pays her respects to them with appropriate ceremony. (*Enter some women who make obeisance. Then exit the women with* ⁸⁵ VITTORIA *and* ANGELICA)

(Enter PANTALONE and the DOTTORE in chains)

THE PRINCE, PANTALONE, AND THE DOTTORE They beg the Prince to show them mercy, with elaborate demonstrations of their sufferings. The Prince calls Gabinetto (*Enter* GABINETTO) and orders him to set them free. ⁹⁰ Gabinetto releases them. (*Exit* GABINETTO) They thank the Prince and tell him how Vittoria has denounced Brunetto. The Prince has Brunetto called.

(Enter BRUNETTO)

THE PRINCE, PANTALONE, THE DOTTORE, AND BRUNETTO The Prince reproves Brunetto, who then explains his position, telling him everything. The ⁹⁵ Prince then orders Pantalone to fetch Vittoria and stands aside to watch the

---

⁸⁰ A porridge or soft moist loaf made from corn meal.

scene. (PANTALONE *goes out and returns with* VITTORIA. PANTALONE *and the* DOTTORE *then go out*)

BRUNETTO, VITTORIA, AND THE PRINCE   Brunetto appeases Vittoria, but the Prince intercedes and rebukes him. The Prince then calls Gabinetto (*Enter* GABINETTO) and instructs him to put Brunetto in prison. He then sends Vittoria to her apartment. (*They all go out*)
(*Enter* TRIVELLINO)

TRIVELLINO   He discourses on the pleasure he is having as Prince. (*Enter* GABINETTO) Gabinetto asks what he should do with Brunetto. Not under- standing what has happened, Trivellino tells him to release him and to fetch Vittoria. (GABINETTO *goes out. A moment later* BRUNETTO *enters*)

TRIVELLINO AND BRUNETTO   Brunetto attempts to thank him. (*Enter* VITTORIA) Vittoria and Brunetto perform their *lazzi* of prostrating themselves and lying on the ground. After their *lazzi,* Trivellino marries them and sends them to the palace to consummate their marriage. (BRUNETTO *and* VITTORIA *go out*)
(*Enter* PANTALONE *and the* DOTTORE)

TRIVELLINO, PANTALONE, AND THE DOTTORE   Trivellino asks them how they happen to be free and sends for Gabinetto and Corte. (*Enter* GABINETTO *and* CORTE) Again Trivellino condemns Pantalone and the Dottore to prison. (*They all go out*)

Act Three

(*Enter the* PRINCE, VITTORIA, *and* BRUNETTO)

THE PRINCE, VITTORIA, AND BRUNETTO   The Prince rages that someone has released them. Brunetto and Vittoria insist that he did it and that he married them. He denies it and calls Gabinetto and Corte. (*Enter* GABINETTO *and* CORTE) The Prince then orders that in an hour Brunetto and Vittoria will be beheaded. (*They all go, leaving the* PRINCE *alone*)
(*Enter a* MESSENGER)

THE PRINCE AND THE MESSENGER   The Messenger presents a petition from Pantalone and the Dottore, who are still in prison. Astonished, the Prince gives his royal seal to him and tells him to go liberate Pantalone and the Dottore instantly. (*They go out*)
(*Enter* TRIVELLINO)

TRIVELLINO   He reflects on his pleasure that Pantalone and the Dottore are in prison. (*Enter* PANTALONE *and the* DOTTORE) They thank him profusely for having released them. He, astounded, asks them who released them. They say that he did, but he denies it and calls Gabinetto. (*Enter* GABINETTO) Trivellino then orders that Pantalone and the Dottore be hanged. (*They all go out, leaving* TRIVELLINO *alone*)
(*Enter* ANGELICA)

TRIVELLINO AND ANGELICA   Angelica kneels before Trivellino, thinking him the Prince, and begs him to show mercy to Vittoria and Brunetto. He doesn't understand. (*Enter* GABINETTO) Gabinetto asks when he should execute Vittoria and Brunetto. Trivellino demands to know who ordered the execution, and when Gabinetto tells him that he did, he denies it. Finally, Trivellino orders Gabinetto to release Vittoria and Brunetto. (GABINETTO *goes* 140 *out*)

(*Enter* VITTORIA *and* BRUNETTO)

TRIVELLINO, ANGELICA, VITTORIA, AND BRUNETTO Vittoria and Brunetto thank Trivellino for sparing their lives. Trivellino takes Angelica by the hand and then sends all of them into the palace. After a *lazzo* Trivellino also 145 goes.

(*Enter* GABINETTO *as executioner, followed by the* PRINCE, VITTORIA, *and* BRUNETTO)

GABINETTO, THE PRINCE, VITTORIA, AND BRUNETTO The Prince rages again at Vittoria and Brunetto, who protest that he set them free. (*Enter* 150 PANTALONE *and the* DOTTORE) Pantalone and the Dottore come in on their way to the scaffold. The Prince is stunned. He demands to know who condemned them; they claim that he did; and he denies it. (*Enter* TRIVELLINO *and* SPINETTA)

THE PRINCE, VITTORIA, BRUNETTO, GABINETTO, PANTALONE, THE DOT- 155 TORE, TRIVELLINO, AND SPINETTA Trivellino performs a *lazzo* while the Prince reels in astonishment. They all perform their *lazzi* concerning who condemned them and who freed them. The Prince then takes charge. (*Enter the* MAGICIAN) The Magician reveals that Brunetto is Angelica's brother. The Prince then gives Vittoria to Brunetto as wife, pardons the Magician, 160 and makes Pantalone take Spinetta as wife.

Christopher Marlowe

*Christopher Marlowe (1564–1593) was the most important
playwright in English before Shakespeare. In his short, stormy life
he wrote poems and six complete plays, and with this work
contributed much to the then crystallizing Elizabethan tradition.
In his tragedies he combined a selection of the highly diverse
materials available to him to produce important early examples of
epic tragedy in* TAMBURLAINE, *of revenge tragedy in* THE JEW
OF MALTA, *of the tragedy of character in* DR. FAUSTUS, *and of
historical tragedy in* EDWARD II. *His use of blank verse as the
verbal medium for his plays settled the question for the dramatists
who followed him of its superiority among the verse forms then
in use in dramatic poetry.*

Chronology

1564 Born in Canterbury.

1579 Enrolled in King's School, Canterbury.

1580 Matriculated at Corpus Christi College, Cambridge.

1584 Received the B.A. degree. He received the M.A. three or four years later.

1587 Cambridge authorities informed by the Queen's Privy Council that rumors of Marlowe's having gone abroad to join the Catholics should be silenced, that, on the contrary, he had been "employed in matters touching the benefit of his country."

Part I of *Tamburlaine* was produced by the Lord Admiral's Men, followed closely by Part II.

1588 Probable year of *Doctor Faustus.* Marlowe fought a duel with William Bradley, who was killed in an ensuing struggle by Thomas Watson. Marlowe and Watson were imprisoned but then released.

1589–93 Wrote *The Jew of Malta, Edward II,* and *The Massacre at Paris.*

1593 Probably transferred his services from the Lord Admiral's to Lord Strange's company, where he would have associated with Shakespeare.

Thomas Kyd, the dramatist, accused Marlowe of blasphemy and atheism. Marlowe was summoned by the Privy Council to answer these charges. On May 30 Marlowe was stabbed to death by Ingram Frizer in a quarrel over a dinner bill. The Coroner's Jury found that Frizer had acted in self-defense.

1604 First extant edition of *Doctor Faustus* published.

1616 Second, considerably revised text of *Doctor Faustus* published.

Selected Bibliography

Bakeless, John Edwin, *The Tragicall History of Christopher Marlowe,* 2 vols., Cambridge, Mass., 1942.

Boas, F. S., *Christopher Marlowe; A Biographical and Critical Study,* Oxford, 1940.

Cole, Douglas, *Suffering and Evil in the Plays of Christopher Marlowe,* Princeton, N.J., 1962.

Davidson, Clifford, "Doctor Faustus of Wittenberg," *Studies in Philology,* LIX (1962), 514–523.

Ellis-Fermor, U. M., *Christopher Marlowe,* London, 1927.

Heilman, Robert B., "The Tragedy of Knowledge: Marlowe's Treatment of Faustus," *Quarterly Review of Literature,* II (1946), 316–32.

Kirschbaum, Leo, "Marlowe's Faustus: A Reconsideration," *Review of English Studies,* XIX (1943), 225–41.

Leech, Clifford, ed., *Marlowe: A Collection of Critical Essays,* Englewood Cliffs, N.J., 1964.

Levin, Harry, *Christopher Marlowe, The Overreacher,* London, 1952.

Rowse, Alfred Leslie, *Christopher Marlowe: His Life and Work,* New York, 1965.

Smith, Warren D., "The Nature of Evil in Doctor Faustus," *Modern Language Review,* LX (1965), 171–175.

Stean, J., *Marlowe, A Critical Study,* Cambridge, 1914.

Waith, Eugene M., *The Herculean Hero in Marlowe, Chapman, Shakespeare, and Dryden,* New York, 1962.

Mechanical devil, such as may have been used in Marlowe's *Doctor Faustus*, Act Two, Scene One. 15th-century manuscript. *Bavarian State Library, Munich.*

THE TRAGICAL HISTORY
OF
DOCTOR FAUSTUS

by Christopher Marlowe

Characters
CHORUS
DOCTOR FAUSTUS
WAGNER, *his servant*
The GOOD *and* EVIL ANGELS
VALDES *and* CORNELIUS, *conjurors and friends to Faustus*
Three Scholars
MEPHISTOPHILIS, *a devil*
THE CLOWN
BALIOL, BELCHER, LUCIFER, BELZEBUB, *and other devils*
THE SEVEN DEADLY SINS
THE POPE
CARDINAL OF LORRAIN
FRIARS
ROBIN, *the ostler*
RAFE
A VINTNER
THE EMPEROR
A KNIGHT *and attendants*
SPIRITS OF ALEXANDER *and his* PARAMOUR
A HORSE-COURSER
THE DUKE *of* VANHOLT *and his* DUCHESS
AN OLD MAN
The spirit of HELEN OF TROY

Prologue

(*Enter* CHORUS)
CHORUS   Not marching in the fields of Thrasimene,
Where Mars did mate the warlike Carthagens;*
Nor sporting in the dalliance of love,
In courts of kings, where state is overturned;
Nor in the pomp of proud audacious deeds,
Intends our Muse to vaunt his heavenly verse: 5

2 Apparently an allusion to an earlier play by Marlowe.

Only this, gentles—we must now perform
The form of Faustus' fortunes, good or bad:
And now to patient judgments we appeal,
And speak for Faustus in his infancy.
Now is he born, of parents base of stock, 10
In Germany, within a town called Rhodes;
At riper years to Wittenberg* he went,
Whereas his kinsmen chiefly brought him up.
So soon he profits in divinity,
The fruitful plot of scholarism graced, 15
That shortly he was graced with doctor's name,
Excelling all and sweetly can dispute
In heavenly matters of theology;
Till swollen with cunning, of a self-conceit,
His waxen wings did mount above his reach, 20
And, melting, heavens conspired his overthrow; .
For, falling to a devilish exercise,
And glutted now with learning's golden gifts,
He surfeits upon cursèd necromancy.
Nothing so sweet as magic is to him, 25
Which he prefers before his chiefest bliss.
And this the man that in his study sits! (*Exit*)

Act One

Scene 1

(FAUSTUS *in his Study*)
FAUSTUS Settle thy studies, Faustus, and begin
To sound the depth of that thou wilt profess;
Having commenced, be a divine in show,
Yet level at the end of every art,
And live and die in Aristotle's works. 5
Sweet Analytics, 'tis thou hast ravished me—
(*Reads*) *Bene disserere est finis logices.**
Is to dispute well logic's chiefest end?
Affords this art no greater miracle?
Then read no more, thou hast attained that end;
A greater subject fitteth Faustus' wit: 10
Bid ὄν χαὶ μὴ ὄν* farewell; Galen* come,
Seeing *Ubi desinit philosophus ibi incipit medicus;**
Be a physician, Faustus, heap up gold,

---

13 A famous Saxon university.
7 "To dispute well is logic's end."
12 (*a*) Aristotle's "being and not-being." (*b*) The medieval authority on medical science.
13 A version of a sentence from Aristotle: "Where the philosopher gives over, there the doctor begins."

And be eternized for some wondrous cure.
(*Reads*) *Summum bonum medicinæ sanitas,*
The end of physic is our body's health.
Why, Faustus, hast thou not attained that end?
Is not thy common talk sound aphorisms?
Are not thy bills* hung up as monuments,
Whereby whole cities have escaped the plague,
And thousand desperate maladies been cured?
Yet art thou still but Faustus and a man.
Couldst thou make men to live eternally,
Or, being dead, raise them to life again,
Then this profession were to be esteemed.
Physic, farewell.—Where is Justinian?
(*Reads*) *Si una eademque res legatur duobus, alter rem, alter valorem rei, etc.**
A pretty case of paltry legacies!
(*Reads*) *Exhæreditare filium non potest pater nisi, etc.**
Such is the subject of the Institute
And universal body of the law.
This study fits a mercenary drudge,
Who aims at nothing but external trash;
Too servile and illiberal for me.
When all is done divinity is best;
Jerome's Bible,* Faustus, view it well.
(*Reads*) *Stipendium peccati mors est.* Ha! *Stipendium,* etc.
The reward of sin is death. That's hard.
(*Reads*) *Si peccasse negamus, fallimur, et nulla est in nobis veritas.*
If we say that we have no sin,
We deceive ourselves, and there's no truth in us.
Why, then, belike we must sin,
And so consequently die.
Ay, we must die an everlasting death.
What docrine call you this, *Che sera sera,*
What will be, shall be? Divinity, adieu!
These metaphysics of magicians
And necromantic books are heavenly:
Lines, circles, letters, and characters:
Ay, these are those that Faustus most desires.
O, what a world of profit and delight,
Of power, of honor, of omnipotence
Is promised to the studious artisan!
All things that move between the quiet poles
Shall be at my command: emperors and kings

---

20 Prescriptions.
28 A ruling from Justinian's *Institutes* (incorrectly cited) ordering the division of a legacy: "If one and the
   same thing is willed to two persons, the thing goes to one, the value of the thing to the other, etc."
30 "A father cannot disinherit a son, unless etc."
37 The Vulgate, translated chiefly by St. Jerome.

Are but obeyed in their several provinces,
Nor can they raise the wind or rend the clouds;
But his dominion that exceeds in this
Stretcheth as far as doth the mind of man,   60
A sound magician is a mighty god:
Here, try thy brains to get a deity.
Wagner!

(Enter WAGNER)

      Commend me to my dearest friends,   65
The German Valdes and Cornelius;
Request them earnestly to visit me.

WAGNER   I will, sir. (*Exit*)

FAUSTUS   Their conference will be a greater help to me
    Than all my labors, plod I ne'er so fast.   70

(Enter the GOOD ANGEL and the EVIL ANGEL)

GOOD ANGEL   O Faustus! lay that damned book aside,
    And gaze not on it, lest it tempt thy soul,
    And heap God's heavy wrath upon thy head.
    Read, read the Scriptures: that is blasphemy.   75

EVIL ANGEL   Go forward, Faustus, in that famous art,
    Wherein all Nature's treasure is contained:
    Be thou on earth as Jove is in the sky,
    Lord and commander of these elements. (*Exeunt* ANGELS)

FAUSTUS   How am I glutted with conceit of this!   80
    Shall I make spirits fetch me what I please,
    Resolve me of all ambiguities,
    Perform what desperate enterprise I will?
    I'll have them fly to India for gold,
    Ransack the ocean for orient pearl,   85
    And search all corners of the new-found world
    For pleasant fruits and princely delicates;
    I'll have them read me strange philosophy
    And tell the secrets of all foreign kings;
    I'll have them wall all Germany with brass,   90
    And make swift Rhine circle fair Wittenberg,
    I'll have them fill the public schools with silk,
    Wherewith the students shall be bravely clad;
    I'll levy soldiers with the coin they bring,
    And chase the Prince of Parma from our land,*   95
    And reign sole king of all the provinces;
    Yea, stranger engines for the brunt of war
    Than was the fiery keel at Antwerp's bridge,*
    I'll make my servile spirits to invent.

(Enter VALDES and CORNELIUS)   100

[95] The Spanish Governor-general (1579–92) of the Netherlands, then part of the Spanish empire.

[98] The fireship with which the Netherlanders destroyed the bridge which Parma had built to complete the blockade of Antwerp.

Come, German Valdes and Cornelius,
And make me blest with your sage conference.
Valdes, sweet Valdes, and Cornelius,
Know that your words have won me at the last
To practise magic and concealed arts: 105
Yet not your words only, but mine own fantasy,
That will receive no object; for my head
But ruminates on necromantic skill.
Philosophy is odious and obscure,
Both law and physic are for petty wits;   110
Divinity is basest of the three,
Unpleasant, harsh, contemptible, and vile:
'Tis magic, magic that hath ravished me.
Then, gentle friends, aid me in this attempt;
And I, that have with subtle syllogisms   115
Gravelled* the pastors of the German church,
And made the flowering pride of Wittenberg
Swarm to my problems, as the infernal spirits
On sweet Musæus,* when he came to hell,
Will be as cunning as Agrippa* was,   120
Whose shadows made all Europe honor him.

VALDES Faustus, these books, thy wit, and our experience
    Shall make all nations to canònize us.
    As Indian Moors obey their Spanish lords,
    So shall the spirits of every element   125
    Be always serviceable to us three;
    Like lions shall they guard us when we please;
    Like Almain rutters* with their horsemen's staves
    Or Lapland giants, trotting by our sides;
    Sometimes like women or unwedded maids,   130
    Shadowing more beauty in their airy brows
    Than have the white breasts of the queen of love:
    From Venice shall they drag huge argosies,
    And from America the golden fleece
    That yearly stuffs old Philip's* treasury,   135
    If learned Faustus will be resolute.

FAUSTUS Valdes, as resolute am I in this
    As thou to live; therefore object it not.

CORNELIUS The miracles that magic will perform
    Will make thee vow to study nothing else.   140

---

116 Nonplussed.
119 A reminiscence of the *Aeneid:* Virgil placed Musaeus, also a poet, in the Elysian fields attended by a
   multitude of spirits.
120 Cornelius Agrippa was thought to have the power to call up the shades of the dead.
128 German horsemen.
135 Philip II of Spain (1556–98).

He that is grounded in astrology,
Enriched with tongues, well seen in minerals,
Hath all the principles magic doth require.
Then doubt not, Faustus, but to be renowned,
And more frequented for this mystery   145
Than heretofore the Delphian Oracle.
The spirits tell me they can dry the sea,
And fetch the treasure of all foreign wrecks,
Ay, all the wealth that our forefathers hid
Within the massy entrails of the earth;   150
Then tell me, Faustus, what shall we three want?
FAUSTUS   Nothing, Cornelius! O, this cheers my soul!
Come, show me some demonstrations magical,
That I may conjure in some bushy grove,
And have these joys in full possession.   155
VALDES   Then haste thee to some solitary grove,
And bear wise Bacon's and Albertus' works,*
The Hebrew Psalter and New Testament;
And whatsoever else is requisite
We will inform thee ere our conference cease.   160
CORNELIUS   Valdes, first let him know the words of art;
And then, all other ceremonies learned,
Faustus may try his cunning by himself.
VALDES   First I'll instruct thee in the rudiments,
And then wilt thou be perfecter than I.   165
FAUSTUS   Then come and dine with me, and after meat,
We'll canvass every quiddity* thereof;
For ere I sleep I'll try what I can do:
This night I'll conjure tho' I die therefore. (*Exeunt*)

Scene 2

Before Faustus' House   170
(*Enter two* SCHOLARS)

1ST SCHOLAR   I wonder what's become of Faustus that was wont to make our
schools ring with *sic probo?**
2ND SCHOLAR   That shall we know, for see here comes his boy.
(*Enter* WAGNER)   175
1ST SCHOLAR   How now, sirrah! Where's thy master?
WAGNER   God in heaven knows!
2ND SCHOLAR   Why, dost not thou know, then?
WAGNER   Yes, I know. But that follows not.

---

157 Roger Bacon (1214?–94) and Albertus Magnus (1193?–1280), both famous scholars also believed to be
magicians.
167 Essential element.
173 "Thus I prove."

1ST SCHOLAR   Go to, sirrah! leave your jesting, and tell us where he is.   180

WAGNER   That follows not necessary by force of argument, which you, being licentiates,* should stand upon: therefore acknowledge your error and be attentive.

2ND SCHOLAR   Why, didst thou not say thou knewest?

WAGNER   Have you any witness of it?   185

1ST SCHOLAR   Yes, sirrah, I heard you.

WAGNER   Ask my fellow if I be a thief.

2ND SCHOLAR   Well, you will not tell us?

WAGNER   Yes, sir, I will tell you; yet if you were not dunces, you would never ask me such a question; for is not he *corpus naturale?* and is not that   190 *mobile?** Then wherefore should you ask me such a question? But that I am by nature phlegmatic, slow to wrath, and prone to lechery (to love, I would say), it were not for you to come within forty feet of the place of execution, although I do not doubt to see you both hanged the next sessions. Thus having triumphed over you, I will set my countenance like a precisian,*   195 and begin to speak thus: Truly, my dear brethren, my master is within at dinner, with Valdes and Cornelius, as this wine, if it could speak, would inform your worships; and so the Lord bless you, preserve you, and keep you, my dear brethren. (*Exit*)

1ST SCHOLAR   O Faustus. Then I fear that which I have long suspected,   200
That thou art fallen in that damned art
For which they two are infamous through the world.

2ND SCHOLAR   Were he a stranger, not allied to me,
The danger of his soul would make me mourn.
But come, let us go and inform the rector.   205
It may be his grave counsel can reclaim him.

1ST SCHOLAR   I fear me nothing will reclaim him now.

2ND SCHOLAR   Yet let us try what we can do. (*Exeunt*)

Scene 3

(*Enter* FAUSTUS *to conjure in a grove*)

FAUSTUS   Now that the gloomy shadow of the night,   210
Longing to view Orion's drizzling look,*
Leaps from the antarctic world unto the sky,
And dims the welkin with her pitchy breath,
Faustus, begin thine incantations,
And try if devils will obey thy hest,   215
Seeing thou hast prayed and sacrificed to them.

---

182 Those who have been licensed to take an advanced degree.

191 "*Corpus naturale seu mobile*" (A body natural or changeable) was the scholastic expression for the subject-matter of physics.

195 A puritan.

211 Another echo of Virgil: the scene in Book I (l. 535) in which Aeneas' ship is swamped when Orion, the star, brings on a storm.

Within this circle is Jehovah's name,
Forward and backward anagrammatized,*
The breviated names of holy saints,
Figures of every adjunct to the heavens,*   220
And characters of signs and erring stars,*
By which the spirits are enforced to rise:
Then fear not, Faustus, but be resolute,
And try the uttermost magic can perform.
   Sint mihi dei Acherontis propitii! Valeat numen triplex Jehovæ! Ignei, aerii, 225
acquatani spiritus, salvete! Orientis princeps Belzebub, inferni ardentis monarcha, et
Demogorgon, propitiamus vos, ut appareat et surgate Mephistophilis. Quid tu
moraris? per Jehovam, Gehennam, et consecratam aquam quam nunc spargo, sig-
numque crucis quod nunc facio, et per vota nostra, ipse nunc surgat nobis dicatus
*Mephistophilis!**
                                                                              230
               (*Enter* MEPHISTOPHILIS)
I charge thee to return and change thy shape;
Thou art too ugly to attend on me.
Go, and return an old Franciscan friar;
That holy shape becomes a devil best. (*Exit* MEPHISTOPHILIS)   235
I see there's virtue in my heavenly words;
Who would not be proficient in this art?
How pliant is this Mephistophilis,
Full of obedience and humility!
Such is the force of magic and my spells: 240
Now, Faustus, thou are conjuror laureat,
That canst command great Mephistophilis:
*Quin redis Mephistophilis fratris imagine.**
        (*Enter* MEPHISTOPHILIS *like a Franciscan Friar*)

MEPHISTOPHILIS   Now, Faustus, what would'st thou have me do?   245
FAUSTUS   I charge thee wait upon me whilst I live,
To do whatever Faustus shall command,
Be it to make the moon drop from her sphere,
Or the ocean to overwhelm the world.
MEPHISTOPHILIS   I am a servant to great Lucifer,   250
And may not follow thee without his leave:
No more than he commands must we perform.
FAUSTUS   Did not he charge thee to appear to me?
MEPHISTOPHILIS   No, I came now hither of mine own accord.

---

[218] Transposed in such a way as to form another word.

[220] The heavenly bodies, seen as parts of a solid firmament.

[221] Signs of the zodiac and planets. "Erring" in this case means wandering.

[230] "May the gods of Acheron be favorable to me! Away with the triple deity of Jehovah! Spirits of fire, air, water, earth, hail! Prince of the East [Lucifer], Belzebub, monarch of burning hell, and Demogorgon, we ask your grace that Mephistophilis may appear and rise. Why do you linger? By Jehovah, hell, and the holy water which I now sprinkle, and the sign of the Cross which I now make, and by our vows, may Mephistophilis himself now rise to do us service."

[243] A rough Latin rendering of the line above: "Go, and return an old Franciscan friar."

FAUSTUS   Did not my conjuring raise thee? Speak.   255
MEPHISTOPHILIS   That was the cause, but yet *per accidens*,*
     For, when we hear one rack* the name of God,
     Abjure the Scriptures and his Saviour Christ,
     We fly in hope to get his glorious soul;
     Nor will we come, unless he use such means   260
     Whereby he is in danger to be damned:
     Therefore the shortest cut for conjuring
     Is stoutly to abjure the Trinity,
     And pray devoutly to the Prince of Hell.
FAUSTUS   So Faustus hath   265
     Already done; and holds this principle,
     There is no chief, but only Belzebub,
     To whom Faustus doth dedicate himself.
     This word "damnation" terrifies not me,
     For I confound hell in Elysium;   270
     My ghost be with the old philosophers!
     But, leaving these vain trifles of men's souls,
     Tell me what is that Lucifer thy lord?
MEPHISTOPHILIS   Arch-regent and commander of all spirits.
FAUSTUS   Was not that Lucifer an angel once?   275
MEPHISTOPHILIS   Yes, Faustus, and most dearly loved of God.
FAUSTUS   How comes it then that he is prince of devils?
MEPHISTOPHILIS   O, by aspiring pride and insolence;
     For which God threw him from the face of heaven.
FAUSTUS   And what are you that live with Lucifer?   280
MEPHISTOPHILIS   Unhappy spirits that fell with Lucifer,
     Conspired against our God with Lucifer,
     And are for ever damned with Lucifer.
FAUSTUS   Where are you damned?
MEPHISTOPHILIS   In hell.   285
FAUSTUS   How comes it then that thou are out of hell?
MEPHISTOPHILIS   Why this is hell, nor am I out of it:
     Think'st thou that I who saw the face of God,
     And tasted the eternal joys of heaven,
     Am not tormented with ten thousand hells,   290
     In being deprived of everlasting bliss?
     O Faustus! leave these frivolous demands,
     Which strike a terror to my fainting soul.
FAUSTUS   What, is great Mephistophilis so passionate
     For being deprived of the joys of heaven?   295
     Learn thou of Faustus manly fortitude,
     And scorn those joys thou never shalt possess.
     Go bear these tidings to great Lucifer:

256 Another scholastic formula: "The cause, but by accident."
257 Torture by anagrammatizing.

Seeing Faustus hath incurred eternal death
By desperate thoughts against Jove's deity,
Say he surrenders up to him his soul,
So he will spare him four and twenty years,
Letting him live in all voluptuousness;
Having thee ever to attend on me;
To give me whatsoever I shall ask,
To tell me whatsoever I demand,
To slay mine enemies, and to aid my friends,
And always be obedient to my will.
Go and return to mighty Lucifer,
And meet me in my study at midnight,
And then resolve me of thy master's mind.

MEPHISTOPHILIS   I will, Faustus. (*Exit*)

FAUSTUS   Had I as many souls as there be stars,
I'd give them all for Mephistophilis.
By him I'll be great Emperor of the world,
And make a bridge through the moving air,
To pass the ocean with a band of men;
I'll join the hills that bind the Afric shore,
And make that country continent to Spain,
And both contributory to my crown.
The Emperor shall not live but by my leave,
Nor any potentate of Germany.
Now that I have obtained what I desire,
I'll live in speculation* of this art
Till Mephistophilis return again. (*Exit*)

Scene 4

(*Enter* WAGNER *and* CLOWN)

WAGNER   Sirrah, boy, come hither.

CLOWN   How, boy! Swowns,* boy! I hope you have seen many boys with such pickadevaunts* as I have; boy, quotha.

WAGNER   Tell me, sirrah, hast thou any comings in?*

CLOWN   Ay, and goings out too. You may see else.

WAGNER   Alas, poor slave! See how poverty jesteth in his nakedness! The villain is bare and out of service, and so hungry that I know he would give his soul to the Devil for a shoulder of mutton though 'twere blood-raw.

CLOWN   How? My soul to the Devil for a shoulder of mutton, though 'twere blood-raw! Not so, good friend. By'r-lady, I had need have it well roasted and good sauce to it, if I pay so dear.

---

324 Contemplative study.
328 Like "zounds," a corruption of the curse "God's wounds."
329 From *pic à devant*, meaning a beard cut to a point.
330 Income.

WAGNER Well, wilt thou serve me, and I'll make thee go like *Qui mihi discipulus?**

CLOWN How, in verse? 340

WAGNER No, sirrah; in beaten silk and stavesacre.*

CLOWN How, how, Knave's acre!* Ay, I thought that was all the land his father left him. Do you hear? I would be sorry to rob you of your living.

WAGNER Sirrah, I say in stavesacre.

CLOWN Oho! Oho! Stavesacre! Why then belike if I were your man I should 345 be full of vermin.

WAGNER So thou shalt, whether thou beest with me or no. But, sirrah, leave your jesting, and bind yourself presently unto me for seven years, or I'll turn all the lice about thee into familiars,* and they shall tear thee in pieces.

CLOWN Do you hear, sir? You may save that labor: they are too familiar 350 with me already: swowns! they are as bold with my flesh as if they had paid for their meat and drink.

WAGNER Well, do you hear, sirrah? Hold, take these guilders.* (*Gives money*)

CLOWN Gridirons! what be they?

WAGNER Why, French crowns. 355

CLOWN Mass, but in the name of French crowns, a man were as good have as many English counters. And what should I do with these?

WAGNER Why, now, sirrah, thou art at an hour's warning, whensoever and wheresoever the Devil shall fetch thee.

CLOWN No, no. Here, take your gridirons again. 360

WAGNER Truly I'll none of them.

CLOWN Truly but you shall.

WAGNER Bear witness I gave them him.

CLOWN Bear witness I give them you again.

WAGNER Well, I will cause two devils presently to fetch thee away—Balio 365 and Belcher!

CLOWN Let your Balio and your Belcher come here, and I'll knock them, they were never so knocked since they were devils! Say I should kill one of them, what would folks say? "Do you see yonder tall* fellow in the round slop* —he has killed the devil." So I should be called Kill-devil all the parish 370 over.

(Enter two DEVILS; *the* CLOWN *runs up and down crying*)

WAGNER Baliol and Belcher! Spirits, away! (*Exeunt* DEVILS)

CLOWN What, are they gone? A vengeance on them, they have vile long nails! There was a he-devil and a she-devil! I'll tell you how you shall know 375 them; all he-devils has horns, and all she-devils has clifts and cloven feet.

WAGNER Well, sirrah, follow me.

---

339 "One who is a student of mine."

341 Silk with some metal stamped into it. "'Stavesacre" is a poison used for killing vermin.

342 A well known, rather disreputable street in London at the time.

349 Familiars were demonic spirits which assisted conjurors, usually taking the form of animals as they did so.

353 Coins.

369 (*a*) Valiant. (*b*) Loose trousers.

CLOWN   But, do you hear—if I should serve you, would you teach me to raise up Banios and Belcheos?

WAGNER   I will teach thee to turn thyself to anything; to a dog, or a cat, or a 380 mouse, or a rat, or anything.

CLOWN   How! a Christian fellow to a dog or a cat, a mouse or a rat! No, no, sir. If you turn me into anything, let it be in the likeness of a little pretty frisking flea, that I may be here and there and everywhere. O, I'll tickle the pretty wenches' plackets;* I'll be amongst them, i' faith. 385

WAGNER   Well, sirrah, come.

CLOWN   But, do you hear, Wagner?

WAGNER   How! Baliol and Belcher!

CLOWN   O Lord! I pray, sir, let Banio and Belcher go sleep.

WAGNER   Villain—call me Master Wagner, and let thy eye be diametarily 390 fixed upon my right heel, with *quasi vestigias nostras insistere.** (*Exit*)

CLOWN   God forgive me, he speaks Dutch fustian.* Well, I'll follow him: I'll serve him, that's flat. (*Exit*)

Act Two

Scene 1

(Enter FAUSTUS in his Study)

FAUSTUS   Now, Faustus, must
   Thou needs be damned, and canst thou not be saved.
   What boots it, then, to think of God or heaven?
   Away with such vain fancies, and despair:
   Despair in God, and trust in Belzebub;
   Now go not backward: Faustus, be resolute: 5
   Why waver'st thou? O, something soundeth in mine ear
   "Abjure this magic, turn to God again!"
   Ay, and Faustus will turn to God again.
   To God?—He loves thee not—
   The God thou serv'st is thine own appetite, 10
   Wherein is fixed the love of Belzebub;
   To him I'll build an altar and a church,
   And offer lukewarm blood of new-born babes.

(Enter GOOD and EVIL ANGELS) 15

EVIL ANGEL   Go forward, Faustus, in that famous art.

GOOD ANGEL   Sweet Faustus, leave that execrable art.

FAUSTUS   Contrition, prayer, repentance! What of these?

GOOD ANGEL   O, they are means to bring thee unto heaven.

EVIL ANGEL   Rather illusions, fruits of lunacy, 20
   That make men foolish that do use them most.

---

385 A slit at the top of a skirt.
391 "As if to tread in my footprints."
392 Jargon, or rhetorical nonsense.

GOOD ANGEL   Sweet Faustus, think of heaven and heavenly things.
EVIL ANGEL   No, Faustus, think of honor and of wealth. (*Exeunt* ANGELS)
FAUSTUS   Wealth!

Why the signiory of Embden* shall be mine.   25
When Mephistophilis shall stand by me,
What God can hurt thee? Faustus, thou are safe:
Cast no more doubts. Mephistophilis, come!
And bring glad tidings from great Lucifer;
Is't not midnight? Come, Mephistophilis;   30
Veni, veni, Mephistophile! *

(*Enter* MEPHISTOPHILIS)

Now tell me, what says Lucifer, thy lord?
MEPHISTOPHILIS   That I shall wait on Faustus whilst he lives,
So he will buy my service with his soul.   35
FAUSTUS   Already Faustus hath hazarded that for thee.
MEPHISTOPHILIS   But now thou must bequeath it solemnly,
And write a deed of gift with thine own blood,
For that security craves great Lucifer.
If thou deny it, I must back to hell.   40
FAUSTUS   Stay, Mephistophilis! and tell me what good
Will my soul do thy lord.
MEPHISTOPHILIS   Enlarge his kingdom.
FAUSTUS   Is that the reason why he tempts us thus?
MEPHISTOPHILIS   *Solamen miseris socios habuisse doloris.* *   45
FAUSTUS   Why, have you any pain that tortures others?
MEPHISTOPHILIS   As great as have the human souls of men.
But tell me, Faustus, shall I have thy soul?
And I will be thy slave, and wait on thee,
And give thee more than thou hast wit to ask.   50
FAUSTUS   Ay, Mephistophilis, I give it him.
MEPHISTOPHILIS   Then, Faustus, stab thine arm courageously,
And bind* thy soul that at some certain day
Great Lucifer may claim it as his own;
And then be thou as great as Lucifer.   55
FAUSTUS (*stabbing his arm*)   Lo, Mephistophilis, for love of thee,
I cut mine arm, and with my proper blood
Assure my soul to be great Lucifer's,
Chief lord and regent of perpetual night!
View here the blood that trickles from mine arm,   60
And let it be propitious for my wish.
MEPHISTOPHILIS   But, Faustus, thou must
Write it in manner of a deed of gift.

---

25 Near the mouth of the Ems, Embden was the chief town of East Friesland in northern Holland.
31 "Come, come, Mephistophilis."
45 "It's a solace to the miserable to have had companions in sorrow."
53 Give a bond for.

FAUSTUS   Ay, so I do. (*Writes*) But, Mephistophilis,
   My blood congeals, and I can write no more.

MEPHISTOPHILIS   I'll fetch thee fire to dissolve it straight. (*Exit*)

FAUSTUS   What might the staying of my blood portend?
   Is it unwilling I should write this bill?
   Why streams it not that I may write afresh?
   Faustus gives to thee his soul. Ah, there it stayed.
   Why should'st thou not? Is not thy soul thine own?
   Then write again, *Faustus gives to thee his soul.*

                    (*Enter* MEPHISTOPHILIS *with a chafer of coals*)

MEPHISTOPHILIS   See, Faustus, here is fire, set it on.

FAUSTUS   So, now the blood begins to clear again;
   Now will I make an end immediately. (*Writes*)

MEPHISTOPHILIS   (*Aside*)   O, what will not I do to obtain his soul.

FAUSTUS   *Consummatum est:* * this bill is ended,
   And Faustus hath bequeathed his soul to Lucifer.
   But what is this inscription on mine arm?
   Homo, fuge! * Whither should I fly?
   If unto God, he'll throw me down to hell.
   My senses are deceived; here's nothing writ—
   Oh yes, I see it plain; even here is writ
   Homo, fuge! Yet shall not Faustus fly.

MEPHISTOPHILIS   I'll fetch him somewhat to delight his mind. (*Exit*)
   (*Re-enter* MEPHISTOPHILIS *with* DEVILS, *giving crowns and rich apparel to*
                    FAUSTUS. *They dance, and then depart*)

FAUSTUS   What means this show? Speak, Mephistophilis.

MEPHISTOPHILIS   Nothing, Faustus, but to delight thy mind,
   And let thee see what magic can perform.

FAUSTUS   But may I raise such spirits when I please?

MEPHISTOPHILIS   Ay, Faustus, and do greater things than these.

FAUSTUS   Then there's enough for a thousand souls.
   Here, Mephistophilis, receive this scroll,
   A deed of gift of body and of soul:
   But yet conditionally that thou perform
   All articles prescribed between us both.

MEPHISTOPHILIS   Faustus, I swear by hell and Lucifer
   To effect all promises between us made.

FAUSTUS   Then hear me read it, Mephistophilis. *On these conditions following.
   First, that Faustus may be a spirit in form and substance. Secondly, that Mephistophilis shall be his servant, and at his command. Thirdly, that Mephistophilis shall
   do for him and bring him whatsoever. Fourthly, that he shall be in his chamber
   or house invisible. Lastly, that he shall appear to the said John Faustus, at all
   times, in what form or shape soever he please. I, John Faustus, of Wittenberg, Doctor,
   by these presents do give both body and soul to Lucifer, Prince of the East, and his*

---

78 "It is finished." From the Gospel of St. John, XIX, 30.
81 "Man, take flight."

minister, Mephistophilis: and furthermore grant unto them that, four and twenty years being expired and these articles above written inviolate, full power to fetch or carry the said John Faustus, body and soul, flesh, blood, or goods, into their 110
habitation wheresoever. By me,

John Faustus.

MEPHISTOPHILIS Speak, Faustus, do you deliver this as your deed?

FAUSTUS Ay, take it, and the Devil give thee good of it!

MEPHISTOPHILIS So, now, Faustus, ask me what thou wilt. 115

FAUSTUS First will I question with thee about hell.
Tell me where is the place that men call hell?

MEPHISTOPHILIS Under the heavens.

FAUSTUS Ay, so are all things else, but whereabouts?

MEPHISTOPHILIS Within the bowels of these elements, 120
Where we are tortured and remain for ever;
Hell hath no limits, nor is circumscribed
In one self place; for where we are is hell,
And where hell is, there must we ever be:
And, to be short, when all the world dissolves, 125
And every creature shall be purified,
All places shall be hell that is not heaven.

FAUSTUS I think hell's a fable.

MEPHISTOPHILIS Ay, think so, till experience change thy mind.

FAUSTUS Why, dost thou think that Faustus shall be damned? 130

MEPHISTOPHILIS Ay, of necessity, for here's the scroll
In which thou hast given thy soul to Lucifer.

FAUSTUS Ay, and body too; but what of that?
Think'st thou that Faustus is so fond to imagine
That, after this life, there is any pain? 135
No, these are trifles and mere old wives' tales.

MEPHISTOPHILIS But I am an instance to prove the contrary,
For I tell I am damned and now in hell.

FAUSTUS How! now in hell?
Nay, and this be hell, I'll willingly be damnèd; 140
What? sleeping, eating, walking, disputing?
But, leaving off this, let me have a wife,
The fairest maid in Germany,
For I am wanton and lascivious,
And cannot live without a wife. 145

MEPHISTOPHILIS How—a wife?
I prithee, Faustus, talk not of a wife.

FAUSTUS Nay, sweet Mephistophilis, fetch me one, for I will have one.

MEPHISTOPHILIS Well—thou wilt have one. Sit there till I come:
I'll fetch thee a wife in the Devil's name. (*Exit*) 150
(*Re-enter* MEPHISTOPHILIS *with a* DEVIL *dressed like a woman, with fireworks*)

MEPHISTOPHILIS Tell me, Faustus, how dost thou like thy wife?

FAUSTUS A plague on her for a hot whore!

MEPHISTOPHILIS Tut, Faustus,

Marriage is but a ceremonial toy; 155
And if thou lovest me, think no more of it.
I'll cull thee out the fairest courtesans,
And bring them every morning to thy bed;
She whom thine eye shall like, thy heart shall have,
Be she as chaste as was Penelope,
And as wise as Saba,* or as beautiful 160
As was bright Lucifer before his fall.
Here, take this book, peruse it thoroughly: (*Gives a book*)
The iterating of these lines brings gold;
The framing of this circle on the ground 165
Brings thunder, whirlwinds, storm, and lightning;
Pronounce this thrice devoutly to thyself,
And men in armor shall appear to thee,
Ready to execute what thou commandest.

FAUSTUS Thanks, Mephistophilis; yet fain would I have a book wherein I 170
might behold all spells and incantations, that I might raise up spirits when
I please.

MEPHISTOPHILIS Here they are, in this book. (*They turn to them*)

FAUSTUS Now would I have a book where I might see all characters and planets
of the heavens, that I might know their motions and dispositions. 175

MEPHISTOPHILIS Here they are too. (*Turn to them*)

FAUSTUS Nay, let me have one book more—and then I have done—wherein
I might see all plants, herbs, and trees that grow upon the earth.

MEPHISTOPHILIS Here they be.

FAUSTUS Thanks, Mephistophilis, for this sweet book.
This will I keep as chary as my life. (*Exeunt*) 180

Scene 2

(*Enter* FAUSTUS *in his Study, and* MEPHISTOPHILIS)

FAUSTUS When I behold the heavens, then I repent,
And curse thee, wicked Mephistophilis,
Because thou hast deprived me of those joys. 185

MEPHISTOPHILIS 'Twas thine own seeking, Faustus, thank thyself.
But think'st thou heaven is such a glorious thing?
I tell thee, Faustus, 'tis not half so fair
As thou, or any man that breathes on earth.

FAUSTUS How prov'st thou that?

MEPHISTOPHILIS 'Twas made for man; then he's more excellent. 190

FAUSTUS If it were made for man, 'twas made for me;
I will renounce this magic and repent.

(*Enter* GOOD ANGEL *and* EVIL ANGEL)

GOOD ANGEL Faustus, repent; yet God will pity thee.

EVIL ANGEL Thou art a spirit; God cannot pity thee. 195

FAUSTUS Who buzzeth in my ears I am a spirit?

161 The Queen of Sheba.

Be I a devil, yet God may pity me;
Ay, God will pity me if I repent.

EVIL ANGEL   Ay, but Faustus never shall repent. (*Exeunt* ANGELS)   200

FAUSTUS   My heart's so hardened I cannot repent.
Scarce can I name salvation, faith, or heaven,
But fearful echoes thunder in mine ears,
"Faustus, thou are damned!" Then swords and knives,
Poison, gun, halters, and envenomed steel   205
Are laid before me to dispatch myself,
And long ere this I should have done the deed,
Had not sweet pleasure conquered deep despair.
Have not I made blind Homer sing to me
Of Alexander's love and Œnon's death?*   210
And hath not he that built the walls of Thebes
With ravishing sound of his melodious harp,*
Made music with my Mephistophilis?
Why should I die, then, or basely despair?
I am resolved: Faustus shall ne'er repent—   215
Come, Mephistophilis, let us dispute again,
And reason of divine astrology.
Speak, are there many spheres above the moon?
Are all celestial bodies but one globe,
As is the substance of this centric earth?   220

MEPHISTOPHILIS   As are the elements, such are the heavens,
Even from the moon unto the imperial orb,
Mutually folded in each other's spheres,
And jointly move upon one axle-tree
Whose termine is termed the world's wide pole;   225
Nor are the names of Saturn, Mars, or Jupiter
Feigned, but are erring stars.

FAUSTUS   But have they all one motion, both *situ et tempore?**

MEPHISTOPHILIS   All move from east to west in twenty-four hours upon the
poles of the world; but differ in their motions upon the poles of the zodiac. 230

FAUSTUS   Tush!
These slender trifles Wagner can decide;
Hath Mephistophilis no greater skill?
Who knows not the double motion of the planets?
The first is finished in a natural day;   235
The second thus: Saturn in thirty years;
Jupiter in twelve; Mars in four; the Sun, Venus, and Mercury in a year; the
moon in twenty-eight days. Tush, these are freshmen's questions. But tell
me, hath every sphere a dominion or *intelligentia?*

MEPHISTOPHILIS   Ay.   240

210 Paris, or Alexander, was the lover of Oenone.
212 Amphion.
228 "In position and time."

FAUSTUS How many heavens, or spheres, are there?

MEPHISTOPHILIS Nine: the seven planets, the firmament, and the empyreal heaven.

FAUSTUS But is there not *coelum igneum et cristallinum?**

MEPHISTOPHILIS No, Faustus, they are but fables. 245

FAUSTUS Resolve me then in this one question: Why are not conjunctions, oppositions, aspects, eclipses, all at one time, but in some years we have more, in some less?

MEPHISTOPHILIS *Per inæqualem motum respectu totius.**

FAUSTUS Well, I am answered. Tell me who made the world. 250

MEPHISTOPHILIS I will not.

FAUSTUS Sweet Mephistophilis, tell me.

MEPHISTOPHILIS Move me not, Faustus.

FAUSTUS Villain, have I not bound thee to tell me anything?

MEPHISTOPHILIS Ay, that is not against our kingdom. 255
This is. Thou art damned; think thou on hell.

FAUSTUS Think, Faustus, upon God that made the world.

MEPHISTOPHILIS Remember this. (*Exit*)

FAUSTUS Ay, go, accursed spirit, to ugly hell.
'Tis thou hast damned distressèd Faustus' soul. 260
Is't not too late?

(*Enter* GOOD ANGEL *and* EVIL ANGEL)

EVIL ANGEL Too late.

GOOD ANGEL Never too late, if Faustus can repent.

EVIL ANGEL If thou repent, devils will tear thee in pieces. 265

GOOD ANGEL Repent, and they shall never raze thy skin. (*Exeunt* ANGELS)

FAUSTUS Ah, Christ, my Saviour, my Saviour,
Seek to save distressed Faustus' soul!

(*Enter* LUCIFER, BELZEBUB, *and* MEPHISTOPHILIS)

LUCIFER Christ cannot save thy soul, for he is just; 270
There's none but I have interest in the same.

FAUSTUS O, what art thou that look'st so terrible?

LUCIFER I am Lucifer,
And this is my companion-prince in hell.

FAUSTUS O Faustus! They are come to fetch thy soul! 275

BELZEBUB We are come to tell thou dost injure us.

LUCIFER Thou call'st on Christ, contrary to thy promise.

BELZEBUB Thou should'st not think of God.

LUCIFER Think of the Devil.

BELZEBUB And his dam too. 280

FAUSTUS Nor will I henceforth: pardon me in this,
And Faustus vows never to look to heaven,
Never to name God, or to pray to him,
To burn his scriptures, slay his ministers,

---

244 "Fiery and crystalline heavens."
249 "By their unequal motion in regard to the whole."

And make my spirits pull his churches down. ₂₈₅

LUCIFER   So shalt thou show thyself an obedient servant, and we will gratify thee for it.

BELZEBUB   Faustus, we are come from hell to show thee some pastime: sit down, and thou shalt behold the Seven Deadly Sins appear in their own proper shapes and likenesses. ₂₉₀

FAUSTUS   That sight will be as pleasing unto me,
As Paradise was to Adam, the first day
Of his creation.

LUCIFER   Talk not of Paradise or creation, but mark the show. Go, Mephistophilis, fetch them in. ₂₉₅

(*Enter* THE SEVEN DEADLY SINS)

BELZEBUB   Now, Faustus, question them of their names and dispositions.

FAUSTUS   That shall I soon. What art thou—the first?

PRIDE   I am Pride. I disdain to have any parents. I am like to Ovid's flea: I can creep into every corner of a wench; sometimes, like a periwig, I sit upon ₃₀₀ her brow; next, like a necklace I hang about her neck; then, like a fan of feathers, I kiss her lips; and then turning myself to a wrought smoke do what I list. But, fie, what a smell is here! I'll not speak another word, unless the ground be perfumed, and covered with cloth of arras.*

FAUSTUS   Thou art a proud knave, indeed! What art thou—the second? ₃₀₅

COVETOUSNESS   I am Covetousness, begotten of an old churl in an old leather bag; and, might I now obtain my wish, this house, you and all, should turn to gold, that I might lock you safe in my chest. O, my sweet gold!

FAUSTUS   And what art thou—the third?

WRATH   I am Wrath. I had neither father nor mother; I leapt out of a lion's ₃₁₀ mouth when I was scarce half an hour old; and ever since I have run up and down the world with this case of rapiers, wounding myself when I could get nobody to fight withal. I was born in hell; and look to it, for some of you shall be my father.

FAUSTUS   What art thou—the fourth? ₃₁₅

ENVY   I am Envy, begotten of a chimney-sweeper and an oyster-wife. I cannot read, and therefore wish all books burned. I am lean with seeing others eat. O, that there would come a famine over all the world, that all might die, and I live alone! then thou should'st see how fat I'd be. But must thou sit and I stand! Come down with a vengeance! ₃₂₀

FAUSTUS   Out, envious wretch! What art thou—the fifth?

GLUTTONY   Who, I, sir? I am Gluttony. My parents are all dead, and the devil a penny they have left me, but a small pension, and that buys me thirty meals a day and ten bevers*—a small trifle to suffice nature. O, I come of a royal pedigree! My father was a Gammon of Bacon, my mother was a ₃₂₅ Hogshead of Claret wine; my godfathers were these, Peter Pickle-herring, and Martin Martlemas-beef.* But my god-mother, O she was a jolly gentle-

---

₃₀₄ A fine cloth woven in Flanders and used for tapestries.
₃₂₄ Snacks.
₃₂₇ Martinmas, the 11th of November, the time when beef which had been salted for the winter was hung.

woman, and well beloved in every good town and city; her name was Mistress Margery March-bee.* Now, Faustus, thou hast heard all my progeny, wilt thou bid me to supper?   330

FAUSTUS   No, I'll see thee hanged: thou wilt eat up all my victuals.

GLUTTONY   Then the Devil choke thee!

FAUSTUS   Choke thyself, glutton! What art thou—the sixth?

SLOTH   Heigh ho! I am Sloth. I was begotten on a sunny bank, where I have lain ever since; and you have done me great injury to bring me from   335 thence: let me be carried thither again by Gluttony and Lechery. Heigh ho! I'll not speak another word for a king's ransom.

FAUSTUS   What are you, Mistress Minx, the seventh and last?

LECHERY   Who, I, sir? I am the one that loves an inch of raw mutton better than an ell of fried stock-fish; and the first letter of my name begins   340 with L.

LUCIFER   Away to hell, away, on Piper!* (*Exeunt the Sins*)
Now, Faustus, how dost thou like this?

FAUSTUS   O, how this sight delights my soul!

LUCIFER   But, Faustus, in hell is all manner of delight.   345

FAUSTUS   O, might I see hell, and return again safe,
How happy were I then!

LUCIFER   Faustus, thou shalt. At midnight I will send for thee.
Meanwhile peruse this book and view it thoroughly,
And thou shalt turn thyself into what shape thou wilt.   350

FAUSTUS   Thanks, mighty Lucifer!
This will I keep as chary as my life.

LUCIFER   Farewell, Faustus, and think on the Devil.

FAUSTUS   Farewell, great Lucifer! Come, Mephistophilis. (*Exeunt omnes*)

Scene 3

(*Enter* ROBIN *the ostler, with a book in his hand*)   355

ROBIN   O, this is admirable! Here have I stolen one of Doctor Faustus' conjuring books, and, in faith, I mean to search some circles for my own use. (*Draws circles on the ground*) Now will I make all the maidens in our parish dance at my pleasure stark naked before me, and so by that means I shall see more than ere I felt or saw yet.   360

(*Enter* RAFE, *calling* ROBIN)

RAFE   Robin, prithee, come away; there's a gentleman tarries to have his horse, and he would have his things rubbed and made clean; he keeps such a chafing with my mistress about it, and she has sent me to look thee out. Prithee, come away.   365

ROBIN   Keep out, keep out, or else you are blown up, you are dismembered, Ralph; keep out, for I am about a roaring piece of work.

RAFE   Come, what doest thou with that same book? Thou canst not read!

ROBIN   Yes, my master and mistress shall find that I can read, he for his fore-

329 A choice ale made in March.
342 Apparently addressed to a musician.

head, she for her private study; she's bound to bear with me, or else my 370
art fails.

RAFE   Why, Robin, what book is that?

ROBIN   What book? Why, the most intolerable book for conjuring that ere
was invented by any brimstone devil.

RAFE   Canst thou conjure with it?   375

ROBIN   I can do all these things easily with it. First, I can make thee drunk
with ippocras* at any tavern in Europe for nothing; that's one of my conjuring works.

RAFE   Our master Parson says that's nothing.

ROBIN   True, Ralph; and more, Ralph, if thou hast any mind to Nan Spit, 380
our kitchen maid, then turn her and wind her to thy own use, as often as
thou wilt, and at midnight.

RAFE   O, brave, Robin! Shall I have Nan Spit, and to mine own use? On that
condition I'll feed thy devil with horse-bread as long as he lives, of free cost.

ROBIN   No more, sweet Ralph; let's go and make clean our boots, which lie 385
foul upon our hands, and then to our conjuring in the devil's name. (*Exeunt*)

Act Three

Prologue

(*Enter the* CHORUS)

CHORUS   Learned Faustus,
To know the secrets of astronomy,
Graven in the book of Jove's high firmament,
Did mount him up to scale Olympus' top,
Where sitting in a chariot burning bright,   5
Drawn by the strength of yoked dragons' necks,
He views the clouds, the planets, and the stars,
The tropic zones, and quarters of the sky,
From the bright circle of the horned moon,
E'en to the height of *Primum mobile;**   10
And whirling round with this circumference,
Within the concave compass of the pole,
From east to west his dragons swiftly glide,
And in eight days did bring him home again.
Not long he stayed within his quiet house,   15
To rest his bones after his weary toil,
But new exploits do hale him out again,
And mounted then upon a dragon's back,
That with his wings did part the subtle air,
He now is gone to prove cosmography,   20
That measures coasts, and kingdoms of the earth,

377 A spiced wine.
10 The Prime Mover.

And, as I guess, will first arrive at Rome,
To see the Pope and manner of his court,
And take some part of holy Peter's feast,
The which this day is highly solemnized. (*Exit*)

25

Scene 1

  (*The* POPE'S *Privy-chamber. Enter* FAUSTUS *and* MEPHISTOPHILIS)

FAUSTUS Having now, my good Mephistophilis,
Passed with delight the stately town of Trier,
Environed round with airy mountain tops,
With walls of flint, and deep entrenched lakes,
Not to be won by any conquering prince;

30

From Paris next, coasting the realm of France,
We saw the river Maine fall into Rhine,
Whose banks are set with groves of fruitful vines;
Then up to Naples, rich Campania,
Whose buildings fair and gorgeous to the eye,

35

The streets straight forth, and paved with finest brick,
Quarters the town in four equivalents;
There we saw learned Maro's golden tomb,*
The way he cut, an English mile in length,
Thorough a rock of stone, in one night's space;

40

From thence to Venice, Padua, and the East,
In one of which a sumptuous temple stands,*
That threats the stars with her aspiring top,
Whose frame is paved with sundry coloured stones,
And roofed aloft with curious work in gold.

45

Thus hitherto hath Faustus spent his time.
But tell me now, what resting-place is this?
Hast thou, as erst I did command,
Conducted me within the walls of Rome?

50

MEPHISTOPHILIS I have, my Faustus; and for proof thereof
This is the goodly palace of the Pope;
And 'cause we are no common guests
I choose his privy chamber for our use.

FAUSTUS I hope his Holiness will bid us welcome.

55

MEPHISTOPHILIS All's one, for we'll be bold with his venison.
But now, my Faustus, that thou may'st perceive
What Rome contains for to delight thine eyes,
Know that this city stands upon seven hills
That underprop the groundwork of the same:

60

Just through the midst runs flowing Tiber's stream,
With winding banks that cut it in two parts:

---

[39] Publius Vergilius Maro, or Virgil, was buried in Naples in 19 B.C. The tomb is located at the end of a promontory through which runs a tunnel which Virgil is supposed to have cut out by magic.
[43] St. Mark's, Venice.

Over the which four stately bridges lean,
That make safe passage to each part of Rome:
Upon the bridge called Ponte Angelo   65
Erected is a castle passing strong,
Where thou shalt see such store of ordnance,
As that the double cannons, forged of brass,
Do match the number of the days contained
Within the compass of one complete year.   70
Beside the gates, and high pyramides,
That Julius Cæsar brought from Africa.

FAUSTUS   Now, by the kingdoms of infernal rule,
Of Styx, of Acheron, and the fiery lake
Of ever-burning Phlegethon,* I swear   75
That I do long to see the monuments
And situation of bright splendent Rome:
Come, therefore, let's away.

MEPHISTOPHILIS   Nay, stay my Faustus; I know you'd see the Pope,
And take some part of holy Peter's feast,   80
Where thou shalt see a troop of bald-pate friars,
Whose *summum bonum* is in belly-cheer.

FAUSTUS   Well, I'm content to compass them some sport,
And by their folly make us merriment.
Then charm me, Mephistophilis, that I   85
May be invisible, to do what I please
Unseen of any whilst I stay in Rome. (MEPHISTOPHILIS *charms him*)

MEPHISTOPHILIS   So, Faustus, now
Do what thou wilt, thou shalt not be discerned.
(*Sound a sennet. Enter the* POPE *and the* CARDINAL *of* LORRAIN *to the*   90
banquet, with FRIARS *attending*)

POPE   My Lord of Lorrain, wilt please you draw near?

FAUSTUS   Fall to, and the devil choke you and you spare!

POPE   How now! Who's that which spake?—Friars, look about.

FRIAR   Here's nobody, if it like your Holiness.   95

POPE   My lord, here is a dainty dish was sent me from the Bishop of Milan.

FAUSTUS   I thank you, sir. (*Snatches it*)

POPE   How now! Who's that which snatched the meat from me? Will no man
look? My Lord, this dish was sent me from the Cardinal of Florence.

FAUSTUS   You say true; I'll ha't. (*Snatches the dish*)   100

POPE   What, again! My lord, I'll drink to your grace.

FAUSTUS   I'll pledge your grace. (*Snatches the cup*)

CARDINAL OF LORRAIN   My Lord, it may be some ghost newly crept out of
purgatory, come to beg a pardon of your Holiness.

POPE   It may be so. Friars, prepare a dirge to lay the fury of this ghost. Once   105
again, my lord, fall to. (*The* POPE *crosseth himself*)

FAUSTUS   What, are you crossing of yourself?

75 The Styx and Acheron are rivers, while the Phlegeton is a lake—all in Hades.

Well, use that trick no more I would advise you. (*Cross again*)
Well, there's the second time. Aware the third,
I give you fair warning. (*Cross again, and* FAUSTUS *hits him a box of the ear;* 110
and they all run away)
Come on, Mephistophilis, what shall we do?

MEPHISTOPHILIS Nay, I know not. We shall be cursed with bell, book, and candle.*

FAUSTUS How! bell, book, and candle—candle, book, and bell, 115
Forward and backward to curse Faustus to hell!
Anon you shall hear a hog grunt, a calf bleat, and an ass bray,
Because it is Saint Peter's holiday.

(*Enter all the* FRIARS *to sing the Dirge*)

FRIAR Come, brethren, let's about our business with good devotion. 120
(*Sing this*) Cursed be he that stole away his Holiness' meat from the table!
Maledicat Dominus!
Cursed be he that struck his Holiness a blow on the face! *Maledicat Dominus!*
Cursed be he that took Friar Sandelo a blow on the pate! *Maledicat Dominus!*
Cursed be he that disturbeth our holy dirge! *Maledicat Dominus!* 125
Cursed be he that took away his Holiness' wine! *Maledicat Dominus! Et omnes
sancti!* * Amen! (MEPHISTOPHILIS *and* FAUSTUS *beat the* FRIARS, *and fling fireworks
among them: and so exeunt*)

Scene 2

(*Enter* ROBIN *and* RAFE *with a silver goblet*)

ROBIN Come, Rafe, did not I tell thee we were for ever made by this Doctor 130
Faustus' book? *Ecce signum,* here's a simple purchase* for horse-keepers; our
horses shall eat no hay as long as this lasts.

RAFE But, Robin, here comes the Vintner.

ROBIN Hush! I'll gull him supernaturally.

(*Enter* VINTNER) 135
Drawer,* I hope all is paid: God be with you; come, Rafe.

VINTNER Soft, sir; a word with you. I must yet have a goblet paid from you,
ere you go.

ROBIN I, a goblet, Rafe; I, a goblet! I scorn you, and you are but a, etc. I, a
goblet! search me. 140

VINTNER I mean so, sir, with your favor. (*Searches him*)

ROBIN How say you now?

VINTNER I must say somewhat to your fellow. You, sir!

RAFE Me, sir! me, sir! search your fill. (VINTNER *searches him*) Now, sir, you may
be ashamed to burden honest men with a matter of truth. 145

VINTNER Well, t'one of you hath this goblet about you.

---

[114] The excommunication ceremony closes with the tolling of the bell, the closing of the book, and the extinguishing of the candle.
[127] "May the Lord curse him. And all the saints."
[131] "Look to the proof. Here's a clear gain. . . ."
[136] He purposely mistakes the vintner for an inn-servant.

ROBIN   (*Aside*) You lie, drawer, 'tis afore me. (*Aloud to* VINTNER)—Sirrah you,
I'll teach you to impeach honest men—stand by—I'll scour you for a goblet!
—stand aside you had best, I charge you in the name of Belzebub.—(*Aside to*
RAFE) Look to the goblet, Rafe   150

VINTNER   What mean you, sirrah?

ROBIN   I'll tell you what I mean. (*Reads from a book*) *Sanctobulorum Periphrasticon*
—nay, I'll tickle you, Vintner. (*Aside to* RAFE) Look to the goblet, Rafe.
(*Reads*) *Polypragmos Belseborams framanto pacostiphos tostu, Mephistophilis, etc.**
    (*Enter* MEPHISTOPHILIS, *sets squibs at their backs, and then exit.*   155
                     They run about)

VINTNER   *O nomine Domine!** what meanest thou, Robin? thou hast no goblet.

RAFE   *Peccatum peccatorum.** Here's thy goblet, good Vintner. (*Gives the goblet to*
                     VINTNER, *who exit*)

ROBIN   *Misericordia pro nobis!** What shall I do? Good Devil, forgive me now,   160
and I'll never rob thy library more.
                     (*Enter to them* MEPHISTOPHILIS)

MEPHISTOPHILIS   Vanish villains, the one like an ape, another like a bear, the
    third an ass for doing this enterprise.
    Monarch of hell, under whose black survey   165
    Great potentates do kneel with awful fear,
    Upon whose altars thousand souls do lie,
    How am I vexed with these villains' charms!
    From Constantinople am I hither come
    Only for pleasure of these damnèd slaves.   170

ROBIN   How, from Constantinople! You have had a great journey: will you
take six-pence in your purse to pay for your supper, and begone?

MEPHISTOPHILIS   Well, villains, for your presumption I transform thee into an
    ape, and thee into a dog and so begone. (*Exit*)

ROBIN   How, into an ape; that's brave! I'll have fine sport with the boys. 175
I'll get nuts and apples enow.

RAFE   And I must be a dog.

ROBIN   I'faith thy head will never be out of the pottage pot. (*Exeunt*)

Act Four

Prologue

                     (*Enter* CHORUS)

CHORUS   When Faustus had with pleasure ta'en the view
    Of rarest things, and royal courts of kings,
    He stay'd his course, and so returned home;
    Where such as bear his absence but with grief,

---

154 Mock-Latin.
157 "In God's name."
158 "Sin of sins."
160 Have mercy on us.

I mean his friends and near'st companions,
Did gratulate his safety with kind words,   5
And in their conference of what befell,
Touching his journey through the world and air,
They put forth questions of astrology,
Which Faustus answered with such skill
As they admired and wondered at his wit.   10
Now is his fame spread forth in every land;
Amongst the rest the Emperor is one,
Carolus the Fifth,* at whose palace now
Faustus is feasted 'mongst his noblemen.
What there he did, in trial of his art,   15
I leave untold; your eyes shall see performed. (*Exit*)

Scene 1

The Court
(*Enter* EMPEROR, FAUSTUS, *and a* KNIGHT *with* ATTENDANTS)

EMPEROR   Master Doctor Faustus, I have heard strange report of thy knowl-   20
edge in the black art, how that none in my empire nor in the whole world
can compare with thee for the rare effects of magic; they say thou hast a
familiar spirit, by whom thou canst accomplish what thou list. This, therefore,
is my request, that thou let me see some proof of thy skill, that mine eyes may
be witnesses to confirm what mine ears have heard reported; and here I   25
swear to thee by the honor of mine imperial crown, that, whatever thou doest,
thou shalt be no ways prejudiced or endamaged.

KNIGHT   (*Aside*) I'faith he looks much like a conjuror.

FAUSTUS   My gracious sovereign, though I must confess myself far inferior to
the report men have published, and nothing answerable to the honor of   30
your imperial majesty, yet for that love and duty binds me thereunto, I am
content to do whatsoever your majesty shall command me.

EMPEROR   Then, Doctor Faustus, mark what I shall say.
As I was sometimes solitary set
Within my closet, sundry thoughts arose
About the honor of mine ancestors,   35
How they had won by prowess such exploits,
Got such riches, subdued so many kingdoms
As we that do succeed, or they that shall
Hereafter possess our throne, shall
(I fear me) ne'er attain to that degree   40
Of high renown and great authority;
Amongst which kings is Alexander the Great,
Chief spectacle of the world's pre-eminence,
The bright shining of whose glorious acts
Lightens the world with his reflecting beams,   45

---

14 Charles V of Spain was the emperor from 1519 to 1566.

As when I hear but motion made of him
It grieves my soul I never saw the man.
If therefore thou by cunning of thine art
Canst raise this man from hollow vaults below,   50
Where lies entombed this famous conqueror,
And bring with him his beauteous paramour,
Both in their right shapes, gesture, and attire
They used to wear during their time of life,
Thou shalt both satisfy my just desire,   55
And give me cause to praise thee whilst I live.

FAUSTUS   My gracious lord, I am ready to accomplish your request so far forth
as by art, and power of my spirit, I am able to perform.

KNIGHT   (*Aside*) I'faith that's just nothing at all.

FAUSTUS   But, if it like your grace, it is not in my ability to present before   60
your eyes the true substantial bodies of those two deceased princes, which
long since are consumed to dust.

KNIGHT   (*Aside*) Ay, marry, Master Doctor, now there's a sign of grace in you,
when you will confess the truth.

FAUSTUS   But such spirits as can lively resemble Alexander and his paramour   65
shall appear before your grace in that manner that they best lived in, in their
most flourishing estate; which I doubt not shall sufficiently content your
imperial majesty.

EMPEROR   Go to, Master Doctor, let me see them presently.

KNIGHT   Do you hear, Master Doctor? You bring Alexander and his para-   70
mour before the Emperor!

FAUSTUS   How then, sir?

KNIGHT   I'faith that's as true as Diana turned me to a stag!

FAUSTUS   No, sir, but when Actæon died, he left the horns for you. Mephistophilis, begone. (*Exit* MEPHISTOPHILIS)   75

KNIGHT   Nay an you go to conjuring, I'll begone. (*Exit* KNIGHT)

FAUSTUS   I'll meet with you anon for interrupting me so. Here they are, my
gracious lord.

(*Enter* MEPHISTOPHILIS *with* SPIRITS *in the shape of* ALEXANDER
and his Paramour)   80

EMPEROR   Master Doctor, I heard this lady while she lived had a wart or mole
in her neck: how shall I know whether it be so or no?

FAUSTUS   Your highness may boldly go and see.

EMPEROR   Sure these are no spirits, but the true substantial bodies of those two
deceased princes. (*Exeunt Spirits*)   85

FAUSTUS   Will't please your highness now to send for the knight that was so
pleasant with me here of late?

EMPEROR   One of you call him forth! (*Exit Attendant*)

(*Enter the* KNIGHT *with a pair of horns on his head*)

How now, sir knight! why I had thought thou had'st been a bachelor,   90
but now I see thou hast a wife, that not only gives thee horns, but makes thee
wear them. Feel on thy head.

KNIGHT   Thou damned wretch and execrable dog,

Bred in the concave of some monstrous rock,
How darest thou thus abuse a gentleman?
Villain, I say, undo what thou hast done!   95

FAUSTUS   O, not so fast, sir; there's no haste; but, good, are you remembered how you crossed me in my conference with the Emperor? I think I have met with you for it.

EMPEROR   Good Master Doctor, at my entreaty release him; he hath done   100 penance sufficient.

FAUSTUS   My gracious lord, not so much for the injury he offered me here in your presence, as to delight you with some mirth, hath Faustus worthily requited this injurious knight; which, being all I desire, I am content to release him of his horns: and, sir knight, hereafter speak well of scholars. Mephistoph- 105 ilis, transform him straight. (MEPHISTOPHILIS *removes the horns*) Now, my good lord, having done my duty I humbly take my leave.

EMPEROR   Farewell, Master Doctor; yet, ere you go,
Expect from me a bounteous reward. (*Exit Emperor*)

Scene 2

A Green, then Faustus' house   110
(*Enter* FAUSTUS *and* MEPHISTOPHILIS)

FAUSTUS   Now, Mephistophilis, the restless course
That Time doth run with calm and silent foot,
Shortening my days and thread of vital life,
Calls for the payment of my latest years: 115
Therefore, sweet Mephistophilis, let us
Make haste to Wittenberg.

MEPHISTOPHILIS   What, will you go on horse-back or on foot?

FAUSTUS   Nay, till I'm past this fair and pleasant green,
I'll walk on foot.   120

(*Enter a* HORSE-COURSER*)

HORSE-COURSER   I have been all this day seeking one Master Fustian: mass, see where he is! God save you, Master Doctor!

FAUSTUS   What, Horse-Courser! You are well met.

HORSE-COURSER   Do you hear, sir? I have brought you forty dollars for your   125 horse.

FAUSTUS   Friend, thou canst not buy so good a horse for so small a price. I have no great need to sell him, but if thou likest him, for ten dollars more take him, because I see thou hast a good mind to him.

HORSE-COURSER   Alas, sir, I have no more.—I pray you speak for me.   130

MEPHISTOPHILIS   I pray you let him have him: he is an honest fellow, and he has a great charge, neither wife nor child.

FAUSTUS   Well, come, give me your money. (HORSE-COURSER *gives* FAUSTUS *the money*) My boy will deliver him to you. But I must tell you one thing before you have him; ride him not into the water at any hand.   135

---

[121] A horse-dealer.

HORSE-COURSER Why, sir, will he not drink of all waters?

FAUSTUS O, yes, he will drink of all waters, but ride him not into the water: ride him over hedge or ditch, or where thou wilt, but not into the water.

HORSE-COURSER Well, sir.—(*Aside*) Now am I made man for ever: I'll not leave my horse for twice forty: if he had but the quality of hey-ding-ding, hey- 140 ding-ding, I'd make a brave living on him: he has a buttock as slick as an eel. Well, good-bye, sir, your boy will deliver him me: but hark you, sir; if my horse be sick or ill at ease, if I bring his water to you, you'll tell me what it is?

FAUSTUS Away, you villain; what, dost think I am a horse-doctor?

(Exit HORSE-COURSER) 145

What are thou, Faustus, but a man condemned to die?
Thy fatal time doth draw to final end;
Despair doth drive distrust unto my thoughts:
Confound these passions with a quiet sleep:
Tush, Christ did call the thief upon the cross;   150
Then rest thee, Faustus, quiet in conceit. (*Sleeps in his chair*)

(Re-enter HORSE-COURSER, all wet, crying)

HORSE-COURSER Alas, alas! Doctor Fustian quotha? Mass, Doctor Lopus* was never such a doctor. Has given me a purgation has purged me of forty dollars; I shall never see them more. But yet, like an ass as I was, I would not be 155 ruled by him, for he bade me I should ride him into no water. Now I, thinking my horse had had some rare quality that he would not have had me known of, I, like a venturous youth, rid him into the deep pond at the town's end. I was no sooner in the middle of the pond, but my horse vanished away, and I sat upon a bottle of hay,* never so near drowning in my life. 160 But I'll seek out my Doctor, and have my forty dollars again, or I'll make it the dearest horse!—O, yonder is his snipper-snapper.—Do you hear? you hey-pass,* where's your master?

MEPHISTOPHILIS Why, sir, what would you? You cannot speak with him.

HORSE-COURSER But I will speak with him.   165

MEPHISTOPHILIS Why, he's fast asleep. Come some other time.

HORSE-COURSER I'll speak with him now, or I'll break his glass windows about his ears.

MEPHISTOPHILIS I tell thee he has not slept this eight nights.

HORSE-COURSER An he have not slept this eight weeks, I'll speak with him. 170

MEPHISTOPHILIS See where he is, fast asleep.

HORSE-COURSER Ay, this is he. God save you, Master Doctor, Master Doctor, Master Doctor Fustian!—Forty dollars, forty dollars for a bottle of hay!

MEPHISTOPHILIS Why, thou seest he hears thee not.

HORSE-COURSER So-ho, ho!—so-ho ho! (*Hollas in his ear*) No, will you not 175 wake? I'll make you wake ere I go. (*Pulls him by the leg, and pulls it away*) Alas, I am undone! What shall I do?

---

153 Doctor Rodrigo Lopez was Queen Elizabeth's private physician. In February of 1594 he was convicted of trying to poison her and executed.
160 A bundle of hay.
163 Juggler.

FAUSTUS   O, my leg, my leg! Help, Mephistophilis! call the officers. My leg, my leg!

MEPHISTOPHILIS   Come, villain, to the constable.   180

HORSE-COURSER   O lord, sir, let me go, and I'll give you forty dollars more.

MEPHISTOPHILIS   Where be they?

HORSE-COURSER   I have none about me. Come to my ostry* and I'll give them you.

MEPHISTOPHILIS   Begone quickly. (HORSE-COURSER *runs away*)   185

FAUSTUS   What, is he gone? Farewell he! Faustus has his leg again, and the horse-courser, I take it, a bottle of hay for his labor. Well, this trick shall cost him forty dollars more.

(*Enter* WAGNER)

How now, Wagner, what's the news with thee?   190

WAGNER   Sir, the Duke of Vanholt doth earnestly entreat your company.

FAUSTUS   The Duke of Vanholt! an honorable gentleman, to whom I must be no niggard of my cunning. Come, Mephistophilis, let's away to him. (*Exeunt*)

Scene 3

Court of the Duke

(*Enter the* DUKE *and the* DUCHESS, FAUSTUS, *and* MEPHISTOPHILIS)   195

DUKE   Thanks, Master Doctor, for these pleasant sights. Nor know I how sufficiently to recompense your great deserts in erecting that castle in the air, the sight whereof so delighted me, as nothing in the world could please me more.

FAUSTUS   I do think myself, good lord, highly recompensed in that it pleaseth   200 your Grace to think well of that which Faustus hath performed. But gracious lady, it may be that you take no delight in those sights; therefore, I pray you tell me, what is the thing you most desire to have; be it in the world, it shall be yours. I have heard that great bellied women do long for things are rare and dainty; what is it, madam? tell me, and you shall have it.   205

DUCHESS   True, Master Doctor; and since I find your courteous intents to pleasure me, I will not hide from you the thing my heart desires; and were it now summer, as it is January and the dead time of the winter, I would desire no better meat than a dish of ripe grapes.

FAUSTUS   Alas, madam, that's nothing! Mephistophilis, begone. (*Exit* MEPHIS-   210 TOPHILIS) Were it a greater thing than this, so it would content you, you should have it.

(*Enter* MEPHISTOPHILIS *with the grapes*)

Here they be, madam; wilt please you taste on them?

DUKE   Believe me, Master Doctor, this makes me wonder above the rest, that   215 being in the dead time of winter, and in the month of January, how you should come by these grapes.

FAUSTUS   If it like your grace, the year is divided into two circles over the whole world, that, when it is here winter with us, in the contrary circle it is summer

---

183 Inn.

with them, as in India, Saba, and farther countries in the East; and by 220
means of a swift spirit that I have I had them brought hither, as you see.—
How do you like them, madam; be they good?

DUCHESS   Believe me, Master Doctor, they be the best grapes that e'er I tasted
in my life before.

FAUSTUS   I am glad they content you so, madam.   225

DUKE   Come, madam, let us in, where you must well reward this learned man
for the great kindness he hath showed to you.

DUCHESS   And so I will, my lord; and, whilst I live, rest beholding for this
courtesy.

FAUSTUS   I humbly thank your grace.   230

DUKE   Come, Master Doctor, follow us and receive your reward. (*Exeunt*)

Act Five

Scene 1

(FAUSTUS' Study. Enter WAGNER solus)

WAGNER   I think my master means to die shortly,
 He has made his will, and given me his wealth,
 His house, his goods, his store of golden plate,
 Besides two thousand ducats ready coined.
 And yet, methinks, if that death were [so] near,   5
 He would not banquet, and carouse and swill
 Amongst the students, as even now he doth,
 Who are at supper with such belly-cheer
 As Wagner ne'er beheld in all his life.
 See where they come! belike the feast is done.   10

(Enter FAUSTUS, with two or three SCHOLARS and MEPHISTOPHILIS)

1ST SCHOLAR   Master Doctor Faustus, since our conference about fair ladies,
which was the beautifullest in all the world, we have determined with ourselves that Helen of Greece was the admirablest lady that ever lived: therefore,
Master Doctor, if you will do us that favor, as to let us see that peerless 15
dame of Greece, whom all the world admires for majesty, we should think
ourselves much beholding unto you.

FAUSTUS   Gentlemen,
 For that I know your friendship is unfeigned,
 It is not Faustus' custom to deny   20
 The just request of those that wish him well,
 You shall behold that peerless dame of Greece,
 No otherwise for pomp or majesty
 Than when Sir Paris crossed the seas with her,
 And brought the spoils to rich Dardania.   25
 Be silent, then, for danger is in words.

(Music sounds and HELEN passeth over the stage)

2ND SCHOLAR   Was this fair Helen, whose admired worth

Made Greece with ten years' wars afflict poor Troy?
Too simple is my wit to tell her praise,
Whom all the world admires for majesty.

3RD SCHOLAR   No marvel though the angry Greeks pursued
With ten years' war the rape of such a queen,
Whose heavenly beauty passeth all compare.

1ST SCHOLAR   Now we have seen the pride of Nature's works,
And only paragon of excellence,
                    (*Enter an* OLD MAN)
We'll take our leaves; and for this glorious deed
Happy and blest be Faustus evermore.

FAUSTUS   Gentlemen, farewell—the same I wish to you.
                (*Exeunt* SCHOLARS *and* WAGNER)

OLD MAN   O gentle Faustus, leave this damned art,
This magic, that will charm thy soul to hell,
And quite bereave thee of salvation.
Though thou hast offended like a man,
Do not persever in it like a devil;
Yet, yet, thou hast an amiable soul,
If sin by custom grow not into nature:
Then, Faustus, will repentence come too late,
Then thou art banished from the sight of heaven;
No mortal can express the pains of hell.
It may be this my exhortation
Seems harsh and all unpleasant; let it not,
For, gentle son, I speak it not in wrath,
Or envy of thee, but in tender love,
And pity of thy future misery.
And so have hope, that this my kind rebuke,
Checking thy body, may amend thy soul.

FAUSTUS   Break heart, drop blood, and mingle it with tears,
Tears falling from repentant heaviness
Of thy most vile and loathsome filthiness,
The stench whereof corrupts the inward soul
With such flagitious crimes of heinous sins
As no commiseration may expel,
But mercy, Faustus, of thy Saviour sweet,
Whose blood alone must wash away thy guilt.
Where art thou, Faustus? wretch, what hast thou done?
Damned art thou, Faustus, damned; despair and die!
Hell claims his right, and with a roaring voice
Says, "Faustus! come! thine hour is almost come!"
And Faustus now will come to do thee right.
                (MEPHISTOPHILIS *gives him a dagger*)

OLD MAN   Ah, stay, good Faustus, stay thy desperate steps!
I see an angel hovers o'er thy head,
And, with a vial full of precious grace,

Offers to pour the same into thy soul:
Then call for mercy, and avoid despair.

FAUSTUS   Ah, my sweet friend, I feel
Thy words do comfort my distressed soul.
Leave me a while to ponder on my sins.   80

OLD MAN   I go, sweet Faustus, but with grief of heart,
Fearing the enemy of thy hapless soul. (*Exit*)

FAUSTUS   Accursed Faustus, where is mercy now?
I do repent; and yet I do despair;
Hell strives with grace for conquest in my breast: 85
What shall I do to shun the snares of death?

MEPHISTOPHILIS   Thou traitor, Faustus, I arrest thy soul
For disobedience to my sovereign lord;
Revolt, or I'll in piecemeal tear thy flesh.

FAUSTUS   I do repent I e'er offended him.   90
Sweet Mephistophilis, entreat thy lord
To pardon my unjust presumption.
And with my blood again I will confirm
My former vow I made to Lucifer.

MEPHISTOPHILIS   Do it, then, Faustus, with unfeigned heart,   95
Lest greater danger do attend thy drift. (FAUSTUS *stabs his arm and writes on a paper with his blood*)

FAUSTUS   Torment, sweet friend, that base and aged man
That durst dissuade me from thy Lucifer,
With greatest torments that our hell affords.   100

MEPHISTOPHILIS   His faith is great; I cannot touch his soul;
But what I may afflict his body with
I will attempt, which is but little worth.

FAUSTUS   One thing, good servant, let me crave of thee,
To glut the longing of my heart's desire—   105
That I might have unto my paramour
That heavenly Helen which I saw of late
Whose sweet embraces may extinguish clean
Those thoughts that do dissuade me from my vow,
And keep my oath I made to Lucifer.   110

MEPHISTOPHILIS   This or what else my Faustus shall desire
Shall be performed in twinkling of an eye.
(*Enter* HELEN)

FAUSTUS   Was this the face that launched a thousand ships
And burnt the topless towers of Ilium?   115
Sweet Helen, make me immortal with a kiss. (*Kisses her*)
Her lips suck forth my soul; see where it flies!—
Come, Helen, come, give me my soul again.
Here will I dwell, for heaven is in these lips,
And all is dross that is not Helena.   120
I will be Paris, and for love of thee, (*Enter the* OLD MAN)
Instead of Troy, shall Wittenberg be sacked;

And I will combat with weak Menelaus,
And wear thy colors on my plumed crest:
Yea, I will wound Achilles in the heel,   125
And then return to Helen for a kiss.
O, thou art fairer than the evening's air
Clad in the beauty of a thousand stars;
Brighter art thou than flaming Jupiter
When he appeared to hapless Semele:*   130
More lovely than the monarch of the sky
In wanton Arethusa's azured arms:*
And none but thou shalt be my paramour! (*Exeunt*)

OLD MAN   Accursed Faustus, miserable man,
That from thy soul exclud'st the grace of heaven,   135
And fly'st the throne of his tribunal seat!

(*Enter* DEVILS)

Satan begins to sift me with his pride:
As in this furnace God shall try my faith,
My faith, vile hell, shall triumph over thee.
Ambitious fiends! see how the heavens smile   140
At your repulse, and laughs your state to scorn!
Hence, hell! for hence I fly unto my God. (*Exeunt*)

Scene 2

(FAUSTUS' *study. Thunder. Enter above* LUCIFER, BELZEBUB, *and*
MEPHISTOPHILIS)   145

LUCIFER   Thus from infernal Dis do we ascend
To view the subjects of our monarchy,
Those souls which sin seals the black sons of hell,
'Mong which as chief, Faustus, we come to thee,
Bringing with us lasting damnation   150
To wait upon thy soul; the time is come
Which makes it forfeit.

MEPHISTOPHILIS   And this gloomy night,
Here in this room will wretched Faustus be.

BELZEBUB   And here we'll stay,
To mark him how he doth demean himself.   155

MEPHISTOPHILIS   How should he, but in desperate lunacy?
Fond worldling, now his heart-blood dries with grief,
His conscience kills it and his labouring brain
Begets a world of idle fantasies,
To over-reach the Devil; but all in vain,   160
His store of pleasures must be sauced with pain.
He and his servant, Wagner, are at hand.

---

130 As a tower of fire.

132 It was the river god Alpheus who made love to Arethusa, a fountain, by mingling with her streams.

Both come from drawing Faustus' latest will.
See where they come! 165

(*Enter* FAUSTUS *and* WAGNER)

FAUSTUS   Say, Wagner, thou hast perused my will,
How dost like it?

WAGNER   Sir, so wondrous well,
As in all humble duty, I do yield 170
My life and lasting service for your love.

(*Enter the* SCHOLARS)

1ST SCHOLAR   Now, worthy Faustus, methinks your looks are changed.

FAUSTUS   O, gentlemen!

2ND SCHOLAR   What ails Faustus? 175

FAUSTUS   Ah, my sweet chamber-fellow, had I lived with thee, then had I
lived still! But now I die eternally. Look, sirs, comes he not? Comes
he not?

1ST SCHOLAR   O my dear Faustus, what imports this fear?

2ND SCHOLAR   Is all our pleasure turned to melancholy? 180

3RD SCHOLAR   He is not well with being over-solitary.

1ST SCHOLAR   If it be so, we'll have physicians to cure him. 'Tis but a surfeit.
Never fear, man.

FAUSTUS   A surfeit of deadly sin that hath damned both body and soul.

2ND SCHOLAR   Yet, Faustus, look up to heaven: remember God's mercies 185
are infinite.

FAUSTUS   But Faustus' offence can ne'er be pardoned: the serpent that tempted
Eve may be saved, but not Faustus. Ah, gentlemen, hear me with patience,
and tremble not at my speeches! Though my heart pants and quivers to
remember that I have been a student here these thirty years, O, would I 190
had never seen Wittenberg, never read book! And what wonders I have
done, all Germany can witness, yea, all the world; for which Faustus hath
lost both Germany and the world, yea heaven itself, heaven, the seat of God,
the throne of the blessed, the kingdom of joy; and must remain in hell for
ever, hell, ah, hell, for ever! Sweet friends! what shall become of Faustus 195
being in hell for ever?

3RD SCHOLAR   Yet, Faustus, call on God.

FAUSTUS   On God, whom Faustus hath abjured! on God, whom Faustus hath
blasphemed! Ah, my God, I would weep, but the Devil draws in my tears.
Gush forth blood instead of tears! Yea, life and soul! O, he stays my 200
tongue! I would lift up my hands, but see, they hold them; they hold them!

ALL   Who, Faustus?

FAUSTUS   Why, Lucifer and Mephistophilis. Ah, gentlemen, I gave them my soul
for my cunning!

ALL   Oh, God forbid! 205

FAUSTUS   God forbade it, indeed; but Faustus hath done it: for vain pleasure
of twenty-four years hath Faustus lost eternal joy and felicity. I writ them
a bill with mine own blood: the date is expired; this is the time, and he will
fetch me.

1ST SCHOLAR   Why did not Faustus tell us of this before, that divines might   210
have prayed for thee?

FAUSTUS   Oft have I thought to have done so: but the Devil threatened to tear
me in pieces if I named God; to fetch me, body and soul, if I once gave ear
to divinity: and now 'tis too late. Gentlemen, away! lest you perish with me.

2ND SCHOLAR   O, what shall we do to save Faustus?   215

FAUSTUS   Talk not of me, but save yourselves, and depart.

3RD SCHOLAR   God will strengthen me. I will stay with Faustus.

1ST SCHOLAR   Tempt not God, sweet friend; but let us into the next room, and
there pray for him.

FAUSTUS   Ay, pray for me, pray for me! and what noise soever ye hear, come   220
not unto me, for nothing can rescue me.

2ND SCHOLAR   Pray thou, and we will pray that God may have mercy upon
thee.

FAUSTUS   Gentlemen, farewell: if I live till morning I'll visit you: if not—
Faustus is gone to hell.   225

ALL   Faustus, farewell. (*Exeunt* SCHOLARS. *The clock strikes eleven*)

FAUSTUS   Ah, Faustus,
Now hast thou but one bare hour to live,
And then thou must be damned perpetually!
Stand still, you ever-moving spheres of heaven,   230
That time may cease, and midnight never come;
Fair Nature's eye, rise, rise again and make
Perpetual day; or let this hour be but
A year, a month, a week, a natural day,
That Faustus may repent and save his soul!   235
*O lente, lente, currite noctis equi!**
The stars move still, time runs, the clock will strike,
The Devil will come, and Faustus must be damned.
Oh, I'll leap up to my God! Who pulls me down?
See, see where Christ's blood streams in the firmament!   240
One drop would save my soul—half a drop: ah, my Christ!
Ah, rend not my heart for naming of my Christ!
Yet will I call on him: O, spare me, Lucifer!—
Where is it now? 'tis gone; and see where God
Stretcheth out his arm, and bends his ireful brows!   245
Mountain and hills come, come and fall on me,
And hide me from the heavy wrath of God!
No! no!
Then will I headlong run into the earth;
Earth gape! O, no, it will not harbor me!   250
You stars that reigned at my nativity,
Whose influence hath allotted death and hell,
Now draw up Faustus like a foggy mist

236 "Slowly, slowly run, ye horses of the night." From Ovid *Amores,* I, 13.

Into the entrails of yon laboring clouds,
That, when you vomit forth into the air,   255
My limbs may issue from their smoky mouths,
So that my soul may but ascend to heaven! (*The clock strikes the half hour*)
Ah, half the hour is past! 'twill all be past anon!
O God!
If thou wilt not have mercy on my soul,   260
Yet for Christ's sake whose blood hath ransomed me,
Impose some end to my incessant pain;
Let Faustus live in hell a thousand years—
A hundred thousand, and—at last—be saved!
O, no end is limited to damned souls!   265
Why wert thou not a creature wanting soul?
Or why is this immortal that thou hast?
Ah, Pythagoras' metempsychosis!* were that true,
This soul should fly from me, and I be changed
Unto some brutish beast! all beasts are happy,   270
For, when they die,
Their souls are soon dissolved in elements;
But mine must live, still to be plagued in hell.
Curst be the parents that engendered me!
No, Faustus: curse thyself; curse Lucifer   275
That hath deprived thee of the joys of heaven. (*The clock strikes twelve*)
O, it strikes, it strikes! Now, body, turn to air,
Or Lucifer will bear thee quick to hell. (*Thunder and lightning*)
O soul, be changed into little water-drops,
And fall into the ocean—ne'er be found.   280
My God! my God! look not so fierce on me!
                    (*Enter* DEVILS)
Adders and serpents, let me breathe awhile!
Ugly hell, gape not! come not, Lucifer!
I'll burn my books!—Ah Mephistophilis! (*Exeunt with him*)   285
                    (*Enter* CHORUS)
CHORUS   Cut is the branch that might have grown full straight,
         And burnèd is Apollo's laurel bough,
         That sometime grew within this learned man.
         Faustus is gone; regard his hellish fall,   290
         Whose fiendful fortune may exhort the wise
         Only to wonder at unlawful things,
         Whose deepness doth entice such forward wits
         To practise more than heavenly power permits. (*Exit*)

              *Terminat hora diem; terminat auctor opus.**   295

268 The doctrine of transmigration of souls, or successive reincarnations.
295 "The hour ends the day; the author completes his work."

94   MARLOWE

Ben Jonson

Ben Jonson (1572–1637) *was the most important and influential
literary figure of Shakespeare's contemporaries. During his long and
productive career he wrote numerous poems and plays, as well as
some criticism, and by his professional example exerted a profound
influence, particularly on a group of talented poets known as the
"Sons of Ben." Although he wrote tragedies—scrupulously
documented historical tragedies based on Roman materials, his
major contribution to English drama consisted of his invention and
perfection of the comic form known as satirical comedy. This form
gave his considerable critical powers the opportunity to play freely
over the foibles and vices of his age, as well as the opportunity to
wed criticism with comic exuberance and verbal brilliance. Variously
described as witty, harsh, hilarious, grotesque, and distressing, such
plays as* THE ALCHEMIST *and* VOLPONE *have always been regarded
as comic classics in English and have long held the stage. In the
last twenty years of his life Jonson virtually abandoned the public
stage to write short musical dramas known as masques.*

Chronology

1572   Born in or near London.

*c.*1583–89   Attended Westminster
School, London.

*c.*1589   Apprenticed as a brick-layer to
his step-father.

*c.*1594   Served against Spain in the
Netherlands.

1597   Probable year of his debut in the
theater as an actor and playwright;
imprisoned for his share in the lost
satiric comedy, *The Isle of Dogs.*

1598   Production of *Every Man in His
Humour* with Shakespeare in a
leading role; fought a duel with
a fellow actor and killed him. Cited
for felonious assault, he was released with the felon's brand on
his thumb.

1599–1601   Wrote his "comical sa-
tires": *Every Man Out of His
Humour, Cynthia's Revels,* and *Poet-
aster.* He engaged in the so-called

"war of the theaters" with Dekker
and Marston, who, in reply to his
attacks, lampooned him in *Satiro-
mastix.*

1603   Composed a series of entertainments for the new king, James I;
arrested on suspicion of treason
for *Sejanus,* a tragedy on Roman
decadence.

1605   Arrested, along with his collaborators, Marston and Chapman,
for his part in *Eastward Ho!*

1605–25   Period of the court masques
and entertainments composed for
court festivals.

1606   *Volpone* produced at the Globe
Theater. Jonson and his wife, who
were Roman Catholics at this
time, were summoned for failing
to take communion in the Church
of England.

1609   *Epicoene, or The Silent Woman*

produced by the Children of the Queen's Revels.

1614 *Bartholomew Fair* performed at the Hope Theater.

1616 Published his plays in a single folio volume entitled *The Works of Benjamin Jonson,* the first such collection in English.

1616–32 Period of the later plays, *The Devil Is an Ass, The Staple of News, The New Inn,* and *The Magnetic Lady.*

1618 Toured Scotland with Drummond of Hawthorneden, who kept a record of their conversations.

1623 His library, containing much unpublished work, destroyed by fire.

1625–32 Period of the later masques and court entertainments and of his bitter rivalry with Inigo Jones, the court architect.

1628 Suffered a paralytic stroke.

1637 Died in London; buried in Westminster Abbey.

Selected Bibliography

Armstrong, William A., "Ben Jonson and Jacobean Stagecraft," *Jacobean Theatre,* ed. John Russell Brown and Bernard Harris (New York, 1960), pp. 43–61.

Barish, Jonas A., "The Double Plot in *Volpone,*" *Modern Philology,* LI (1953), 83–92.

————, *Ben Jonson and the Language of Prose Comedy,* Cambridge, Mass., 1960.

Chute, Marchette, *Ben Jonson of Westminster,* New York, 1953.

Davison, P. H., "*Volpone* and the Old Comedy," *Modern Language Quarterly,* XXIV (1963), 151–157.

Enck, John J., *Jonson and the Comic Truth,* Madison, Wisc., 1957.

Goldberg, S. L., "Folly into Crime: The Catastrophe of *Volpone,*" *Modern Language Quarterly,* XX (1959), 233–42.

Knights, L. C., *Drama and Society in the Age of Jonson,* New York, 1937.

Levin, Harry, "Jonson's Metempsychosis," *Philological Quarterly,* XXII (1943), 231–39.

Partridge, Edward B., *The Broken Compass: A Study of the Major Comedies of Ben Jonson,* Cambridge, Mass., 1958.

Redwine, James D., Jr., "Beyond Psychology: The Moral Basis of Jonson's Theory of Humour Characterization," *English Literary History,* XXVII (1961), 316–334.

Swinburne, Algernon C., *A Study of Ben Jonson,* London, 1889.

Thayer, C. G., *Ben Jonson: Studies in the Plays,* Norman, Okla., 1963.

VOLPONE OR THE FOX

by Ben Jonson

Characters
VOLPONE, *a Magnifico*
MOSCA, *his Parasite*
VOLTORE, *an Advocate*
CORBACCIO, *an old Gentleman*
CORVINO, *a Merchant*
BONARIO, *son to Corbaccio*
SIR POLITICK WOULD-BE, *a Knight*
PEREGRINE, *a Gentleman Traveller*
NANO, *a Dwarf*
CASTRONE, *an Eunuch*
ANDROGYNO, *an Hermaphrodite*
COMMANDADORI, *Officers of Justice*
MERCATORI, *three Merchants*
AVOCATORI, *four Magistrates*
NOTARIO, *the Register*
LADY WOULD-BE, *Sir Politick's Wife*
CELIA, *Corvino's Wife*
SERVITORI, SERVANTS, *two* WAITING-WOMEN, *and* CITIZENS

Venice

The Argument

Volpone,* childless, rich, feigns sick, despairs,
Offers his state to hopes of several heirs,
Lies languishing; his parasite receives
Presents of all, assures, deludes, then weaves
Other cross plots, which ope themselves, are told.
New tricks for safety are sought; they thrive; when bold,   5
Each tempts the other again, and all are sold.

Now, luck yet send us, and a little wit
    Will serve to make our play hit;
(According to the palates of the season)
    Here is rhyme, not empty of reason.   10
This we were bid to credit from our poet,
    Whose true scope, if you would know it,

[1] Many of Jonson's characters have "humour" names, that is, names descriptive of their dominant character traits. Hence *Volpone* means fox; *Mosca*, fly; *Voltore*, vulture; *Corbaccio*, raven; *Corvino*, crow; *Bonario*, agreeable one; and *Peregrine*, wanderer.

In all his poems still hath been this measure,
    To mix profit with your pleasure;   15
And not as some (whose throats their envy failing)
    Cry hoarsely, All he writes is railing:
And when his plays come forth, think they can flout them,
    With saying, he was a year about them.
To these there needs no lie, but this his creature,   20
    Which was, two months since, no feature;
And, though he dares give them five lives to mend it,
    'Tis known, five weeks fully penn'd it,
From his own hand, without a co-adjutor,*
    Novice, journey-man, or tutor.   25
Yet thus much I can give you as a token
    Of his play's worth, no eggs are broken;
Nor quaking custards* with fierce teeth affrighted,
    Wherewith your rout are so delighted;
Nor hales he in a gull,* old ends reciting,   30
    To stop gaps in his loose writing;
With such a deal of monstrous and forced action,
    As might make Bethlem* a faction.
Nor made he his play, for jests, stolen from each table,
    But makes jests to fit his fable;   35
And so presents quick comedy, refined,
    As best critics have designed;
The laws of time, place, persons he observeth,
    From no needful rule he swerveth.
All gall and copperas* from his ink he draineth,   40
    Only a little salt remaineth,
Wherewith he'll rub your cheeks, till, red with laughter,
    They shall look fresh a week after.

Act One

A Room in Volpone's House
(Enter VOLPONE and MOSCA)

VOLPONE   Good morning to the day; and next, my gold:
    Open the shrine, that I may see my saint.
    (MOSCA *withdraws the curtain, and discovers piles of gold, plate, jewels, etc.*)
    Hail the world's soul, and mine! More glad than is
    The teeming earth to see the long'd-for sun   5
    Peep through the horns of the celestial Ram,*

24 Fellow-worker or helper.
28 Huge pudding pies; that is, cowards.
30 A fool or dupe.
33 Bedlam, an insane asylum.
40 Substances used in making ink: "gall" was associated with bitterness, "copperas" with metallic quality.
6 A sign of the zodiac.

Am I, to view thy splendour, darkening his;
That, lying here, amongst my other hoards,
Show'st like a flame, by night, or like the day
Struck out of chaos, when all darkness fled
Unto the centre. O, thou son of Sol,   10
But brighter than thy father, let me kiss,
With adoration, thee, and every relic
Of sacred treasure, in this blessed room.
Well did wise poets, by thy glorious name,
Title that age which they would have the best;   15
Thou being the best of things, and far transcending
All style of joy, in children, parents, friends,
Or any other waking dream on earth:
Thy looks, when they to Venus did ascribe,*   20
They should have given her twenty thousand Cupids;
Such are thy beauties and our loves! Dear saint,
Riches, the dumb god, that giv'st all men tongues,
Thou canst do nought, and yet mak'st men do all things;
The price of souls, even hell, with thee to boot,   25
Is made worth heaven. Thou art virtue, fame,
Honour, and all things else. Who can get thee,
He shall be noble, valiant, honest, wise—
MOSCA   And what he will, sir. Riches are in fortune
A greater good than wisdom is in nature.   30
VOLPONE   True, my beloved Mosca. Yet I glory
More in the cunning purchase* of my wealth,
Than in the glad possession, since I gain
No common way; I use no trade, no venture;
I wound no earth with plough-shares, fat no beasts,   35
To feed the shambles;* have no mills for iron,
Oil, corn, or men, to grind them into powder:
I blow no subtle* glass, expose no ships
To threat'nings of the furrow-faced sea;
I turn no monies in the public bank,   40
Nor usure* private.
MOSCA   No, sir, nor devour
Soft prodigals. You shall have some will swallow
A melting heir as glibly as your Dutch
Will pills of butter, and ne'er purge for it;*   45
Tear forth the fathers of poor families
Out of their beds, and coffin them alive

---

20 That is, when they described Venus as golden. Venus was the mother and constant companion of Cupid.
32 Acquisition.
36 Slaughterhouses.
38 Fine or delicate.
41 Lend at usurous or exhorbitant rates.
45 The Dutch were reputedly very fond of butter, which was thought, apparently, to be a purgative.

In some kind, clasping prison, where their bones
May be forth-coming, when the flesh is rotten:
But your sweet nature doth abhor these courses;   50
You loathe the widow's or the orphan's tears
Should wash your pavements, or their piteous cries
Ring in your roofs, and beat the air for vengeance.

VOLPONE   Right, Mosca; I do loathe it.

MOSCA   And besides, sir,   55
You are not like the thresher that doth stand
With a huge flail, watching a heap of corn,
And, hungry, dares not taste the smallest grain,
But feeds on mallows,* and such bitter herbs;
Nor like the merchant, who hath fill'd his vaults   60
With Romagnia, and rich Candian wines,*
Yet drinks the lees of Lombard's vinegar:*
You will lie not in straw, whilst moths and worms
Feed on your sumptuous hangings and soft beds;
You know the use of riches, and dare give now   65
From that bright heap, to me, your poor observer,
Or to your dwarf, or your hermaphrodite,*
Your eunuch, or what other household trifle
Your pleasure allows maintenance—

VOLPONE   Hold thee, Mosca, (*Gives him money*)   70
Take of my hand; thou strik'st on truth in all,
And they are envious term thee parasite.
Call forth my dwarf, my eunuch, and my fool,
And let them make me sport. (*Exit* MOSCA) What should I do,
But cocker up my genius,* and live free   75
To all delights my fortune calls me to?
I have no wife, no parent, child, ally,
To give my substance to; but whom I make
Must be my heir: and this makes men observe me.
Women and men of every sex and age,   80
That bring me presents, send me plate,* coin, jewels,
With hope that when I die (which they expect
Each greedy minute), it shall then return
Ten-fold upon them; whilst some, covetous
Above the rest, seek to engross* me whole,   85
And counter-work* the one unto the other,
Contend in gifts, as they would seem in love:

59 Common wild plants.
61 "Romagnia" was a sweet wine; "Candian" were wines from Crete.
62 Cheap sour wine from Lombardy.
67 One combining the sexual characteristics of both sexes.
75 That is, indulge my inclination.
81 Utensils made of silver and gold.
85 Monopolize.
86 Oppose.

All which I suffer, playing with their hopes,
And am content to coin them into profit,
And look upon their kindness, and take more,   90
And look on that; still bearing them in hand,
Letting the cherry knock against their lips,
And draw it by their mouths, and back again.
How now!

      (*Re-enter* MOSCA *with* NANO, ANDROGYNO, *and* CASTRONE)   95

NANO Now, room for fresh gamesters, who do will you to know,
    They do bring you neither play or university show;
And therefore do entreat you, that whatsoever they rehearse,
    May not fare a whit the worse, for the false pace of the verse.
If you wonder at this, you will wonder more ere we pass,   100
    For know, here is inclosed the soul of Pythagoras,*
That juggler divine, as hereafter shall follow;
    Which soul, fast and loose, sir, came first from Apollo,*
And was breath'd into Æthalides, Mercurius his son,
    Where it had the gift to remember all that ever was done.   105
From thence it fled forth, and made quick transmigration
    To goldly-lock'd Euphorbus, who was killed in good fashion,
At the siege of old Troy, by the cuckold of Sparta.*
    Hermotimus was next (I find it in my charta)
To whom it did pass, where no sooner it was missing   110
    But with one Pyrrhus of Delos it learn'd to go a fishing;
And thence did it enter the sophist of Greece.*
    From Pythagore, she went into a beautiful piece,
Hight* Aspasia, the meretrix;* and the next toss of her
    Was again of a whore, she became a philosopher,   115
Crates the cynic, as it self doth relate it:
    Since kings, knights, and beggars, knaves, lords, and fools got it,
Besides ox and ass, camel, mule, goat, and brock,*
    In all which it hath spoke, as in the cobbler's cock.*
But I come not here to discourse of that matter,   120
    Or his one, two, or three, or his great oath, BY QUATER!*
His musics, his trigon,* his golden thigh,
    Or his telling how elements shift,* but I

---

101 Greek philosopher and mathematician (*fl.* 497 B.C.); he is associated with the doctrine of transmigration
   of souls.
103 God of the sun, music, prophecy, and archery. The movements of Pythagoras from creature to creature
   are traced in what follows.
108 Menelaus, husband to Helen of Troy.
112 Pythagoras.
114 (*a*) Named. (*b*) Prostitute.
118 Badger.
119 In Lucian's dialogue *The Cock*, the soul of Pythagoras, dwelling in the cock, tells the cobbler of his
   previous transmigrations.
121 "By four."
122 Triangle.
123 Characteristic of the Pythagorean system.

Would ask, how of late thou hast suffered translation
And shifted thy coat in these days of reformation?   125
ANDROGYNO   Like one of the reformed, a fool, as you see,
Counting all old doctrine* heresy.
NANO   But not on thine own forbid meats hast thou ventured?
ANDROGYNO   On fish, when first a Carthusian* I enter'd.
NANO   Why, then thy dogmatical silence* hath left thee?   130
ANDROGYNO   Of that an obstreperous lawyer bereft me.
NANO   O wonderful change, when sir lawyer forsook thee!
For Pythagore's sake, what body then took thee?
ANDROGYNO   A good dull mule.
NANO   And how! By that means   135
Thou wert brought to allow of the eating of beans?*
ANDROGYNO   Yes.
NANO   But from the mule into whom didst thou pass?
ANDROGYNO   Into a very strange beast, by some writers call'd an ass;
By others, a precise, pure illuminate* brother,   140
Of those devour flesh, and sometimes one another;
And will drop you forth a libel, or a sanctified lie,
Betwixt every spoonful of a nativity-pie.*
NANO   Now quit thee, for heaven, of that profane nation,
And gently report thy next transmigration.   145
ANDROGYNO   To the same that I am.
NANO   A creature of delight?
And, what is more than a fool, an hermaphrodite!
Now, prithee, sweet soul, in all thy variation,
Which body would'st thou chose, to keep up thy station?   150
ANDROGYNO   Troth, this I am in; even here would I tarry.
NANO   'Cause here the delight of each sex thou canst vary?
ANDROGYNO   Alas, those pleasures be stale and forsaken;
No, 'tis your fool wherewith I am so taken,
The only one creature that I can call blessed;   155
For all other forms I have proved most distressed.
NANO   Spoke true, as thou wert in Pythagoras still.
This learned opinion we celebrate will,
Fellow eunuch, as behoves us, with all our wit and art,
To dignify that whereof ourselves are so great and special a part.   160
VOLPONE   Now, very, very pretty! Mosca, this
Was thy invention?
MOSCA   If it please my patron,
Not else.

127 The doctrine of Roman Catholicism.
129 An austere order of monks.
130 Pythagoras required his followers to observe five years of silence.
136 Pythagoras forbade the eating of beans.
140 Inspired.
143 Puritan term for Christmas pie.

VOLPONE   It doth, good Mosca.

MOSCA   Then it was, sir.

(NANO and CASTRONE sing)

NANO *and*   Fools, they are the only nation
CASTRONE   Worth men's envy or admiration;
           Free from care or sorrow-taking,   170
           Selves and others merry making:
           All they speak or do is sterling.
           Your fool he is your great man's darling,
           And your ladies' sport and pleasure;
           Tongue and bauble are his treasure.   175
           E'en his face begetteth laughter,
           And he speaks truth free from slaughter;*
           He's the grace of every feast,
           And sometimes the chiefest guest;
           Hath his trencher* and his stool,   180
           When wit waits upon the fool.
              O, who would not be
              He, he, he? (*Knocking without*)

VOLPONE   Who's that? Away! (*Exeunt* NANO *and* CASTRONE)
   Look, Mosca. Fool, begone! (*Exit* ANDROGYNO)   185

MOSCA   'Tis signior Voltore, the advocate;
   I know him by his knock.

VOLPONE   Fetch me my gown,
   My furs and night-caps; say, my couch is changing,
   And let him entertain himself awhile   190
   Without i' the gallery. (*Exit* MOSCA) Now, now, my clients
   Begin their visitation! Vulture, kite,
   Raven, and gorcrow,* all my birds of prey,
   That think me turning carcass, now they come;
   I am not for them yet—   195

(Re-enter MOSCA, with the gown, etc.)
Now now! the news?

MOSCA   A piece of plate, sir.

VOLPONE   Of what bigness?

MOSCA   Huge,   200
   Massy, and antique, with your name inscribed,
   And arms* engraven.

VOLPONE   Good! And not a fox
   Stretch'd on the earth, with fine delusive sleights,
   Mocking a gaping crow? Ha, Mosca!   205

MOSCA   Sharp, sir.

VOLPONE   Give me my furs. (*Puts on his sick dress*) Why dost thou laugh so, man?

---

177 With impunity.
180 Wooden plate.
193 Carrion crow.
202 Coat of arms.

MOSCA I cannot choose, sir, when I apprehend
What thoughts he has without now, as he walks:
That this might be the last gift he should give;   210
That this would fetch you; if you died to-day,
And gave him all, what he should be to-morrow;
What large return would come of all his ventures;
How he should worship'd be, and reverenced;*
Ride with his furs, and foot-cloths;* waited on   215
By herds of fools, and clients; have clear way
Made for his mule,* as letter'd* as himself;
Be call'd the great and learned advocate:
And then concludes, there's nought impossible.
VOLPONE Yes, to be learned, Mosca.   220
MOSCA O, no: rich
Implies it. Hood an ass with reverend purple,
So you can hide his two ambitious ears,
And he shall pass for a cathedral doctor.*
VOLPONE My caps, my caps, good Mosca. Fetch him in.   225
MOSCA Stay, sir; your ointment for your eyes.
VOLPONE That's true;
Dispatch, dispatch: I long to have possession
Of my new present.
MOSCA That, and thousands more,   230
I hope to see you lord of.
VOLPONE Thanks, kind Mosca.
MOSCA And that, when I am lost in blended dust,
And hundred such as I am, in succession—
VOLPONE Nay, that were too much, Mosca.   235
MOSCA You shall live,
Still, to delude these harpies.*
VOLPONE Loving Mosca!
'Tis well; my pillow now, and let him enter. (*Exit* MOSCA)
Now, my feign'd cough, my phthisic,* and my gout,   240
My apoplexy, palsy, and catarrhs,
Help, with your forced functions, this my posture,
Wherein, this three year, I have milk'd their hopes.
He comes; I hear him—Uh! (*coughing*) uh! uh! uh! O—
          (*Re-enter* MOSCA, *introducing* VOLTORE, *with a piece of Plate*)   245
MOSCA You still are what you were, sir. Only you,
Of all the rest, are he commands his love,
And you do wisely to preserve it thus,

---

214 Regarded with deep respect.
215 Ornamented cloths draped over a horse.
217 (*a*) Officials in the law often used mules.   (*b*) Literate.
224 A physician who holds a professorial chair.
237 Rapacious birds; hence grasping people.
240 Pulmonary consumption.

With early visitation, and kind notes*
Of your good meaning to him, which, I know,   250
Cannot but come most grateful!* Patron! Sir!
Here's signior Voltore is come—
VOLPONE (*Faintly*) What say you?
MOSCA Sir, signior Voltore is come this morning
To visit you.   255
VOLPONE I thank him.
MOSCA And hath brought
A piece of antique plate, bought of St. Mark,*
With which he here presents you.
VOLPONE He is welcome.   260
Pray him to come more often.
MOSCA Yes.
VOLTORE What says he?
MOSCA He thanks you, and desires you see him often.
VOLPONE Mosca.   265
MOSCA My patron?
VOLPONE Bring him near, where is he?
I long to feel his hand.
MOSCA The plate is here, sir.
VOLTORE How fare you, sir?   270
VOLPONE I thank you, signior Voltore;
Where is the plate? Mine eyes are bad.
VOLTORE (*Putting it into his hands*) I'm sorry,
To see you still thus weak.
MOSCA (*Aside*) That he's not weaker.   275
VOLPONE You are too munificent.
VOLTORE No, sir; would to heaven,
I could as well give health to you, as that plate!
VOLPONE You give, sir, what you can. I thank you. Your love
Hath taste* in this, and shall not be unanswer'd: 280
I pray you see me often.
VOLTORE Yes, I shall, sir.
VOLPONE Be not far from me.
MOSCA Do you observe that, sir?
VOLPONE Hearken unto me still; it will concern you.   285
MOSCA You are a happy man, sir; know your good.
VOLPONE I cannot now last long—
MOSCA (*Aside*) You are his heir, sir.
VOLTORE Am I?
VOLPONE I feel me going; Uh! Uh! Uh! Uh!   290
I'm sailing to my port, Uh! Uh! Uh! Uh!

---

[249] Signs or indications.
[251] Acceptable.
[258] Bought on the Piazza San Marco, Venice.
[280] Is tested.

And I am glad I am so near my haven.

MOSCA Alas, kind gentleman! Well, we must all go—

VOLTORE But, Mosca—

MOSCA Age will conquer. 295

VOLTORE 'Pray thee, hear me:
Am I inscribed his heir for certain?

MOSCA Are you!
I do beseech you, sir, you will vouchsafe
To write me in your family.* All my hopes 300
Depend upon your worship. I am lost,
Except the rising sun do shine on me.

VOLTORE It shall both shine, and warm thee, Mosca.

MOSCA Sir,
I am a man, that hath not done your love 305
All the worst offices: here I wear your keys,
See all your coffers and your caskets lock'd,
Keep the poor inventory of your jewels,
Your plate and monies; am your steward, sir,
Husband your goods here. 310

VOLTORE But am I sole heir?

MOSCA Without a partner, sir; confirm'd this morning:
The wax is warm yet, and the ink scarce dry
Upon the parchment.

VOLTORE Happy, happy, me! 315
By what good chance, sweet Mosca?

MOSCA Your desert, sir;
I know no second cause.

VOLTORE Thy modesty
Is loath to know it; well, we shall requite it. 320

MOSCA He ever liked your course, sir; that first took him.
I oft have heard him say, how he admired
Men of your large* profession, that could speak
To every cause, and things mere* contraries,
Till they were hoarse again, yet all be law; 325
That, with most quick agility, could turn,
And return; make knots, and undo them;
Give forked counsel; take provoking* gold
On either hand, and put it up: these men,
He knew, would thrive with their humility. 330
And, for his part, he thought he should be blest
To have his heir of such a suffering spirit,
So wise, so grave, of so perplex'd a tongue,
And loud withal, that would not wag, nor scarce

300 That is, enlist me as a servant in your house.
323 Liberal.
324 Complete.
328 Both exciting and irritating because used for bribes.

Lie still, without a fee; when every word   335
Your worship but lets fall, is a chequin!*— (*Knocking without*)
Who's that? One knocks; I would not have you seen, sir.
And yet—pretend you came, and went in haste;
I'll fashion an excuse——and, gentle sir,
When you do come to swim in golden lard,   340
Up to the arms in honey, that your chin
Is borne up stiff, with fatness of the flood,
Think on your vassal;* but remember me:
I have not been your worst of clients.

VOLTORE Mosca!—   345

MOSCA When will you have your inventory brought, sir?
Or see a copy of the will?—Anon!—*
I'll bring them to you, sir. Away, be gone,
Put business in your face. (*Exit* VOLTORE)

VOLPONE (*Springing up*) Excellent Mosca!   350
Come hither, let me kiss thee.

MOSCA Keep you still, sir.
Here is Corbaccio.

VOLPONE Set the plate away:
The vulture's gone, and the old raven's come!   355

MOSCA Betake you to your silence, and your sleep.
Stand there and multiply. (*Putting the plate to the rest*) Now, shall we see
A wretch who is indeed more impotent
Than this can feign to be; yet hopes to hop
Over his grave—   360

(*Enter* CORBACCIO)
Signior Corbaccio!
You're very welcome, sir.

CORBACCIO How does your patron?

MOSCA Troth, as he did, sir; no amends.   365

CORBACCIO What! Mends he?

MOSCA No, sir: he's rather worse.

CORBACCIO That's well. Where is he?

MOSCA Upon his couch, sir, newly fall'n asleep.

CORBACCIO Does he sleep well?   370

MOSCA No wink, sir, all this night.
Nor yesterday; but slumbers.

CORBACCIO Good! he should take
Some counsel of physicians: I have brought him
An opiate* here, from mine own doctor.   375

MOSCA He will not hear of drugs.

CORBACCIO Why? I myself

---

336 A Venetian gold coin.
343 Servant.
347 Right away.
375 A narcotic used to induce sleep.

Stood by while it was made, saw all the ingredients:
And know it cannot but most gently work:
My life for his, 'tis but to make him sleep.   380
VOLPONE (*Aside*) Ay, his last sleep, if he would take it.
MOSCA Sir,
He has no faith in physic.*
CORBACCIO Say you, say you?
MOSCA He has no faith in physic: he does think   385
Most of your doctors are the greater danger,
And worse disease, to escape. I often have
Heard him protest, that your physician
Should never be his heir.
CORBACCIO Not I his heir?   390
MOSCA Not your physician, sir.
CORBACCIO O, no, no, no,
I do not mean it.
MOSCA No, sir, nor their fees
He cannot brook: he says, they flay a man,   395
Before they kill him.
CORBACCIO Right, I do conceive* you.
MOSCA And then they do it by experiment;*
For which the law not only doth absolve them,
But gives them great reward: and he is loth   400
To hire his death so.
CORBACCIO It is true, they kill
With as much license as a judge.
MOSCA Nay, more;
For he but kills, sir, where the law condemns,   405
And these can kill him too.
CORBACCIO Ay, or me;
Or any man. How does his apoplex?
Is that strong on him still?
MOSCA Most violent.   410
His speech is broken, and his eyes are set,
His face drawn longer than 'twas wont—
CORBACCIO How! How!
Stronger than he was wont?
MOSCA No, sir: his face   415
Drawn longer than 'twas wont.
CORBACCIO O, good!
MOSCA His mouth
Is ever gaping, and his eyelids hang.
CORBACCIO Good.   420

383 Medicine.
397 Understand.
398 That is, they practise as an experiment.

108 JONSON

MOSCA   A freezing numbness stiffens all his joints,
  And makes the colour of his flesh like lead.
CORBACCIO   'Tis good.
MOSCA   His pulse beats slow, and dull.
CORBACCIO   Good symptoms still.   425
MOSCA   And from his brain—
CORBACCIO   Ha? How? Not from his brain?
MOSCA   Yes, sir, and from his brain—
CORBACCIO   I conceive you; good.
MOSCA   Flows a cold sweat, with a continual rheum,*   430
  Forth the resolved* corners of his eyes.
CORBACCIO   Is't possible? Yet I am better, ha!
  How does he, with the swimming of his head?
MOSCA   O, sir, 'tis past the scotomy;* he now
  Hath lost his feeling, and hath left to snort:*   435
  You hardly can perceive him that he breathes.
CORBACCIO   Excellent, excellent! Sure I shall outlast him;
  This makes me young again, a score of years.
MOSCA   I was a coming for you, sir.
CORBACCIO   Has he made his will?   440
  What has he given me?
MOSCA   No, sir.
CORBACCIO   Nothing? Ha?
MOSCA   He has not made his will, sir.
CORBACCIO   Oh, oh, oh!   445
  What then did Voltore, the lawyer, here?
MOSCA   He smelt a carcass, sir, when he but heard
  My master was about his testament
  (As I did urge him to it for your good)—
CORBACCIO   He came unto him, did he? I thought so.   450
MOSCA   Yes, and presented him this piece of plate.
CORBACCIO   To be his heir?
MOSCA   I do not know, sir.
CORBACCIO   True,
  I know it too.   455
MOSCA (*Aside*)   By your own scale, sir.
CORBACCIO   Well,
  I shall prevent him, yet. See, Mosca, look,
  Here, I have brought a bag of bright chequines,
  Will quite weigh down his plate.   460
MOSCA (*Taking the bag*)   Yea, marry,* sir.

  430 Watery discharge.
  431 Softened; dissolved by fluid.
  434 Dizziness and dimness of vision.
  435 That is, given up snorting.
  461 Indeed.

This is true physic, this your sacred medicine;
No talk of opiates, to this great elixir!*
CORBACCIO 'Tis *aurum palpabile,* if not *potabile.**
MOSCA It shall be minister'd to him, in his bowl. 465
CORBACCIO Ay, do, do, do.
MOSCA Most blessed cordial!
This will recover him.
CORBACCIO Yes, do, do, do.
MOSCA I think it were not best, sir. 470
CORBACCIO What?
MOSCA To recover him.
CORBACCIO O, no, no, no; by no means.
MOSCA Why, sir, this
Will work some strange effect, if he but feel it. 475
CORBACCIO 'Tis true, therefore forbear; I'll take my venture:*
Give me it again.
MOSCA At no hand, pardon me;
You shall not do yourself that wrong, sir. I
Will so advise you, you shall have it all. 480
CORBACCIO How?
MOSCA All, sir; 'tis your right, your own; no man
Can claim a part: 'tis yours, without a rival,
Decreed by destiny.
CORBACCIO How, how, good Mosca? 485
MOSCA I'll tell you, sir. This fit he shall recover.
CORBACCIO I do conceive you.
MOSCA And, on first advantage
Of his gain'd sense, will I re-importune him
Unto the making of his testament: 490
And show him this. (*Pointing to the money*)
CORBACCIO Good, good.
MOSCA 'Tis better yet,
If you will hear, sir.
CORBACCIO Yes, with all my heart. 495
MOSCA Now, would I counsel you, make home with speed;
There, frame a will, whereto you shall inscribe
My master your sole heir.
CORBACCIO And disinherit
My son? 500
MOSCA O, sir, the better: for that colour*
Shall make it much more taking.
CORBACCIO O, but colour?
MOSCA This will, sir, you shall send it unto me.

463 A drug or concoction supposedly capable of lengthening life.
464 That is, the gold can be felt, if not drunk.
476 Investment.
501 Appearance.

Now, when I come to inforce,* as I will do,   505
Your cares, your watchings,* and your many prayers,
Your more than many gifts, your this day's present,
And last, produce your will, where, without thought
Or least regard unto your proper* issue,
A son so brave,* and highly meriting,   510
The stream of your diverted love hath thrown you
Upon my master, and made him your heir:
He cannot be so stupid, or stone-dead,
But out of conscience, and mere gratitude—
CORBACCIO   He must pronounce me his?   515
MOSCA   'Tis true.
CORBACCIO   This plot
Did I think on before.
MOSCA   I do believe it.
CORBACCIO   Do you not believe it?   520
MOSCA   Yes, sir.
CORBACCIO   Mine own project.
MOSCA   Which, when he hath done, sir—
CORBACCIO   Publish'd me his heir?
MOSCA   And you so certain to survive him—   525
CORBACCIO   Ay.
MOSCA   Being so lusty a man—
CORBACCIO   'Tis true.
MOSCA   Yes, sir—
CORBACCIO   I thought on that too. See, how he should be   530
The very organ to express my thoughts!
MOSCA   You have not only done yourself a good—
CORBACCIO   But multiplied it on my son.
MOSCA   'Tis right, sir.
CORBACCIO   Still, my invention.   535
MOSCA   'Las, sir! heaven knows,
It hath been all my study, all my care
(I e'en grow gray withal) how to work things—
CORBACCIO   I do conceive, sweet Mosca.
MOSCA   You are he,   540
For whom I labour here.
CORBACCIO   Ay, do, do, do:
I'll straight about it. (*Going*)
MOSCA   Rook go with you,* raven!
CORBACCIO   I know thee honest.   545
MOSCA (*Aside*)   You do lie, sir!

505 Urge.
506 Bedside vigils.
509 Own.
510 Fine.
544 That is, be rooked or duped.

CORBACCIO   And—

MOSCA   Your knowledge is no better than your ears, sir.

CORBACCIO   I do not doubt, to be a father to thee.

MOSCA   Nor I to gull my brother of his blessing.   550

CORBACCIO   I may have my youth restored to me, why not?

MOSCA   Your worship is a precious ass!

CORBACCIO   What say'st thou?

MOSCA   I do desire your worship to make haste, sir.

CORBACCIO   'Tis done, 'tis done; I go. (*Exit*)   555

VOLPONE   (*Leaping from his couch*)   O, I shall burst!
    Let out my sides, let out my sides—

MOSCA   Contain
    Your flux of laughter, sir: you know this hope
    Is such a bait, it covers any hook.   560

VOLPONE   O, but thy working, and thy placing it!
    I cannot hold; good rascal, let me kiss thee:
    I never knew thee in so rare a humour.

MOSCA   Alas, sir, I but do as I am taught;
    Follow your grave instructions; give them words;   565
    Pour oil into their ears, and send them hence.

VOLPONE   'Tis true, 'tis true. What a rare punishment
    Is avarice to itself!

MOSCA   Ay, with our help, sir.

VOLPONE   So many cares, so many maladies,   570
    So many fears attending on old age,
    Yea, death so often call'd on, as no wish
    Can be more frequent with them, their limbs faint,
    Their senses dull, their seeing, hearing, going,*
    All dead before them; yea, their very teeth,   575
    Their instruments of eating, failing them:
    Yet this is reckon'd life! Nay, here was one,
    Is now gone home, that wishes to live longer!
    Feels not his gout, nor palsy; feigns himself
    Younger by scores of years, flatters his age   580
    With confident belying it, hopes he may,
    With charms, like Æson,* have his youth restored:
    And with these thoughts so battens,* as if fate
    Would be as easily cheated on, as he,
    And all turns air! (*Knocking within*) Who's that there, now? A third!   585

MOSCA   Close, to your couch again; I hear his voice.
    It is Corvino, our spruce merchant.

VOLPONE (*Lies down as before*)   Dead.

MOSCA   Another bout, sir, with your eyes. (*Anointing them*)—Who's there?
                         (*Enter* CORVINO)   590

---

574 Walking.

582 Father of Jason; Medea, Jason's wife, rejuvenated Aeson through magic.

583 Gluts himself.

Signior Corvino! Come most wish'd for! O,
How happy were you, if you knew it, now!

CORVINO   Why? What? Wherein?

MOSCA   The tardy hour is come, sir.

CORVINO   He is not dead?

MOSCA   Not dead, sir, but as good;   595
   He knows no man.

CORVINO   How shall I do then?

MOSCA   Why, sir?

CORVINO   I have brought him here a pearl.   600

MOSCA   Perhaps he has
   So much remembrance left, as to know you, sir:
   He still calls on you; nothing but your name
   Is in his mouth. Is your pearl orient,* sir?

CORVINO   Venice was never owner of the like.   605

VOLPONE (*Faintly*)   Signior Corvino!

MOSCA   Hark.

VOLPONE   Signior Corvino!

MOSCA   He calls you; step and give it to him.—He's here sir,
   And he has brought you a rich pearl.   610

CORVINO   How do you, sir?
   Tell him, it doubles the twelfth carat.*

MOSCA   Sir,
   He cannot understand, his hearing's gone;
   And yet it comforts him to see you—   615

CORVINO   Say,
   I have a diamond for him, too.

MOSCA   Best show it, sir;
   Put it into his hand; 'tis only there
   He apprehends: he has his feeling, yet.   620
   See how he grasps it!

CORVINO   'Las, good gentleman!
   How pitiful the sight is!

MOSCA   Tut! Forget, sir.
   The weeping of an heir should still be laughter   625
   Under a visor.

CORVINO   Why, am I his heir?

MOSCA   Sir, I am sworn, I may not show the will
   Till he be dead; but here has been Corbaccio,
   Here has been Voltore, here were others too,
   I cannot number 'em, they were so many,   630
   All gaping here for legacies; but I,
   Taking the vantage* of his naming you,
   Signior Corvino, Signior Corvino, took

---

604 Of the best quality.

612 That is, is more than 24 carats.

633 Benefit.

Paper, and pen, and ink, and there I asked him,   635
Whom he would have his heir? *Corvino.* Who
Should be executor? *Corvino.* And,
To any question he was silent to,
I still interpreted the nods he made,
Through weakness, for consent: and sent home th' others,   640
Nothing bequeath'd them, but to cry and curse.

CORVINO   O, my dear Mosca! (*They embrace*) Does he not perceive us?

MOSCA   No more than a blind harper.* He knows no man,
No face of friend, nor name of any servant,
Who 'twas that fed him last, or gave him drink: 645
Not those he hath begotten, or brought up,
Can he remember.

CORVINO   Has he children?

MOSCA   Bastards,
Some dozen, or more, that he begot on beggars,   650
Gypsies, and Jews, and black-moors,* when he was drunk.
Knew you not that, sir? 'Tis the common fable.
The dwarf, the fool, the eunuch, are all his;
He's the true father of his family.
In all, save me: but he has given them nothing.   655

CORVINO   That's well, that's well! Art sure he does not hear us?

MOSCA   Sure, sir! Why, look you, credit your own sense.
(*Shouts in* VOLPONE'S *ear*) The pox* approach and add to your diseases,
If it would send you hence the sooner, sir.
For your incontinence, it hath deserv'd it   660
Thoroughly, and thoroughly, and the plague to boot!—
You may come near, sir.—Would you would once close
Those filthy eyes of yours, that flow with slime
Like two frog-pits; and those same hanging cheeks,
Cover'd with hide instead of skin—Nay, help, sir—   665
That look like frozen dish-clouts* set on end!

CORVINO (*Aloud*)   Or like an old smoked wall, on which the rain
Ran down in streaks!

MOSCA   Excellent, sir! speak out:
You may be louder yet; a culverin*   670
Discharged in his ear would hardly bore it.

CORVINO   His nose is like a common sewer, still running.

MOSCA   'Tis good! And what his mouth?

CORVINO   A very draught.*

MOSCA   O, stop it up—   675

---

643 Harpist.
651 Negroes or dark-skinned persons.
658 Syphilis.
666 Dish-cloths.
670 Cannon.
674 Stream.

CORVINO   By no means.
MOSCA   'Pray you, let me.
   Faith, I could stifle him rarely* with a pillow,
   As well as any woman that should keep him.*
CORVINO   Do as you will; but I'll be gone.   680
MOSCA   Be so;
   It is your presence makes him last so long.
CORVINO   I pray you, use no violence.
MOSCA   No, sir? Why?
   Why should you be thus scrupulous, pray you, sir?   685
CORVINO   Nay, at your discretion.
MOSCA   Well, good sir, begone.
CORVINO   I will not trouble him now, to take my pearl.
MOSCA   Puh! Nor your diamond. What a needless care
   Is this afflicts you? Is not all here yours?   690
   Am not I here, whom you have made your creature?
   That owe my being to you?
CORVINO   Grateful Mosca!
   Thou art my friend, my fellow, my companion,
   My partner, and shalt share in all my fortunes.   695
MOSCA   Excepting one.
CORVINO   What's that?
MOSCA   Your gallant wife, sir,— (*Exit* CORVINO)
   Now is he gone: we had no other means
   To shoot him hence, but this.   700
VOLPONE   My divine Mosca!
   Thou hast to-day outgone thyself. (*Knocking within*) Who's there?
   I will be troubled with no more. Prepare
   Me music, dances, banquets, all delights;
   The Turk is not more sensual in his pleasures,   705
   Than will Volpone. (*Exit* MOSCA) Let me see; a pearl!
   A diamond! Plate! Chequines! Good morning's purchase.*
   Why, this is better than rob churches, yet;
   Or fat* by eating once a month, a man—
                (*Re-enter* MOSCA)   710
   Who is't?
MOSCA   The beauteous lady Would-be, sir,
   Wife to the English knight, sir Politick Would-be,
   (This is the style,* sir, is directed me,)
   Hath sent to know how you have slept to-night,   715
   And if you would be visited?

---

678 Splendidly.
679 Watch over him.
707 Loot.
709 Growing fat.
714 Manner of address.

VOLPONE Not now:
   Some three hours hence—
MOSCA I told the squire so much.
VOLPONE When I am high with mirth and wine; then, then.   720
   'Fore heaven, I wonder at the desperate valour
   Of the bold English, that they dare let loose
   Their wives to all encounters!
MOSCA Sir, this knight
   Had not his name for nothing, he is *politic,**   725
   And knows, howe'er his wife affect strange airs,
   She hath not yet the face* to be dishonest.
   But had she signior Corvino's wife's face—
VOLPONE Has she so rare a face?
MOSCA O, sir, the wonder,   730
   The blazing star of Italy! A wench
   Of the first year! A beauty ripe as harvest!
   Whose skin is whiter than a swan all over,
   Than silver, snow, or lilies! A soft lip,
   Would tempt you to eternity of kissing!   735
   And flesh that melteth in the touch to blood!
   Bright as your gold, and lovely as your gold!
VOLPONE Why had not I known this before?
MOSCA Alas, sir,
   Myself but yesterday discover'd it.   740
VOLPONE How might I see her?
MOSCA O, not possible;
   She's kept as warily* as is your gold;
   Never does come abroad, never takes air,
   But at a window. All her looks are sweet,   745
   As the first grapes or cherries, and are watch'd
   As near* as they are.
VOLPONE I must see her.
MOSCA Sir,
   There is a guard of spies ten thick upon her,   750
   All his whole household; each of which is set
   Upon his fellow, and have all their charge,*
   When he goes out, when he comes in, examined.
VOLPONE I will go see her, though but at her window.
MOSCA In some disguise, then.   755
VOLPONE That is true. I must
   Maintain mine own shape still the same: we'll think. (*Exeunt*)

725 Crafty.
727 Audacity.
743 Carefully.
747 Closely.
752 Duties, hence activities.

Act Two

Scene 1

St. Mark's Square; a retired corner before Corvino's House.
(*Enter* SIR POLITICK WOULD-BE *and* PEREGRINE)

SIR POLITICK   Sir, to a wise man, all the world's his soil.
It is not Italy, nor France, nor Europe,
That must bound me, if my fates call me forth.   5
Yet, I protest, it is no salt* desire
Of seeing countries, shifting a religion,
Nor any disaffection to the state
Where I was bred, and unto which I owe
My dearest plots, hath brought me out; much less,   10
That idle, antique, stale, gray-headed project
Of knowing men's minds and manners, with Ulysses!*
But a peculiar humour* of my wife's
Laid for this height of Venice, to observe,
To quote, to learn the language, and so forth—   15
I hope you travel, sir, with license?*

PEREGRINE   Yes.

SIR POLITICK   I dare the safelier converse——How long, sir,
: Since you left England?

PEREGRINE   Seven weeks.   20

SIR POLITICK   So lately!
You have not been with my lord ambassador?

PEREGRINE   Not yet, sir.

SIR POLITICK   Pray you, what news, sir, vents our climate?*
I heard last night a most strange thing reported   25
By some of my lord's followers, and I long
To hear how 'twill be seconded.

PEREGRINE   What was't, sir?

SIR POLITICK   Marry, sir, of a raven that should build
In a ship royal of the king's.   30

PEREGRINE (*Aside*)   This fellow,
Does he gull me, trow? Or is gull'd? Your name, sir?

SIR POLITICK   My name is Politick Would-be.

PEREGRINE (*Aside*)   O, that speaks him.—
A knight, sir?   35

SIR POLITICK   A poor knight, sir.

PEREGRINE   Your lady
Lies here in Venice, for intelligence

---

⁶ Inordinate or excessive.
¹² The hero of the *Odyssey* is notorious for his wanderings.
¹³ Whim.
¹⁶ With official permission.
²⁴ Circulates.

Of tires,* and fashions, and behaviour,
Among the courtezans? The fine lady Would-be?   40
SIR POLITICK   Yes, sir; the spider and the bee, ofttimes,
Suck from one flower.
PEREGRINE   Good sir Politick,
I cry you mercy;* I have heard much of you:
'Tis true, sir, of your raven.   45
SIR POLITICK   On your knowledge?
PEREGRINE   Yes, and your lion's whelping in the Tower.*
SIR POLITICK   Another whelp!
PEREGRINE   Another, sir.
SIR POLITICK   Now heaven!   50
What prodigies be these? The fires at Berwick!*
And the new star! These things concurring, strange,
And full of omen! Saw you those meteors?
PEREGRINE   I did, sir.
SIR POLITICK   Fearful! Pray you, sir, confirm me,   55
Were there three porpoises seen above the bridge,
As they give out?
PEREGRINE   Six, and a sturgeon, sir.
SIR POLITICK   I am astonish'd.
PEREGRINE   Nay, sir, be not so;   60
I'll tell you a greater prodigy* than these.
SIR POLITICK   What should these things portend?
PEREGRINE   The very day
(Let me be sure) that I put forth from London,
There was a whale discover'd in the river,
As high as Woolwich,* that had waited there,   65
Few know how many months, for the subversion
Of the Stode fleet.
SIR POLITICK   Is't possible? Believe it,
'Twas either sent from Spain, or the archdukes.*   70
Spinola's whale,* upon my life, my credit!
Will they not leave these projects? Worthy sir,
Some other news.
PEREGRINE   Faith, Stone the fool is dead,
And they do lack* a tavern fool extremely.   75

39 Dress.
44 Beg your pardon.
47 Bearing offspring in the Tower of London.
51 There were reports of ghost-armies threatening the borders of Scotland near Berwick.
61 Omen or portent.
66 That is, as far up as Woolwich, a town in Kent.
70 The rulers of the Spanish Netherlands.
71 Spinola, a Spanish general, was believed to have contrived many secret weapons for use against England,
   including a whale which was supposed to inundate London.
75 Miss.

SIR POLITICK Is Mass* Stone dead?

PEREGRINE He's dead, sir; why, I hope
    You thought him not immortal?—(*Aside*) O, this knight,
    Were he well known, would be a precious thing
    To fit our English stage: he that should write   80
    But such a fellow, should be thought to feign
    Extremely, if not maliciously.

SIR POLITICK Stone dead!

PEREGRINE Dead.—Lord! How deeply, sir, you apprehend it.*
    He was no kinsman to you?   85

SIR POLITICK That I know of.
    Well! The same fellow was an unknown fool.

PEREGRINE And yet you knew him, it seems?

SIR POLITICK I did so. Sir,
    I knew him one of the most dangerous heads   90
    Living within the state, and so I held him.

PEREGRINE Indeed, sir?

SIR POLITICK While he lived, in action.
    He has received weekly intelligence,
    Upon my knowledge, out of the Low Countries,   95
    For all parts of the world, in cabbages;
    And those dispensed again to ambassadors,
    In oranges, musk-melons, apricocks,
    Lemons, pome-citrons,* and such-like; sometimes
    In Colchester oysters, and your Selsey cockles.*   100

PEREGRINE You make me wonder.

SIR POLITICK Sir, upon my knowledge.
    Nay, I've observed him, at your public ordinary,*
    Take his advertisement from a traveller,
    A conceal'd statesman, in a trencher of meat;   105
    And instantly, before the meal was done,
    Convey an answer in a tooth-pick.

PEREGRINE Strange!
    How could this be, sir?

SIR POLITICK Why, the meat was cut   110
    So like his character, and so laid, as he
    Must easily read the cipher.*

PEREGRINE I have heard,
    He could not read, sir.

SIR POLITICK So 'twas given out,   115

---

[76] Master.
[84] Take it to heart.
[99] Fruit resembling lemons.
[100] A type of mussel.
[103] Tavern.
[112] That is, the meat was cut into figures corresponding to his secret code.

In policy,* by those that did employ him:
But he could read, and had your languages,
And to't, as sound a noddle—*

PEREGRINE   I have heard, sir,
That your baboons were spies, and that they were   120
A kind of subtle nation near to China.

SIR POLITICK   Ay, ay, your *Mamaluchi*.* Faith, they had
Their hand in a French plot or two; but they
Were so extremely given to women, as
They made discovery of all: yet I   125
Had my advices* here, on Wednesday last,
From one of their own coat,* they were return'd,
Made their relations,* as the fashion is,
And now stand fair for fresh employment.

PEREGRINE (*Aside*)   'Heart!   130
This sir Pol will be ignorant of nothing.
It seems, sir, you know all.

SIR POLITICK   Not all, sir, but
I have some general notions. I do love
To note and to observe: though I live out,   135
Free from the active torrent, yet I'd mark
The currents and the passages of things,
For mine own private use; and know the ebbs
And flows of state.

PEREGRINE   Believe it, sir, I hold   140
Myself in no small tie* unto my fortunes,
For casting me thus luckily upon you,
Whose knowledge, if your bounty equal it,
May do me great assistance, in instruction
For my behaviour, and my bearing, which   145
Is yet so rude and raw.

SIR POLITICK   Why, came you forth
Empty of rules for travel?

PEREGRINE   Faith, I had
Some common ones, from out that vulgar* grammar,   150
Which he that cried* Italian to me, taught me.

SIR POLITICK   Why, this it is that spoils all our brave bloods,*
Trusting our hopeful gentry unto pedants,
Fellows of outside, and mere bark. You seem

---

116 For political reasons.   118 Head.
122 Converted slaves in Moslem countries.
126 Dispatches.
127 Class.
128 That is, gave their reports.
141 Deeply indebted.
150 Common.
151 Pronounced loudly.
152 Fine young men.

To be a gentleman, of ingenuous* race.   155
I not profess it, but my fate hath been
To be, where I have been consulted with,
In this high kind,* touching some great men's sons,
Persons of blood and honour.—
    (*Enter* MOSCA *and* NANO *disguised, followed by persons with materials*   160
                    for erecting a Stage)

PEREGRINE Who be these, sir?

MOSCA Under that window, there 't must be. The same.

SIR POLITICK Fellows, to mount a bank.* Did your instructor
In the dear tongues,* never discourse to you   165
  Of the Italian mountebanks?*

PEREGRINE Yes, sir.

SIR POLITICK Why,
Here you shall see one.

PEREGRINE They are quacksalvers: 170
Fellows that live by venting* oils and rugs.

SIR POLITICK Was that the character he gave you of them?

PEREGRINE As I remember.

SIR POLITICK Pity his ignorance.
They are the only knowing men of Europe!   175
Great general scholars, excellent physicians,
Most admired statesmen, professed favourites,
And cabinet counsellors to the greatest princes;
The only languaged men of all the world!

PEREGRINE And I have heard, they are most lewd* imposters;   180
Made all of terms and shreds;* no less beliers*
Of great men's favours, than their own vile med'cines;
Which they will utter* upon monstrous oaths:
Selling that drug for two-pence, ere they part,
Which they have valued at twelve crowns before.   185

SIR POLITICK Sir, calumnies are answer'd best with silence.
Yourself shall judge.—Who is it mounts, my friends?

MOSCA Scoto of Mantua,* sir.

SIR POLITICK Is't he? Nay, then
I'll proudly promise, sir, you shall behold   190
Another man than has been phant'sied* to you.

---

155 Noble.
158 In this important matter.
164 Bench or small stage.
165 Respected languages.
166 Sellers of medicines, etc., who attracted clients by giving entertaining speeches.
171 Selling.
180 Ignorant and low.
181 (*a*) Technical jargon and clichés. (*b*) One who misinterprets or falsifies.
183 Sell.
188 A famous Italian comedian.
191 Described.

I wonder yet, that he should mount his bank,
Here in this nook, that has been wont t'appear
In face of the Piazza!—Here he comes.

(*Enter* VOLPONE, *disguised as a mountebank Doctor, and followed by a*   195
crowd of people)

VOLPONE (*To* NANO)   Mount, zany.*

MOB   Follow, follow, follow, follow!

SIR POLITICK   See how the people follow him! He's a man
May write ten thousand crowns in bank here. Note,   200
(VOLPONE *mounts the Stage*)
Mark but his gesture:—I do use to observe
The state he keeps* in getting up.

PEREGRINE   'Tis worth it, sir.

VOLPONE   Most noble gentlemen, and my worthy patrons! It may seem   205
strange, that I, your Scoto Mantuano, who was ever wont to fix my bank
in face of the public Piazza, near the shelter of the Portico to the Procuratia,
should now, after eight months' absence from this illustrious city of Venice,
humbly retire myself into an obscure nook of the Piazza.

SIR POLITICK   Did not I now object the same?   210

PEREGRINE   Peace, sir.

VOLPONE   Let me tell you: I am not, as your Lombard proverb saith, cold on
my feet;* or content to part with my commodities at a cheaper rate, than
I accustomed: look not for it. Nor that the calumnious reports of that impudent detractor, and shame to our profession, (Alessandro Buttone,   215
I mean) who gave out, in public, I was condemned a *sforzato* to the galleys,
for poisoning the cardinal Bembo's*———cook, hath at all attached,* much
less dejected me. No, no, worthy gentlemen; to tell you true, I cannot endure
to see the rabble of these ground *ciarlitani,* that spread their cloaks on the
pavement, as if they meant to do feats of activity,* and then come in   220
lamely, with their mouldy tales out of Boccacio, like stale Tabarine, the
fabulist:* some of them discoursing their travels, and of their tedious captivity
in the Turks' gallies, when, indeed, were the truth known, they were the
Christians' gallies, where very temperately they eat bread, and drunk water,
as a wholesome penance, enjoined them by their confessors, for base   225
pilferies.

SIR POLITICK   Note but his bearing, and contempt of these.

VOLPONE   These turdy-facy-nasty-paty-lousy-fartical rogues, with one poor groat's-
worth* of unprepared antimony, finely wrapt up in several *scartoccios,* are

---

[197] Clown; one of a group of *commedia dell' arte* servants.

[203] That is, the ritual he observes.

[213] Poverty-stricken or desperate.

[216] Convict.

[217] (*a*) An illustrious cardinal of the time (1470–1547). The allusion here is to his mistress.   (*b*) Put on
trial.

[219] Common mountebanks.

[220] Acrobatic feats.

[222] Probably Tabarin (fl. early 17th century), a famous French clown.

[229] (*a*) An English groat was worth four pence.   (*b*) Paper wrappings.

able, very well, to kill their twenty a week, and play; yet, these meagre, 230
starved spirits, who have half stopt the organs of their minds with earthy
oppilations,* want not their favourers among your shrivell'd salad-eating
artizans, who are overjoyed that they may have their half-pe'rth* of physic;
though it purge them into another world, it makes no matter.

SIR POLITICK Excellent! have you heard better language, sir? 235

VOLPONE Well, let them go. And, gentlemen, honourable gentlemen, know,
that for this time, our bank, being thus removed from the clamours of the
*canaglia,** shall be the scene of pleasure and delight; for I have nothing to
sell, little or nothing to sell.

SIR POLITICK I told you, sir, his end. 240

PEREGRINE You did so, sir.

VOLPONE I protest, I, and my six servants, are not able to make of this precious
liquor, so fast as it is fetch'd away from my lodging by gentlemen of your
city; strangers of the Terrafirma;* worshipful merchants; ay, and senators
too: who, ever since my arrival, have detained me to their uses, by their 245
splendidous liberalities. And worthily. For, what avails your rich man to have
his magazines stuffed with *moscadelli,** or of the purest grape, when his
physicians prescribe him, on pain of death, to drink nothing but water cocted*
with aniseeds? O, health! Health! The blessing of the rich! The riches of
the poor! Who can buy thee at too dear a rate, since there is no enjoying 250
this world without thee? Be not then so sparing of your purses, honourable
gentlemen, as to abridge the natural course of life—

PEREGRINE You see his end.

SIR POLITICK Ay, is't not good?

VOLPONE For, when a humid flux,* or catarrh, by the mutability of air, falls 255
from your head into an arm or shoulder, or any other part; take you a ducket,*
or your chequin of gold, and apply to the place affected: see what good effect
it can work. No, no, 'tis this blessed unguento,* this rare extraction, that
hath only power to disperse all malignant humours,* that proceed either of
hot, cold, moist, or windy causes— 260

PEREGRINE I would he had put in dry too.

SIR POLITICK 'Pray you, observe.

VOLPONE To fortify the most indigest and crude* stomach, ay, were it of one
that, through extreme weakness, vomited blood, applying only a warm napkin
to the place, after the unction and fricace;*—for the vertigine* in the 265
head, putting but a drop into your nostrils, likewise behind the ears; a most

232 Obstructions.
233 Half-pennyworth.
238 Pack of dogs; rabble.
244 The continental territory controlled by Venice.
247 Muscatel wines.
248 Boiled.
255 Discharge.
256 Ducat; a gold or silver coin.
258 Ointment.
259 Bodily fluids.
263 Queasy.
265 (a) Massage. (b) Dizziness.

sovereign and approved remedy: the *mal caduco,** cramps, convulsions, paralysies, epilepsies, *tremor-cordia,** retired nerves,* ill vapours of the spleen, stopping of the liver, the stone,* the strangury,* *hernia ventosa,** *iliaca passio;** stops a dysenteria immediately; easeth the torsion* of the small guts; and 270 cures *melancholia hypondriaca,** being taken and applied according to my printed receipt. (*Pointing to his bill and his vial*) For, this is the physician, this the medicine; this counsels, this cures; this gives the direction, this works the effect; and, in sum, both together may be termed an abstract of the theorick and practick in the Æsculapian art.* 'Twill cost you eight crowns. 275 And,—Zan Fritada, prithee sing a verse extempore in honour of it.

SIR POLITICK   How do you like him, sir?

PEREGRINE   Most strangely, I!

SIR POLITICK   Is not his language rare?

PEREGRINE   But alchemy,   280
I never heard the like; or Broughton's books.*

(NANO *sings*)

NANO   Had old Hippocrates, or Galen,*
That to their books put med'cines all in,
But known this secret, they had never   285
(Of which they will be guilty ever)
Been murderers of so much paper,
Or wasted many a hurtless taper;
No Indian drug had e'er been famed,
Tobacco, sassafras not named;   290
Ne* yet, of guacum* one small stick, sir,
Nor Raymund Lully's great elixir.*
Ne had been known the Danish Gonswart,*
Or Paracelsus,* with his long sword.

PEREGRINE   All this, yet, will not do; eight crowns is high.   295

VOLPONE   No more.—Gentlemen, if I had but time to discourse to you the miraculous effects of this my oil, surnamed *Oglio del Scoto;* with the countless catalogue of those I have cured of the aforesaid, and many more diseases; the patents and privileges of all the princes and commonwealths of Christendom; or but the depositions of those that appeared on my part, before 300 the signiory of the *Sanita** and most learned College of Physicians; where

267 Falling sickness; a kind of epilepsy.
268 (*a*) Heart palpitations.   (*b*) Shrunken sinews.
269 (*a*) Kidney.   (*b*) Painful urination.   (*c*) Gassy tumor.   (*d*) Intestinal cramp.
270 Convulsion.
271 Extreme morbid depression.
275 Medicine.
281 Complex studies in rabbinical scholarship.*
283 Ancient physicians.
291 (*a*) Nor.   (*b*) A medicinal bark.
292 Lully was an alchemist and physician (*c*.1235–1315) who was supposed to have found the elixir of life.
293 Apparently, another famous alchemist-physician of the time.
294 A famous German physician (1493–1541), half-quack, half-scientist.
301 The Board of Health in Venice.

I was authorised, upon notice taken of the admirable virtues of my medicaments, and mine own excellency in matter of rare and unknown secrets, not only to disperse them publicly in this famous city, but in all the territories, that happily joy under the government of the most pious and magnificent 305 states of Italy. But may some other gallant fellow say, O, there be divers* that make professions to have as good, and as experimented receipts* as yours: indeed, very many have assayed, like apes, in imitation of that, which is really and essentially in me, to make of this oil; bestowed great cost in furnaces, stills, alembecks,* continual fires, and preparation of the ingre- 310 dients (as indeed there goes to it six hundred several simples,* besides some quantity of human fat, for the conglutination, which we buy of the anatomists,*) but, when these practitioners come to the last decoction, blow, blow, puff, puff, and all flies in *fumo:** ha, ha, ha! Poor wretches! I rather pity their folly and indiscretion, than their loss of time and money; for these may 315 be recovered by industry: but to be a fool born is a disease incurable.

For myself, I always from my youth have endeavoured to get the rarest secrets, and book them, either in exchange, or for money: I spared nor cost nor labour, where any thing was worthy to be learned. And, gentlemen, honourable gentlemen, I will undertake, by virtue of chemical art, out 320 of the honourable hat that covers your head, to extract the four elements; that is to say, the fire, air, water, and earth, and return you your felt without burn or stain. For, whilst others have been at the Balloo,* I have been at my book; and am now past the craggy paths of study, and come to the flowery plains of honour and reputation. 325

SIR POLITICK   I do assure you, sir, that is his aim.

VOLPONE   But to our price—

PEREGRINE   And that withal, sir Politick.

VOLPONE   You all know, honourable gentlemen, I never valued this *ampulla,* or vial, at less than eight crowns; but for this time, I am content to be 330 deprived of it for six: six crowns is the price, and less in courtesy I know you cannot offer me; take it or leave it, howsoever, both it and I am at your service. I ask you not as the value of the thing, for then I should demand of you a thousand crowns, so the cardinals Montalto, Fernese, the great Duke of Tuscany, my gossip,* with divers other princes, have given me; but 335 I despise money. Only to show my affection to you, honourable gentlemen, and your illustrious State here, I have neglected the messages of these princes, mine own offices, framed my journey hither, only to present you with the fruits of my travels.—Tune your voices once more to the touch of your instruments, and give the honourable assembly some delightful recrea- 340 tion.

306 Several.   307 Tested formulas.
310 Part of a still.
311 Medicinal herbs.
313 Students of dissection.
314 Smoke.
323 Venetian game of ball.
335 God-fathers.

PEREGRINE What monstrous and most painful circumstance
  Is here, to get some three or four *gazettes,**
  Some three-pence in the whole! For that 'twill come to.
       (NANO *sings*)   345
NANO You that would last long, list to my song,
  Make no more coil,* but buy of this oil.
  Would you be ever fair and young?
  Stout of teeth, and strong of tongue?
  Tart* of palate? Quick of ear?   350
  Sharp of sight? Of nostril clear?
  Moist of hand? And light of foot?
  Or, I will come nearer to't,
  Would you live free from all diseases?
  Do the act your mistress pleases,   355
  Yet fright all aches from your bones?
  Here's a medicine for the nones.*

VOLPONE Well, I am in a humour at this time to make a present of the small
quantity my coffer contains; to the rich in courtesy, and to the poor for
God's sake. Wherefore now mark: I ask'd you six crowns; and six crowns, 360
at other times, you have paid me; you shall not give me six crowns, nor five,
not four, nor three, nor two, nor one; nor half a ducat; no, nor a *moccinigo.**
Sixpence it will cost you, or six hundred pound—expect no lower price,
for, by the banner of my front,* I will not bate a *bagatine,**—that I will have,
only, a pledge of your loves, to carry something from amongst you, to 365
show I am not contemn'd by you. Therefore, now, toss your handkerchiefs,
cheerfully, cheerfully; and be advertised, that the first heroic spirit that deigns
to grace me with a handkerchief, I will give it a little remembrance of something, beside, shall please it better, than if I had presented it with a double
pistolet.*   370

PEREGRINE Will you be that *heroic spark,** sir Pol?
   (CELIA *at a window above, throws down her handkerchief*)
  O, see! the window has prevented you.

VOLPONE Lady, I kiss your bounty; and for this timely grace you have done
your poor Scoto of Mantua, I will return you, over and above my oil, 375
a secret of that high and inestimable nature, shall make you for ever enamour'd on that minute, wherein your eye first descended on so mean, yet
not altogether to be despised, an object. Here is a powder conceal'd in this
paper, of which, if I should speak to the worth, nine thousand volumes were

---

343 Venetian coins of little value.
347 Fuss.
350 Keen.
357 Purpose.
362 Small Italian coin.
364 (*a*) Apparently, proclaimed reputation (for honesty?). (*b*) Another small Italian coin. That is, I will
  not subtract a *bagatine.*
370 Spanish gold coin.
371 Young gentleman.

but as one page, that page as a line, that line as a word; so short is this 380
pilgrimage of man (which some call life) to the expressing of it. Would
I reflect on the price? Why, the whole world is but as an empire, that empire
as a province, that province as a bank, that bank as a private purse to the
purchase of it. I will only tell you; it is the powder that made Venus a goddess
(given her by Apollo) that kept her perpetually young, clear'd her 385
wrinkles, firm'd her gums, fill'd her skin, colour'd her hair; from her derived
to Helen, and at the sack of Troy unfortunately lost: till now, in this our
age, it was as happily recovered, by a studious antiquary, out of some ruins
of Asia, who sent a moiety* of it to the court of France (but much sophisticated*), wherewith the ladies there, now, colour their hair. The rest, of 390
this present, remains with me; extracted to a quintessence: so that, wherever
it but touches, in youth it perpetually preserves, in age restores the complexion; seats your teeth, did they dance like virginal jacks,* firm as a wall;
makes them white as ivory, that were black as—

(Enter CORVINO) 395

CORVINO Spight o' the devil, and my shame! Come down here;
　　Come down.—No house but mine to make your scene?*
　　Signior Flaminio, will you down, sir? Down?
　　What, is my wife your Franciscina,* sir?
　　No windows on the whole Piazza, here, 400
　　To make your properties, but mine? But mine?

(Beats away VOLPONE, NANO, etc.)

　　Heart! Ere to-morrow I shall be new-christen'd,
　　And call'd the Pantalone di Besogniosi,*
　　About the town. 405

PEREGRINE What should this mean, sir Pol?
SIR POLITICK Some trick of state, believe it. I will home.
PEREGRINE It may be some design on you.
SIR POLITICK I know not,
　　I'll stand upon my guard. 410
PEREGRINE It is your best, sir.
SIR POLITICK This three weeks, all my advices, all my letters,
　　They have been intercepted.
PEREGRINE Indeed, sir!
　　Best have a care. 415
SIR POLITICK Nay, so I will.
PEREGRINE This knight,
　　I may not lose him, for my mirth, till night. (Exeunt)

---

389 Half.
390 Adulterated.
393 The pieces of wood in a spinet which hold the quills which, in turn, pluck the strings.
397 Stage.
399 The hoydenish maid-servant of the commedia dell' arte.
404 Another commedia character; frequently an old, cuckolded husband.

Scene 2

A Room in Volpone's House
(*Enter* VOLPONE *and* MOSCA)

VOLPONE   O, I am wounded!

MOSCA   Where, sir?

VOLPONE   Not without;
Those blows were nothing: I could bear them ever.
But angry Cupid, bolting from her eyes,   425
Hath shot himself into me like a flame;
Where, now, he flings about his burning heat,
As in a furnace an ambitious* fire,
Whose vent is stopt. The fight is all within me.
I cannot live, except thou help me, Mosca;   430
My liver* melts, and I, without the hope
Of some soft air, from her refreshing breath,
Am but a heap of cinders.

MOSCA   'Las, good sir,
Would you had never seen her!   435

VOLPONE   Nay, would thou
Had'st never told me of her!

MOSCA   Sir, 'tis true;
I do confess I was unfortunate,
And you unhappy: but I'm bound in conscience,   440
No less than duty, to effect my best
To your release of torment, and I will, sir.

VOLPONE   Dear Mosca, shall I hope?

MOSCA   Sir, more than dear,
I will not bid you to despair of aught   445
Within a human compass.*

VOLPONE   O, there spoke
My better angel. Mosca, take my keys,
Gold, plate, and jewels, all's at thy devotion;*
Employ them how thou wilt; nay, coin me too: 450
So thou, in this, but crown my longings, Mosca.

MOSCA   Use but your patience.

VOLPONE   So I have.

MOSCA   I doubt not
To bring success to your desires.   455

VOLPONE   Nay, then,
I not repent me of my late* disguise.

MOSCA   If you can horn* him, sir, you need not.

---

428 Swelling.
431 Believed to be the seat of erotic passion.
446 The range of human craft.
449 Disposal.
457 Recent.
458 Make him a cuckold. Horns were the traditional sign of the cuckold.

VOLPONE True:

Besides, I never meant him for my heir.— 460
Is not the colour of my beard and eyebrows
To make me known?

MOSCA No jot.

VOLPONE I did it well.

MOSCA So well, would I could follow you in mine, 465
With half the happiness!—(*Aside*) And yet I would
Escape your epilogue.*

VOLPONE But were they gull'd
With a belief that I was Scoto?

MOSCA Sir, 470
Scoto himself could hardly have distinguish'd!
I have not time to flatter you now; we'll part;
And as I prosper, so applaud my art. (*Exeunt*)

Scene 3

A Room in Corvino's House
(*Enter* CORVINO, *with his sword in his hand, dragging in* CELIA) 475

CORVINO Death of mine honour, with the city's fool!
A juggling, tooth-drawing, prating* mountebank!
And at a public window! Where, whilst he,
With his strain'd action, and his dole of faces,*
To his drug-lecture draws your itching ears, 480
A crew of old, unmarried, noted letchers,
Stood leering up like satyrs;* and you smile
Most graciously, and fan your favours forth,
To give your hot spectators satisfaction!
What, was your mountebank their call? Their whistle? 485
Or were you enamour'd on his copper rings,
His saffron jewel with the toad-stone* in't,
Or his embroider'd suit, with the cope-stitch,*
Made of a hearse cloth?* Or his old tilt-feather?*
Or his starch'd beard? Well, you shall have him, yes! 490
He shall come home, and minister unto you
The fricace for the mother.* Or, let me see,
I think you'd rather mount; would you not mount?
Why, if you'll mount, you may; yes, truly, you may:
And so you may be seen, down to the foot. 495

---

[467] Here, the beating he took.
[477] Chattering.
[479] Repertory of set facial expressions.
[482] Notoriously lascivious creatures; half-man, half-goat.
[487] A stone presumably taken from a toad's head and having the power to charm.
[488] Decorative stitch for ceremonial robes.
[489] (*a*) Coffin-cloth or shroud.   (*b*) A feather worn at a jousting tournament.
[492] Hysteria.

Get you a cittern,* lady Vanity,
And be a dealer with the virtuous man;
Make one: I'll but protest myself a cuckold,
And save your dowry. I'm a Dutchman, I!
For, if you thought me an Italian,   500
You would be damn'd, ere you did this, you whore!
Thou'dst tremble, to imagine, that the murder
Of father, mother, brother, all thy race,
Should follow, as the subject of my justice!

CELIA   Good sir, have patience.   505

CORVINO   What couldst thou propose
Less to thyself, than in this heat of wrath,
And stung with my dishonour, I should strike
This steel into thee, with as many stabs,
As thou wert gaz'd upon with goatish eyes?   510

CELIA   Alas, sir, be appeased! I could not think
My being at the window should more now
Move your impatience, than at other times.

CORVINO   No? Not to seek and entertain a parley
With a known knave, before a multitude!   515
You were an actor with your handkerchief,
Which he most sweetly kissed in the receipt,
And might, no doubt, return it with a letter,
And point the place where you might meet; your sister's,
Your mother's, or your aunt's might serve the turn.   520

CELIA   Why, dear sir, when do I make these excuses,
Or ever stir abroad, but to the church?
And that so seldom—

CORVINO   Well, it shall be less;
And thy restraint before was liberty,   525
To what I now decree: and therefore, mark me.
First, I will have this bawdy light damm'd up;
And till't be done, some two or three yards off,
I'll chalk a line: o'er which if thou but chance
To set thy desperate foot, more hell, more horror,   530
More wild remorseless rage shall seize on thee,
Than on a conjuror, that had needless left
His circle's safety ere his devil was laid.*
Then here's a lock* which I will hang upon thee,
And, now I think on't, I will keep thee backwards;   535
Thy lodging shall be backwards; thy walks backwards;
Thy prospect, all be backwards; and no pleasure,
That thou shalt know but backwards: nay, since you force

---

496 Zither.

533 When a conjuror called up a devil, he protected himself from him by remaining within a magic circle.
    "Laid" here means driven off.

534 Chastity belt.

My honest nature, know, it is your own,
Being too open, makes me use you thus.   540
Since you will not contain your subtle nostrils
In a sweet room, but they must snuff the air
Of rank and sweaty passengers.* (*Knocking within*)—One knocks.
Away, and be not seen, pain of thy life;
Nor look toward the window: if thou dost—   545
Nay, stay, hear this—let me not prosper, whore,
But I will make thee an anatomy,*
Dissect thee mine own self, and read a lecture
Upon thee to the city, and in public.
Away!— (*Exit* CELIA)   550

(Enter SERVANT)

       Who's there?

SERVANT   'Tis signior Mosca, sir.

CORVINO   Let him come in. (*Exit* SERVANT) His master's dead: there's yet
Some good to help the bad.—   555

(Enter MOSCA)
My Mosca, welcome!

I guess your news.

MOSCA   I fear you cannot, sir.

CORVINO   Is't not his death?   560

MOSCA   Rather the contrary.

CORVINO   Not his recovery?

MOSCA   Yes, sir.

CORVINO   I am curs'd,
I am betwitch'd, my crosses* meet to vex me.   565
How? How? How? How?

MOSCA   Why, sir, with Scoto's oil;
Corbaccio and Voltore brought of it,
Whilst I was busy in an inner room—

CORVINO   Death! That damn'd mountebank! But for the law,   570
Now, I could kill the rascal: it cannot be,
His oil should have that virtue.* Have not I
Known him a common rogue, come fiddling in
To the *osteria*,* with a tumbling* whore,
And, when he has done all his forced tricks, been glad   575
Of a poor spoonful of dead wine, with flies in't?
It cannot be. All his ingredients
Are a sheep's gall, a roasted bitch's marrow,
Some few sod earwigs,* pounded caterpillars,

<hr>

543 Passersby.

547 That is, use your corpse for an anatomy demonstration.

565 Afflictions.

572 Power.

574 (*a*) Inn. (*b*) Acrobatic.

579 Insects which presumably crawled into the ear.

A little capon's grease, and fasting spittle:*   580
    I know them to a dram.*
MOSCA   I know not, sir;
    But some on't, there, they pour'd into his ears,
    Some in his nostrils, and recover'd him;
    Applying but the fricace.   585
CORVINO   Pox o' that fricace!
MOSCA   And since, to seem the more officious*
    And flatt'ring of his health, there, they have had,
    At extreme fees, the college of physicians
    Consulting on him, how they might restore him;   590
    Where one would have a cataplasm* of spices,
    Another a flay'd ape clapp'd to his breast,
    A third would have it a dog, a fourth an oil,
    With wild cats' skins: at last, they all resolved
    That, to preserve him, was no other means,   595
    But some young woman must be straight sought out,
    Lusty, and full of juice, to sleep by him;
    And to this service, most unhappily,
    And most unwillingly, am I now employ'd,
    Which here I thought to pre-acquaint you with,   600
    For your advice, since it concerns you most;
    Because, I would not do that thing might cross
    Your ends, on whom I have my whole dependance, sir:
    Yet, if I do it not, they may delate*
    My slackness to my patron, work me out   605
    Of his opinion; and there all your hopes,
    Ventures, or whatsoever, are all frustrate!
    I do but tell you, sir. Besides, they are all
    Now striving, who shall first present him. Therefore—
    I could entreat you, briefly conclude somewhat;   610
    Prevent them if you can.
CORVINO   Death to my hopes,
    This is my villainous fortune! Best to hire
    Some common courtezan.
MOSCA   Ay, I thought on that, sir.   615
    But they are all so subtle, full of art—
    And age again doting and flexible,
    So as—I cannot tell—we may, perchance,
    Light on a quean* may cheat us all.
CORVINO   'Tis true.   620

---

580 The saliva of a person who has been fasting.
581 That is, down to the finest details.
587 Zealous.
591 Poultice or plaster.
604 Relate.
619 Prostitute.

MOSCA No, no: it must be one that has no tricks, sir,
    Some simple thing, a creature made unto it;
    Some wench you may command. Have you no kinswoman?
    Odso*—Think, think, think, think, think, think, think, sir.
    One o' the doctors offer'd there his daughter.   625

CORVINO How!

MOSCA Yes, signior Lupo,* the physician.

CORVINO His daughter!

MOSCA And a virgin, sir. Why, alas,
    He knows the state of 's body, what it is;   630
    That nought can warm his blood, sir, but a fever;
    Nor any incantation raise his spirit:
    A long forgetfulness hath seized that part.
    Besides sir, who shall know it? Some one or two—

CORVINO I pray thee give me leave. (*Walks aside*) If any man   635
    But I had had this luck—The thing in't self,
    I know, is nothing—Wherefore should not I
    As well command my blood and my affections,
    As this dull doctor? In the point of honour,
    The cases are all one of wife and daughter.   640

MOSCA   (*Aside*) I hear him coming.*

CORVINO She shall do't: 'tis done.
    Slight!* If this doctor, who is not engaged,
    Unless 't be for his counsel, which is nothing,
    Offer his daughter, what should I, that am   645
    So deeply in? I will prevent him: Wretch!
    Covetous wretch!—Mosca, I have determined.

MOSCA How, sir?

CORVINO We'll make all sure. The party you wot* of
    Shall be mine own wife, Mosca.   650

MOSCA Sir, the thing;
    But that I would not seem to counsel you,
    I should have motion'd* to you, at the first:
    And make your count, you have cut all their throats.
    Why, 'tis directly taking a possession!   655
    And in his next fit, we may let him go.
    'Tis but to pull the pillow from his head,
    And he is throttled: it had been done before,
    But for your scrupulous doubts.

CORVINO Ay, a plague on't,   660
    My conscience fools my wit! Well, I'll be brief,

---

624 God's so', probably from "God's son"; a mild curse.

627 Another "humour" name: the wolf.

641 Coming around.

643 A trifling matter.

649 Know.

653 Proposed.

And so be thou, lest they should be before us:
Go home, prepare him, tell him with what zeal
And willingness I do it; swear it was
On the first hearing, as thou may'st do, truly,   665
Mine own free motion.
MOSCA   Sir, I warrant you,
   I'll so possess him with it, that the rest
   Of his starv'd clients shall be banish'd all;
   And only you received. But come not, sir,   670
   Until I send, for I have something else
   To ripen for your good, you must not know't.
CORVINO   But do not you forget to send now.
MOSCA   Fear not. (*Exit*)
CORVINO   Where are you, wife? My Celia! Wife!   675
               (*Re-enter* CELIA)
                     —What, blubbering?
   Come, dry those tears. I think thou thought'st me in earnest;
   Ha! By this light I talk'd so but to try thee.
   Methinks the lightness* of the occasion   680
   Should have confirm'd thee. Come, I am not jealous.
CELIA   No?
CORVINO   Faith I am not, I, nor never was;
   It is a poor unprofitable humour.
   Do not I know, if women have a will,   685
   They'll do 'gainst all the watches of the world,
   And that the fiercest spies are tamed with gold?
   Tut, I am confident in thee, thou shalt see't;
   And see, I'll give thee cause too, to believe it.
   Come kiss me. Go, and make thee ready, straight,   690
   In all thy best attire, thy choicest jewels,
   Put them all on, and, with them, thy best looks:
   We are invited to a solemn feast,
   At old Volpone's, where it shall appear
   How far I am free from jealousy or fear. (*Exeunt*)   695

Act Three

Scene 1

A Street
(*Enter* MOSCA)
MOSCA   I fear, I shall begin to grow in love
   With my dear self, and my most properous parts,*
   They do so spring and burgeon; I can feel   5
   A whimsy in my blood: I know not how,

680 Triviality.
4 Propitious talents.

Success hath made me wanton.* I could skip
Out of my skin, now, like a subtle snake,
I am so limber. O! your parasite
Is a most precious thing, dropped from above,   10
Not bred 'mongst clods and clodpoles,* here on earth.
I muse, the mystery was not made a science,
It is so liberally professed!* Almost
All the wise world is little else, in nature,
But parasites or sub-parasites.—And yet,   15
I mean not those that have your bare town-art,
To know who's fit to feed them; have no house,
No family, no care, and therefore mould
Tales for men's ears, to bait that sense; or get
Kitchen-invention,* and some stale receipts   20
To please the belly, and the groin; nor those,
With their court dog-tricks, that can fawn and fleer,*
Make their revenue out of legs and faces,
Echo my lord, and lick away a moth:*
But your fine elegant rascal, that can rise,   25
And stoop, almost together, like an arrow;
Shoot through the air as nimbly as a star;
Turn short as doth a swallow; and be here,
And there, and here, and yonder, all at once;
Present to any humour, all occasion;   30
And change a visor, swifter than a thought!
This is the creature had the art born with him;
Toils not to learn it, but doth practise it
Out of most excellent nature:* and such sparks
Are the true parasites, others but their zanies.   35
              (*Enter* BONARIO)
Who's this? Bonario, old Corbaccio's son?
The person I was bound to seek.—Fair sir,
You are happily met.
BONARIO   That cannot be by thee.   40
MOSCA Why, sir?
BONARIO Nay, pray thee, know thy way, and leave me:
    I would be loath to interchange discourse
    With such a mate* as thou art.
MOSCA Courteous sir,   45
    Scorn not my poverty.

7 Frisky.
11 Numbskulls.
13 Widely practised.
20 Cooking skill.
22 Criticize wittily.
24 That is, keep moths off his lord.
34 Out of natural inclination.
44 Low fellow.

BONARIO Not I, by heaven;
　　　But thou shalt give me leave to hate thy baseness.
MOSCA Baseness!
BONARIO Ay; answer me, is not thy sloth　　　　　　　　　　50
　　　Sufficient argument? Thy flattery?
　　　Thy means of feeding?
MOSCA Heaven be good to me!
　　　These imputations are too common, sir,
　　　And easily stuck on virtue when she's poor.　　　　　　55
　　　You are unequal* to me, and however
　　　Your sentence may be righteous, yet you are not
　　　That, ere you know me, thus proceed in censure:
　　　St. Mark bear witness 'gainst you, 'tis inhuman. (*Weeps*)
BONARIO (*Aside*) What! Does he weep? The sign is soft and good:　　60
　　　I do repent me that I was so harsh.
MOSCA 'Tis true, that, sway'd by strong necessity,
　　　I am enforced to eat my careful* bread
　　　With too much obsequy;* 'tis true, beside,
　　　That I am fain to spin mine own poor raiment　　　　　65
　　　Out of my mere observance,* being not born
　　　To a free fortune: but that I have done
　　　Base offices, in rending friends asunder,
　　　Dividing families, betraying counsels,
　　　Whispering false lies, or mining* men with praises,　　70
　　　Train'd their credulity* with perjuries,
　　　Corrupted chastity, or am in love
　　　With mine own tender ease, but would not rather
　　　Prove* the most rugged, and laborious course,
　　　That might redeem my present estimation,　　　　　75
　　　Let me here perish, in all hope of goodness.
BONARIO (*Aside*) This cannot be a personated* passion.—
　　　I was to blame, so to mistake thy nature;
　　　Prithee, forgive me: and speak out thy business.
MOSCA Sir, it concerns you; and though I may seem,　　　80
　　　At first, to make a main* offence in manners,
　　　And in my gratitude unto my master;
　　　Yet, for the pure love, which I bear all right,
　　　And hatred of the wrong, I must reveal it.
　　　This very hour your father is in purpose　　　　　85
　　　To disinherit you—

56 Unjust.
63 Eaten with anxiety.
64 Obsequiousness.
66 That is, from what I can manage in service.
70 Undermining.
71 That is, entrapped their faith.
74 Undergo.
77 Counterfeited.
81 Great.

BONARIO   How!

MOSCA   And thrust you forth,
As a mere stranger to his blood; 'tis true, sir,
The work no way engageth me, but, as   90
I claim an interest in the general state
Of goodness and true virtue, which I hear
To abound in you: and, for which mere respect,*
Without a second aim, sir, I have done it.

BONARIO   This tale hath lost thee much of the late trust   95
Thou hadst with me; it is impossible:
I know not how to lend it any thought,
My father should be so unnatural.

MOSCA   It is a confidence that well becomes,
Your piety; and form'd, no doubt, it is   100
From your own simple* innocence: which makes
Your wrong more monstrous and abhorr'd. But, sir,
I now will tell you more. This very minute,
It is, or will be doing; and, if you
Shall be but pleased to go with me, I'll bring you,   105
I dare not say where you shall see, but where
Your ear shall be a witness of the deed;
Hear yourself written bastard, and professed
The common issue of the earth.*

BONARIO   I am amazed!   110

MOSCA   Sir, if I do it not, draw your just sword,
And score your vengeance on my front* and face:
Mark me your villain: you have too much wrong,
And I do suffer for you, sir. My heart
Weeps blood in anguish—   115

BONARIO   Lead; I follow thee. (*Exeunt*)

Scene 2

A Room in Volpone's House
(*Enter* VOLPONE)

VOLPONE   Mosca stays long, methinks.—Bring forth your sports,
And help to make the wretched time more sweet.   120
        (*Enter* NANO, ANDROGYNO, *and* CASTRONE)

NANO   Dwarf, fool, and eunuch, well met here we be.
A question it were now, whether* of us three,
Being all the known delicates* of a rich man,
In pleasing him, claim the precedency can?   125

93 That is, only out of this consideration.
101 Honest or open.
109 A nobody, without a known family.
112 Forehead.
123 Which.
124 Favorites.

CASTRONE   I claim for myself.

ANDROGYNO   And so doth the fool.

NANO   'Tis foolish indeed: let me set you both to school.
   First for your dwarf, he's little and witty,
   And every thing, as it is little, is pretty; 130
   Else why do men say to a creature of my shape,
   So soon as they see him, It's a pretty little ape?
   And why a pretty ape, but for pleasing imitation
   Of greater men's actions, in a ridiculous fashion?
   Beside, this feat* body of mine doth not crave 135
   Half the meat, drink, and cloth, one of your bulks will have.
   Admit your fool's face be the mother of laughter,
   Yet, for his brain, it must always come after:
   And though that do feed him, it's a pitiful case,
   His body is beholding to such a bad face. (*Knocking within*) 140

VOLPONE   Who's there? My couch; away! Look! Nano, see:

       (*Exeunt* ANDROGYNO *and* CASTRONE)
   Give me my caps, first——go, enquire. (*Exit* NANO)—Now, Cupid
   Send* it be Mosca, and with fair return!

NANO (*Within*)   It is the beauteous madam— 145

VOLPONE   Would-be—is it?

NANO   The same.

VOLPONE   Now torment on me! Squire her in;
   For she will enter, or dwell here for ever.
   Nay, quickly. (*Retires to his couch*)—That my fit were past! I fear 150
   A second hell too, that my loathing this
   Will quite expel my appetite to the other.*
   Would she were taking now her tedious leave.
   Lord, how it threats me what I am to suffer!

       (*Re-enter* NANO, *with* LADY POLITICK WOULD-BE) 155

LADY POLITICK   I thank you, good sir. 'Pray you signify*
   Unto your patron, I am here.—This band*
   Shows not my neck enough.—I trouble you, sir;
   Let me request you, bid one of my women
   Come hither to me.—In good faith, I am dressed 160
   Most favourably to-day! It is no matter:
   'Tis well enough.—

       (*Enter* 1ST WAITING-WOMAN)
       Look, see, these petulant things,
   How they have done this! 165

VOLPONE (*Aside*)   I do feel the fever
   Entering in at mine ears. O, for a charm,

135 Graceful.
144 Let or grant.
152 That is, Celia.
156 Inform.
157 Ruff, a pleated collar.

To fright it hence!

LADY POLITICK   Come nearer: is this curl
    In his right place, or this? Why is this higher
    Than all the rest? You have not wash'd your eyes, yet!
    Or do they not stand even in your head?
    Where is your fellow? Call her. (*Exit* 1ST WOMAN)

NANO   Now, St. Mark
    Deliver us! Anon, she'll beat her women,
    Because her nose is red.

                (*Re-enter* 1ST *with* 2ND WOMAN)

LADY POLITICK   I pray you, view
    This tire, forsooth:* are all things apt,* or no?

1ST WOMAN   One hair, a little, here, sticks out, forsooth.

LADY POLITICK   Does't so, forsooth! and where was your dear sight,
    When it did so, forsooth! What now! Bird-eyed?
    And you, too? 'Pray you, both approach and mend it.
    Now, by that light, I muse* you are not ashamed!
    I, that have preach'd these things so oft unto you,
    Read you the principles, argued all the grounds,
    Disputed every fitness, every grace,
    Call'd you to counsel of so frequent dressings—

NANO (*Aside*)   More carefully than of your fame or honour.

LADY POLITICK   Made you acquainted, what an ample dowry
    The knowledge of these things would be unto you,
    Able, alone, to get you noble husbands
    At your return: and you thus to neglect it!
    Besides, you seeing what a curious nation
    The Italians are, what will they say of me?
    The English lady cannot dress herself.
    Here's a fine imputation to our country!
    Well, go your ways, and stay in the next room.
    This fucus* was too coarse too; it's no matter.—
    Good sir, you'll give them entertainment?

           (*Exeunt* NANO *and* WAITING-WOMAN)

VOLPONE   The storm comes toward me.

LADY POLITICK (*Goes to the couch*)   How does my Volpone?

VOLPONE   Troubled with noise, I cannot sleep; I dreamt
    That a strange fury enter'd, now, my house,
    And, with the dreadful tempest of her breath,
    Did cleave my roof asunder.

LADY POLITICK   Believe me, and I
    Had the most fearful dream, could I remember't—

VOLPONE (*Aside*)   Out of my fate! I have given her the occasion
    How to torment me: she will tell me hers.

---

179 (*a*) In truth.   (*b*) Fitting or becoming.
184 Wonder.
199 Cosmetic.

LADY POLITICK   Me thought, the golden mediocrity,*
    Polite and delicate—
VOLPONE   O, if you do love me,
    No more: I sweat, and suffer, at the mention   215
    Of any dream; feel how I tremble yet.
LADY POLITICK   Alas, good soul! the passion of the heart.*
    Seed-pearl* were good now, boil'd with syrup of apples,
    Tincture of gold, and coral, citron-pills,
    Your elicampane root,* myrobalanes—*   220
VOLPONE (Aside)   Ah me, I have ta'en a grass-hopper by the wing!
LADY POLITICK   Burnt silk, and amber: You have muscadel
    Good in the house—
VOLPONE   You will not drink, and part?
LADY POLITICK   No, fear not that. I doubt, we shall not get   225
    Some English saffron, half a dram would serve;
    Your sixteen cloves, a little musk, dried mints,
    Bugloss,* and barleymeal—
VOLPONE (Aside)   She's in again!
    Before I feign'd diseases, now I have one.   230
LADY POLITICK   And these applied with a right* scarlet cloth.
VOLPONE (Aside)   Another flood of words! A very torrent!
LADY POLITICK   Shall I, sir, make you a poultice?
VOLPONE   No, no, no,
    I'm very well, you need prescribe no more.   235
LADY POLITICK   I have a little studied physic; but now,
    I'm all for music, save, in the forenoons,
    An hour or two for painting. I would have
    A lady, indeed, to have all, letters and arts,
    Be able to discourse, to write, to paint,   240
    But principal,* as Plato holds, your music
    (And so does wise Pythagoras, I take it)
    Is your true rapture: when there is consent*
    In face, in voice, and clothes: and is, indeed,
    Our sex's chiefest ornament.   245
VOLPONE   The poet
    As old in time as Plato, and as knowing,
    Says, that your highest female grace is silence.
LADY POLITICK   Which of your poets? Petrarch, or Tasso, or Dante?
    Guarini? Ariosto? Aretine?   250
    Cieco di Hadria? I have read them all.

212 Golden mean.
217 Heartburn.
218 A tiny pearl resembling a seed.
220 (a) A medicinal herb.   (b) A fruit that was used medicinally.
228 Another plant; related to the prickly ox-tongue.
231 Straight.
241 Chiefly.
243 Harmony.

VOLPONE (*Aside*) Is every thing a cause to my destruction?

LADY POLITICK I think I have two or three of them about me.

VOLPONE (*Aside*) The sun, the sea, will sooner both stand still
    Than her eternal tongue! nothing can 'scape it. 255

LADY POLITICK Here's *Pastor Fido*—

VOLPONE (*Aside*) Profess obstinate silence;
    That's now my safest.

LADY POLITICK All our English writers,
    I mean such as are happy* in the Italian, 260
    Will deign to steal out of this author, mainly:
    Almost as much as from Montagnié:*
    He has so modern and facile a vein,
    Fitting the time, and catching the court-ear!
    Your Petrarch is more passionate, yet he, 265
    In days of sonnetting, trusted them with much:
    Dante is hard, and few can understand him.
    But, for a desperate* wit, there's Aretine;*
    Only, his pictures are a little obscene—
    You mark me not. 270

VOLPONE Alas, my mind's perturb'd.

LADY POLITICK Why, in such cases, we must cure ourselves,
    Make use of our philosophy—

VOLPONE Oh me!

LADY POLITICK And as we find our passions do rebel, 275
    Encounter* them with reason, or divert them,
    By giving scope unto some other humour
    Of lesser danger: as, in politic bodies,
    There's nothing more doth overwhelm the judgment,
    And cloud the understanding, than too much 280
    Settling and fixing, and, as 'twere subsiding
    Upon one object. For the incorporating
    Of these same outward things, into that part,
    Which we call mental, leaves some certain *fæces**
    That stop the organs, and as Plato says, 285
    Assassinate our knowledge.

VOLPONE (*Aside*) Now, the spirit
    Of patience help me!

LADY POLITICK Come, in faith, I must
    Visit you more a days; and make you well: 290
    Laugh and be lusty.

VOLPONE (*Aside*) My good angel save me!

---

256 *Il Pastor Fido* (*The Faithful Shepherd*), Guarini's celebrated pastoral play.

260 Fluent.

262 Michel de Montaigne (1533–92), French essayist and philosopher.

268 (*a*) Outrageous. (*b*) Pietro Aretino (1492–1556).

276 Oppose.

284 Dregs or sediment.

LADY POLITICK   There was but one sole man in all the world,
      With whom I e'er could sympathise; and he
      Would lie you,* often, three, four hours together   295
      To hear me speak; and be sometimes so rapt,
      As he would answer me quite from the purpose,
      Like you, and you are like him, just. I'll discourse,
      An't be but only, sir, to bring you asleep,
      How we did spend our time and loves together,   300
      For some six years.
VOLPONE   Oh, oh, oh, oh, oh, oh!
LADY POLITICK   For we were *cœtanei,** and brought up—
VOLPONE   Some power, some fate, some fortunes rescue me!
                              (*Enter* MOSCA)   305
MOSCA   God save you, madam!
LADY POLITICK   Good sir.
VOLPONE   Mosca! Welcome,
      Welcome to my redemption.
MOSCA   Why, sir?   310
VOLPONE   Oh,
      Rid me of this my torture, quickly, there;
      My madam, with the everlasting voice:
      The bells, in time of pestilence, ne'er made
      Like noise, or were in that perpetual motion!   315
      The Cock-pit* comes not near it. All my house,
      But now, steam'd like a bath with her thick breath,
      A lawyer could not have been heard; nor scarce
      Another woman, such a hail of words
      She has let fall. For hell's sake, rid her hence.   320
MOSCA   Has she presented?*
VOLPONE   O, I do not care;
      I'll take her absence, upon any price,
      With any loss.
MOSCA   Madam—   325
LADY POLITICK   I have brought your patron
      A toy,* a cap here, of mine own work.
MOSCA   'Tis well.
      I had forgot to tell you, I saw your knight.
      Where you would little think it.—   330
LADY POLITICK   Where?
MOSCA   Marry,
      Where yet, if you make haste, you may apprehend
      Rowing upon the water in a gondole
      With the most cunning courtezan of Venice.   335

295 That is, lie for you.
303 Contemporaries.
316 Arena for cock-fights.
321 Presented her gift.   327 Trifle.

LADY POLITICK Is't true?

MOSCA Pursue them, and believe your eyes:
Leave me, to make your gift. (*Exit* LADY POLITICK *hastily*)
      —I knew 'twould take:
For, lightly,* they that use themselves most license,   340
Are still most jealous.

VOLPONE Mosca, hearty thanks,
For thy quick fiction, and delivery of me.
Now to my hopes, what say'st thou?
     (*Re-enter* LADY POLITICK WOULD-BE)   345

LADY POLITICK But do you hear, sir?—

VOLPONE Again! I fear a paroxysm.

LADY POLITICK Which way
Row'd they together?

MOSCA Toward the Rialto.*   350

LADY POLITICK I pray you lend me your dwarf.

MOSCA I pray you take him.— (*Exit* LADY POLITICK)
Your hopes, sir, are like happy blossoms, fair,
And promise timely* fruit, if you will stay
But the maturing; keep you at your couch,   355
Corbaccio will arrive straight, with the Will;
When he is gone, I'll tell you more. (*Exit*)

VOLPONE My blood,
My spirits are return'd; I am alive:
And like your wanton gamester at *primero*,*   360
Whose thought had whisper'd to him, not go less,
Methinks I lie, and draw—for an encounter. (*The scene closes upon* VOLPONE)

Scene 3

The Passage leading to Volpone's Chamber
(*Enter* MOSCA *and* BONARIO)

MOSCA Sir, here conceal'd, (*Shows him a closet*) you may hear all. But, pray you, 365
Have patience, sir; (*Knocking within*)—the same's your father knocks:
I am compell'd to leave you. (*Exit*)

BONARIO Do so.—Yet
Cannot my thought imagine this a truth. (*Goes into the closet*)

Scene 4

Another Part of the same   370
(*Enter* MOSCA *and* CORVINO, CELIA *following*)

MOSCA Death on me! you are come too soon, what meant you?
Did not I say, I would send?

340 Commonly.
350 A bridge over the Grand Canal in Venice.
354 Early.
360 A card game. In the following lines he uses the language of the game—"go less," "lie," and "draw"—
as he plans for Celia.

CORVINO   Yes, but I fear'd
　　You might forget it, and then they prevent us.　　　　　　375
MOSCA (*Aside*)   Prevent! Did e'er man haste so, for his horns?
　　A courtier would not ply it so, for a place.*
　　Well, now there is no helping it, stay here;
　　I'll presently return. (*Exit*)
CORVINO   Where are you, Celia?　　　　　　　　　　　　380
　　You know not wherefore I have brought you hither?
CELIO   Not well, except you told me.
CORVINO   Now, I will:
　　Hark hither. (*Exeunt*)

Scene 5

　　　　　　　A Closet opening into a Gallery　　　　　　385
　　　　　　　　(*Enter* MOSCA *and* BONARIO)
MOSCA   Sir, your father hath sent word,
　　It will be half an hour ere he come;
　　And therefore, if you please to walk the while
　　Into that gallery—at the upper end,　　　　　　　　　390
　　There are some books to entertain the time:
　　And I'll take care no man shall come unto you, sir.
BONARIO   Yes, I will stay there.—(*Aside*) I do doubt this fellow. (*Exit*)
MOSCA (*Looking after him*)   There; he is far enough; he can hear nothing:
　　And, for his father, I can keep him off. (*Exit*)　　　　395

Scene 6

　　　　　Volpone's Chamber.—Volpone on his couch. Mosca sitting by him
　　　　　　　　(*Enter* CORVINO, *forcing in* CELIA)
CORVINO   Nay, now, there is no starting back; and therefore,
　　Resolve upon it: I have so decreed.
　　It must be done. Nor would I move't* afore,　　　　　400
　　Because I would avoid all shifts and tricks,
　　That might deny me.
CELIA   Sir, let me beseech you,
　　Affect not these strange trials; if you doubt
　　My chastity, why, lock me up for ever;　　　　　　　405
　　Make me the heir of darkness. Let me live,
　　Where I may please your fears, if not your trust.
CORVINO   Believe it, I have no such humour, I.
　　All that I speak I mean; yet I 'm not mad;
　　Nor horn-mad, see you? Go to, show yourself　　　　410
　　Obedient, and a wife.
CELIA   O heaven!
CORVINO   I say it,
　　Do so.

³⁷⁷ Position at court.　　　⁴⁰⁰ Propose it.

CELIA Was this the train?*

CORVINO I've told you reasons;
   What the physicians have set down: how much,   415
   It may concern me; what my engagements are;
   My means; and the necessity of those means,
   For my recovery: wherefore, if you be
   Loyal, and mine, be won, respect my venture.   420

CELIA Before your honour?

CORVINO Honour! Tut, a breath:
   There's no such thing in nature: a mere term
   Invented to awe fools. What is my gold
   The worse for touching, clothes for being look'd on?   425
   Why, this is no more. An old decrepit wretch,
   That has no sense, no sinew; takes his meat
   With others' fingers;* only knows to gape,
   When you do scald his gums; a voice, a shadow;
   And, what can this man hurt you?   430

CELIA (Aside) Lord! What spirit
   Is this hath enter'd him?

CORVINO And for your fame,
   That's such a jig;* as if I would go tell it,
   Cry it on the Piazza! Who shall know it,   435
   But he that cannot speak it, and this fellow,
   Whose lips are in my pocket?* Save yourself
   (If you'll proclaim't, you may), I know no other
   Shall come to know it.

CELIA Are heaven and saints then nothing?   440
   Will they be blind or stupid?

CORVINO How!

CELIA Good sir,
   Be jealous still, emulate them; and think
   What hate they burn with toward every sin.   445

CORVINO I grant you: if I thought it were a sin,
   I would not urge you. Should I offer this
   To some young Frenchman, or hot Tuscan blood
   That had read Aretine, conn'd all his prints,*   450
   Knew every quirk within lust's labyrinth,
   And were professed critic* in lechery;
   And I would look upon him, and applaud him,
   This were a sin: but here, 'tis contrary,
   A pious work, mere charity for physic,   455

---

415 Sequel; that is, "Is this what we've come to?"
429 With the help of others.
435 Farce.
438 That is, who is my servant.
450 Studied his pornographic pictures.
452 Expert.

And honest polity, to assure mine own.

CELIA O heaven! Canst thou suffer such a change?

VOLPONE Thou art mine honour, Mosca, and my pride,
My joy, my tickling,* my delight! Go bring them.

MOSCA (*Advancing*) Please you draw near, sir.   460

CORVINO Come on, what—
You will not be rebellious? By that light—

MOSCA Sir,
Signior Corvino, here, is come to see you.

VOLPONE Oh!   465

MOSCA And hearing of the consultation had
So lately, for your health, is come to offer,
Or rather, sir, to prostitute—

CORVINO Thanks, sweet Mosca.

MOSCA Freely, unask'd, or unintreated—   470

CORVINO Well.

MOSCA As the true fervent instance of his love,
His own most fair and proper wife; the beauty,
Only of price* in Venice—

CORVINO 'Tis well urged.   475

MOSCA To be your comfortress, and to preserve you.

VOLPONE Alas, I am past, already! Pray you, thank him
For his good care and promptness; but for that,
'Tis a vain labour e'en fight 'gainst heaven;
Applying fire to stone—uh, uh, uh, uh! (*Coughing*)   480
Making a dead leaf grow again. I take
His wishes gently, though; and you may tell him,
What I have done for him: marry, my state is hopeless.
Will him to pray for me; and to use his fortune
With reverence, when he comes to't.   485

MOSCA Do you hear, sir?
Go to him with your wife.

CORVINO Heart of my father!
Wilt thou persist thus? Come, I pray thee, come.
Thou seest 'tis nothing, Celia. By this hand,   490
I shall grow violent. Come, do't, I say.

CELIA Sir, kill me, rather: I will take down poison,
Eat burning coals, do any thing.—

CORVINO Be damn'd!
Heart, I will drag thee hence, home, by the hair;   495
Cry thee a strumpet through the streets; rip up
Thy mouth unto thine ears; and slit thy nose,
Like a raw rochet!*—Do not tempt me; come,
Yield, I am loth—Death! I will buy some slave

---

474 The only precious beauty.
498 Fish.

Whom I will kill, and bind thee to him, alive; 500
And at my window hang you forth, devising
Some monstrous crime, which I, in capital letters,
Will eat into thy flesh with aquafortis,*
And burning corsives,* on this stubborn breast.
Now, by the blood thou hast incensed, I'll do it! 505
CELIA Sir, what you please, you may, I am your martyr.
CORVINO Be not thus obstinate, I have not deserved it:
Think who it is entreats you. 'Prithee, sweet;—
Good faith, thou shalt have jewels, gowns, attires,
What thou wilt think, and ask. Do but go kiss him. 510
Or touch him, but. For my sake.—At my suit.—
This once.—No! Not! I shall remember this.
Will you disgrace me thus? Do you thirst my undoing?
MOSCA Nay, gentle lady, be advised.
CORVINO No, no. 515
She has watch'd her time. Ods precious, this is scurvy,*
'Tis very scurvy; and you are—
MOSCA Nay, good sir.
CORVINO An arrant* locust, by heaven, a locust!
Whore, crocodile, that hast thy tears prepared,
Expecting how thou'lt bid them flow— 520
MOSCA Nay, 'pray you, sir!
She will consider.
CELIA Would my life would serve
To satisfy—
CORVINO S'death! If she would but speak to him, 525
And save my reputation, it were somewhat;
But spightfully to affect* my utter ruin!
MOSCA Ay, now you have put your fortune in her hands.
Why i'faith, it is her modesty, I must quit* her.
If you were absent, she would be more cunning; 530
I know it: and dare undertake* for her.
What woman can before her husband? 'Pray you,
Let us depart, and leave her here.
CORVINO Sweet Celia,
Thou may'st redeem all, yet; I'll say no more: 535
If not, esteem yourself as lost. Nay, stay there.
                (*Shuts the door, and exit with* MOSCA)
CELIA O God, and his good angels! Whither, whither,
Is shame fled human breasts? That with such ease, 540

503 Acid.
504 Corrosives.
516 Contemptible.
519 Notorious.
528 Seek.
530 Acquit.
532 Promise or pledge.

Men dare put off your honours, and their own?
Is that, which ever was a cause of life,
Now placed beneath the basest circumstance,
And modesty an exile made, for money?

VOLPONE Ay, in Corvino, and such earth-fed minds, (*Leaping from his couch*)   545
That never tasted the true heaven of love.
Assure thee, Celia, he that would sell thee,
Only for hope of gain, and that uncertain,
He would have sold his part of Paradise
For ready money, had he met a cope-man.*   550
Why art thou mazed to see me thus revived?
Rather applaud thy beauty's miracle;
'Tis thy great work: that hath, not now alone,
But sundry times raised me, in several shapes,
And, but this morning, like a mountebank,   555
To see thee at thy window. Ay, before
I would have left my practice,* for thy love,
In varying figures, I would have contended
With the blue Proteus,* or the horned flood.*
Now art thou welcome.   560

CELIA Sir!

VOLPONE Nay, fly me not.
Nor let thy false imagination
That I was bed-rid, make thee think I am so:
Thou shalt not find it. I am, now, as fresh,   565
As hot, as high, and in as jovial plight,*
As when, in that so celebrated scene,
At recitation of our comedy,
For entertainment of the great Valois,*
I acted young Antinous;* and attracted   570
The eyes and ears of all the ladies present,
To admire each graceful gesture, note, and footing.

(*Sings*)   Come, my Celia, let us prove,*
While we can, the sports of love,
Time will not be ours for ever,   575
He, at length, our good will sever;
Spend not then his gifts in vain.
Suns, that set, may rise again;
But if once we lose this light,
'Tis with us perpetual night.   580

---

550 Tradesman.
557 Scheming.
559 (*a*) A sea god who was continually changing form.   (*b*) Sea or river god with horns.
566 Condition.
569 Henry III of France, who was in Venice in 1594.
570 Famous for his good looks.
573 Practise or try.

Why should we defer our joys?
Fame and rumour are but toys.
Cannot we delude the eyes
Of a few poor household spies?
Or his easier ears beguile,
Thus removed by our wile?—
'Tis no sin love's fruits to steal:
But the sweet thefts to reveal;
To be taken, to be seen,
These have crimes accounted been.

CELIA   Some serene* blast me, or dire lightning strike
   This my offending face!

VOLPONE   Why droops my Celia?
   Thou hast, in place of a base husband, found
   A worthy lover: use thy fortune well,
   With secrecy and pleasure. See, behold,
   What thou art queen of; not in expectation,
   As I feed others: but possess'd and crown'd.
   See, here, a rope of pearl; and each, more orient
   Than that the brave Ægyptian queen caroused:*
   Dissolve and drink them. See, a carbuncle,*
   May put out both the eyes of our St. Mark;
   A diamond, would have bought Lollia Paulina,*
   When she came in like star-light, hid with jewels,
   That were the spoils of provinces; take these,
   And wear, and lose them: yet remains an ear-ring
   To purchase them again, and this whole state.
   A gem but worth a private patrimony*
   Is nothing: we will eat such at a meal.
   The heads of parrots, tongues of nightingales,
   The brains of peacocks, and of ostriches,
   Shall be our food: and, could we get the phœnix,*
   Though nature lost her kind, she were our dish.

CELIA   Good sir, these things might move a mind affected
   With such delights; but I, whose innocence
   Is all I can think wealthy, or worth th' enjoying,
   And which, once lost, I have nought to lose beyond it,
   Cannot be taken with these sensual baits:
   If you have conscience—

VOLPONE   'Tis the beggar's virtue;
   If thou hast wisdom, hear me, Celia.

591 A noxious dew or mist.

600 Cleopatra drank pearls dissolved in vinegar to win a bet with Antony.

601 Precious red stone.

603 The wife of a Roman ruler, she was reputed to have dressed in stolen finery.

608 Inheritance.

612 A mythical bird, only one of which existed at a time and which was consumed by fire and then re-born
in its own ashes.

Thy baths shall be the juice of July-flowers,
Spirit of roses, and of violets,
The milk of unicorns, and panthers' breath
Gather'd in bags, and mixt with Cretan wines.   625
Our drink shall be prepared gold and amber;
Which we will take, until my roof whirl round
With the vertigo: and my dwarf shall dance,
My eunuch sing, my fool make up the antic.*
Whilst we, in changed shapes, act Ovid's tales,   630
Thou, like Europa now, and I like Jove,*
Then I like Mars, and thou like Erycine:*
So, of the rest, till we have quite run through,
And wearied all the fables of the gods.
Then will I have thee in more modern forms,   635
Attired like some sprightly dame of France,
Brave Tuscan lady, or proud Spanish beauty;
Sometimes, unto the Persian sophy's* wife;
Or the grand signior's* mistress; and, for change,
To one of our most artful courtezans,   640
Or some quick* Negro, or cold Russian;
And I will meet thee in as many shapes:
Where we may so transfuse* our wandering souls
Out at our lips, and score up sums of pleasures,

(*Sings*)   That the curious shall not know   645
            How to tell them as they flow;
            And the envious, when they find
            What their number is, be pined.*
CELIA   If you have ears that will be pierced—or eyes
That can be open'd—a heart that may be touch'd—   650
Or any part that yet sounds man about you—
If you have touch of holy saints—or heaven—
Do me the grace to let me 'scape—if not,
Be bountiful and kill me. You do know,
I am a creature, hither ill betray'd,   655
By one, whose shame I would forget it were:
If you will deign me neither of these graces,
Yet feed your wrath, sir, rather than your lust
(It is a vice comes nearer manliness)
And punish that unhappy crime of nature,   660

629 Grotesque dance.
631 Jove, in the form of a bull, abducted Europa.
632 Mars and Venus, another famous pair of lovers.
638 Shah's.
639 Sultan of Turkey.
641 Vigorous.
643 Cause to flow from one to the other.
648 Pine with envy.

Which you miscall my beauty: flay my face,
Or poison it with ointments, for seducing
Your blood to this rebellion. Rub these hands,
With what may cause an eating leprosy,
E'en to my bones and marrow: any thing,   665
That may disfavour* me, save in my honour—
And I will kneel to you, pray for you, pay down
A thousand hourly vows, sir, for your health;
Report, and think you virtuous—

VOLPONE Think me cold,   670
Frozen and impotent, and so report me?
That I had Nestor's hernia,* thou wouldst think.
I do degenerate, and abuse my nation,
To play with opportunity thus long;
I should have done the act, and then have parley'd.*   675
Yield, or I'll force thee. (*Seizes her*)

CELIA O! just God!

VOLPONE In vain—

BONARIO (*Rushing in*) Forbear, foul ravisher, libidinous swine!
Free the forced lady, or thou diest, impostor.   680
But that I'm loath to snatch thy punishment
Out of the hand of justice, thou shouldst, yet,
Be made the timely sacrifice of vengeance,
Before this altar, and this dross,* thy idol.—
Lady, let's quit the place, it is the den   685
Of villainy; fear nought, you have a guard:
And he, ere long, shall meet his just reward. (*Exeunt* BONARIO *and* CELIA)

VOLPONE Fall on me, roof, and bury me in ruin!
Become my grave, that wert my shelter! O!
I am unmask'd, unspirited,* undone,   690
Betray'd to beggary, to infamy—
                      (*Enter* MOSCA, *wounded and bleeding*)

MOSCA Where shall I run, most wretched shame of men,
To beat out my unlucky brains?

VOLPONE Here, here.   695
What! Dost thou bleed?

MOSCA O that his well-driv'n sword
Had been so courteous to have cleft me down
Unto the navel, ere I lived to see
My life, my hopes, my spirits, my patron, all   700
Thus desperately engaged,* by my error!

---

666 Disfigure.
672 The impotence of old age.
675 Talked.
684 Garbage.
690 Despondent.
701 Entangled.

VOLPONE Woe on thy fortune!

MOSCA And my follies, sir.

VOLPONE Thou hast made me miserable.

MOSCA And myself, sir.   705
    Who would have thought he would have hearken'd so?

VOLPONE What shall we do?

MOSCA I know not; if my heart
    Could expiate the mischance, I'd pluck it out.
    Will you be pleased to hang me, or cut my throat?   710
    And I'll requite you, sir. Let's die like Romans,*
    Since we have lived like Grecians.* (*Knocking within*)

VOLPONE Hark! Who's there?
    I hear some footing; officers, the *saffi,**
    Come to apprehend us! I do feel the brand   715
    Hissing already at my forehead; now,
    Mine ears are boring.*

MOSCA To your couch, sir, you,
    Make that place good, however. (**VOLPONE** *lies down, as before*) Guilty men
    Suspect what they deserve still.   720

(Enter CORBACCIO)

    Signior Corbaccio!

CORBACCIO Why, how now, Mosca?

MOSCA O, undone, amazed, sir.
    Your son, I know not by what accident,   725
    Acquainted with your purpose to my patron,
    Touching your Will, and making him your heir,
    Enter'd our house with violence, his sword drawn
    Sought for you, call'd you wretch, unnatural,
    Vow'd he would kill you.   730

CORBACCIO Me!

MOSCA Yes, and my patron.

CORBACCIO This act shall disinherit him indeed;
    Here is the Will.

MOSCA 'Tis well, sir.   735

CORBACCIO Right and well:
    Be you as careful now for me.

(Enter VOLTORE, behind)

MOSCA My life, sir,
    Is not more tender'd;* I am only yours.   740

CORBACCIO How does he? Will he die shortly, think'st thou?

MOSCA I fear
    He'll outlast May.

---

711 By suicide.
712 Extravagantly.
714 Venetian police.
717 Being pierced.
740 Cared for.

CORBACCIO To-day?

MOSCA No, last out May, sir.

CORBACCIO Could'st thou not give him a dram?

MOSCA O, by no means, sir.

CORBACCIO Nay, I'll not bid you.

VOLTORE (*Coming forward*) This is a knave, I see.

MOSCA (*Seeing* VOLTORE. *Aside*) How, signior Voltore! did he hear me?   750

VOLTORE Parasite!

MOSCA Who's that?—O, sir, most timely welcome—

VOLTORE Scarce,
   To the discovery of your tricks, I fear.
   You are his, *only?* And mine also, are you not?   755

MOSCA Who? I, sir?

VOLTORE You, sir. What device is this
   About a Will?

MOSCA A plot for you, sir.

VOLTORE Come,   760
   Put not your foists* upon me; I shall scent them.

MOSCA Did you not hear it?

VOLTORE Yes, I hear Corbaccio
   Hath made your patron there his heir.

MOSCA 'Tis true,   765
   By my device, drawn to it by my plot,
   With hope—

VOLTORE Your patron should reciprocate?
   And you have promised?

MOSCA For your good, I did, sir.   770
   Nay, more, I told his son, brought, hid him here,
   Where he might hear his father pass the deed;
   Being persuaded to it by this thought, sir,
   That the unnaturalness, first, of the act,
   And then his father's oft disclaiming* in him   775
   (Which I did mean t'help on), would sure enrage him
   To do some violence upon his parent.
   On which the law should take sufficient hold,
   And you be stated* in a double hope:
   Truth be my comfort, and my conscience,   780
   My only aim was to dig you a fortune
   Out of these two old rotten sepulchres—

VOLTORE I cry thee mercy, Mosca.

MOSCA Worth your patience,
   And your great merit, sir. And see the change!   785

VOLTORE Why, what success?

MOSCA Most hapless! You must help, sir.

761 Tricks.
775 Repudiating.
779 Installed.

Whilst we expected the old raven, in comes
Corvino's wife, sent hither by her husband—
VOLTORE   What, with a present?   790
MOSCA   No, sir, on visitation
(I'll tell you how anon); and staying long,
The youth he grows impatient, rushes forth,
Seizeth the lady, wounds me, makes her swear
(Or he would murder her, that was his vow)   795
To affirm my patron to have done her rape:
Which how unlike it is, you see! And hence,
With that pretext he's gone, to accuse his father,
Defame my patron, defeat you—
VOLTORE   Where is her husband?   800
Let him be sent for straight.
MOSCA   Sir, I'll go fetch him.
VOLTORE   Bring him to the Scrutineo.*
MOSCA   Sir, I will.
VOLTORE   This must be stopped.   805
MOSCA   O you do nobly, sir.
Alas, 'twas labour'd all, sir, for your good;
Nor was there want of counsel in the plot:
But fortune can, at any time, o'erthrow
The projects of a hundred learned clerks,* sir.   810
CORBACCIO (*Listening*)   What's that?
VOLTORE   Will't please you, sir, to go along?
                    (*Exit* CORBACCIO, *followed by* VOLTORE)
MOSCA   Patron, go in, and pray for our success.
VOLPONE (*Rising from his couch*)   Need makes devotion: heaven your labour 815
                              bless! (*Exeunt*)

Act Four

Scene 1

A Street
(*Enter* SIR POLITICK WOULD-BE *and* PEREGRINE)
SIR POLITICK   I told you, sir, it* was a plot; you see
What observation is! You mention'd me
For some instructions: I will tell you, sir,   5
(Since we are met here in the height of Venice)
Some few particulars I have set down,
Only for this meridian,* fit to be known
Of your crude traveller; and they are these.
I will not touch, sir, at your phrase, or clothes,   10

803 The Venetian Senate House.
810 Scholars.
3 Corvino's driving Volpone away from his window.
8 Sphere or geographical area.

For they are old.

PEREGRINE Sir, I have better.

SIR POLITICK Pardon,
    I meant, as they are themes.*

PEREGRINE O, sir, proceed:
    I'll slander you no more of wit, good sir.

SIR POLITICK First, for your garb, it must be grave and serious,
    Very reserv'd and lock'd; not tell a secret
    On any terms, not to your father; scarce
    A fable, but with caution: made sure choice
    Both of your company, and discourse; beware
    You never speak a truth—

PEREGRINE How!

SIR POLITICK Not to strangers,
    For those be they you must converse with most;
    Others I would not know, sir, but at distance,
    So as I still might be a saver in them:*
    You shall have tricks else passed upon you hourly.
    And then, for your religion, profess none,
    But wonder at the diversity, of all:
    And, for your part, protest, were there no other
    But simply the laws o' the land, you could content you
    Nic. Machiavel,* and Monsieur Bodin,* both
    Were of this mind. Then must you learn the use
    And handling of your silver fork at meals,
    The metal* of your glass (these are main matters
    With your Italian); and to know the hour
    When you must eat your melons, and your figs.

PEREGRINE Is that a point of state too?

SIR POLITICK Here it is:
    For your Venetian, if he see a man
    Preposterous* in the least, he has him straight;
    He has; he strips him. I'll acquaint you, sir,
    I now have lived here, 'tis some fourteen months
    Within the first week of my landing here,
    All took me for a citizen of Venice,
    I knew the forms so well—

PEREGRINE (*Aside*) And nothing else.

SIR POLITICK I had read Contarini,* took me a house,

---

[14] Topics of discussion.

[27] That is, so that I might keep their acquaintance.

[33] (*a*) Machiavelli was reputed to be an atheist. (*b*) A French political economist (1530–96) who supported religious toleration.

[36] Material.

[42] Unconventional.

[49] Could allude to any of several members of the Contarini family, many of whom produced books; probably intends Vincenzo Contarini (1577–1617), however, who published a book of readings from classical literature.

Dealt with my Jews to furnish it with moveables—
Well, if I could but find one man, one man
To mine own heart, whom I durst trust, I would—
PEREGRINE   What, what, sir?
SIR POLITICK   Make him rich; make him a fortune:
He should not think again. I would command it.
PEREGRINE   As how?
SIR POLITICK   With certain projects that I have;
Which I may not discover.
PEREGRINE (*Aside*)   If I had
But one to wager with, I would lay odds now,
He tells me instantly.
SIR POLITICK   One is, and that
I care not greatly who knows, to serve the state
Of Venice with red herrings for three years,
And at a certain rate, from Rotterdam,
Where I have correspondence. There's a letter,
Sent me from one o' the states,* and to that purpose:
He cannot write his name, but that's his mark.
PEREGRINE   He is a chandler?*
SIR POLITICK   No, a cheesemonger.
There are some others too with whom I treat
About the same negociation;
And I will undertake it: for 'tis thus.
I'll do't with ease, I have cast* it all: Your hoy*
Carries but three men in her, and a boy;
And she shall make me three returns a year:
So, if there come but one of three, I save;
If two, I can defalc:*—but this is now,
If my main project fail.
PEREGRINE   Then you have others?
SIR POLITICK   I should be loath to draw the subtle air
Of such a place, without my thousand aims.
I'll not dissemble, sir: where'er I come,
I love to be considerative;* and 'tis true,
I have at my free hours thought upon
Some certain goods unto the state of Venice,
Which I do call *my Cautions;* and, sir, which
I mean, in hope of pension, to propound
To the Great Council, then unto the Forty,
So to the Ten.* My means are made already—

[67] The States General of Holland.
[69] A candle-merchant.
[74] (*a*) Calculated.   (*b*) Small boat.
[78] Reduce expenses.
[84] Thoughtful.
[87] Precautions.
[90] Ruling bodies and councils.

PEREGRINE By whom?

SIR POLITICK Sir, one that, though his place be obscure,
    Yet he can sway, and they will hear him. He's
    A *commandador*.*

PEREGRINE What! A common serjeant?   95

SIR POLITICK Sir, such as they are, put it in their mouths,
    What they should say, sometimes as well as greater:
    I think I have my notes to show you— (*Searching his pockets*)

PEREGRINE Good sir.

SIR POLITICK But you shall swear unto me, on your gentry,*   100
    Not to anticipate—

PEREGRINE I, sir!

SIR POLITICK Nor reveal
    A circumstance——My paper is not with me.

PEREGRINE O, but you can remember, sir.   105

SIR POLITICK My first is
    Concerning tinder-boxes. You must know,
    No family is here without its box.
    Now, sir, it being so portable a thing,
    Put case,* that you or I were ill affected   110
    Unto the state, sir; with it in our pockets,
    Might not I go into the Arsenal,
    Or you, come out again, and none the wiser?

PEREGRINE Except yourself, sir.

SIR POLITICK Go to,* then. I therefore   115
    Advertise to the state, how fit it were,
    That none but such as were known patriots,
    Sound lovers of their country, should be suffer'd
    To enjoy them in their houses; and even those
    Seal'd at some office, and at such a bigness   120
    As might not lurk in pockets.

PEREGRINE Admirable!

SIR POLITICK My next is, how to enquire, and be resolv'd,
    By present* demonstration, whether a ship,
    Newly arrived from Soria,* or from   125
    Any suspected part of all the Levant,*
    Be guilty of the plague: and where they use
    To lie out forty, fifty days, sometimes,
    About the Lazaretto,* for their trial;
    I'll save that charge and loss unto the merchant,   130
    And in an hour clear the doubt.

94 An officer attached to the government of Venice.
100 Good breeding.
110 Assume.
115 Come, come.
124 Immediate.
125 A province in Spain.
126 The east.   129 A quarantine area.

PEREGRINE Indeed, sir!

SIR POLITICK Or—I will lose my labour.

PEREGRINE 'My faith, that's much.

SIR POLITICK Nay, sir, conceive me. It will cost me in onions,   135
    Some thirty livres—*

PEREGRINE Which is one pound sterling.

SIR POLITICK Beside my water-works: for this I do, sir.
    First, I bring in your ship 'twixt two brick walls;
    But those the state shall venture: On the one   140
    I strain* me a fair tarpaulin, and in that
    I stick my onions, cut in halves; the other
    Is full of loop-holes, out at which I thrust
    The noses of my bellows; and those bellows
    I keep, with water-works, in perpetual motion   145
    (Which is the easiest matter of a hundred).
    Now, sir, your onion, which doth naturally
    Attract the infection, and your bellows blowing
    The air upon him,* will show, instantly,
    By his changed colour, if there be contagion;   150
    Or else remain as fair as at the first.
    —Now it is known, 'tis nothing.

PEREGRINE You are right, sir.

SIR POLITICK I would I had my note.

PEREGRINE 'Faith, so would I: 155
    But you have done well for once, sir.

SIR POLITICK Were I false,
    Or would be made so, I could show you reasons
    How I could sell this state now to the Turk,
    Spite of their galleys or their— (*Examining his papers*)   160

PEREGRINE Pray you, sir Pol.

SIR POLITICK I have them not about me.

PEREGRINE That I fear'd:
    They are there, sir?

SIR POLITICK No, this is my diary,   165
    Wherein I note my actions of the day.

PEREGRINE Pray you, let's see, sir. What is here? (*Reads*) *Notandum*,*
    A rat had gnawn my spur-leathers; notwithstanding,
    I put on new, and did go forth: but first
    I threw three beans over the threshold. *Item*,*   170
    I went and bought two tooth-picks, whereof one
    I burst immediately, in a discourse
    With a Dutch merchant, 'bout *ragion del stato*.*

136 Old French money.
141 Stretch.
149 It.
167 "Note."
170 "And in addition."   173 Affairs of state.

From him I went and paid a *moccinigo*
For piecing* my silk stockings; by the way
I cheapen'd sprats;* and at St. Mark's I urined.   175
'Faith, these are politic notes!
SIR POLITICK Sir, I do slip*
No action of my life, but thus I quote it.
PEREGRINE Believe me, it is wise!   180
SIR POLITICK Nay, sir, read forth.

(*Enter, at a distance,* LADY POLITICK WOULD-BE, NANO, *and two*
WAITING-WOMEN)

LADY POLITICK Where should this loose knight be, trow? Sure he's housed.
NANO Why, then he's fast.*   185
LADY POLITICK Ay, he plays both* with me.
I pray you stay. This heat will do more harm
To my complexion, than his heart is worth.
(I do not care to hinder, but to take him.)
How it comes off! (*Rubbing her cheeks*)   190
1ST WOMAN My master's yonder.
LADY POLITICK Where?
2ND WOMAN With a young gentleman.
LADY POLITICK That same's the party;
In man's apparel! 'Pray you, sir, jog* my knight: 195
I will be tender to his reputation,
However he demerit.*
SIR POLITICK (*Seeing her*) My lady!
PEREGRINE Where?
SIR POLITICK 'Tis she indeed, sir; you shall know her. She is,   200
Were she not mine, a lady of that merit,
For fashion and behaviour; and for beauty
I durst compare—
PEREGRINE It seems you are not jealous,
That dare commend her.   205
SIR POLITICK Nay, and for discourse—
PEREGRINE Being your wife, she cannot miss that.
SIR POLITICK (*Introducing* PEREGRINE) Madam,
Here is a gentleman, pray you, use him fairly;
He seems a youth, but he is—   210
LADY POLITICK None?
SIR POLITICK Yes, one
Has put his face as soon into the world—
LADY POLITICK You mean, as early? But to-day?

175 Mending.
176 Small fish.
178 Pass over.
185 Secure.
186 Both fast and loose.
195 Nudge.
197 That is, however much he is at fault.

SIR POLITICK How's this?

LADY POLITICK Why, in this habit, sir; you apprehend me.
    Well, master Would-be, this doth not become you;
    I had thought the odour, sir, of your good name
    Had been more precious to you; that you would not
    Have done this dire massacre on your honour;   220
    One of your gravity and rank besides!
    But knights, I see, care little for the oath
    They make to ladies; chiefly, their own ladies.

SIR POLITICK Now, by my spurs, the symbol of my knighthood,—

PEREGRINE (*Aside*) Lord, how his brain is humbled for an oath!   225

SIR POLITICK I reach you not.*

LADY POLITICK Right, sir, your policy*
    May bear it through thus.—(*To* PEREGRINE) Sir, a word with you.
    I would be loath to contest publicly
    With any gentlewoman, or to seem   230
    Forward, or violent, as the courtier* says;
    It comes too near rusticity in a lady,
    Which I would shun by all means: and however
    I may deserve from master Would-be, yet
    T'have one fair gentlewoman thus be made   235
    The unkind instrument to wrong another,
    And one she knows not, ay, and to persevere;
    In my poor judgment, is not warranted
    From being a solecism* in our sex,
    If not in manners.   240

PEREGRINE How is this!

SIR POLITICK Sweet madam,
    Come nearer to your aim.

LADY POLITICK Marry, and will, sir.
    Since you provoke me with your impudence,   245
    And laughter of your light land-siren here,
    Your Sporus,* your hermaphrodite—

PEREGRINE What's here?
    Poetic fury, and historic storms!

SIR POLITICK The gentleman, believe it, is of worth,   250
    And of our nation.

LADY POLITICK Ay, your White-friars* nation!
    Come, I blush for you, master Would-be, I;
    And am asham'd you should have no more forehead,*

---

226 That is, I don't understand you.

227 Cunning.

231 Baldassare Castiglione (1478–1529), whose book *The Courtier* set forth the rules for the courtier's conduct.

239 Impropriety.

247 A court favorite whom Nero had castrated and then married in a mock-ceremony.

252 A precinct of London well known for its criminals.

254 Shame.

Than thus to be the patron, or St. George,   255
To a lewd harlot, a base fricatrice,*
A female devil, in a male outside.
SIR POLITICK Nay,
An you be such a one, I must bid adieu
To your delights. The case appears too liquid.* (*Exit*)   260
LADY POLITICK Ay, you may carry't clear, with your state-face!*—
But for your carnival concupiscence,*
Who here is fled for liberty of conscience,
From furious persecution of the marshal,*
Her will I dis'ple.*   265
PEREGRINE This is fine, i'faith!
And do you use this often? Is this part
Of your wit's exercise, 'gainst you have occasion?*
Madam—
LADY POLITICK Go to, sir.   270
PEREGRINE Do you hear me, lady?
Why, if your knight have set you to beg shirts,
Or to invite me home, you might have done it
A nearer way,* by far.
LADY POLITICK This cannot work you   275
Out of my snare.
PEREGRINE Why, am I in it, then?
Indeed your husband told me you were fair,
And so you are; only your nose inclines,
That side that's next the sun, to the queen-apple.*   280
LADY POLITICK This cannot be endur'd by any patience.
                          (*Enter* MOSCA)
MOSCA What is the matter, madam?
LADY POLITICK If the senate
Right not my quest in this, I will protest them   285
To all the world, no aristocracy.
MOSCA What is the injury, lady?
LADY POLITICK Why, the callet*
You told me of, here I have ta'en disguised.
MOSCA Who? This? What means your ladyship? The creature   290
I mention'd to you is apprehended now,
Before the senate; you shall see her—

256 Prostitute.
260 Clear.
261 Official appearance.
262 That is, this woman as lewd as carnival-time.
264 Lady Would-Be assumes that Peregrine, like the Puritans, has fled England for greater freedom.
265 Discipline.
268 That is, in preparation for the time when you'll need it.
274 A more direct way.
280 That is, your nose is red.
288 Whore.

LADY POLITICK   Where?

MOSCA   I'll bring you to her. This young gentleman,
   I saw him land this morning at the port.   295

LADY POLITICK   Is't possible! How has my judgment wander'd?
   Sir, I must, blushing, say to you, I have err'd;
   And plead your pardon.

PEREGRINE   What, more changes yet?

LADY POLITICK   I hope you have not the malice to remember   300
   A gentlewoman's passion. If you stay
   In Venice here, please you to use me,* sir—

MOSCA   Will you go, madam?

LADY POLITICK   'Pray you, sir, use me; in faith,
   The more you see me, the more I shall conceive   305
   You have forgot our quarrel.

      (*Exeunt* LADY WOULD-BE, MOSCA, NANO, *and* WAITING-WOMEN)

PEREGRINE   This is rare!
   Sir Politick Would-be? No; sir Politick Bawd,
   To bring me thus acquainted with his wife!   310
   Well, wise sir Pol, since you have practised thus
   Upon my freshman-ship, I'll try your salt-head,*
   What proof it is against a counter-plot. (*Exit*)

Scene 2

The Scrutineo, or Senate-House
     (*Enter* VOLTORE, CORBACCIO, CORVINO, *and* MOSCA)   315

VOLTORE   Well, now you know the carriage* of the business,
   Your constancy is all that is required
   Unto the safety of it.

MOSCA   Is the lie
   Safely convey'd amongst us? Is that sure?   320
   Knows every man his burden?

CORVINO   Yes.

MOSCA   Then shrink not.

CORVINO   But knows the advocate the truth?

MOSCA   O, sir,   325
   By no means; I devised a formal* tale,
   That salv'd your reputation. But be valiant, sir.

CORVINO   I fear no one but him, that this his pleading
   Should make him stand a co-heir—

MOSCA   Co-halter!*   330
   Hang him; we will but use his tongue, his noise,
   As we do croakers* here.

302 Frequent my company.
312 Experience.   316 Conduct.
326 Circumstantial.
330 "Halter" in the sense of hangman's noose.
332 Corbaccio.

CORVINO Ay, what shall he do?

MOSCA When we have done, you mean?

CORVINO Yes.   335

MOSCA Why, we'll think:
Sell him for mummia;* he's half dust already. (*To* VOLTORE)
Do you not smile, to see this buffalo,*
How he doth sport it with his head?—(*Aside*) I should,
If all were well and past.—(*To* CORBACCIO) Sir, only you   340
Are he that shall enjoy the crop of all,
And these not know for whom they toil.

CORBACCIO Ay, peace.

MOSCA (*Turning to* CORVINO) But you shall eat it. (*Aside*) Much!—(*To*
VOLTORE) Worshipful sir,   345
Mercury sit upon your thundering tongue,
Or the French Hercules,* and make your language
As conquering as his club, to beat along,
(As with a tempest) flat, our adversaries;
But much more yours, sir.   350

VOLTORE Here they come, have done.

MOSCA I have another witness, if you need, sir,
I can produce.

VOLTORE Who is it?

MOSCA Sir, I have her.   355

    (*Enter* AVOCATORI *and take their seats,* BONARIO, CELIA, NOTARIO,
        COMMANDADORI, SAFFI, *and other* OFFICERS *of justice*)

1ST AVOC. The like of this the senate never heard of.

2ND AVOC. 'Twill come most strange to them when we report it.

4TH AVOC. The gentlewoman has been ever held   360
Of unreproved name.

3RD AVOC. So has the youth.

4TH AVOC. The more unnatural part that of his father.

2ND AVOC. More of the husband.

1ST AVOC. I not know to give   365
His act a name, it is so monstrous!

4TH AVOC. But the impostor, he's a thing created
To exceed example!

1ST AVOC. And all after-times!*

2ND AVOC. I never heard a true voluptuary   370
Described, but him.

3RD AVOC. Appear yet those were cited?

NOTARIO All but the old magnifico, Volpone.

1ST AVOC. Why is not he here?

MOSCA Please your fatherhoods,   375

---

[337] Dead flesh that was ground to powder and used in medicines.

[338] That is, with horns; Corvino.

[347] Patron of eloquence.

[369] Future time.

Here is his advocate: himself's so weak,
So feeble—

4TH AVOC.   What are you?

BONARIO   His parasite,
His knave, his pander: I beseech the court,   380
He may be forced to come, that your grave eyes
May bear strong witness of his strange impostures.*

VOLTORE   Upon my faith and credit with your virtues,
He is not able to endure the air.

2ND AVOC.   Bring him, however.   385

3RD AVOC.   We will see him.

4TH AVOC.   Fetch him.

VOLTORE   Your fatherhoods' fit pleasures be obey'd; (*Exeunt* OFFICERS)
But sure, the sight will rather move your pities,
Than indignation. May it please the court,   390
In the mean time, he may be heard in me;
I know this place most void of prejudice,
And therefore crave it, since we have no reason
To fear our truth should hurt our cause.

3RD AVOC.   Speak free.   395

VOLTORE   Then know, most honour'd fathers, I must now
Discover to your strangely abused ears,
The most prodigious and most frontless* piece
Of solid impudence, and treachery,
That ever vicious nature yet brought forth   400
To shame the state of Venice. This lewd woman
(That wants no artificial looks or tears
To help the vizor she has now put on),
Hath long been known a close* adulteress
To that lascivious youth there; not suspected,   405
I say, but known, and taken in the act
With him; and by this man, the easy husband,
Pardon'd; whose timeless* bounty makes him now
Stand here, the most unhappy, innocent person,
That ever man's own goodness made accused.   410
For these, not knowing how to owe* a gift
Of that dear grace,* but with their shame; being placed
So above all powers of their gratitude,
Began to hate the benefit; and, in place
Of thanks, devise to extirp* the memory   415
Of such an act. Wherein I pray your fatherhoods

382 Frauds.
398 Shameless.
404 Secret.
408 Badly timed.
411 Own.
412 Preciousness.
415 Root out.

To observe the malice, yea, the rage of creatures
Discover'd in their evils; and what heart
Such take, even from their crimes:—but that anon
Will more appear.—This gentleman, the father,   420
Hearing of this foul fact, with many others,
Which daily struck at his too tender ears,
And grieved in nothing more than that he could not
Preserve himself a parent (his son's ills
Growing to that strange flood), at last decreed   425
To disinherit him.

1ST AVOC.   These be strange turns!

2ND AVOC.   The young man's fame was ever fair and honest.

VOLTORE   So much more full of danger is his vice,
That can beguile so under shade of virtue.   430
But, as I said, my honour'd sires, his father
Having this settled purpose (by what means
To him betray'd, we know not), and this day
Appointed for the deed, that parricide
(I cannot style him better), by confederacy   435
Preparing this his paramour to be there,
Enter'd Volpone's house (who was the man,
Your fatherhoods must understand, design'd
For the inheritance), there sought his father:—
But with what purpose sought he him, my lords?   440
I tremble to pronounce it, that a son
Unto a father, and to such a father,
Should have so foul, felonious intent!
It was to murder him: when being prevented
By his more happy absence, what then did he?   445
Not check his wicked thoughts; no, now new deeds
(Mischief doth never end where it begins),
An act of horror, fathers! He dragg'd forth
The aged gentleman that had there lain bed-rid
Three years and more, out of his innocent couch,   450
Naked upon the floor, there left him; wounded
His servant in the face; and, with this strumpet
The stale* to his forged practice, who was glad
To be so active—I shall here desire
Your fatherhoods to note but my collections,*   455
As most remarkable—thought at once to stop
His father's ends, discredit his free choice
In the old gentleman, redeem themselves,
By laying infamy upon this man,
To whom, with blushing, they should owe their lives.   460

1ST AVOC.   What proofs have you of this?

453 Decoy.
455 Conclusion.

BONARIO   Most honoured fathers,
    I humbly crave there be no credit given
    To this man's mercenary tongue.
2ND AVOC.   Forbear.   465
BONARIO   His soul moves in his fee.
3RD AVOC.   O, sir.
BONARIO   This fellow,
    For six sols* more, would plead against his Maker.
1ST AVOC.   You do forget yourself.   470
VOLTORE   Nay, nay, grave fathers,
    Let him have scope: can any man imagine
    That he will spare his accuser, that would not
    Have spared his parent?
1ST AVOC.   Well, produce your proofs.   475
CELIA   I would I could forget I were a creature.
VOLTORE   Signior Corbaccio! (CORBACCIO *comes forward*)
4TH AVOC.   What is he?
VOLTORE   The father.
2ND AVOC.   Has he had an oath?   480
NOTARIO   Yes.
CORBACCIO   What must I do now?
NOTARIO   Your testimony's craved.
CORBACCIO   Speak to the knave?
    I'll have my mouth first stopped with earth; my heart   485
    Abhors his knowledge:* I disclaim in him.
1ST AVOC.   But for what cause?
CORBACCIO   The mere portent* of nature!
    He is an utter stranger to my loins.
BONARIO   Have they made you to this?   490
CORBACCIO   I will not hear thee,
    Monster of men, swine, goat, wolf, parricide!
    Speak not, thou viper.
BONARIO   Sir, I will sit down,
    And rather wish my innocence should suffer,   495
    Than I resist the authority of a father.
VOLTORE   Signior Corvino! (CORVINO *comes forward*)
2ND AVOC.   This is strange.
1ST AVOC.   Who's this?
NOTARIO   The husband.   500
4TH AVOC.   Is he sworn?
NOTARIO   He is.
3RD AVOC.   Speak, then.
CORVINO   This woman, please your fatherhoods, is a whore,

469 Pence.
486 Knowing him.
488 Monster.

Of most hot exercise, more than a partridge,*   505
    Upon record—
1ST AVOC.   No more.
CORVINO   Neighs like a jennet.*
NOTARIO   Preserve the honour of the court.
CORVINO   I shall,   510
    And modesty of your most reverend ears.
    And yet I hope that I may say, these eyes
    Have seen her glued unto that piece of cedar,
    That fine well-timber'd gallant; and that here (*Points to his own forehead*)
    The letters may be read, thorough the horn,*   515
    That makes the story perfect.
MOSCA   Excellent! sir.
CORVINO (*Aside to* MOSCA)   There is no shame in this now, is there?
MOSCA   None.
CORVINO   Or if I said, I hoped that she were onward   520
    To her damnation, if there be a hell
    Greater than whore and woman; a good catholic
    May make the doubt.
3RD AVOC.   His grief hath made him frantic.
1ST AVOC.   Remove him hence.
2ND AVOC.   Look to the woman. (CELIA *swoons*)   525
CORVINO   Rare!
    Prettily feign'd, again!
4TH AVOC.   Stand from about her.
1ST AVOC.   Give her the air.
3RD AVOC. (*To* MOSCA)   What can you say?   530
MOSCA   My wound,
    May it please your wisdoms, speaks for me, received
    In aid of my good patron, when he missed
    His sought-for father, when that well-taught dame   535
    Had her cue given to her, to cry out, A rape!
BONARIO   O, most laid* impudence! Fathers—
3RD AVOC.   Sir, be silent;
    You had your hearing free, so must they theirs.
2ND AVOC.   I do begin to doubt the imposture here.   540
4TH AVOC.   This woman has too many moods.
VOLTORE   Grave fathers,
    She is a creature of a most professed
    And prostituted lewdness.
CORVINO   Most impetuous,   545
    Unsatisfied, grave fathers!

---

505 Reputed to be lascivious.
508 A mare in heat.
515 The letter "V," sign of the cuckold.
537 Well planned.

VOLTORE May her feignings
Not take your wisdoms: but this day she baited
A stranger, a grave knight, with her loose eyes,
And more lascivious kisses. This man saw them   550
Together on the water, in a gondola.

MOSCA Here is the lady herself, that saw them too,
Without; who then had in the open streets
Pursued them, but for saving her knight's honour.

1ST AVOC. Produce that lady.   555

2ND AVOC. Let her come. (*Exit* MOSCA)

4TH AVOC. These things,
They strike with wonder.

3RD AVOC. I am turn'd a stone.

           (*Re-enter* MOSCA *with* LADY WOULD-BE)   560

MOSCA Be resolute, madam.

LADY POLITICK Ay, this same is she. (*Pointing to* CELIA)
Out, thou camelion* harlot! Now thine eyes
Vie tears with the hyæna.* Dar'st thou look
Upon my wronged face?—I cry your pardons,   565
I fear I have forgettingly transgressed
Against the dignity of the court—

2ND AVOC. No, madam.

LADY POLITICK And been exorbitant*—

2ND AVOC. You have not, lady.   570

4TH AVOC. These proofs are strong.

LADY POLITICK Surely, I had no purpose
To scandalise your honours, or my sex's.

3RD AVOC. We do believe it.

LADY POLITICK Surely, you may believe it.   575

2ND AVOC. Madam, we do.

LADY POLITICK Indeed you may; my breeding
Is not so coarse—

4TH AVOC. We know it.

LADY POLITICK To offend   580
With pertinacy*—

3RD AVOC. Lady—

LADY POLITICK Such a presence!
No surely.

1ST AVOC. We well think it.   585

LADY POLITICK You may think it.

1ST AVOC. Let her o'ercome. What witnesses have you
To make good your report?

BONARIO Our consciences.

---

563 Chameleon, hence changeable.
564 The hyena, notorious for its cunning, was reputed to imitate human voices, laughter, and tears.
569 Out of order.
581 Impertinence.

CELIA   And heaven, that never fails the innocent.
4TH AVOC.   These are no testimonies.
BONARIO   Not in your courts,
        Where multitude, and clamour overcomes.
1ST AVOC.   Nay, then you do wax insolent.
                    (*Re-enter* OFFICERS, *bearing* VOLPONE *on a couch*)   595
VOLTORE   Here, here,
        The testimony comes, that will convince,
        And put to utter dumbness their bold tongues.
        See here, grave fathers, here's the ravisher,
        The rider on men's wives, the great imposter,   600
        The grand voluptuary! Do you not think
        These limbs should affect venery?* Or these eyes
        Covet a concubine? Pray you mark these hands;
        Are they not fit to stroke a lady's breasts?—
        Perhaps he doth dissemble!   605
BONARIO   So he does.
VOLTORE   Would you have him tortured?
BONARIO   I would have him proved.
VOLTORE   Best try him then with goads,* or burning irons;
        Put him to the *strappado:** I have heard   610
        The rack hath cured the gout; 'faith, give it him,
        And help him of a malady; be courteous.
        I'll undertake, before these honour'd fathers,
        He shall have yet as many left diseases,
        As she has known adulterers, or thou strumpets.—   615
        O, most equal* hearers, if these deeds,
        Acts of this bold and most exorbitant strain,
        May pass with sufferance, what one citizen
        But owes the forfeit of his life, yea, fame,
        To him that dares traduce him? Which of you   620
        Are safe, my honour'd fathers? I would ask,
        With leave of your grave fatherhoods, if their plot
        Have any face or colour like to truth?
        Or if, unto the dullest nostril here,
        It smell not rank, and most abhorred slander?   625
        I crave your care of this good gentleman,
        Whose life is much endanger'd by their fable;
        And as for them, I will conclude with this,
        That vicious persons, when they're hot and flesh'd*
        In impious acts, their constancy abounds: 630
        Damn'd deeds are done with greatest confidence.

---

602 Sexual pleasure.
609 Pointed sticks.
610 Instrument for stretching and breaking the limbs.
616 Just.
629 Hardened.

1ST AVOC. Take them to custody, and sever them.

2ND AVOC. 'Tis pity two such prodigies should live.

1ST AVOC. Let the old gentleman be return'd with care.

(Exeunt OFFICERS with VOLPONE) 635

I'm sorry your credulity hath wrong'd him.

4TH AVOC. These are two creatures!

3RD AVOC. I've an earthquake in me.

2ND AVOC. Their shame, even in their cradles, fled their faces.

4TH AVOC. (To VOLTORE) You have done a worthy service to the state, sir, 640
In their discovery.

1ST AVOC. You shall hear, ere night,
What punishment the court decrees upon them. (Exeunt AVOCATORI,
NOTARIO, and OFFICERS with BONARIO and CELIA)

VOLTORE We thank your fatherhoods.—How like you it? 645

MOSCA Rare.
I'd have your tongue, sir, tipped with gold for this;
I'd have you be the heir to the whole city;
The earth I'd have want* men, ere you want living:
They're bound to erect your statue in St. Mark's. 650
Signior Corvino, I would have you go
And show yourself, that you have conquer'd.

CORVINO Yes.

MOSCA It was much better that you should profess
Yourself a cuckold thus, than that the other 655
Should have been proved.

CORVINO Nay, I consider'd that:
Now it is her fault.

MOSCA Then, it had been yours.

CORVINO True; I do doubt this advocate still. 660

MOSCA I'faith
You need not, I dare ease you of that care.

CORVINO I trust thee, Mosca. (Exit)

MOSCA As your own soul, sir.

CORBACCIO Mosca! 665

MOSCA Now for your business, sir.

CORBACCIO How! Have you business?

MOSCA Yes, your's, sir.

CORBACCIO O, none else?

MOSCA None else, not I. 670

CORBACCIO Be careful, then.

MOSCA Rest you with both your eyes, sir.

CORBACCIO Dispatch it.

MOSCA Instantly.

CORBACCIO And look that all, 675
Whatever, be put in, jewels, plate, moneys,
Household stuff, bedding, curtains.

[649] Lack.

170 JONSON

MOSCA   Curtain-rings, sir:
    Only the advocate's fee must be deducted.
CORBACCIO   I'll pay him now; you'll be too prodigal.   680
MOSCA   Sir, I must tender it.
CORBACCIO   Two chequines is well.
MOSCA   No, six, sir.
CORBACCIO   'Tis too much.
MOSCA   He talk'd a great while;   685
    You must consider that, sir.
CORBACCIO   Well, there's three—
MOSCA   I'll give it him.
CORBACCIO   Do so, and there's for thee. (*Exit*)
MOSCA   (*Aside*)   Bountiful bones! What horrid strange offence   690
    Did he commit 'gainst nature, in his youth,
    Worthy this age?—(*To* VOLTORE) You see, sir, how I work
    Unto your ends; take you no notice.
VOLTORE   No,
    I'll leave you. (*Exit*)   695
MOSCA   All is yours, the devil and all:
    Good advocate!—Madam, I'll bring you home.
LADY POLITICK   No, I'll go see your patron.
MOSCA   That you shall not:
    I'll tell you why. My purpose is to urge   700
    My patron to reform his Will; and for
    The zeal you have shown to-day, whereas before
    You were but third or fourth, you shall be now
    Put in the first: which would appear as begg'd,
    If you were present. Therefore—   705
LADY POLITICK   You shall sway me. (*Exeunt*)

Act Five

Scene 1

A Room in Volpone's House
(*Enter* VOLPONE)

VOLPONE   Well, I am here, and all this brunt* is past.
    I ne'er was in dislike with my disguise
    'Till this fled moment: here 'twas good, in private;
    But in your public,—*cave** whilst I breathe.   5
    'Fore God, my left leg 'gan to have the cramp,
    And I apprehended straight some power had struck me
    With a dead palsy:* Well! I must be merry,
    And shake it off. A many of these fears   10

3 Stress.
6 "Beware."
9 Paralysis.

Would put me into some villainous disease,
Should they come thick upon me: I'll prevent 'em.
Give me a bowl of lusty wine, to fright
This humour from my heart. (*Drinks*)—Hum, hum, hum!
'Tis almost gone already; I shall conquer.   15
Any device, now, of rare ingenious knavery,
That would possess me with a violent laughter,
Would make me up again. (*Drinks again*)—So, so, so, so!
This heat is life; 'tis blood by this time:—Mosca!
          (*Enter* MOSCA)   20
MOSCA How now, sir? Does the day look clear again?
  Are we recover'd, and wrought* out of error,
  Into our way, to see our path before us?
  Is our trade free once more?
VOLPONE Exquisite Mosca!   25
MOSCA Was it not carried learnedly?
VOLPONE And stoutly:
  Good wits are greatest in extremities.
MOSCA It were a folly beyond thought, to trust
  Any grand act unto a cowardly spirit: 30
  You are not taken with it enough, methinks.
VOLPONE O, more than if I had enjoy'd the wench:
  The pleasure of all woman-kind's not like it.
MOSCA Why now you speak, sir. We must here be fix'd;
  Here we must rest; this is our master-piece;   35
  We cannot think to go beyond this.
VOLPONE True,
  Thou hast play'd thy prize, my precious Mosca.
MOSCA Nay, sir,
  To gull the court—   40
VOLPONE And quite divert the torrent
  Upon the innocent.
MOSCA Yes, and to make
  So rare a music out of discords—
VOLPONE Right.   45
  That yet to me's the strangest, how thou hast borne it!
  That these, being so divided 'mongst themselves,
  Should not scent somewhat, or in me or thee,
  Or doubt their own side.
MOSCA True, they will not see't.   50
  Too much light blinds them, I think. Each of them
  Is so possessed and stuffed with his own hopes,
  That any thing unto the contrary,
  Never so true, or never so apparent,
  Never so palpable, they will resist it—   55
VOLPONE Like a temptation of the devil.

²² Dug.

MOSCA   Right, sir.
Merchants may talk of trade, and your great signiors
Of land that yields well; but if Italy
Have any glebe* more fruitful than these fellows,
I am deceiv'd. Did not your advocate rare?

VOLPONE   O—*My most honour'd fathers, my grave fathers,*
Under correction of your fatherhoods,
What face of truth is here? If these strange deeds
May pass, most honour'd fathers—I had much ado
To forbear laughing.

MOSCA   It seem'd to me, you sweat, sir.

VOLPONE   In troth, I did a little.

MOSCA   But confess, sir,
Were you not daunted?

VOLPONE   In good faith, I was
A little in a mist, but not dejected;
Never, but still my self.

MOSCA   I think it, sir.
Now, so truth help me, I must needs say this, sir,
And out of conscience for your advocate,
He has taken pains, in faith, sir, and deserv'd
(In my poor judgment, I speak it under favour,
Not to contrary you, sir), very richly—
Well—to be cozen'd.*

VOLPONE   Troth, and I think so too,
By that I heard him, in the latter end.

MOSCA   O, but before, sir: had you heard him first
Draw it to certain heads,* then aggravate,*
Then use his vehement figures*—I look'd still
When he would shift a shirt:* and, doing this
Out of pure love, no hope of gain—

VOLPONE   'Tis right.
I cannot answer him, Mosca, as I would,
Not yet; but for thy sake, at thy entreaty,
I will begin, even now—to vex them all,
This very instant.

MOSCA   Good sir.

VOLPONE   Call the dwarf
And eunuch forth.

MOSCA   Castrone, Nano!

(*Enter* CASTRONE *and* NANO)

NANO   Here.

60 Soil.
80 Cheated.
84 (*a*) That is, arrange the speech in different ways. (*b*) Stress or emphasize.
85 Rhetorical devices.
86 By gesturing wildly.

VOLPONE   Shall we have a jig now?

MOSCA   What you please, sir.   100

VOLPONE   Go,
    Straight give out about the streets, you two,
    That I am dead; do it with constancy,
    Sadly, do you hear? impute it to the grief
    Of this late slander. (*Exeunt* CASTRONE *and* NANO)   105

MOSCA   What do you mean, sir?

VOLPONE   O,
    I shall have instantly my Vulture, Crow,
    Raven, come flying hither, on the news,
    To peck for carrion, my she-wolf, and all,   110
    Greedy, and full of expectation—

MOSCA   And then to have it ravish'd from their mouths!

VOLPONE   'Tis true. I will have thee put on a gown,
    And take upon thee, as thou wert mine heir:
    Show them a will: Open that chest, and reach   115
    Forth one of those that has the blanks; I'll straight
    Put in thy name.

MOSCA   It will be rare, sir. (*Gives him a paper*)

VOLPONE   Ay,
    When they ev'n gape, and find themselves deluded—   120

MOSCA   Yes.

VOLPONE   And thou use them scurvily!
    Dispatch, get on thy gown.

MOSCA (*Putting on a gown*)   But what, sir, if they ask
    After the body?   125

VOLPONE   Say, it was corrupted.

MOSCA   I'll say, it stunk, sir; and was fain* to have it
    Coffin'd up instantly, and sent away.

VOLPONE   Any thing; what thou wilt. Hold, here's my will.
    Get thee a cap, a count-book, pen and ink,   130
    Papers afore thee; sit as thou wert taking
    An inventory of parcels: I'll get up
    Behind the curtain, on a stool, and hearken;
    Sometime peep over, see how they do look,
    With what degrees their blood doth leave their faces.   135
    O, 'twill afford me a rare meal of laughter!

MOSCA (*Putting on a cap, and setting out the table, etc.*)
    Your advocate will turn stark dull upon it.

VOLPONE   It will take off his oratory's edge.

MOSCA   But your *clarissimo,** old round-back, he   140
    Will crump* you like a hog-louse, with the touch.

---

[127] Obliged.

[140] Venetian grandee; here Corbaccio.

[141] That is, he will bend you like a hog-louse (woodlouse).

174   JONSON

VOLPONE And what Corvino?

MOSCA O, sir, look for him,
To-morrow morning, with a rope and dagger,
To visit all the streets; he must run mad.
My lady too, that came into the court,   145
To bear false witness for your worship—

VOLPONE Yes,
And kiss'd me 'fore the fathers, when my face
Flow'd all with oils.

MOSCA And sweat, sir. Why, your gold   150
Is such another med'cine, it dries up
All those offensive savours:* it transforms
The most deformed, and restores them lovely,
As 'twere the strange poetical girdle.* Jove   155
Could not invent t' himself a shroud more subtle
To pass Acrisius' guards.* It is the thing
Makes all the world her grace, her youth, her beauty.

VOLPONE I think she loves me.

MOSCA Who? The lady, sir?   160
She's jealous of you.

VOLPONE Dost thou say so? (*Knocking within*)

MOSCA Hark,
There's some already.

VOLPONE Look.

MOSCA It is the Vulture;   165
He has the quickest scent.

VOLPONE I'll to my place,
Thou to thy posture. (*Goes behind the curtain*)

MOSCA I am set.

VOLPONE But, Mosca,   170
Play the artificer* now, torture them rarely.

(*Enter* VOLTORE)

VOLTORE How now, my Mosca?

MOSCA (*Writing*) Turkey carpets, nine—   175

VOLTORE Taking an inventory! That is well.

MOSCA Two suits* of bedding, tissue—*

VOLTORE Where's the Will?
Let me read that the while.

(*Enter* SERVANTS, *with* CORBACCIO *in a chair*)   180

CORBACCIO So, set me down,
And get you home. (*Exeunt* SERVANTS)

---

153 Smells.

155 Venus' belt, with love and beauty woven into it.

157 Jove entered the chamber of Danaë, Acrisius' daughter, as a shower of gold.

172 Trickster.

177 (*a*) Sets.   (*b*) Cloth with gold thread.

VOLTORE Is he come now, to trouble us?

MOSCA Of cloth of gold, two more—

CORBACCIO Is it done, Mosca? 185

MOSCA Of several velvets eight—

VOLTORE I like his care.

CORBACCIO Dost thou not hear?

(Enter CORVINO*)*

CORBACCIO Ha! is the hour come, Mosca? 190

VOLPONE *(Peeping over the curtain)* Ay, now they muster.

CORVINO What does the advocate here,
Or this Corbaccio?

CORBACCIO What do these here?

(Enter LADY POLITICK WOULD-BE*)* 195

LADY POLITICK Mosca!
Is his thread spun?

MOSCA Eight chests of linen—

VOLPONE O,
My fine dame Would-be, too! 200

CORVINO Mosca, the Will,
That I may show it these, and rid them hence.

MOSCA Six chests of diaper,* four of damask.—There. *(Gives them the Will
carelessly, over his shoulder)*

CORBACCIO Is that the Will? 205

MOSCA Down-beds and bolsters—

VOLPONE Rare!
Be busy still. Now they begin to flutter:
They never think of me. Look, see, see, see!
How their swift eyes run over the long deed, 210
Unto the name, and to the legacies,
What is bequeathed them there—

MOSCA Ten suits of hangings—

VOLPONE Ay, in their garters,* Mosca. Now their hopes
Are at the gasp.* 215

VOLTORE Mosca the heir!

CORBACCIO What's that?

VOLPONE My advocate is dumb; look to my merchant.
He has heard of some strange storm, a ship is lost,
He faints; my lady will swoon. Old glazen eyes, 220
He hath not reach'd his despair yet.

CORBACCIO All these
Are out of hope; I am, sure, the man. *(Takes the Will)*

CORVINO But, Mosca—

MOSCA Two cabinets. 225

---

203 Fine linen.
214 That is, they will hang themselves in their garters.
215 Near death.

CORVINO Is this in earnest?

MOSCA One
Of ebony—

CORVINO Or do you but delude me?

MOSCA The other, mother of pearl—I am very busy. 230
Good faith, it is a fortune thrown upon me—
Item, one salt* of agate—not my seeking.

LADY POLITICK Do you hear, sir?

MOSCA A perfumed box—'Pray you forbear,
You see I'm troubled—made of an onyx— 235

LADY POLITICK How!

MOSCA To-morrow or next day, I shall be at leisure
To talk with you all.

CORVINO Is this my large hope's issue?

LADY POLITICK Sir, I must have a fairer answer. 240

MOSCA Madam!
Marry, and shall: 'pray you, fairly quit my house.
Nay, raise no tempest with your looks; but hark you,
Remember what your ladyship offer'd me
To put you in an heir; go to, think on it: 245
And what you said e'en your best madams did
For maintenance; and why not you? Enough.
Go home, and use the poor sir Pol, your knight, well,
For fear I tell some riddles; go, be melancholy. (*Exit* LADY WOULD-BE)

VOLPONE O, my fine devil! 250

CORVINO Mosca, 'pray you a word.

MOSCA Lord! Will you not take your dispatch hence yet?
Methinks, of all, you should have been the example.
Why should you stay here? With what thoughts, what promise?
Hear you; do you not know, I know you an ass, 255
And that you would most fain have been a wittol,*
If fortune would have let you? That you are
A declared cuckold, on good terms? This pearl,
You'll say, was yours? Right. This diamond?
I'll not deny't, but thank you. Much here else? 260
It may be so. Why, think that these good works
May help to hide your bad. I'll not betray you;
Although you be but extraordinary,
And have it only in title,* it sufficeth:
Go home, be melancholy too, or mad. (*Exit* CORVINO) 265

VOLPONE Rare Mosca! How his villainy becomes him!

VOLTORE Certain he doth delude all these for me.

CORBACCIO Mosca the heir!

---

232 Salt-cellar.
256 Willing cuckold.
264 That is, although you are only a cuckold in name.

VOLPONE   O, his four eyes have found it.

CORBACCIO   I am cozen'd, cheated, by a parasite slave; 270
   Harlot, thou hast gull'd me.

MOSCA   Yes, sir. Stop your mouth,
   Or I shall draw the only tooth is left.
   Are not you he, that filthy covetous wretch,
   With the three legs, that here, in hope of prey, 275
   Have, any time this three years, snuff'd about,
   With your most grovelling nose, and would have hired
   Me to the poisoning of my patron, sir?
   Are not you he that have to-day in court
   Profess'd the disinheriting of your son? 280
   Perjured yourself? Go home, and die, and stink.
   If you but croak a syllable, all comes out:
   Away, and call your porters! (*Exit* CORBACCIO) Go, go, stink.

VOLPONE   Excellent varlet!*

VOLTORE   Now, my faithful Mosca, 285
   I find thy constancy.

MOSCA   Sir!

VOLTORE   Sincere.

MOSCA (*Writing*)   A table
   Of porphyry*—I marle* you'll be thus troublesome. 290

VOLTORE   Nay, leave off now, they are gone.

MOSCA   Why, who are you?
   What! Who did send for you? O, cry you mercy,
   Reverend sir! Good faith, I am grieved for you,
   That any chance of mine should thus defeat 295
   Your (I must needs say) most deserving travails:
   But I protest, sir, it was cast upon me,
   And I could almost wish to be without it,
   But that the will o' the dead must be observ'd.
   Marry, my joy is that you need it not; 300
   You have a gift, sir (thank your education),
   Will never let you want; while there are men,
   And malice, to breed causes.* Would I had
   But half the like, for all my fortune, sir!
   If I have any suits (as I do hope, 305
   Things being so easy and direct, I shall not),
   I will make bold with your obstreperous aid,
   Conceive me,—for your fee, sir. In mean time,
   You that have so much law, I know have the conscience
   Not to be covetous of what is mine. 310
   Good sir, I thank you for my plate; 'twill help

---

284 Rascal.
290 (*a*) Beautiful red stone.   (*b*) Marvel.
303 Lawsuits.

To set up a young man. Good faith, you look
As you were costive;* best go home and purge, sir. (*Exit* VOLTORE)
VOLPONE (*Comes from behind the curtain*)   Bid him eat lettuce well. My witty
                                                            mischief,   315
Let me embrace thee. O that I could now
Transform thee to a Venus!—Mosca, go,
Straight take my habit of clarissimo,
And walk the streets; be seen, torment them more:
We must pursue, as well as plot. Who would   320
Have lost this feast?
MOSCA   I doubt it will lose them.
VOLPONE   O, my recovery shall recover all.
That I could now but think on some disguise
To meet them in, and ask them questions: 325
How I would vex them still at every turn!
MOSCA   Sir, I can fit you.
VOLPONE   Canst thou?
MOSCA   Yes, I know
One o' the commandadori, sir, so like you;   330
Him will I straight make drunk, and bring you his habit.
VOLPONE   A rare disguise, and answering thy brain!
O, I will be a sharp disease unto them.
MOSCA   Sir, you must look for curses—
VOLPONE   Till they burst;   335
The Fox fares ever best when he is curst. (*Exeunt*)

Scene 2

A Hall in Sir Politick's House
(*Enter* PEREGRINE *disguised, and three* MERCHANTS)

PEREGRINE   Am I enough disguised?
1ST MERCHANT   I warrant you.*   340
PEREGRINE   All my ambition is to fright him only.
2ND MERCHANT   If you could ship him away, 'twere excellent.
3RD MERCHANT   To Zant,* or to Aleppo?*
PEREGRINE   Yes, and have his
Adventures put i' the Book of Voyages,   345
And his gull'd story* register'd for truth.
Well, gentlemen, when I am in a while,
And that you think us warm in our discourse,
Know your approaches.
1ST MERCHANT   Trust it to our care. (*Exeunt* MERCHANTS)   350
                        (*Enter* WAITING-WOMAN)
PEREGRINE   Save you, fair lady! Is sir Pol within?

---

313 Constipated.
340 Assure you.
343 (*a*) An island west of Greece.   (*b*) A city in Syria.
346 The story of his gulling.

WOMAN I do not know, sir.

PEREGRINE Pray you say unto him,
Here is a merchant, upon earnest business,   355
Desires to speak with him.

WOMAN I will see, sir. (*Exit*)

PEREGRINE I pray you.—
I see the family is all female here.

(Re-enter WAITING-WOMAN)   360

WOMAN He says, sir, he has weighty affairs of state,
That now require him whole; some other time
You may possess him.

PEREGRINE Pray you say again,
If those require him whole, these will exact* him,   365
Whereof I bring him tidings. (*Exit* WOMAN)—What might be
His grave affair of state now? How to make
Bolognian sausages here in Venice, sparing
One o' the ingredients?

(Re-enter WAITING-WOMAN)   370

WOMAN Sir, he says, he knows
By your word *tidings*,* that you are no statesman,
And therefore wills you stay.

PEREGRINE Sweet, pray you return him;
I have not read so many proclamations,   375
And studied them for words, as he has done—
But—here he deigns to come. (*Exit* WOMAN)

(Enter SIR POLITICK)

SIR POLITICK Sir, I must crave
Your courteous pardon. There hath chanced to-day,   380
Unkind disaster 'twixt my lady and me;
And I was penning my apology,
To give her satisfaction, as you came now.

PEREGRINE Sir, I am grieved I bring you worse disaster:
The gentleman you met at the port to-day,   385
That told you, he was newly arrived—

SIR POLITICK Ay, was
A fugitive punk?*

PEREGRINE No, sir, a spy set on you;
And he has made relation to the senate,   390
That you professed to him to have a plot
To sell the State of Venice to the Turk.

SIR POLITICK O me!

PEREGRINE For which, warrants are sign'd by this time,
To apprehend you, and to search your study   395
For papers—

---

365 Demand.
372 A statesman would probably have said "intelligence."
388 Prostitute.

SIR POLITICK   Alas, sir, I have none, but notes
   Drawn out of play-books—
PEREGRINE   All the better, sir.
SIR POLITICK   And some essays. What shall I do?   400
PEREGRINE   Sir, best
   Convey yourself into a sugar-chest;
   Or, if you could lie round, a frail* were rare,
   And I could send you aboard.
SIR POLITICK   Sir, I but talk'd so,
   For discourse sake merely. (*Knocking within*)   405
PEREGRINE   Hark! They are there.
SIR POLITICK   I am a wretch, a wretch!
PEREGRINE   What will you do, sir?
   Have you ne'er a currant-butt* to leap into?
   They'll put you to the rack; you must be sudden.   410
SIR POLITICK   Sir, I have an engine*—
3RD MERCHANT (*Within*)   Sir Politick Would-be!
2ND MERCHANT (*Within*)   Where is he?
SIR POLITICK   That I have thought upon before time.
PEREGRINE   What is it?   415
SIR POLITICK   I shall ne'er endure the torture.
   Marry, it is, sir, of a tortoise-shell,
   Fitted for these extremities: pray you, sir, help me.
   Here I've a place, sir, to put back my legs,
   Please you to lay it on, sir (*Lies down while* PEREGRINE *places the shell upon*   420
                                     him)—with this cap,
   And my black gloves. I'll lie, sir, like a tortoise,
   'Till they are gone.
PEREGRINE   And call you this an engine?
SIR POLITICK   Mine own device——Good sir, bid my wife's women   425
   To burn my papers. (*Exit* PEREGRINE)
                    (*The three* MERCHANTS *rush in*)
1ST MERCHANT   Where is he hid?
3RD MERCHANT   We must,
   And will sure find him.   430
2ND MERCHANT   Which is his study?
                    (*Re-enter* PEREGRINE)
1ST MERCHANT   What
   Are you, sir?
PEREGRINE   I am a merchant, that came here   435
   To look upon this tortoise.
3RD MERCHANT   How!
1ST MERCHANT   St. Mark!
   What beast is this?
                                    440

---

[403] Fig-basket.
[410] Barrel for currants.
[412] Contrivance.

PEREGRINE   It is a fish.

2ND MERCHANT   Come out here!

PEREGRINE   Nay, you may strike him, sir, and tread upon him;
    He'll bear a cart.

1ST MERCHANT   What, to run over him?   445

PEREGRINE   Yes, sir.

3RD MERCHANT   Let's jump upon him.

2ND MERCHANT   Can he not go?

PEREGRINE   He creeps; sir.

1ST MERCHANT   Let's see him creep.   450

PEREGRINE   No, good sir, you will hurt him.

2ND MERCHANT   Heart, I will see him creep, or prick his guts.

3RD MERCHANT   Come out here!

PEREGRINE (*Aside to* SIR POLITICK)   Pray you, sir!—Creep a little.

1ST MERCHANT   Forth.   455

2ND MERCHANT   Yet farther.

PEREGRINE   Good, sir!—Creep.

2ND MERCHANT   We'll see his legs. (*They pull off the shell and discover him*)

3RD MERCHANT   Ods so, he has garters!

1ST MERCHANT   Ay, and gloves!   460

2ND MERCHANT   Is this
    Your fearful tortoise?

PEREGRINE (*Discovering himself*)   Now, sir Pol, we are even;
    For your next project I shall be prepared:
    I am sorry for the funeral of your notes, sir.   465

1ST MERCHANT   'Twere a rare motion* to be seen in Fleet-street.

2ND MERCHANT   Ay, in the Term.*

1ST MERCHANT   Or Smithfield, in the fair.

3RD MERCHANT   Methinks 'tis but a melancholy sight.

PEREGRINE   Farewell, most politic tortoise!   470
                (*Exeunt* PEREGRINE *and* MERCHANTS)
                (*Re-enter* WAITING-WOMAN)

SIR POLITICK   Where's my lady?
    Knows she of this?

WOMAN   I know not, sir.   475

SIR POLITICK   Inquire.—
    O, I shall be the fable of all feasts,
    The freight of the *gazetti,** ship-boy's tale;
    And, which is worst, even talk for ordinaries.

WOMAN   My lady's come most melancholy home,   480
    And says, sir, she will straight to sea for physic.

SIR POLITICK   And I to shun this place and clime for ever,
    Creeping with house on back, and think it well
    To shrink my poor head in my politic shell. (*Exeunt*)

466 Spectacle.
467 When the lawcourts were in session and visitors came to London.
478 That is, the subject of all the newspapers.

Scene 3

A Room in Volpone's House
(*Enter* MOSCA *in the habit of a Clarissimo, and* VOLPONE *in that of a Commandadore*)

VOLPONE Am I then like him?

MOSCA O, sir, you are he:
No man can sever you.

VOLPONE Good.

MOSCA But what am I?

VOLPONE 'Fore heaven, a brave *clarissimo;* thou becom'st it!
Pity thou wert not born one.

MOSCA (*Aside*) If I hold

495

My made one, 'twill be well.

VOLPONE I'll go and see
What news first at the court (*Exit*)

MOSCA Do so. My Fox
Is out of his hole, and ere he shall re-enter,

500

I'll make him languish in his borrow'd case,*
Except he come to composition* with me.—
Androgyno, Castrone, Nano!
(*Enter* ANDROGYNO, CASTRONE, *and* NANO)

ALL Here.

505

MOSCA Go, recreate yourselves abroad; go sport.—(*Exeunt*)
So, now I have the keys, and am possessed.
Since he will needs be dead afore his time,
I'll bury him, or gain by him: I am his heir,
And so will keep me, till he share at least.

510

To cozen him of all, were but a cheat
Well placed; no man would construe it a sin:
Let his sport pay for't. This is call'd the Fox-trap. (*Exit*)

Scene 4

A Street
(*Enter* CORBACCIO *and* CORVINO)

515

CORBACCIO They say, the court is set.

CORVINO We must maintain
Our first tale good, for both our reputations.

CORBACCIO Why, mine's no tale: my son would there have kill'd me.

CORVINO That's true, I had forgot:—(*Aside*) mine is, I'm sure.

520

But for your Will, sir.

CORBACCIO Ay, I'll come upon him
For that hereafter, now his patron's dead.
(*Enter* VOLPONE)

501 Disguise.
502 That is, comes to an understanding.

VOLPONE   Signior Corvino! And Corbaccio! Sir,   ⁵²⁵
   Much joy unto you.
CORVINO   Of what?
VOLPONE   The sudden good
   Dropped down upon you—
CORBACCIO   Where?   ⁵³⁰
VOLPONE   And none knows how,
   From old Volpone, sir.
CORBACCIO   Out, arrant knave!
VOLPONE   Let not your too much wealth, sir, make you furious.
CORBACCIO   Away, thou varlet!   ⁵³⁵
VOLPONE   Why, sir?
CORBACCIO   Dost thou mock me?
VOLPONE   You mock the world, sir; did you not change wills?
CORBACCIO   Out, harlot!
VOLPONE   O! Belike* you are the man,   ⁵⁴⁰
   Signior Corvino? 'Faith, you carry it well;
   You grow not mad withal; I love your spirit.
   You are not over-leaven'd with your fortune.
   You should have some would swell now, like a wine-fat,
   With such an autumn——Did he give you all, sir?   ⁵⁴⁵
CORVINO   Avoid, you rascal!
VOLPONE   Troth, your wife has shown
   Herself a very* woman; but you are well,
   You need not care, you have a good estate,
   To bear it out, sir, better by this chance: ⁵⁵⁰
   Except Corbaccio have a share.
CORBACCIO   Hence, varlet.
VOLPONE   You will not be acknown,* sir; why, 'tis wise.
   Thus do all gamesters, at all games, dissemble:
   No man will seem to win. (*Exeunt* CORVINO *and* CORBACCIO)—Here   ⁵⁵⁵
                                                    comes my vulture,
   Heaving his beak up in the air, and snuffing.
                    (*Enter* VOLTORE)
VOLTORE   Outstripped thus, by a parasite! A slave,
   Would run on errands, and make legs for crumbs!   ⁵⁶⁰
   Well, what I'll do—
VOLPONE   The court stays for your worship.
   I e'en rejoice, sir at your worship's happiness,
   And that it fell into so learned hands,
   That understand the fingering—   ⁵⁶⁵
VOLTORE   What do you mean?

<hr>

540 Most likely.
548 True.
553 Recognized.

VOLPONE   I mean to be a suitor to your worship,
    For the small tenement, out of reparations,*
    That, to the end of your long row of houses,
    By the Piscaria:* it was, in Volpone's time,   570
    Your predecessor, ere he grew diseased,
    A handsome, pretty, custom'd* bawdy-house
    As any was in Venice, none dispraised;*
    But fell with him: his body and that house
    Decay'd together.   575
VOLTORE   Come, sir, leave your prating.
VOLPONE   Why, if your worship give me but your hand,*
    That I may have the refusal, I have done.
    'Tis a mere toy to you, sir; candle-rents;*
    As your learn'd worship knows—   580
VOLTORE   What do I know?
VOLPONE   Marry, no end of your wealth, sir: God decrease it!
VOLTORE   Mistaking knave! What, mock'st thou my misfortune? (*Exit*)
VOLPONE   His blessing on your heart, sir; would 'twere more!—
    Now to my first again, at the next corner. (*Exit*)   585

Scene 5

Another part of the Street
(*Enter* CORBACCIO *and* CORVINO;—MOSCA *passes over the Stage, before them*)
CORBACCIO   See, in our habit! See the impudent varlet!
CORVINO   That I could shoot mine eyes at him like gunstones!*
                    (*Enter* VOLPONE)   590
VOLPONE   But is this true, sir, of the parasite?
CORBACCIO   Again, to afflict us! Monster!
VOLPONE   In good faith, sir,
    I'm heartily grieved, a beard of your grave length
    Should be so over-reach'd.* I never brook'd   595
    That parasite's hair; methought his nose should cozen:
    There still was somewhat in his look, did promise
    The bane of a *clarissimo*.
CORBACCIO   Knave—
VOLPONE   Methinks   600
    Yet you, that are so traded in the world,
    A witty merchant, the fine bird, Corvino,

---

568 In disrepair.
570 Fishmarket.
572 Popular.
573 That is, no one disparaged it.
577 Signature.
579 Money from dilapidated property.
589 Cannonballs.
595 Outwitted.

That have such moral emblems on your name,*
Should not have sung your shame, and dropped your cheese,
To let the Fox laugh at your emptiness.*   605
CORVINO Sirrah, you think the privilege of the place,
And your red saucy cap, that seems to me
Nail'd to your jolt-head* with those two *chequines*,*
Can warrant your abuses; come you hither:
You shall perceive, sir, I dare beat you; approach.   610
VOLPONE No haste, sir, I do know your valour well,
Since you durst publish what you are, sir.
CORVINO Tarry,
I'd speak with you.
VOLPONE Sir, sir, another time—   615
CORVINO Nay, now.
VOLPONE O god, sir! I were a wise man,
Would stand the fury of a distracted* cuckold.
                    (*As he is running off, re-enter* MOSCA)
CORBACCIO What, come again?   620
VOLPONE Upon 'em, Mosca; save me.
CORBACCIO The air's infected where he breathes.
CORVINO Let's fly him. (*Exeunt* CORVINO *and* CORBACCIO)
VOLPONE Excellent basilisk!* Turn upon the vulture.
                    (*Enter* VOLTORE)   625
VOLTORE Well, flesh-fly, it is summer with you now;
Your winter will come on.
MOSCA Good advocate,
Prithee not rail, nor threaten out of place thus;
Thou'lt make a solecism, as madam says.   630
Get you a biggin* more, your brain breaks loose. (*Exit*)
VOLTORE Well, sir.
VOLPONE Would you have me beat the insolent slave,
Throw dirt upon his first good clothes?
VOLTORE This same   635
Is doubtless some familiar.*
VOLPONE Sir, the court,
In troth, stays for you. I am mad, a mule
That never read Justinian, should get up,
And ride an advocate. Had you no quirk*   640

603 Pictures, using crows, that taught moral lessons.
605 An allusion to Aesop's fable of the fox and the crow. The fox flattered the crow and caused him to drop
his cheese.
608 (*a*) Blockhead. (*b*) Gilt buttons.
618 Deranged.
624 A fabulous king of serpents whose look and breath were fatal.
631 Lawyer's skullcap.
636 Assisting devil.
640 Trick.

To avoid gullage, sir, by such a creature?
I hope you do but jest; he has not done it.
'Tis but confederacy, to blind the rest.
You are the heir.

VOLTORE   A strange, officious,   645
Troublesome knave! Thou dost torment me.

VOLPONE   I know—
It cannot be, sir, that you should be cozen'd;
'Tis not within with the wit of man to do it;
You are so wise, so prudent; and 'tis fit   650
That wealth and wisdom still should go together. (*Exeunt*)

Scene 6

The Scrutineo or Senate-House

(*Enter* AVOCATORI, NOTARIO, BONARIO, CELIA, CORBACCIO, CORVINO,
COMMANDADORI, SAFFI, *etc.*)

1ST AVOC.   Are all the parties here?   655

NOTARIO   All but the advocate.

2ND AVOC.   And here he comes.

(*Enter* VOLTORE *and* VOLPONE)

1ST AVOC.   Then bring them forth to sentence.

VOLTORE   O, my most honour'd fathers, let your mercy   660
Once win upon your justice, to forgive—
I am distracted—

VOLPONE (*Aside*)   What will he do now?

VOLTORE   O,
I know not which to address myself to first;
Whether your fatherhoods, or these innocents—   665

CORVINO (*Aside*)   Will he betray himself?

VOLTORE   Whom equally
I have abused, out of most covetous ends—

CORVINO   The man is mad!   670

CORBACCIO   What's that?

CORVINO   He is possessed.

VOLTORE   For which, now struck in conscience, here, I prostrate
Myself at your offended feet, for pardon.

1ST AND 2ND AVOC.   Arise.

CELIA   O heaven, how just thou art!   675

VOLPONE (*Aside*)   I am caught
In mine own noose—

CORVINO (*To* CORBACCIO)   Be constant, sir: nought now
Can help, but impudence.   680

1ST AVOC.   Speak forward.

COMMANDADORI   Silence!

VOLTORE   It is not passion in me, reverend fathers,
But only conscience, conscience, my good sires,

That makes me now tell truth. That parasite,   685
That knave, hath been the instrument of all.
1ST AVOC. Where is that knave? Fetch him.
VOLPONE I go. (*Exit*)
CORVINO Grave fathers,
This man's distracted; he confessed it now: 690
For, hoping to be old Volpone's heir,
Who now is dead—
3RD AVOC. How!
2ND AVOC. Is Volpone dead?
CORVINO Dead since, grave fathers.   695
BONARIO O sure vengeance!
1ST AVOC. Stay,
Then he was no deceiver.
VOLTORE O no, none:
The parasite, grave fathers.   700
CORVINO He does speak
Out of mere envy, 'cause the servant's made
The thing he gaped* for: please your fatherhoods,
This is the truth, though I'll not justify,
The other, but he may be some-deal* faulty.   705
VOLTORE Ay, to your hopes, as well as mine, Corvino:
But I'll use modesty. Pleaseth your wisdoms,
To view these certain* notes, and but confer* them;
As I hope favour, they shall speak clear truth.
CORVINO The devil has enter'd him!   710
BONARIO Or bides in you.
4TH AVOC. We have done ill, by a public officer
To send for him, if he be heir.
2ND AVOC. For whom?
4TH AVOC. Him that they call the parasite.   715
3RD AVOC. 'Tis true,
He is a man of great estate, now left.
4TH AVOC. Go you, and learn his name; and say, the court
Entreats his presence here, but to the clearing
Of some few doubts. (*Exit* NOTARY)   720
2ND AVOC. This same's a labyrinth!
1ST AVOC. Stand you unto your first report?
CORVINO My state,
My life, my fame—
BONARIO Where is it?   725
CORVINO Are at the stake.
1ST AVOC. Is yours so too?

703 Longed for.
705 Somewhat.
708 (*a*) Particular. (*b*) Compare.

CORBACCIO   The advocate's a knave,
    And has a forked tongue—
2ND AVOC.   Speak to the point.   730
CORBACCIO   So is the parasite, too.
1ST AVOC.   This is confusion.
VOLTORE   I do beseech your fatherhoods, read but those—
                        (*Giving them papers*)
CORVINO   And credit nothing the false spirit hath writ: 735
    It cannot be, but he's possessed, grave fathers. (*The scene closes*)

Scene 7

A Street

(*Enter* VOLPONE)

VOLPONE   To make a snare for mine own neck! and run
    My head into it, wilfully! With laughter!   740
    When I had newly 'scaped, was free, and clear,
    Out of mere wantonness! O, the dull devil
    Was in this brain of mine, when I devised it,
    And Mosca gave it second; he must now
    Help to sear up this vein, or we bleed dead.—   745
            (*Enter* NANO, ANDROGYNO, *and* CASTRONE)
    How now! Who let you loose? Whither go you now?
    What, to buy gingerbread, or to drown kitlings?*
NANO   Sir, master Mosca call'd us out of doors,
    And bid us all go play, and took the keys.   750
ANDROGYNO   Yes.
VOLPONE   Did master Mosca take the keys? Why so!
    I'm farther in. These are my fine conceits!*
    I must be merry, with a mischief to me!
    What a vile wretch was I, that could not bear   755
    My fortune soberly? I must have my crotchets,*
    And my conundrums!* Well, go you, and seek him:
    His meaning may be truer than my fear.*
    Bid him, he straight come to me to the court;
    Thither will I, and, if 't be possible,   760
    Unscrew my advocate, upon new hopes:
    When I provoked him, then I lost myself. (*Exeunt*)

748 Kittens.
753 Notions.
756 Fancies.
757 Riddles.
758 That is, he may be more faithful than I think.

Scene 8

The Scrutineo, or Senate-House

(AVOCATORI, BONARIO, CELIA, CORBACCIO, CORVINO, COMMANDADORI, SAFFI, *etc., as before*)

765

1ST AVOC. These things can ne'er be reconciled. He, here, (*Showing the papers*)
Professeth, that the gentleman was wrong'd,
And that the gentlewoman was brought thither,
Forced by her husband, and there left.

VOLTORE Most true. 770

CELIA How ready is heaven to those that pray!

1ST AVOC. But that
Volpone would have ravish'd her, he holds
Utterly false, knowing his impotence.

CORVINO Grave fathers, he's possessed; again, I say, 775
Possessed: nay, if there be possession, and
Obsession, he has both.

3RD AVOC. Here comes our officer.

(*Enter* VOLPONE)

VOLPONE The parasite will straight be here, grave fathers. 780

4TH AVOC. You might invent some other name, sir varlet.

3RD AVOC. Did not the notary meet him?

VOLPONE Not that I know.

4TH AVOC. His coming will clear all.

2ND AVOC. Yet, it is misty. 785

VOLTORE May't please your fatherhoods—

VOLPONE (*Whispers to* VOLTORE) Sir, the parasite
Will'd me to tell you, that his master lives;
That you are still the man; your hopes the same;
And this was only a jest— 790

VOLTORE How?

VOLPONE Sir, to try
If you were firm, and how you stood affected.

VOLTORE Art sure he lives?

VOLPONE Do I live, sir? 795

VOLTORE O me!
I was too violent.

VOLPONE Sir, you may redeem it.
They said, you were possessed; fall down, and seem so:
I'll help to make it good. (VOLTORE *falls*)—God bless the man!— 800
Stop your wind hard, and swell—See, see, see, see!
He vomits crooked pins! His eyes are set,
Like a dead hare's hung in a poulter's shop!
His mouth's running away!* Do you see, signior?
Now it is in his belly.* 805

---

804 Distorted.
805 All symptoms attributed to demonic possession.

190 JONSON

CORVINO   Ay, the devil!

VOLPONE   Now in his throat.

CORVINO   Ay, I perceive it plain.

VOLPONE   'Twill out, 'twill out! Stand clear. See where it flies,
          In shape of a blue toad, with a bat's wings!
          Do you not see it, sir?

CORBACCIO   What? I think I do.

CORVINO   'Tis too manifest.

VOLPONE   Look! He comes to himself!

VOLTORE   Where am I?

VOLPONE   Take good heart, the worst is past, sir.
          You are dispossessed.

1ST AVOC.   What accident is this!

2ND AVOC.   Sudden, and full of wonder!

3RD AVOC.   If he were
            Possessed, as it appears, all this is nothing.

CORVINO   He has been often subject to these fits.

1ST AVOC.   Show him that writing:—do you know it, sir?

VOLPONE (*Whispers to* VOLTORE)   Deny it, sir, forswear it; know it not.

VOLTORE   Yes, I do know it well, it is my hand;
          But all that it contains is false.

BONARIO   O practice!

2ND AVOC.   What maze is this!

1ST AVOC.   Is he not guilty then,
            Whom you there name the parasite?

VOLTORE   Grave fathers,
          No more than his good patron, old Volpone.

4TH AVOC.   Why, he is dead.

VOLTORE   O no, my honour'd fathers,
          He lives—

1ST AVOC.   How! Lives?

VOLTORE   Lives.

2ND AVOC.   This is subtler yet!

3RD AVOC.   You said he was dead.

VOLTORE   Never.

3RD AVOC.   You said so.

CORVINO   I heard so.

4TH AVOC.   Here comes the gentleman; make him way.

(*Enter* MOSCA)

3RD AVOC.   A stool.

4TH AVOC. (*Aside*)   A proper man; and, were Volpone dead,
          A fit match for my daughter.

3RD AVOC.   Give him way.

VOLPONE (*Aside to* MOSCA)   Mosca, I was almost lost; the advocate
          Had betrayed all; but now it is recovered;
          All's on the hinge again——Say, I am living.

MOSCA   What busy knave is this!—Most reverend fathers,

I sooner had attended your grave pleasures,
But that my order for the funeral
Of my dear patron, did require me—   855
VOLPONE (*Aside*) Mosca!
MOSCA Whom I intend to bury like a gentleman.
VOLPONE (*Aside*) Ay, quick,* and cozen me of all.
2ND AVOC. Still stranger!
More intricate!   860
1ST AVOC. And come about again!
4TH AVOC. (*Aside*) It is a match, my daughter is bestow'd.
MOSCA (*Aside to* VOLPONE) Will you give me half?
VOLPONE First, I'll be hang'd.
MOSCA I know   865
Your voice is good, cry not so loud.
1ST AVOC. Demand*
The advocate.—Sir, did you not affirm
Volpone was alive?
VOLPONE Yes, and he is;   870
This gentleman told me so. (*Aside to* MOSCA)—Thou shalt have half.—
MOSCA Whose drunkard is this same? Speak, some that know him:
I never saw his face. (*Aside to* VOLPONE)—I cannot now
Afford it you so cheap.
VOLPONE No!   875
1ST AVOC. What say you?
VOLTORE The officer told me.
VOLPONE I did, grave fathers,
And will maintain he lives, with mine own life,
And that this creature (*Points to* MOSCA) told me. (*Aside*)—I was born   880
With all good stars my enemies.
MOSCA Most grave fathers,
If such an insolence as this must pass
Upon me, I am silent: 'twas not this
For which you sent, I hope.   885
2ND AVOC. Take him away.
VOLPONE Mosca!
3RD AVOC. Let him be whipped.
VOLPONE Wilt thou betray me?
Cozen me?   890
3RD AVOC. And taught to bear himself
Toward a person of his rank.
4TH AVOC. Away. (*The Officers seize* VOLPONE)
MOSCA I humbly thank your fatherhoods.
VOLPONE (*Aside*) Soft, soft:* Whipped!   895

858 Alive.
867 Question.
895 Gently.

And lose all that I have! If I confess,
It cannot be much more.

4TH AVOC.   Sir, are you married?

VOLPONE   They'll be allied anon; I must be resolute:
The Fox shall here uncase. (*Throws off his disguise*)

MOSCA   Patron!

VOLPONE   Nay, now
My ruins shall not come alone: your match
I'll hinder sure: my substance shall not glue you,
Nor screw you into a family.

MOSCA   Why, patron!

VOLPONE   I am Volpone, and this is my knave; (*Pointing to* MOSCA)
This, (*To* VOLTORE) his own knave; this, (*To* CORBACCIO) avarice's fool;
This, (*To* CORVINO) a chimera* of wittol, fool, and knave:
And, reverend fathers, since we all can hope
Nought but a sentence, let's not now despair it.
You hear me brief.

CORVINO   May it please your fatherhoods—

COMMANDADORI   Silence.

1ST AVOC.   The knot is now undone by miracle.

2ND AVOC.   Nothing can be more clear.

3RD AVOC.   Or can more prove
These innocent.

1ST AVOC.   Give them their liberty.

BONARIO   Heaven could not long let such gross crimes be hid.

2ND AVOC.   If this be held the high-way to get riches,
May I be poor!

3RD AVOC.   This is not the gain, but torment.

1ST AVOC.   These possess wealth, as sick men possess fevers,
Which trulier may be said to possess them.

2ND AVOC.   Disrobe that parasite.

CORVINO AND MOSCA   Most honour'd fathers!—

1ST AVOC.   Can you plead aught to stay the course of justice?
If you can, speak.

CORVINO AND VOLTORE   We beg favour.

CELIA   And mercy.

1ST AVOC.   You hurt your innocence, suing for the guilty.
Stand forth; and first the parasite: You appear
T'have been the chiefest minister, if not plotter,
In all these lewd impostures; and now, lastly,
Have with your impudence abused the court,
And habit of a gentleman of Venice,
Being a fellow of no birth or blood:
For which our sentence is, first, thou be whipped;
Then live perpetual prisoner in our galleys.

VOLPONE   I thank you for him.

---

909 A mythical creature, part lion, goat, and snake.

MOSCA   Bane* to thy wolvish nature!

1ST AVOC.   Deliver him to the saffi. (MOSCA *is carried out*)—Thou, Volpone,
   By blood and rank a gentleman, canst not fall
   Under like censure; but our judgment on thee   945
   Is, that thy substance all be straight confiscate
   To the hospital of the *Incurabili:**
   And, since the most was gotten by imposture,
   By feigning lame, gout, palsy, and such diseases,
   Thou art to lie in prison, cramp'd with irons,   950
   Till thou be'st sick and lame indeed.—Remove him.
                   (*He is taken from the Bar*)

VOLPONE   This is call'd mortifying of a Fox.

1ST AVOC.   Thou, Voltore, to take away the scandal
   Thou hast given all worthy men of thy profession,   955
   Art banish'd from their fellowship, and our state.
   Corbaccio!—Bring him near—We here possess
   Thy son of all thy state, and confine thee
   To the monastery of San Spirito;
   Where, since thou knowest not how to live well here,   960
   Thou shalt be learn'd to die well.

CORBACCIO   Ah! What said he?

COMMANDADORI   You shall know anon, sir.

1ST AVOC.   Thou, Corvino, shalt
   Be straight embark'd from thine own house, and row'd   965
   Round about Venice, through the Grand Canal,
   Wearing a cap, with fair long ass's ears,
   Instead of horns; and so to mount, a paper
   Pinn'd on thy breast, to the *Berlina**—

CORVINO   Yes,   970
   And have mine eyes beat out with stinking fish,
   Bruised fruit, and rotten eggs—'Tis well. I am glad
   I shall not see my shame yet.

1ST AVOC.   And to expiate
   Thy wrongs done to thy wife, thou art to send her   975
   Home to her father, with her dowry trebled:
   And these are all your judgments.

ALL   Honour'd fathers.—

1ST AVOC.   Which may not be revoked. Now you begin,
   When crimes are done, and past, and to be punish'd,   980
   To think what your crimes are: away with them.
   Let all that see these vices thus rewarded,
   Take heart, and love to study 'em! Mischiefs feed
   Like beasts, till they be fat, and then they bleed. (*Exeunt*)
                   (VOLPONE *comes forward*)   985

---

942 Curse.

947 Incurables.

969 Pillory, or instrument in which a malefactor is exhibited publicly.

VOLPONE The seasoning of a play, is the applause.
Now, though the Fox be punish'd by the laws,
He yet doth hope, there is no suffering due,
For any fact which he hath done 'gainst you;
If there be, censure him; here he doubtful stands: 990
If not, fare jovially, and clap your hands. (*Exit*)

John Webster

John Webster (c.1580–1634) *is generally regarded as the Jacobean tragedian* par excellence. *An extremely painstaking and slow writer, he probably wrote only three plays on his own, but the two most famous,* THE WHITE DEVIL *and* THE DUCHESS OF MALFI, *illustrate Jacobean tragedy perfectly. Though their macabre features reflect some of the pessimism associated with the post-Elizabethan era, the stunning vitality of characterization in these plays make them romantic tragedies of great power. Webster collaborated with other dramatists on comedies, histories, and pageants, and himself wrote a number of poems, but his reputation virtually rests on* THE WHITE DEVIL *and* THE DUCHESS OF MALFI.

Chronology

*c.*1580 Born, possibly the son of a London tailor. He later became a member of the Merchant Taylors' Company.

1602 Wrote for Philip Henslowe's company, collaborating with Drayton and others on *Caesar's Fall* and with Dekker and others on other plays.

1604 Contributed the "Induction" to Marston's *The Malcontent.*

1605–07 Appears to have had a share in *Westward Ho!* and *Northward Ho!* These plays, along with *Sir Thomas Wyatt,* were published as by Webster and Dekker.

1612 Published *The White Devil* and contributed prefatory verses to Heywood's *Apology For Actors;* published *A Monumental Column,* an elegy on the death of Prince Henry.

1614 Probable year of the composition of *The Duchess of Malfi.*

1615 Probably contributed "characters" to Sir Thomas Overbury's *Characters.*

*c.*1621 Possibly contributed to *Anything For A Quiet Life,* ascribed to Middleton.

1623 Published *The Duchess of Malfi* and *The Devil's Law Case.*

1624 Wrote *Monuments of Honour,* a pageant for the Merchant Taylors, and collaborated with John Ford on *The Late Murder of the Son Upon the Mother,* now lost.

1625 May have collaborated with Rowley on *A Cure for a Cuckold,* now lost, and with Massinger and Ford on *The Fair Maid of the Inn.*

1625–34 Wrote, probably in collaboration, *Appius and Virginia.*

1634 Conjectural year of his death.

Selected Bibliography

Bogard, Travis, *The Tragic Satire of John Webster,* Berkeley, Calif., 1955.

Boklund, Gunnar, *The Duchess of Malfi: Sources, Themes, Characters,* Cambridge, Mass., 1962.

Brooke, Rupert, *John Webster and the Elizabethan Drama,* New York, 1916.

Calderwood, James L., *"The Duchess of Malfi:* Styles of Ceremony," *Essays in Criticism,* XII (1962), 133–147.

Davies, Cecil W., "The Structure of *The Duchess of Malfi:* An Approach," *English,* XII (1958), 89–93.

Leech, Clifford, *John Webster, A Critical Study,* London, 1951.

————, *Webster: The Duchess of Malfi (Studies in English Literature,* 8), New York, 1963.

Mulryne, J. R., *"The White Devil* and *The Duchess of Malfi,"* Jacobean *Theatre,* eds. John Russell Brown and Bernard Harris (New York, 1960), pp. 201–225.

Ribner, Irving, "Webster's Italian Tragedies," *Tulane Drama Review,* V (1961), 106–118.

Stoll, E. E., *John Webster,* Boston, 1905.

Thayer, C. G., "The Ambiguity of Bosola," *Studies in Philology,* LIV (1957), 162–171.

Title page for *A Game at Chess* (1625?) by Thomas Middleton.
Photo Henry E. Huntington Library, San Marino, California

THE TRAGEDY OF THE DUCHESS OF MALFI

by John Webster

Characters

FERDINAND, *Duke of Calabria*
THE CARDINAL, *his Brother*
ANTONIO BOLOGNA, *Steward of the household to the Duchess*
DELIO, *his Friend*
DANIEL DE BOSOLA, *Gentleman of the horse to the Duchess*
CASTRUCCIO
MARQUIS OF PESCARA
COUNT MALATESTE
SILVIO, *a Lord, of Milan*
RODERIGO   *Gentlemen attending on the Duchess*
GRISOLAN
DOCTOR
Several Madmen, Pilgrims, Executioners, Officers, Attendants, &c.
DUCHESS OF MALFI, *sister of Ferdinand and the Cardinal*
CARIOLA, *her Woman*
JULIA, *Castruccio's Wife and the Cardinal's Mistress*
Old Lady, Ladies, and Children

Amalfi, Rome, and Milan

Act One

Scene 1

Amalfi. The Presence-chamber in the Duchess's Palace
(*Enter* ANTONIO *and* DELIO)

DELIO You are welcome to your country, dear Antonio;
 You have been long in France, and you return
 A very formal Frenchman in your habit:
 How do you like the French court?
ANTONIO   I admire it:
 In seeking to reduce both state and people
 To a fix'd order, their judicious king
 Begins at home; quits* first his royal palace

⁸ Frees.

Of flattering sycophants, of dissolute
And infamous persons,—which* he sweetly terms   10
His master's masterpiece, the work of Heaven;
Considering duly that a prince's court
Is like a common fountain, whence should flow
Pure silver drops in general, but if 't chance
Some curs'd example poison't near the head,   15
Death and diseases through the whole land spread.
And what is't makes this blessed government
But a most provident council, who dare freely
Inform him the corruption of the times?
Though some o' th' court hold it presumption   20
To instruct princes what they ought to do,
It is a noble duty to inform them
What they ought to foresee.—Here comes Bosola, (*Enter* BOSOLA)
The only court-gall; yet I observe his railing
Is not for simple love of piety: 25
Indeed he rails at those things which he wants,
Would be as lecherous, covetous, or proud,
Bloody, or envious, as any man,
If he had means to be so.—Here's the Cardinal.
                  (*Enter the* CARDINAL)   30

BOSOLA   I do haunt you still.

CARDINAL   So.

BOSOLA   I have done you better service than to be slighted thus. Miserable age,
where only the reward of doing well is the doing of it!

CARDINAL   You enforce your merit too much.   35

BOSOLA   I fell into the galleys in your service; where, for two years together,
I wore two towels instead of a shirt, with a knot on the shoulder, after the
fashion of a Roman mantle. Slighted thus? I will thrive some way: black-
birds fatten best in hard weather; why not I in these dog-days?*

CARDINAL   Would you could become honest!   40

BOSOLA   With all your divinity, do but direct me the way to it. I have known
many travel far for it, and yet return as arrant knaves as they went forth,
because they carried themselves always along with them. (*Exit* CARDINAL)
Are you gone? Some fellows, they say, are possessed with the devil, but this
great fellow were able to possess the greatest devil, and make him worse. 45

ANTONIO   He hath denied thee some suit?

BOSOLA   He and his brother are like plum-trees that grow crooked over standing-
pools;* they are rich and o'er-laden with fruit, but none but crows, pies,*
and caterpillars feed on them. Could I be one of their flattering panders,
I would hang on their ears like a horseleech, till I were full, and then 50
drop off. I pray, leave me. Who would rely upon these miserable depend-
encies, in expectation to be advanc'd tomorrow? What creature ever fed

---

10 And this.
39 The period of sultry weather between early July and September, hence days of stagnation, or evil days.
48 (*a*) Stagnant pools. (*b*) Magpies.

worse than hoping Tantalus?* Nor ever died any man more fearfully than
he that hop'd for a pardon. There are rewards for hawks and dogs when
they have done us service; but for a soldier that hazards his limbs in a 55
battle, nothing but a kind of geometry in his last supportation.*

DELIO Geometry?

BOSOLA Aye, to hang in a fair pair of slings, take his latter swing in the world
upon an honourable pair of crutches, from hospital to hospital. Fare ye well,
sir: and yet do not you scorn us, for places in the court are but like beds 60
in the hospital, where this man's head lies at that man's foot, and so lower
and lower. (*Exit*)

DELIO I knew this fellow seven years in the galleys
For a notorious murder; and 'twas thought
The Cardinal suborn'd it: he was releas'd   65
By the French general, Gaston de Foix,*
When he recover'd Naples.

ANTONIO   'Tis great pity
He should be thus neglected: I have heard
He's very valiant. This foul melancholy   70
Will poison all his goodness; for, I'll tell you,
If too immoderate sleep be truly said
To be an inward rust unto the soul,
It then doth follow want of action
Breeds all black malcontents; and their close rearing,   75
Like moths in cloth, do hurt for want of wearing.

        (*Enter* SILVIO, CASTRUCCIO, RODERIGO, GRISOLAN, *and Attendants*)

DELIO The presence 'gins to fill: you promis'd me
To make me the partaker of the natures
Of some of your great courtiers.   80

ANTONIO   The lord Cardinal's,
And other strangers' that are now in court?
I shall.—Here comes the great Calabrian duke.

              (*Enter* FERDINAND)

FERDINAND Who took the ring oftenest?*   85

SILVIO Antonio Bologna, my lord.

FERDINAND Our sister duchess's great-master of her household? Give him the
jewel. When shall we leave this sportive action, and fall to action indeed?

CASTRUCCIO Methinks, my lord, you should not desire to go to war in person.

FERDINAND Now for some gravity:—why, my lord?   90

CASTRUCCIO It is fitting a soldier arise to be a prince, but not necessary a prince
descend to be a captain.

FERDINAND No?

---

53 Tantalus was punished in Hades by being condemned to stand in water up to his chin and beneath
     fruit-laden branches, with the fruit and water receding at each attempt to eat or drink.
56 This expression draws on the idiom "To hang by geometry," which referred to clothes hanging awk-
     wardly and angularly on a person.
66 A well- known young military leader (*c.*1512), who had nothing to do, however, with taking Naples.
85 Alludes to tilting at the ring, or trying to pick off the ring on the point of one's lance.

CASTRUCCIO   No, my lord; he were far better do it by a deputy.

FERDINAND   Why should he not as well sleep or eat by a deputy? This might take idle, offensive, and base office from him, where as the other deprives him of honour.

CASTRUCCIO   Believe my experience, that realm is never long in quiet where the ruler is a soldier.

FERDINAND   Thou told'st me thy wife could not endure fighting.

CASTRUCCIO   True, my lord.

FERDINAND   And of a jest she broke of a captain she met full of wounds: I have forgot it.

CASTRUCCIO   She told him, my lord, he was a pitiful fellow, to lie, like the children of Ismael, all in tents.*

FERDINAND   Why, there's a wit were able to undo all the chirurgeons* o' the city; for although gallants should quarrel, and had drawn their weapons, and were ready to go to it, yet her persuasions would make them put up.

CASTRUCCIO   That she would, my lord.

FERDINAND   How do you like my Spanish gennet?

RODERIGO   He is all fire.

FERDINAND   I am of Pliny's opinion,* I think he was begot by the wind; he runs as if he were ballast'd with quick-silver.

SILVIO   True, my lord, he reels from the tilt often.*

RODERIGO AND GRISOLAN   Ha, ha, ha!

FERDINAND   Why do you laugh? Methinks you that are courtiers should be my touchwood, take fire when I give fire; that is, laugh when I laugh, were the subject never so witty.

CASTRUCCIO   True, my lord: I myself have heard a very good jest, and have scorn'd to seem to have so silly a wit as to understand it.

FERDINAND   But I can laugh at your fool, my lord.

CASTRUCCIO   He cannot speak, you know, but he makes faces. My lady cannot abide him.

FERDINAND   No?

CASTRUCCIO   Nor endure to be in merry company; for she says too much laughing, and too much company, fills her too full of the wrinkle.

FERDINAND   I would, then, have a mathematical instrument made for her face, that she might not laugh out of compass.*—I shall shortly visit you at Milan, Lord Silvio.

SILVIO   Your grace shall arrive most welcome.

FERDINAND   You are a good horseman, Antonio: you have excellent riders in France. What do you think of good horsemanship?

ANTONIO   Nobly, my lord: as out of the Grecian horse* issued many famous

---

105 With many wounds. A "tent" was a roll of lint which was placed in a wound.

106 Surgeons.

112 Pliny the Elder, the Roman scholar (23-79 A.D.). The opinion was that especially fast horses were conceived by the west wind.

114 Apparently, he means the horse was skittish.

128 Beyond bounds.

133 The wooden horse at Troy.

princes, so out of brave horsemanship arise the first sparks of growing resolution, that raise the mind to noble action. 135

FERDINAND You have bespoke it worthily.

SILVIO Your brother, the lord Cardinal, and sister duchess.

(*Re-enter* CARDINAL, *with* DUCHESS, CARIOLA, *and* JULIA)

CARDINAL Are the galleys come about?

GRISOLAN   They are, my lord. 140

FERDINAND Here's the Lord Silvio is come to take his leave.

DELIO (*Aside to* ANTONIO) Now, sir, your promise; what's that Cardinal?
I mean his temper? They say he's a brave fellow,
Will play his five thousand crowns at tennis, dance,
Court ladies, and one that hath fought single combats. 145

ANTONIO Some such flashes superficially hang on him for form; but observe his inward character: he is a melancholy churchman; the spring* in his face is nothing but the engendering of toads; where he is jealous of any man, he lays worse plots for them than ever was impos'd on Hercules,* for he strews in his way flatterers, panders, intelligencers,* atheists, and a thousand 150 such political monsters. He should have been Pope; but instead of coming to it by the primitive decency of the Church, he did bestow bribes so largely and so impudently as if he would have carried it away without Heaven's knowledge. Some good he hath done——

DELIO You have given too much of him. What's his brother? 155

ANTONIO The duke there? A most perverse and turbulent nature:
What appears in him mirth is merely outside;
If he laughs heartily, it is to laugh
All honesty out of fashion.

DELIO   Twins? 160

ANTONIO   In quality.
He speaks with others' tongues, and hears men's suits
With others' ears; will seem to sleep o' th' bench
Only to entrap offenders in their answers;
Dooms men to death by information; 165
Rewards by hearsay.

DELIO   Then the law to him
Is like a foul black cobweb to a spider,—
He makes of it his dwelling and a prison
To entangle those shall feed him. 170

ANTONIO   Most true:
He never pays debts unless they be shrewd turns,
And those he will confess that he doth owe.
Last, for his brother there, the Cardinal,
They that do flatter him most, say oracles 175
Hang at his lips; and verily I believe them,

---

147 "Spring" in the sense of pool.
149 The labors imposed on Hercules.
150 Informers.

For the devil speaks in them.
But for their sister, the right noble duchess,
You never fixed your eye on three fair medals
Cast in one figure, of so different temper.   180
For her discourse, it is so full of rapture,
You only will begin, then to be sorry
When she doth end her speech, and wish, in wonder,
She held it less vain-glory to talk much,
Than your penance to hear her: whilst she speaks,   185
She throws upon a man so sweet a look,
That it were able to raise one to a galliard*
That lay in a dead palsy, and to dote
On that sweet countenance; but in that look
There speaketh so divine a continence   190
As cuts off all lascivious and vain hope.
Her days are practis'd in such noble virtue,
That sure her nights, nay, more, her very sleeps,
Are more in heaven than other ladies' shrifts.
Let all sweet ladies break their flattering glasses,   195
And dress themselves in her.*

DELIO   Fie, Antonio,
You play the wire-drawer* with her commendations.

ANTONIO I'll case the picture up: only thus much;
All her particular worth grows to this sum,—   200
She stains the time past, lights the time to come.

CARIOLA You must attend my lady in the gallery,
Some half an hour hence.

ANTONIO   I shall. (*Exeunt* ANTONIO *and* DELIO)

FERDINAND Sister, I have a suit to you.   205

DUCHESS   To me, sir?

FERDINAND A gentleman here, Daniel de Bosola,
One that was in the galleys—

DUCHESS   Yes, I know him.

FERDINAND A worthy fellow he is: pray, let me entreat for   210
The provisorship of your horse.

DUCHESS   Your knowledge of him
Commends him and prefers him.

FERDINAND   Call him hither. (*Exit Attendant*)
We are now upon parting. Good Lord Silvio,   215
Do us commend to all our noble friends
At the leaguer.*

SILVIO   Sir, I shall.

DUCHESS   You are for Milan?

---

187 A lively dance.
196 Dress themselves by looking at her rather than at looking glasses.
198 Spin out at tedious length.
217 Camp.

SILVIO   I am.   220
DUCHESS   Bring the caroches.* We'll bring you down
    To the haven. (*Exeunt all but* FERDINAND *and the* CARDINAL)
CARDINAL   Be sure you entertain* that Bosola
    For your intelligence: I would not be seen in 't;
    And therefore many times I have slighted him   225
    When he did court our furtherance, as this morning.
FERDINAND   Antonio, the great-master of her household,
    Had been far fitter.
CARDINAL   You are deceiv'd in him:
    His nature is too honest for such business.   230
    He comes: I'll leave you. (*Exit*)
                         (*Re-enter* BOSOLA)
BOSOLA   I was lur'd to you.
FERDINAND   My brother, here, the Cardinal could never
    Abide you.   235
BOSOLA   Never since he was in my debt.
FERDINAND   Maybe some oblique character in your face
    Made him suspect you.
BOSOLA   Doth he study physiognomy?
    There's no more credit to be given to th' face   240
    Than to a sick man's urine, which some call
    The physician's whore because she cozens* him.
    He did suspect me wrongfully.
FERDINAND   For that
    You must give great men leave to take their times.   245
    Distrust doth cause us seldom be deceiv'd:
    You see the oft shaking of the cedar-tree
    Fastens it more at root.
BOSOLA   Yet take heed:
    For to suspect a friend unworthily   250
    Instructs him the next way to suspect you,
    And prompts him to deceive you.
FERDINAND (*Giving him money*)   There's gold.
BOSOLA   So:
    What follows? Never rained such showers as these   255
    Without thunderbolts i' th' tail of them: whose throat must I cut?
FERDINAND   Your inclination to shed blood rides post
    Before my occasion to use you. I give you that
    To live i' th' court here, and observe the duchess;
    To note all the particulars of her haviour,   260
    What suitors do solicit her for marriage,
    And whom she best affects. She's a young widow:
    I would not have her marry again.

221 Coaches.
223 Make use of.
242 Cheats.

BOSOLA	No, sir?
FERDINAND	Do not you ask the reason; but be satisfied

I say I would not.

BOSOLA	It seems you would create me

One of your familiars.

FERDINAND	Familiar? what's that?

BOSOLA Why, a very quaint invisible devil in flesh,
An intelligencer.

FERDINAND   Such a kind of thriving thing
I would wish thee; and ere long thou may'st arrive
At a higher place by 't.

BOSOLA   Take your devils,
Which hell calls angels; these curs'd gifts would make
You a corrupter, me an impudent traitor;
And should I take these, they'd take me to hell.

FERDINAND Sir, I'll take nothing from you that I have given:
There is a place that I procur'd for you
This morning, the provisorship o' th' horse;
Have you heard on 't?

BOSOLA   No.

FERDINAND 'Tis yours: is't not worth thanks?

BOSOLA I would have you curse yourself now, that your bounty,
Which makes men truly noble, e'er should make me
A villain. Oh, that to avoid ingratitude
For the good deed you have done me, I must do
All the ill man can invent! Thus the devil
Candies all sins o'er; and what heaven terms vile,
That names he complimental.*

FERDINAND   Be yourself;
Keep your old garb of melancholy; 'twill express
You envy those that stand above your reach,
Yet strive not to come near 'em: this will gain
Access to private lodgings, where yourself
May, like a politic* dormouse—

BOSOLA   As I have seen some
Feed in a lord's dish, half asleep, not seeming
To listen to any talk; and yet these rogues
Have cut his throat in a dream. What's my place?
The provisorship o' th' horse? Say, then, my corruption
Grew out of horse-dung: I am your creature.

FERDINAND   Away! (*Exit*)

BOSOLA Let good men, for good deeds, covet good fame,
Since place and riches oft are bribes of shame:
Sometimes the devil doth preach. (*Exit*)

291 Required by courtesy.
297 Prudent.

Scene 2

A Gallery in the Duchess's Palace

(*Enter* FERDINAND, DUCHESS, CARDINAL, *and* CARIOLA)

CARDINAL We are to part from you; and your own discretion   310
Must now be your director.

FERDINAND   You are a widow:
You know already what man is; and therefore
Let not youth, high promotion, eloquence—

CARDINAL   No,   315
Nor any thing without the addition, honour,
Sway your high blood.

FERDINAND Marry? They are most luxurious*
Will wed twice.

CARDINAL   Oh, fie!   320

FERDINAND   Their livers are more spotted
Than Laban's sheep.*

DUCHESS   Diamonds are of most value,
They say, that have passed through most jewellers' hands.

FERDINAND Whores, by that rule, are precious.   325

DUCHESS   Will you hear me?
I'll never marry.

CARDINAL   So most widows say;
But commonly that motion lasts no longer
Than the turning of an hour-glass: the funeral sermon
And it end both together.   330

FERDINAND   Now hear me:
You live in a rank pasture, here, i' th' court;
There is a kind of honey-dew that's deadly;
'Twill poison your fame; look to't: be not cunning;   335
For they whose faces do belie their hearts
Are witches ere they arrive at twenty years,
Aye, and give the devil suck.

DUCHESS   This is terrible good counsel.

FERDINAND Hypocrisy is woven of a fine small thread,   340
Subtler than Vulcan's engine:* yet, believe't,
Your darkest actions, nay, your privat'st thoughts,
Will come to light.

CARDINAL   You may flatter yourself,
And take your own choice; privately be married   345
Under the eaves of night—

FERDINAND   Think'st the best voyage

---

318 Lascivious.

322 The liver was thought to be the seat of erotic passion. Laban's spotted sheep were very numerous (*Genesis,* XXX).

341 The net in which he caught Mars and Venus.

That e'er you made; like the irregular crab,
Which, though 't goes backward, thinks that it goes right
Because it goes its own way; but observe,   350
Such weddings may more properly be said
To be executed than celebrated.
CARDINAL   The marriage night
Is the entrance into some prison.
FERDINAND   And those joys,   355
Those lustful pleasures, are like heavy sleeps
Which do forerun man's mischief.
CARDINAL   Fare you well.
Wisdom begins at the end: remember it. (*Exit*)
DUCHESS   I think this speech between you both was studied,   360
It came so roundly off.
FERDINAND   You are my sister;
This was my father's poniard, do you see?
I'd be loath to see 't look rusty, 'cause 'twas his.
I would have you to give o'er these chargeable* revels: 365
A visor and a mask are whispering-rooms*
That were never built for goodness. Fare ye well.
And women like that part which, like the lamprey,
Hath never a bone in 't.
DUCHESS   Fie, sir!   370
FERDINAND   Nay,
I mean the tongue; variety of courtship:
What cannot a neat knave with a smooth tale
Make a woman believe? Farewell, lusty widow. (*Exit*)
DUCHESS   Shall this move me? If all my royal kindred   375
Lay in my way unto this marriage,
I'd make them my low footsteps: and even now,
Even in this hate, as men in some great battles,
By apprehending danger, have achiev'd
Almost impossible actions (I have heard soldiers say so),   380
So I through frights and threatenings will assay
This dangerous venture. Let old wives report
I wink'd* and chose a husband.—Cariola,
To thy known secrecy I have given up
More than my life—my fame.   385
CARIOLA   Both shall be safe;
For I'll conceal this secret from the world
As warily as those that trade in poison
Keep poison from their children.
DUCHESS   Thy protestation   390

365 Expensive.
366 And were frequently worn at revels.
383 Chose blindly, with eyes closed.

Is ingenious* and hearty: I believe it.
Is Antonio come?

CARIOLA   He attends you.

DUCHESS   Good dear soul,
Leave me; but place thyself behind the arras,*
Where thou mayst overhear us. Wish me good speed;   395
For I am going into a wilderness
Where I shall find nor path nor friendly clue
To be my guide. (CARIOLA *goes behind the arras*)
                              (*Enter* ANTONIO)
                    I sent for you: sit down;   400
Take pen and ink, and write: are you ready?

ANTONIO   Yes.

DUCHESS   What did I say?

ANTONIO   That I should write somewhat.

DUCHESS   Oh, I remember.   405
After these triumphs* and this large expense,
It's fit, like thrifty husbands, we inquire
What's laid up for to-morrow.

ANTONIO   So please your beauteous excellence.

DUCHESS   Beauteous?   410
Indeed, I thank you: I look young for your sake;
You have ta'en my cares upon you.

ANTONIO   I'll fetch your grace
The particulars of your revenue and expense.

DUCHESS   Oh, you are an upright treasurer: but you mistook;   415
For when I said I meant to make inquiry
What's laid up for to-morrow, I did mean
What's laid up yonder for me.

ANTONIO   Where?

DUCHESS   In heaven,   420
I am making my will (as 'tis fit princes should
In perfect memory), and, I pray, sir, tell me,
Were not one better make it smiling, thus,
Than in deep groans and terrible ghastly looks,
As if the gifts we parted with procur'd   425
That violent distraction?

ANTONIO   Oh, much better.

DUCHESS   If I had a husband now, this care were quit:
But I intend to make you overseer.
What good deed shall we first remember? Say.   430

ANTONIO   Begin with that first good deed began i' th' world
After man's creation, the sacrament of marriage:

391 Ingenuous.
395 Curtain or tapestry.
407 Festivities.

I'd have you first provide for a good husband;
Give him all.   435

DUCHESS   All?
ANTONIO   Yes, your excellent self.
DUCHESS   In a winding-sheet?*
ANTONIO   In a couple.
DUCHESS   Saint Winfred,   440
That were a strange will!
ANTONIO   'Twere stranger if there were no will in you
To marry again.
DUCHESS   What do you think of marriage?
ANTONIO   I take't, as those that deny purgatory;   445
It locally contains or Heaven or hell;
There's no third place in 't.
DUCHESS   How do you affect it?
ANTONIO   My banishment, feeling my melancholy,
Would often reason thus.   450
DUCHESS   Pray, let's hear it.
ANTONIO   Say a man never marry, nor have children,
What takes that from him? Only the bare name
Of being a father, or the weak delight
To see the little wanton ride a cock-horse   455
Upon a painted stick, or hear him chatter
Like a taught starling.
DUCHESS   Fie, fie, what's all this?
One of your eyes is blood-shot; use my ring to 't,
They say 'tis very sovereign: 'twas my wedding-ring,   460
And I did vow never to part with it
But to my second husband.
ANTONIO   You have parted with it now.
DUCHESS   Yes, to help your eyesight.
ANTONIO   You have made me stark blind.   465
DUCHESS
ANTONIO   There is a saucy and ambitious devil
Is dancing in this circle.
DUCHESS   Remove him.
ANTONIO   How?   470
DUCHESS   There needs small conjuration, when your finger
May do it: this; is it fit? (*She puts the ring upon his finger: he kneels*)
ANTONIO   What said you?
DUCHESS   Sir,
This goodly roof of yours is too low built;   475
I cannot stand upright in 't nor discourse,
Without I raise it higher: raise yourself;
Or, if you please, my hand to help you: so. (*Raises him*)
ANTONIO   Ambition, madam, is a great man's madness,

438 A sheet such as dead bodies were wrapped in.

That is not kept in chains and close-pent rooms,
But in fair lightsome lodgings, and is girt
With the wild noise of prattling visitants,
Which makes it lunatic beyond all cure.
Conceive not I am so stupid but I aim*
Whereto your favours tend: but he's a fool
That, being a-cold, would thrust his hands i' th' fire
To warm them.

DUCHESS   So, now the ground's broke,
You may discover what a wealthy mine
I make you lord of.

ANTONIO   O my unworthiness!

DUCHESS   You were ill to sell yourself:
This darkening of your worth is not like that
Which tradesmen use i' th' city, their false lights
Are to rid bad wares off: and I must tell you,
If you will know where breathes a complete man
(I speak it without flattery), turn your eyes,
And progress through yourself.

ANTONIO   Were there nor heaven
Nor hell, I should be honest: I have long serv'd virtue,
And ne'er ta'en wages of her.

DUCHESS   Now she pays it.
The misery of us that are born great!
We are forc'd to woo, because none dare woo us;
And as a tyrant doubles with his words,
And fearfully equivocates, so we
Are forc'd to express our violent passions
In riddles and in dreams, and leave the path
Of simple virtue, which was never made
To seem the thing it is not. Go, go brag
You have left me heartless; mine is in your bosom:
I hope 'twill multiply love there. You do tremble:
Make not your heart so dead a piece of flesh,
To fear more than to love me. Sir, be confident:
What is 't distracts you? This is flesh and blood, sir;
'Tis not the figure cut in alabaster
Kneels at my husband's tomb. Awake, awake, man!
I do here put off all vain ceremony,
And only do appear to you a young widow
That claims you for her husband, and, like a widow,
I use but half a blush in 't.

ANTONIO   Truth speak for me,
I will remain the constant sanctuary
Of your good name.

DUCHESS   I thank you, gentle love:

484 Guess.

And 'cause you shall not come to me in debt,
Being now my steward, here upon your lips
I sign your *Quietus est.** This you should have begg'd now:
I have seen children oft eat sweetmeats thus,
As fearful to devour them too soon.   530

ANTONIO   But for your brothers?
DUCHESS   Do not think of them:
                    (*She puts her arms around him*)
All discord without* this circumference   535
Is only to be pitied, and not fear'd:
Yet, should they know it, time will easily
Scatter the tempest.

ANTONIO   These words should be mine,
And all the parts you have spoke, if some part of it
Would not have savour'd flattery.   540

DUCHESS   Kneel.
                    (CARIOLA *comes from behind the arras*)

ANTONIO   Ha!
DUCHESS   Be not amazed; this woman's of my counsel:
I have heard lawyers say, a contract in a chamber,   545
*Per verba de presenti,** is absolute marriage. (*She and* ANTONIO *kneel*)
Bless, heaven, this sacred gordian,* which let violence
Never untwine!

ANTONIO   And may our sweet affections, like the spheres,
Be still in motion!   550

DUCHESS   Quickening,* and make
The like soft music!

ANTONIO   That we may imitate the loving palms,*
Best emblem of a peaceful marriage, that ne'er   555
Bore fruit, divided!

DUCHESS OF   What can the Church force more?
ANTONIO   That fortune may not know an accident,
Either of joy or sorrow, to divide
Our fixed wishes!   560

DUCHESS   How can the Church build faster?
We now are man and wife, and 'tis the Church
That must but echo this.—Maid, stand apart:
I now am blind.*

ANTONIO   What's your conceit in this?
DUCHESS   I would have you lead your fortune by the hand?   565

---

528 Acquittance.
534 Outside.
546 By canon law a man and woman were married at the moment they mutually recognized they were.
547 A famous knot.
551 Engendering with life.
553 An allusion to the lore of plant breeding.
563 Like love and/or fortune; or perhaps blind to the consequences.

Unto your marriage bed:
(You speak in me this, for we now are one:)
We'll only lie, and talk together, and plot
To appease my humorous kindred; and if you please,
Like the old tale in 'Alexander and Lodowick',*
Lay a naked sword between us, keep us chaste.   570
Oh, let me shroud my blushes in your bosom,
Since 'tis the treasury of all my secrets! (*Exeunt* DUCHESS *and* ANTONIO)
CARIOLA   Whether the spirit of greatness or of woman
Reign most in her, I know not; but it shows
A fearful madness: I owe her much of pity. (*Exit*)   575

Act Two

Scene 1

A Room in the Palace of the Duchess
(*Enter* BOSOLA *and* CASTRUCCIO)

BOSOLA   You say you would fain be taken for an eminent courtier?
CASTRUCCIO   'Tis the very main of my ambition.
BOSOLA   Let me see: you have a reasonable good face for 't already, and your   5
nightcap* expresses your ears sufficient largely. I would have you learn to
twirl the strings of your band with a good grace, and in a set speech, at th'
end of every sentence, to hum three or four times, or blow your nose till it
smart again, to recover your memory. When you come to be a president in
criminal causes, if you smile upon a prisoner, hang him, but if you frown   10
upon him and threaten him, let him be sure to scape the gallows.
CASTRUCCIO   I would be a very merry president.
BOSOLA   Do not sup o' nights; 'twill beget you an admirable wit.
CASTRUCCIO   Rather it would make me have a good stomach to quarrel; for they
say, your roaring boys* eat meat seldom, and that makes them so valiant.   15
But how shall I know whether the people take me for an eminent fellow?
BOSOLA   I will teach a trick to know it: give out you lie a-dying, and if you hear
the common people curse you, be sure you are taken for one of the prime
nightcaps.*

(*Enter an* OLD LADY)
You come from painting now.   20
OLD LADY   From what?
BOSOLA   Why, from your scurvy face-physic. To behold thee not painted inclines
somewhat near a miracle; these in thy face here were deep ruts and foul
sloughs the last progress.* There was a lady in France that, having had the   25

---

570 A ballad on the subject of two faithful friends.
6 Lawyer's coif.
15 Elizabethan bullies.
19 Lawyers.
25 State procession.

small-pox, flayed the skin off her face to make it more level; and whereas before she look'd like a nutmeg-grater, after she resembled an abortive hedge-hog.*

OLD LADY   Do you call this painting?

BOSOLA   No, no, but I call it careening* of an old morphewed* lady, to make 30 her disembogue* again: there's rough-cast phrase to your plastic.*

OLD LADY   It seems you are well acquainted with my closet.

BOSOLA   One would suspect it for a shop of witchcraft, to find in it the fat of serpents, spawn of snakes, Jews' spittle, and their young children's ordure; and all these for the face. I would sooner eat a dead pigeon taken from the 35 soles of the feet of one sick of the plague than kiss one of you fasting.* Here are two of you, whose sin of your youth is the very patrimony of the physician; makes him renew his foot-cloth* with the spring, and change his high-priced courtezan with the fall of the leaf. I do wonder you do not loathe yourselves. Observe my meditation now. 40

What thing is in this outward form of man
To be belov'd? We account it ominous,
If nature do produce a colt, or lamb,
A fawn, or goat, in any limb resembling
A man, and fly from 't as a prodigy: 45
Man stands amaz'd to see his deformity
In any other creature but himself.
But in our own flesh, though we bear diseases
Which have their true names only ta'en from beasts,
As the most ulcerous wolf and swinish measle, 50
Though we are eaten up of lice and worms,
And though continually we bear about us
A rotten and dead body, we delight
To hide it in rich tissue: all our fear,
Nay, all our terror, is lest our physician 55
Should put us in the ground to be made sweet—
Your wife's gone to Rome: you two couple, and get you
To the wells at Lucca to recover your aches.
I have other work on foot. (*Exeunt* CASTRUCCIO *and* OLD LADY)
                    I observe our duchess 60
Is sick a-days, she pukes, her stomach seethes,
The fins of her eye-lids look most teeming blue,
She wanes i' th' cheek, and waxes fat i' th' flank,
And, contrary to our Italian fashion,
Wears a loose-bodied gown. There's somewhat in 't. 65
I have a trick may chance discover it,

28 A premature porcupine.

30 (*a*) Turning a ship on its side to scrape the paint. (*b*) Leprous.

31 (*a*) To discharge for service, as a ship is discharged after repairs to set out for new prizes. (*b*) "Rough-cast" refers to a rough mixture of lime and gravel, here for modelling, or "plastic."

36 When they are fasting and therefore most offensive.

38 An ornamental cloth draped over a horse.

A pretty one; I have bought some apricocks,
The first our spring yields.

(Enter ANTONIO *and* DELIO, *talking together apart)*

DELIO   And so long since married?   70
You amaze me.

ANTONIO   Let me seal your lips for ever:
For did I think that anything but th' air
Could carry these words from you, I should wish
You had no breath at all.—*(To* BOSOLA*)* Now, sir, in your contemplation?   75
You are studying to become a great wise fellow?

BOSOLA   Oh, sir, the opinion of wisdom is a foul tetter* that runs all over a man's
body: if simplicity direct us to have no evil, it directs us to a happy being; for
the subtlest folly proceeds from the subtlest wisdom: let me be simply
honest.
                                                                                80

ANTONIO   I do understand your inside.

BOSOLA   Do you so?

ANTONIO   Because you would not seem to appear to th' world
Puff'd up with your preferment, you continue
This out-of-fashion melancholy: leave it, leave it.
                                                                                85

BOSOLA   Give me leave to be honest in any phrase, in any compliment
whatsoever. Shall I confess myself to you? I look no higher than I can
reach: they are the gods that must ride on winged horses. A lawyer's mule
of a slow pace will both suit my disposition and business; for, mark me,
when a man's mind rides faster than his horse can gallop, they quickly   90
both tire.

ANTONIO   You would look up to heaven, but I think
The devil, that rules i' th' air, stands in your light.

BOSOLA   Oh, sir, you are lord of the ascendant,* chief man with the duchess; a
duke was your cousin-german remov'd. Say you were lineally descended   95
from King Pepin,* or he himself, what of this? Search the heads of the greatest rivers in the world, you shall find them but bubbles of water. Some would
think the souls of princes were brought forth by some more weighty cause
than those of meaner persons: they are deceiv'd, there's the same hand to
them; the like passions sway them; the same reason that makes a vicar go   100
to law for a tithe-pig,* and undo his neighbours, makes them spoil a whole
province, and batter down goodly cities with the cannon.

(Enter DUCHESS *and* LADIES*)*

DUCHESS   Your arm, Antonio: do I not grow fat?
I am exceeding short-winded.—Bosola,
I would have you, sir, provide for me a litter;   105
Such a one as the Duchess of Florence rode in.

BOSOLA   The duchess used one when she was great with child.

---

⁷⁷ Skin disease.

⁹⁴ By astrological calculation. The rising planet, or sign, is in Antonio's "mansion"; hence both are dominant for a time.

⁹⁶ King of the Franks (c.714–768).

¹⁰¹ A pig paid as tax, usually to support the church.

DUCHESS   I think she did.—Come hither, mend my ruff;
        Here, when?*   110
        Thou art such a tedious lady; and thy breath smells
        Of lemon-peels;* would thou hadst done! Shall I swoon
        Under thy fingers! I am so troubled
        With the mother!*
BOSOLA (*Aside*)   I fear too much.   115
DUCHESS   I have heard you say
        That the French courtiers wear their hats on 'fore
        The king.
ANTONIO   I have seen it.
DUCHESS   In the presence?   120
ANTONIO   Yes.
DUCHESS   Why should not we bring up that fashion? 'Tis
        Ceremony more than duty that consists
        In the removing of a piece of felt:
        Be you the example to the rest o' th' court;   125
        Put on your hat first.
ANTONIO   You must pardon me:
        I have seen, in colder countries than in France,
        Nobles stand bare to th' prince; and the distinction
        Methought show'd reverently.   130
BOSOLA   I have a present for your grace.
DUCHESS   For me, sir?
BOSOLA   Apricocks, madam.
DUCHESS   O, sir, where are they?
        I have heard of none to-year.*   135
BOSOLA (*Aside*)   Good; her colour rises.
DUCHESS   Indeed, I thank you: they are wondrous fair ones.
        What an unskilful fellow is our gardener!
        We shall have none this month.
BOSOLA   Will not your grace pare them?   140
DUCHESS   No: they taste of musk, methinks; indeed they do.
BOSOLA   I know not: yet I wish your grace had pared 'em.
DUCHESS   Why?
BOSOLA   I forgot to tell you, the knave gardener,
        Only to raise his profit by them the sooner,   145
        Did ripen them in horse-dung.
DUCHESS   O, you jest.—
        You shall judge: pray taste one.
ANTONIO   Indeed, madam,
        I do not love the fruit.   150

110 A common exclamation of impatience.
112 Used for sweetening the breath.
114 With hysteria.
135 This year.

DUCHESS   Sir, you are loath
  To rob us of our dainties: 'tis a delicate fruit;
  They say they are restorative.

BOSOLA   'Tis a pretty art,
  This grafting.

DUCHESS   'Tis so; a bettering of nature.

BOSOLA To make a pippin grow upon a crab,*
  A damson on a blackthorn.—(*Aside*) How greedily she eats them!
  A whirlwind strike off these bawd farthingales!*
  For, but for that and the loose-bodied gown,
  I should have discovered apparently
  The young springal* cutting a caper in her belly.

DUCHESS I thank you, Bosola: they were right good ones,
  If they do not make me sick.

ANTONIO   How now, madam?

DUCHESS This green fruit and my stomach are not friends:
  How they swell me!

BOSOLA (*Aside*)   Nay, you are too much swelled already.

DUCHESS Oh, I am in an extreme cold sweat!

BOSOLA   I am very sorry.

DUCHESS Lights to my chamber!—O good Antonio,
  I fear I am undone!

DELIO   Lights there, lights!
    (*Exeunt* DUCHESS *and* LADIES. *Exit, on the other side,* BOSOLA)

ANTONIO O my most trusty Delio, we are lost!
  I fear she's fall'n in labour; and there's left
  No time for her remove.

DELIO   Have you prepar'd
  Those ladies to attend her? And procur'd
  That politic safe conveyance for the midwife
  Your duchess plotted?

ANTONIO I have.

DELIO   Make use, then, of this forc'd occasion:
  Give out that Bosola hath poison'd her
  With these apricocks; that will give some colour
  For her keeping close.

ANTONIO   Fie, fie, the physicians
  Will then flock to her.

DELIO   For that you may pretend
  She'll use some prepar'd antidote of her own,
  Lest the physicians should re-poison her.

ANTONIO I am lost in amazement: I know not what to think on 't. (*Exeunt*)

155

160

165

170

175

180

185

190

---

157 Apples.
159 Hooped petticoats.
162 Stripling.

Scene 2

A Hall in the same Palace
(*Enter* BOSOLA)

BOSOLA So, so, there's no question but her tetchiness and most vulturous 195
eating of the apricocks are apparent signs of breeding.

(*Enter an* OLD LADY)

Now?

OLD LADY I am in haste, sir.

BOSOLA There was a young waiting-woman had a monstrous desire to see the 200
glass-house*——

OLD LADY Nay, pray let me go.

BOSOLA And it was only to know what strange instrument it was should swell
up a glass to the fashion of a woman's belly.

OLD LADY I will hear no more of the glass-house. You are still abusing 205
women?

BOSOLA Who, I? No; only, by the way now and then, mention your frailties.
The orange-tree bears ripe and green fruit and blossoms all together; and
some of you give entertainment for pure love, but more for more precious
reward. The lusty spring smells well; but drooping autumn tastes well. 210
If we have the same golden showers that rained in the time of Jupiter the
thunderer, you have the same Danaës* still, to hold up their laps to receive
them. Didst thou never study the mathematics?

OLD LADY What's that, sir?

BOSOLA Why, to know the trick how to make a many lines meet in one 215
centre. Go, go, give your foster-daughters good counsel: tell them, that the
devil takes delight to hang at a woman's girdle, like a false rusty watch, that
she cannot discern how the time passes. (*Exit* OLD LADY)

(*Enter* ANTONIO, DELIO, RODERIGO, *and* GRISOLAN)

ANTONIO Shut up the court-gates.   220

RODERIGO   Why, sir? what's the danger?

ANTONIO Shut up the posterns presently, and call
All the officers o' th' court.

GRISOLAN   I shall instantly. (*Exit*)

ANTONIO Who keeps the key o' th' park gate?   225

RODERIGO   Forobosco.

ANTONIO Let him bring 't presently.

(*Re-enter* GRISOLAN *with* SERVANTS)

1ST SERVANT O, gentlemen o' the court, the foulest treason!

BOSOLA (*Aside*) If that these apricocks should be poison'd now,   230
Without my knowledge!

1ST SERVANT   There was taken even now
A Switzer* in the duchess' bed chamber—

---

201 Glass-making factory.
212 Jupiter came to Danaë as a shower of gold.
233 A Swiss mercenary soldier common in Italy at the time.

2ND SERVANT   A Switzer?

1ST SERVANT With a pistol in his great cod-piece.*   235

BOSOLA   Ha, ha, ha!

1ST SERVANT The cod-piece was the case for 't.

2ND SERVANT   There was
A cunning traitor: who would have search'd his cod-piece?

1ST SERVANT True, if he had kept out of the ladies' chambers: 240
And all the moulds of his buttons were leaden bullets.

2ND SERVANT O wicked cannibal!*
A fire-lock in 's cod-piece!

1ST SERVANT   'Twas a French plot
Upon my life.

2ND SERVANT   To see what the devil can do!   245

ANTONIO Are all the officers here?

SERVANTS   We are.

ANTONIO   Gentlemen,
We have lost much plate you know; and but this evening
Jewels, to the value of four thousand ducats,   250
Are missing in the duchess' cabinet.
Are the gates shut?

SERVANTS   Yes.

ANTONIO   'Tis the duchess' pleasure   255
Each officer be lock'd into his chamber
Till the sun-rising; and to send the keys
Of all their chests and of their outward doors
Into her bed-chamber. She is very sick.

RODERIGO At her pleasure.   260

ANTONIO   She entreats you take 't not ill:
The innocent shall be the more approv'd by it.

BOSOLA Gentleman o' th' wood-yard, where's your Switzer now?

1ST SERVANT By this hand, 'twas credibly reported by one o' th' black guard.*
                (*Exeunt all except* ANTONIO *and* DELIO)   265

DELIO How fares it with the duchess?

ANTONIO   She's expos'd
Unto the worst of torture, pain, and fear.

DELIO Speak to her all happy comfort.

ANTONIO How I do play the fool with mine own danger!   270
You are this night, dear friend, to post to Rome:
My life lies in your service.

DELIO   Do not doubt me.

ANTONIO Oh, 'tis far from me: and yet fear presents me
Somewhat that looks like danger.   275

DELIO   Believe it,

---

235 A detachable part of a man's hose, at the genitals.
242 Savage.
264 Kitchen helpers.

'Tis but the shadow of your fear, no more;
How superstitiously we mind our evils!
The throwing down salt, or crossing of a hare,
Bleeding at nose, the stumbling of a horse,   280
Or singing of a cricket, are of power
To daunt whole man in us. Sir, fare you well:
I wish you all the joys of a bless'd father:
And, for my faith, lay this unto your breast,—
Old friends, like old swords, still are trusted best. (*Exit*)   285
                    (*Enter* CARIOLA)
CARIOLA   Sir, you are the happy father of a son:
    Your wife commends him to you.
ANTONIO   Blessèd comfort!—
    For Heaven's sake tend her well: I'll presently   290
    Go set a figure for 's nativity.* (*Exeunt*)

Scene 3

                    The Courtyard of the same Palace
                    (*Enter* BOSOLA, *with a dark lantern*)
BOSOLA   Sure I did hear a woman shriek: list, ha!
    And the sound came, if I receiv'd it right,   295
    From the duchess' lodgings. There's some stratagem
    In the confining all our courtiers
    To their several wards: I must have part of it;
    My intelligence will freeze else. List, again!
    It may be 'twas the melancholy bird,   300
    Best friend of silence and of solitariness,
    The owl, that scream'd so.—Ha! Antonio?
                (*Enter* ANTONIO *with a Candle, his Sword drawn*)
ANTONIO   I heard some noise.—Who's there? What art thou? Speak.
BOSOLA   Antonio? Put not your face nor body   305
    To such a forc'd expression of fear:
    I am Bosola, your friend.
ANTONIO   Bosola!—
    (*Aside*) This mole* does undermine me.—Heard you not
    A noise even now?   310
BOSOLA   From whence?
ANTONIO   From the duchess' lodging.
BOSOLA   Not I: did you?
ANTONIO   I did, or else I dream'd.
BOSOLA   Let's walk towards it.   315
ANTONIO   No: it may be 'twas
    But the rising of the wind.

---

291 Have his horoscope cast.
309 One who plants explosives.

BOSOLA   Very likely.
Methinks 'tis very cold, and yet you sweat:
You look wildly.

ANTONIO   I have been setting a figure   320
For the duchess' jewels.

BOSOLA   Ah, and how falls your question?
Do you find it radical?*

ANTONIO   What's that to you?   325
'Tis rather to be questioned what design,
When all men were commanded to their lodgings,
Makes you a night-walker.

BOSOLA   In sooth, I'll tell you:
Now all the court's asleep, I thought the devil
Had least to do here; I came to say my prayers;   330
And if it do offend you I do so,
You are a fine courtier.

ANTONIO (*Aside*) This fellow will undo me.—
You gave the duchess apricocks to-day:
Pray Heaven they were not poison'd!   335

BOSOLA   Poison'd? A Spanish fig*
For the imputation!

ANTONIO   Traitors are ever confident
Till they are discover'd. There were jewels stol'n too: 340
In my conceit, none are to be suspected
More than yourself.

BOSOLA   You are a false steward.

ANTONIO Saucy slave, I'll pull thee up by the roots.

BOSOLA Maybe the ruin will crush you to pieces.   345

ANTONIO You are an impudent snake indeed, sir:
Are you scarce warm, and do you show your sting?
You libel well, sir.

BOSOLA   No, sir: copy it out,
And I will set my hand to't.*   350

ANTONIO (*Aside*)   My nose bleeds.
One that were superstitious would count
This ominous, when it merely comes by chance:
Two letters,* that are wrought here for my name,
Are drown'd in blood!   355
Mere accident.—For you, sir, I'll take order
I' th' morn you shall be safe:—(*Aside*) 'tis that must colour
Her lying-in: —sir, this door you pass not:

---

324 Conclusive.

337 A "fig" was an indecent gesture of contempt.

350 This passage is obscure. But it seems to contain Bosola's proposal that, to prove his innocence, he will
   sign a statement concerning the jewels.

354 Probably initials on his handkerchief.

I do not hold it fit that you come near
The duchess' lodgings, till you have quit* yourself.— 360
(*Aside*) The great are like the base, nay, they are the same,
When they seek shameful ways to avoid shame. (*Exit*)

BOSOLA Antonio hereabout did drop a paper:—
Some of your help, false friend: (*Opening his lantern*) —Oh, here it is.
What's here? a child's nativity calculated? (*Reads*) 365
    "The duchess was deliver'd of a son, 'tween the hours twelve and one in
the night, *Anno Dom.* 1504,"—that's this year—"*decimo nono Decembris,*"—
that's this night,—"taken according to the meridian of Malfi,"—that's our
duchess: happy discovery!—"The lord of the first house being combust in
the ascendant, signifies short life; and Mars being in a human sign, join'd 370
to the tail of the Dragon, in the eighth house, doth threaten a violent death.
Caetera non scrutantur."*
Why, now 'tis most apparent: this precise* fellow
Is the duchess' bawd:—I have it to my wish!
This is a parcel of intelligency 375
Our courtiers were cas'd up for: it needs must follow
That I must be committed on pretence
Of poisoning her; which I'll endure, and laugh at.
If one could find the father now! but that
Time will discover. Old Castruccio 380
I' th' morning posts to Rome: by him I'll send
A letter that shall make her brothers' galls
O'erflow their livers. This was a thrifty way.
Though lust do mask in ne'er so strange disguise,
She's oft found witty, but is never wise. (*Exit*) 385

Scene 4

A Room in the Palace of the Cardinal at Rome
(*Enter* CARDINAL *and* JULIA)

CARDINAL Sit: thou art my best of wishes. Prithee, tell me
What trick didst thou invent to come to Rome
Without thy husband. 390

JULIA   Why, my lord, I told him
I came to visit an old anchorite*
Here for devotion.

CARDINAL   Thou art a witty false one,—
I mean to him. 395

JULIA   You have prevailed with me
Beyond my strongest thoughts. I would not now
Find you inconstant.

<hr>

360 Acquitted.
372 "The rest has not been investigated."
373 Puritanical.
392 Religious recluse.

CARDINAL   Do not put thyself
   To such a voluntary torture, which proceeds   400
   Out of your own guilt.
JULIA   How, my lord?
CARDINAL   You fear
   My constancy, because you have approved
   Those giddy and wild turnings in yourself.   405
JULIA   Did you e'er find them?
CARDINAL   Sooth, generally for women;
   A man might strive to make glass malleable,
   Ere he should make them fixed.
JULIA   So, my lord.   410
CARDINAL   We had need go borrow that fantastic glass
   Invented by Galileo the Florentine*
   To view another spacious world i' th' moon,
   And look to find a constant woman there.
JULIA   This is very well, my lord.   415
CARDINAL   Why do you weep?
   Are tears your justification? The self-same tears
   Will fall into your husband's bosom, lady,
   With a loud protestation that you love him
   Above the world. Come, I'll love you wisely,   420
   That's jealously, since I am very certain
   You cannot make me cuckold.
JULIA   I'll go home
   To my husband.
CARDINAL   You may thank me, lady,   425
   I have taken you off your melancholy perch,
   Bore you upon my fist, and show'd you game,
   And let you fly at it.*—I pray thee, kiss me.—
   When thou wast with thy husband, thou wast watch'd
   Like a tame elephant:—still you are to thank me:—   430
   Thou hadst only kisses from him and high feeding;
   But what delight was that? 'Twas just like one
   That hath a little fingering on the lute,
   Yet cannot tune it:—still you are to thank me.
JULIA   You told me of a piteous wound i' th' heart   435
   And a sick liver, when you wooed me first,
   And spake like one in physic.*
CARDINAL   Who's that?—
                (*Enter* SERVANT)
   Rest firm, for my affection to thee,   440
   Lightning moves slow to 't.*

412 In 1609 Galileo devised, not the first, but an early effective telescope. Here an anachronism.
428 The metaphor is from falconry.
437 Being treated with medicines.
441 In comparison to it.

SERVANT Madam, a gentleman
That's come post from Malfi desires to see you.
CARDINAL Let him enter: I'll withdraw. (*Exit*)
SERVANT He says   445
Your husband, old Castruccio, is come to Rome,
Most pitifully tir'd with riding post. (*Exit*)
                    (*Enter* DELIO)
JULIA Signior Delio! (*Aside*) 'Tis one of my old suitors.
DELIO I was bold to come and see you.   450
JULIA Sir, you are welcome.
DELIO Do you lie here?
JULIA Sure, your own experience
Will satisfy you no: our Roman prelates
Do not keep lodging for ladies.   455
DELIO Very well:
I have brought you no commendations from your husband,
For I know none by him.
JULIA I hear he's come to Rome.
DELIO I never knew man and beast, of a horse and a knight, 460
So weary of each other: if he had had a good back,
He would have undertook to have borne his horse,
His breech was so pitifully sore.
JULIA Your laughter
Is my pity.   465
DELIO Lady, I know not whether
You want money, but I have brought you some.
JULIA From my husband?
DELIO No, from mine own allowance.
JULIA I must hear the condition, ere I be bound to take it.   470
DELIO Look on't, 'tis gold: hath it not a fine colour?
JULIA I have a bird more beautiful.
DELIO Try the sound on 't.
JULIA A lute-string far exceeds it:
It hath no smell, like cassia or civet;*   475
Nor is it physical,* though some fond doctors
Persuade us seethe 't in cullises.* I'll tell you,
This is a creature bred by——
                    (*Re-enter* SERVANT)
SERVANT Your husband's come,   480
Hath deliver'd a letter to the Duke of Calabria
That, to my thinking, hath put him out of his wits. (*Exit*)
JULIA Sir, you hear:
Pray, let me know your business and your suit

---

475 "Cassia" is a coarse cinnamon; "civet" a musky substance obtained from the civet cat and used in
   perfumes.
476 Good for the health.
477 Boil it in strengthening broths.

As briefly as can be.   485

DELIO   With good speed: I would wish you,
   At such time as you are non-resident
   With your husband, my mistress.

JULIA   Sir, I'll go ask my husband if I shall,
   And straight return your answer. (*Exit*)   490

DELIO   Very fine!
   Is this her wit, or honesty, that speaks thus?
   I heard one say the duke was highly mov'd
   With a letter sent from Malfi. I do fear
   Antonio is betray'd: how fearfully   495
   Shows his ambition now! unfortunate fortune!
   They pass through whirlpools, and deep woes do shun,
   Who the event weigh ere the action's done. (*Exit*)

Scene 5

Another Room in the same Palace
(*Enter* CARDINAL, *and* FERDINAND *with a letter*)   500

FERDINAND   I have this night digged up a mandrake.*

CARDINAL   Say you?

FERDINAND   And I am grown mad with 't.

CARDINAL   What's the prodigy?

FERDINAND   Read there,—a sister damn'd: she's loose i' th' hilts;*   505
   Grown a notorious strumpet.

CARDINAL   Speak lower.

FERDINAND   Lower?
   Rogues do not whisper 't now, but seek to publish 't
   (As servants do the bounty of their lords)   510
   Aloud; and with a covetous searching eye,
   To mark who note them. O, confusion seize her!
   She hath had most cunning bawds to serve her turn,
   And more secure conveyances for lust
   Than towns of garrison for service.   515

CARDINAL   Is 't possible?
   Can this be certain?

FERDINAND   Rhubarb, oh, for rhubarb
   To purge this choler! here's the cursèd day
   To prompt my memory; and here 't shall stick   520
   Till of her bleeding heart I make a sponge
   To wipe it out.

CARDINAL   Why do you make yourself
   So wild a tempest?

FERDINAND   Would I could be one,   525
   That I might toss her palace 'bout her ears,

---

501 Madness was supposed to follow eating the mandrake.
505 Unchaste.

Root up her goodly forests, blast her meads,*
And lay her general territory as waste
As she hath done her honours.

CARDINAL   Shall our blood,   530
The royal blood of Arragon and Castile,
Be thus attainted?

FERDINAND   Apply desperate physic:
We must not now use balsamum, but fire,
The smarting cupping-glass,* for that 's the mean   535
To purge infected blood, such blood as hers.
There is a kind of pity in mine eye,—
I'll give it to my handkercher; and now 'tis here,
I'll bequeath this to her bastard.

CARDINAL   What to do?   540

FERDINAND Why, to make soft lint for his mother's wounds,
When I have hewed her to pieces.

CARDINAL   Curs'd creature!
Unequal nature, to place women's hearts
So far upon the left side!*   545

FERDINAND   Foolish men,
That e'er will trust their honour in a bark
Made of so slight weak bulrush as is woman,
Apt every minute to sink it!

CARDINAL Thus ignorance, when it hath purchas'd* honour, 550
It cannot wield it.

FERDINAND   Methinks I see her laughing—
Excellent hyena! Talk to me somewhat, quickly,
Or my imagination will carry me
To see her in the shameful act of sin.   555

CARDINAL With whom?

FERDINAND Happily* with some strong-thigh'd bargeman,
Or one o' the woodyard that can quoit the sledge*
Or toss the bar, or else some lovely squire
That carries coals up to her privy lodgings.   560

CARDINAL You fly beyond your reason.

FERDINAND   Go to, mistress!
'Tis not your whore's milk that shall quench my wild fire,
But your whore's blood.

CARDINAL How idly shows this rage, which carries you, 565
As men convey'd by witches through the air,
On violent whirlwinds! This intemperate noise

---

527 Meadows.

535 Hot cups or cupped glasses were applied to draw off poisons.

545 It was a common belief that a fool's heart was on the left side, a wise man's on the right.

550 Obtained.

557 Or "haply," that is, by chance.

558 Throw the hammer.

Fitly resembles deaf men's shrill discourse,
Who talk aloud, thinking all other men
To have their imperfection.   570
FERDINAND   Have not you
    My palsy?
CARDINAL   Yes, I can be angry, but
    Without this rupture: there is not in nature
    A thing that makes man so deform'd, so beastly,   575
    As doth intemperate anger. Chide yourself.
    You have divers men who never yet express'd
    Their strong desire of rest but by unrest,
    By vexing of themselves. Come, put yourself
    In tune.   580
FERDINAND   So; I will only study to seem
    The thing I am not. I could kill her now,
    In you, or in myself; for I do think
    It is some sin in us heaven doth revenge
    By her.   585
CARDINAL   Are you stark mad?
FERDINAND   I would have their bodies
    Burnt in a coal-pit with the ventage stopp'd,
    That their curs'd smoke might not ascend to heaven;
    Or dip the sheets they lie in in pitch or sulphur,   590
    Wrap them in 't, and then light them like a match;
    Or else to boil their bastard to a cullis,
    And give 't his lecherous father to renew
    The sin of his back.
CARDINAL   I'll leave you.   595
FERDINAND   Nay, I have done.
    I am confident, had I been damn'd in hell,
    And should have heard of this, it would have put me
    Into a cold sweat. In, in; I'll go sleep.
    Till I know who leaps my sister, I'll not stir: 600
    That known, I'll find scorpions to string* my whips,
    And fix her in a general eclipse.* (*Exeunt*)

Act Three

Scene 1

A Room in the Palace of the Duchess
(*Enter* ANTONIO *and* DELIO)

ANTONIO   Our noble friend, my most beloved Delio!
    Oh, you have been a stranger long at court;
    Came you along with the Lord Ferdinand?   5

---

601 Attach to.
602 Total eclipse.

DELIO I did, sir: and how fares your noble duchess?

ANTONIO Right fortunately well: she 's an excellent
    Feeder of pedigrees; since you last saw her,
    She hath had two children more, a son and daughter.

DELIO Methinks 'twas yesterday: let me but wink,   10
    And not behold your face, which to mine eye
    Is somewhat leaner, verily I should dream
    It were within this half-hour.

ANTONIO You have not been in law, friend Delio,
    Nor in prison, nor a suitor at the court,   15
    Nor begged the reversion of some great man's place,
    Nor troubled with an old wife, which doth make
    Your time so insensibly hasten.

DELIO   Pray, sir, tell me,
    Hath not this news arriv'd yet to the ear   20
    Of the Lord Cardinal?

ANTONIO   I fear it hath:
    The Lord Ferdinand, that 's newly come to court,
    Doth bear himself right dangerously.

DELIO   Pray, why?   25

ANTONIO He is so quiet that he seems to sleep
    The tempest out, as dormice do in winter:
    Those houses that are haunted are most still
    Till the devil be up.

DELIO   What say the common people?   30

ANTONIO The common rabble do directly say
    She is a strumpet.

DELIO   And your graver heads
    Which would be politic, what censure* they?

ANTONIO They do observe I grow to infinite purchase,*   35
    The left hand way, and all suppose the duchess
    Would amend it, if she could; for, say they,
    Great princes, though they grudge their officers
    Should have such large and unconfined means
    To get wealth under them, will not complain,   40
    Lest thereby they should make them odious
    Unto the people; for other obligation
    Of love or marriage between her and me
    They never dream of.

DELIO   The Lord Ferdinand   45
    Is going to bed.

           (*Enter* DUCHESS, FERDINAND, *and* BOSOLA)

FERDINAND I'll instantly to bed,
    For I am weary.—I am to bespeak
    A husband for you.   50

34 Think.
35 Wealth.

DUCHESS   For me, sir? Pray, who is 't?
FERDINAND   The great Count Malateste.
DUCHESS   Fie upon him!
    A count? He 's a mere stick of sugar-candy;
    You may look quite thorough him. When I choose   55
    A husband, I will marry for your honour.
FERDINAND   You shall do well in 't.—How is 't, worthy Antonio?
DUCHESS   But, sir, I am to have private conference with you
    About a scandalous report is spread
    Touching mine honour.   60
FERDINAND   Let me be ever deaf to 't:
    One of Pasquil's paper bullets,* court-calumny,
    A pestilent air, which princes' palaces
    Are seldom purged of. Yet, say that it were true,
    I pour it in your bosom, my fix'd love   65
    Would strongly excuse, extenuate, nay, deny
    Faults, were they apparent in you. Go, be safe
    In your own innocency.
DUCHESS (*Aside*)   O bless'd comfort!
    This deadly air is purg'd. (*Exeunt* DUCHESS, ANTONIO, *and* DELIO)   70
FERDINAND   Her guilt treads on
    Hot-burning coulters.*—Now, Bosola,
    How thrives our intelligence?
BOSOLA   Sir, uncertainly;
    'Tis rumour'd she hath had three bastards, but
    By whom we may go read i' th' stars.   75
FERDINAND   Why, some
    Hold opinion all things are written there.
BOSOLA   Yes, if we could find spectacles to read them.
    I do suspect there hath been some sorcery
    Us'd on the duchess.   80
FERDINAND   Sorcery? to what purpose?
BOSOLA   To make her dote on some desertless fellow
    She shames to acknowledge.
FERDINAND   Can your faith give way   85
    To think there 's power in potions or in charms,
    To make us love whether we will or no?
BOSOLA   Most certainly.
FERDINAND   Away! these are mere gulleries, horrid things,
    Invented by some cheating mountebanks   90
    To abuse us. Do you think that herbs or charms
    Can force the will? Some trials have been made
    In this foolish practice, but the ingredients

---

62 Pasquillo was a sharp-tongued Roman schoolmaster in the 15th century, to whose statue students fixed
   satirical verses.

72 A "coulter" was the iron blade in front of the plough-share. In the ordeal by red-hot plough-shares, the
   accused walked over nine of them to prove her chastity.

Were lenitive* poisons, such as are of force
To make the patient mad; and straight the witch   95
Swears by equivocation they are in love.
The witchcraft lies in her rank blood. This night
I will force confession from her. You told me
You had got, within these two days, a false key
Into her bed-chamber.   100

BOSOLA   I have.

FERDINAND   As I would wish.

BOSOLA   What do you intend to do?

FERDINAND   Can you guess?

BOSOLA   No.   105

FERDINAND   Do not ask, then:
He that can compass me, and know my drifts,
May say he hath put a girdle 'bout the world,
And sounded all her quicksands.

BOSOLA   I do not   110
Think so.

FERDINAND   What do you think, then, pray?

BOSOLA   That you
Are your own chronicle too much, and grossly
Flatter yourself.   115

FERDINAND   Give me thy hand; I thank thee:
I never gave pension but to flatterers,
Till I entertained thee. Farewell.
That friend a great man's ruin strongly checks,
Who rails into his belief all his defects. (*Exeunt*)   120

Scene 2

The Bedchamber of the Duchess
(*Enter* DUCHESS, ANTONIO, *and* CARIOLA)

DUCHESS   Bring me the casket hither, and the glass.—
You get no lodging here to-night, my lord.

ANTONIO   Indeed, I must persuade one.   125

DUCHESS   Very good:
I hope in time 'twill grow into a custom,
That noblemen shall come with cap and knee*
To purchase a night's lodging of their wives.

ANTONIO   I must lie here.   130

DUCHESS   Must! you are a lord of misrule.*

ANTONIO   Indeed, my rule is only in the night.

DUCHESS   To what use will you put me?

ANTONIO   We'll sleep together.

DUCHESS   Alas,   135

94 Soothing.
128 With cap in hand and bended knee.
131 Lord of the Christmas revels.

What pleasure can two lovers find in sleep!

CARIOLA   My lord, I lie with her often; and I know
    She'll much disquiet you.

ANTONIO   See, you are complain'd of.

CARIOLA   For she 's the sprawling'st bedfellow.   140

ANTONIO   I shall like her
    The better for that.

CARIOLA   Sir, shall I ask you a question?

ANTONIO   I pray thee, Cariola.

CARIOLA   Wherefore still, when you lie   145
    With my lady, do you rise so early?

ANTONIO   Labouring men
    Count the clock oftenest, Cariola, are glad
    When their task's ended.

DUCHESS   I'll stop your mouth. (*Kisses him*)   150

ANTONIO   Nay, that 's but one; Venus had two soft doves
    To draw her chariot; I must have another—(*She kisses him again*)
    When wilt thou marry, Cariola?

CARIOLA   Never, my lord.

ANTONIO   Oh, fie upon this single life! Forgo it.   155
    We read how Daphne, for her peevish flight,
    Became a fruitless bay-tree; Syrinx turn'd
    To the pale empty reed; Anaxarete
    Was frozen into marble:* whereas those
    Which married, or prov'd kind unto their friends,   160
    Were by a gracious influence transhap'd
    Into the olive, pomegranate, mulberry,
    Became flowers, precious stones, or eminent stars.

CARIOLA   This is a vain poetry: but I pray you tell me,
    If there were propos'd me, wisdom, riches, and beauty,   165
    In three several young men, which should I choose?

ANTONIO   'Tis a hard question: this was Paris' case,*
    And he was blind in 't, and there was great cause;
    For how was 't possible he could judge right,
    Having three amorous goddesses in view,   170
    And they stark naked? 'Twas a motion*
    Were able to benight the apprehension
    Of the severest counsellor of Europe.
    Now I look on both your faces, so well form'd,
    It puts me in mind of a question I would ask.   175

CARIOLA   What is 't?

ANTONIO   I do wonder why hard-favour'd ladies,
    For the most part, keep worse-favour'd waiting-women
    To attend them, and cannot endure fair ones.

---

[159] Daphne was wooed by Apollo, Syrinx by Pan, Anaxerete by Iphis.

[167] In the Contest for the Golden Apple, when he had to choose among Juno, Athena, and Venus.

[171] Spectacle.

DUCHESS Oh, that's soon answer'd.   180
    Did you ever in your life know an ill painter
    Desire to have his dwelling next door to the shop
    Of an excellent picture-maker? 'Twould disgrace
    His face-making, and undo him. I prithee,
    When were we so merry?—My hair tangles.   185
ANTONIO Pray thee, Cariola, let 's steal forth the room,
    And let her talk to herself: I have divers times
    Serv'd her the like, when she hath chaf'd extremely.
    I love to see her angry. Softly, Cariola. (*Exeunt* ANTONIO *and* CARIOLA)
DUCHESS Doth not the colour of my hair 'gin to change?   190
    When I wax grey, I shall have all the court
    Powder their hair with arras,* to be like me.
    You have cause to love me; I enter'd you into my heart
    Before you would vouchsafe to call for the keys.
                    (*Enter* FERDINAND *behind*)   195
    We shall one day have my brothers take you napping;
    Methinks his presence, being now in court,
    Should make you keep your own bed; but you'll say
    Love mix'd with fear is sweetest. I'll assure you,
    You shall get no more children till my brothers   200
    Consent to be your gossips.* Have you lost your tongue?
    'Tis welcome: (*She turns and sees* FERDINAND)
    For know, whether I am doom'd to live or die,
    I can do both like a prince.
FERDINAND   Die, then, quickly! (*Giving her a poniard*) 205
    Virtue, where art thou hid? What hideous thing
    Is it that doth eclipse thee?
DUCHESS   Pray, sir, hear me.
FERDINAND Or is it true thou art but a bare name,
    And no essential thing?   210
DUCHESS   Sir,—
FERDINAND   Do not speak.
DUCHESS No, sir: I will plant my soul in mine ears, to hear you.
FERDINAND O most imperfect light of human reason,
    That mak'st us so unhappy to foresee   215
    What we can least prevent! Pursue thy wishes,
    And glory in them: there 's in shame no comfort
    But to be past all bounds and sense of shame.
DUCHESS I pray, sir, hear me: I am married.
FERDINAND   So!   220
DUCHESS Happily, not to your liking: but for that,
    Alas, your shears do come untimely now
    To clip the bird's wings that's already flown!
    Will you see my husband?

192 A white powder.
201 God-parents to your children.

FERDINAND   Yes, if I could change
    Eyes with a basilisk.*
DUCHESS   Sure, you came hither
    By his confederacy.
FERDINAND   The howling of a wolf
    Is music to thee,* screech-owl: prithee, peace.—   230
    Whate'er thou art that hast enjoy'd my sister,
    For I am sure thou hear'st me, for thine own sake
    Let me not know thee. I came hither prepar'd
    To work thy discovery, yet am now persuaded
    It would beget such violent effects   235
    As would damn us both. I would not for ten millions
    I had beheld thee: therefore use all means
    I never may have knowledge of thy name;
    Enjoy thy lust still, and a wretched life,
    On that condition.—And for thee, vile woman,   240
    If thou do wish thy lecher may grow old
    In thy embracements, I would have thee build
    Such a room for him as our anchorites
    To holier use inhabit. Let not the sun
    Shine on him till he 's dead; let dogs and monkeys   245
    Only converse with him, and such dumb things
    To whom nature denies use to sound his name;
    Do not keep a *paraquito,* * lest she learn it;
    If thou do love him, cut out thine own tongue,
    Lest it bewray him.   250
DUCHESS   Why might not I marry?
    I have not gone about in this to create
    Any new world or custom.
FERDINAND   Thou art undone;
    And thou hast ta'en that massy sheet of lead   255
    That hid thy husband's bones, and folded it
    About my heart.
DUCHESS   Mine bleeds for 't.
FERDINAND   Thine? Thy heart?
    What should I name 't unless a hollow bullet   260
    Fill'd with unquenchable wild-fire?
DUCHESS   You are in this
    Too strict; and were you not my princely brother,
    I would say too wilful: my reputation
    Is safe.   ●   265
FERDINAND   Dost thou know what reputation is?
    I'll tell thee,—to small purpose, since the instruction
    Comes now too late.

---

226 A fabulous king of serpents whose look or breath was fatal.
230 Compared to thee.
248 Parakeet.

Upon a time Reputation, Love, and Death,
Would travel o'er the world; and it was concluded 270
That they should part, and take three several ways.
Death told them, they should find him in great battles,
Or cities plagu'd with plagues: Love gives them counsel
To inquire for him 'mongst unambitious shepherds,
Where dowries were not talk'd of, and sometimes 275
'Mongst quiet kindred that had nothing left
By their dead parents: "Stay," quoth Reputation,
"Do not forsake me; for it is my nature,
If once I part from any man I meet,
I am never found again." And so for you: 280
You have shook hands with Reputation,
And made him invisible. So, fare you well:
I will never see you more.

DUCHESS   Why should only I,
Of all the other princes of the world, 285
Be cas'd up, like a holy relic? I have youth
And a little beauty.

FERDINAND   So you have some virgins
That are witches. I will never see thee more. (*Exit*)
        (*Re-enter* ANTONIO *with a pistol, and* CARIOLA) 290

DUCHESS   You saw this apparition?

ANTONIO   Yes: we are
Betray'd. How came he hither?—I should turn
This to thee, for that. (*Pointing the pistol at* CARIOLA)

CARIOLA   Pray, sir, do; and when 295
That you have cleft my heart, you shall read there
Mine innocence.

DUCHESS   That gallery gave him entrance.

ANTONIO   I would this terrible thing would come again,
That, standing on my guard, I might relate 300
My warrantable love.—(*She shows the poniard*) Ha! what means this?

DUCHESS   He left this with me.

ANTONIO   And it seems did wish
You would use it on yourself.

DUCHESS   His action seem'd 305
To intend so much.

ANTONIO   This hath a handle to 't.
As well as a point: turn it towards him, and
So fasten the keen edge in his rank gall. (*Knocking within*)
How now! Who knocks? More earthquakes? 310

DUCHESS   I stand
As if a mine beneath my feet were ready
To be blown up.

CARIOLA   'Tis Bosola.

DUCHESS   Away! 315

O misery! Methinks unjust actions
Should wear these masks and curtains, and not we.
You must instantly part hence: I have fashion'd it
Already. (*Exit* ANTONIO)

(*Enter* BOSOLA)

BOSOLA The duke your brother is ta'en up in a whirlwind,   320
Hath took horse, and 's rid post to Rome.
DUCHESS   So late?
BOSOLA He told me, as he mounted into th' saddle,
You were undone.
DUCHESS Indeed, I am very near it.   325
BOSOLA   What 's the matter?
DUCHESS Antonio, the master of our household,
Hath dealt so falsely with me in 's accounts:
My brother stood engag'd with me for money
Ta'en up of certain Neapolitan Jews,   330
And Antonio lets the bonds be forfeit.*
BOSOLA Strange!—(*Aside*) This is cunning.
DUCHESS   And hereupon
My brother's bills at Naples are protested
Against.—Call up our officers.   335
BOSOLA   I shall. (*Exit*)

(*Re-enter* ANTONIO)

DUCHESS The place that you must fly to is Ancona:
Hire a house there; I'll send after you
My treasure and my jewels. Our weak safety   340
Runs upon enginous wheels:* short syllables
Must stand for periods. I must now accuse you
Of such a feigned crime as Tasso calls
Magnanima menzogna, a noble lie,*
Cause it must shield our honours.—Hark! they are coming.   345

(*Re-enter* BOSOLA *and* OFFICERS)

ANTONIO Will your grace hear me?
DUCHESS I have got well by you; you have yielded me
A million of loss: I am like to inherit
The people's curses for your stewardship.   350
You had the trick in audit-time to be sick,
Till I had sign'd your *quietus;** and that cur'd you
Without help of a doctor.—Gentlemen,
I would have this man be an example to you all;
So shall you hold my favour; I pray, let him;*   355

---

332 Presumably, Ferdinand had offered security for money which the Duchess had borrowed of Neapolitan
Jews. By not making the necessary payments, Antonio had made Ferdinand's notes ("bills") forfeit.
342 That is, is rapidly leaving us.
345 From *Jerusalem Delivered* by Torquato Tasso (1544–1595). A Christian maiden, Sofronia, takes the blame
for something of which she is innocent to save her fellows.
353 Receipt.
356 Let him go.

For h'as done that, alas, you would not think of,
And, because I intend to be rid of him,
I mean not to publish.—Use your fortune elsewhere.

ANTONIO   I am strongly arm'd to brook my overthrow;   360
As commonly men bear with a hard year,
I will not blame the cause on 't; but do think
The necessity of my malevolent star
Procures this, not her humour. Oh, the inconstant
And rotten ground of service! You may see,   365
'Tis even like him, that in a winter night,
Takes a long slumber o'er a dying fire,
As loath to part from 't; yet parts thence as cold
As when he first sat down.

DUCHESS   We do confiscate,   370
Towards the satisfying of your accounts,
All that you have.

ANTONIO   I am all yours: and 'tis very fit
All mine should be so.

DUCHESS   So, sir, you have your pass.   375

ANTONIO   You may see, gentlemen, what 'tis to serve
A prince with body and soul. (*Exit*)

BOSOLA   Here's an example for extortion: what moisture is drawn out of the
sea, when foul weather comes, pours down, and runs into the sea again.

DUCHESS   I would know what are your opinions of this Antonio.   380

2ND OFFICER   He could not abide to see a pig's head gaping: I thought your
grace would find him a Jew.

3RD OFFICER   I would you had been his officer, for your own sake.

4TH OFFICER   You would have had more money.

1ST OFFICER   He stopped his ears with black wool, and to those came to him   385
for money said he was thick of hearing.

2ND OFFICER   Some said he was an hermaphrodite, for he could not abide a
woman.

4TH OFFICER   How scurvy proud he would look when the treasury was full!
Well, let him go!   390

1ST OFFICER   Yes, and the chippings of the buttery* fly after him, to scour his
gold chain!*

DUCHESS   Leave us. (*Exeunt* OFFICERS) What do you think of these?

BOSOLA   That these are rogues that in 's prosperity, but to have waited on his
fortune, could have wish'd his dirty stirrup riveted through their noses,   395
and follow'd after 's mule, like a bear in a ring; would have prostituted their
daughters to his lust; made their first-born intelligencers; thought none
happy but such as were born under his blest planet, and wore his livery:
and do these lice drop off now? Well, never look to have the like again: he
hath left a sort of flattering rogues behind him; their doom must follow.   400

391 Bread crumbs.
392 A steward's normal badge of office.

Princes pay flatterers in their own money: flatterers dissemble their vices, and they dissemble their lies;* that 's justice. Alas, poor gentleman!

DUCHESS Poor? he hath amply fill'd his coffers.

BOSOLA Sure, he was too honest. Pluto, the god of riches, when he 's sent by Jupiter to any man, he goes limping, to signify that wealth that comes 405 on God's name comes slowly; but when he 's sent on the devil's errand, he rides post and comes in by scuttles.* Let me show you what a most un-valued* jewel you have in a wanton humour thrown away, to bless the man shall find him. He was an excellent courtier and most faithful; a soldier that thought it as beastly to know his own value too little as devilish 410 to acknowledge it too much. Both his virtue and form deserv'd a far better fortune: his discourse rather delighted to judge itself than show itself: his breast was fill'd with all perfection, and yet it seem'd a private whispering-room, it made so little noise of 't.

DUCHESS But he was basely descended.

BOSOLA Will you make yourself a mercenary herald,* rather to examine men's 415 pedigrees than virtues? You shall want him: for know, an honest statesman to a prince is like a cedar planted by a spring; the spring bathes the tree's root, the grateful tree rewards it with his shadow: you have not done so. I would sooner swim to the Bermoothes* on two politicians' rotten 420 bladders, tied together with an intelligencer's heart-string, than depend on so changeable a prince's favour. Fare thee well, Antonio! since the malice of the world would needs down with thee, it cannot be said yet that any ill happened unto thee, considering thy fall was accompanied with virtue.

DUCHESS Oh, you render me excellent music!

BOSOLA Say you? 425

DUCHESS This good one that you speak of is my husband.

BOSOLA Do I not dream? Can this ambitious age
Have so much goodness in 't as to prefer
A man merely for worth, without these shadows
Of wealth and painted honours? Possible? 430

DUCHESS I have had three children by him.

BOSOLA Fortunate lady!
For you have made your private nuptial bed
The humble and fair seminary* of peace.
No question but many an unbeneficed* scholar 435
Shall pray for you for this deed, and rejoice
That some preferment in the world can yet
Arise from merit. The virgins of your land
That have no dowries shall hope your example 440

---

402 That is, flatterers pretend that princes have no vices, and princes pretend that flatterers tell no lies.
407 By short, quick steps.
408 Invaluable.
416 An official who authenticated pedigrees.
420 The Bermudas, famous for storms.
435 Seedplot.
436 Unsupported; without funds or patron.

Will raise them to rich husbands. Should you want
Soldiers, 'twould make the very Turks and Moors
Turn Christians, and serve you for this act.
Last, the neglected poets of your time,
In honour of this trophy of a man,   445
Raised by that curious engine, your white hand,
Shall thank you, in your grave, for 't; and make that
More reverend than all the cabinets*
Of living princes. For Antonio,
His fame shall likewise flow from many a pen,   450
When heralds shall want coats to sell to men.*

DUCHESS   As I taste comfort in this friendly speech,
So would I find concealment.

BOSOLA   Oh, the secret of my prince,
Which I will wear on th' inside of my heart!   455

DUCHESS   You shall take charge of all my coin and jewels,
And follow him; for he retires himself
To Ancona.

BOSOLA   So.

DUCHESS   Whither, within few days,   460
I mean to follow thee.

BOSOLA   Let me think:
I would wish your grace to feign a pilgrimage
To our Lady of Loretto, scarce seven leagues
From fair Ancona; so may you depart   465
Your country with more honour, and your flight
Will seem a princely progress,* retaining
Your usual train about you.

DUCHESS   Sir, your direction
Shall lead me by the hand.   470

CARIOLA   In my opinion,
She were better progress to the baths at Lucca,
Or go visit the Spa in Germany;
For, if you will believe me, I do not like
This jesting with religion, this feigned   475
Pilgrimage.

DUCHESS   Thou art a superstitious fool:
Prepare us instantly for our departure.
Past sorrows, let us moderately lament them;
For those to come, seek wisely to prevent them.   480

(*Exeunt* DUCHESS *and* CARIOLA)

BOSOLA   A politician is the devil's quilted* anvil;
He fashions all sins on him, and the blows

---

448 Private council-chambers.
451 Heralds sometimes sold honors and coats of arms.
467 Procession.
482 Muffled.

Are never heard: he may work in a lady's chamber,
As here for proof. What rests but I reveal
All to my lord? Oh, this base quality   485
Of intelligencer! why, every quality i' th' world
Prefers* but gain or commendation:
Now for this act I am certain to be rais'd,
And men that paint weeds to the life are prais'd. (*Exit*)   490

Scene 3

A Room in the Cardinal's Palace at Rome

(*Enter* CARDINAL, FERDINAND, MALATESTE, PESCARA, SILVIO, *and* DELIO)

CARDINAL   Must we turn soldier, then?

MALATESTE   The emperor
Hearing your worth that way, ere you attain'd   495
This reverend garment, joins you in commission
With the right fortunate soldier the Marquis of Pescara,
And the famous Lannoy.

CARDINAL   He that had the honour
Of taking the French king prisoner?   500

MALTESTE   The same
Here's a plot* drawn for a new fortification
At Naples. (*They talk apart*)

FERDINAND   This great Count Malateste, I perceive,
Hath got employment?   505

DELIO   No employment, my lord;
A marginal note in the muster-book, that he is
A voluntary lord.*

FERDINAND   He 's no soldier?

DELIO   He has worn gunpowder* in 's hollow tooth for the toothache. 510

SILVIO   He comes to the leaguer with a full intent
To eat fresh beef and garlic, means to stay
Till the scent be gone, and straight return to court.

DELIO   He hath read all the late service as the city chronicle relates it; and keeps
two pewterers* going, only to express battles in model.   515

SILVIO   Then he'll fight by the book.

DELIO   By the almanac, I think, to choose good days and shun the critical; that's
his mistress's scarf.

SILVIO   Yes, he protests he would do much for that taffeta.

DELIO   I think he would run away from a battle, to save it from taking*   520
prisoner.

SILVIO   He is horribly afraid gunpowder will spoil the perfume on 't.

488 Produces.
502 Plan.
508 A voluntary.
510 Used as a pain-killer.
515 Metal-workers.
520 Being taken.

DELIO I saw a Dutchman break his pate once for calling him pot-gun,* he made
his head have a bore in 't like a musket.

SILVIO I would he had made a touchhole to 't. He is indeed a guarded 525
sumpter-cloth,* only for the remove of the court.*

(*Enter* BOSOLA *and speaks to* FERDINAND *and the* CARDINAL)

PESCARA Bosola arriv'd? What should be the business?
Some falling-out amongst the cardinals.
These factions amongst great men, they are like   530
Foxes; when their heads are divided,
They carry fire in their tails, and all the country
About them goes to wrack for 't.*

SILVIO   What 's that Bosola?

DELIO I knew him in Padua—a fantastical scholar, like such who study to 535
know how many knots was in Hercules' club, of what colour Achilles' beard
was, or whether Hector were not troubled with the toothache. He hath
studied himself half blear-ey'd to know the true symmetry of Caesar's nose
by a shoeing-horn; and this he did to gain the name of a speculative man.

PESCARA Mark Prince Ferdinand: 540
A very salamander lives in 's eye,
To mock the eager violence of fire.

SILVIO That Cardinal hath made more bad faces with his oppression than ever
Michael Angelo made good ones: he lifts up 's nose, like a foul porpoise
before a storm.*   545

PESCARA The Lord Ferdinand laughs.

DELIO Like a deadly cannon that lightens
Ere it smokes.

PESCARA These are your true pangs of death,
The pangs of life, that struggle with great statesmen.   550

DELIO In such a deformed silence witches whisper
Their charms.

CARDINAL Doth she make religion her riding-hood
To keep her from the sun and tempest?

FERDINAND   That,   555
That damns her. Methinks her fault and beauty,
Blended together, show like leprosy,
The whiter, the fouler. I make it a question
Whether her beggarly brats were ever christened.

CARDINAL I will instantly solicit the state of Ancona   560
To have them banish'd.

FERDINAND   You are for Loretto?
I shall not be at your ceremony; fare you well.—

---

523 Popgun, hence filled with air.
526 (*a*) An ornamental horse cloth. (*b*) Journeys made by the court.
533 An allusion to the jackals which Samson tied tail to tail and used to set fire to the Philistines' fields.
545 Porpoises were thought to forebode storms in this way.

Write to the Duke of Malfi, my young nephew
She had by her first husband, and acquaint him
With's mother's honesty.

BOSOLA   I will.

FERDINAND   Antonio!
A slave that only smell'd of ink and counters,
And never in 's life look'd like a gentleman,
But in the audit-time.—Go, go presently,
Draw me out an hundred and fifty of our horse,
And meet me at the fort-bridge. (*Exeunt*)

Scene 4

The Shrine of Our Lady of Loretto
(*Enter* TWO PILGRIMS)

1ST PILGRIM   I have not seen a goodlier shrine than this;
Yet I have visited many.

2ND PILGRIM   The Cardinal of Arragon
Is this day to resign his cardinal's hat:
His sister duchess likewise is arriv'd
To pay her vow of pilgrimage. I expect
A noble ceremony.

1ST PILGRIM   No question.
—They come.
(*Here the ceremony of the* CARDINAL'S *instalment, in the habit of a soldier, is
performed in delivering up his cross, hat, robes, and ring, at the shrine, and
investing him with sword, helmet, shield, and spurs; then* ANTONIO, *the*
DUCHESS, *and their children, having presented themselves at the shrine, are, by
a form of banishment in dumb-show expressed towards them by the* CARDINAL
*and the state of Ancona, banished: during all which ceremony, this ditty is sung,
to very solemn music, by divers churchmen*)
Arms and honours deck thy story,
To thy fame's eternal glory!
Adverse fortune ever fly thee;
No disastrous fate come nigh thee!

I alone will sing thy praises,
Whom to honour virtue raises;
And thy study, that divine is,
Bent to martial discipline is.
Lay aside all those robes lie by thee;
Crown thy arts with arms, they'll beautify thee.

O worthy of worthiest name, adorn'd in this manner,
Lead bravely thy forces on under war's warlike banner!
Oh, mayst thou prove fortunate in all martial courses!
Guide thou still by skill in arts and forces!

Victory attend thee nigh, whilst fame sings loud thy powers;
Triumphant conquest crown thy head, and blessings pour down showers!
                    (*Exeunt all except the* TWO PILGRIMS)

1ST PILGRIM Here 's a strange turn of state! Who would have thought
So great a lady would have match'd herself   610
Unto so mean a person? Yet the Cardinal
Bears himself much too cruel.
2ND PILGRIM   They are banish'd.
1ST PILGRIM But I would ask what power hath this state
Of Ancona to determine of a free prince?   615
2ND PILGRIM They are a free state, sir, and her brother show'd
How that the Pope, fore-hearing of her looseness,
Hath seiz'd into th' protection of the Church
The dukedom which she held as dowager.
1ST PILGRIM But by what justice?   620
2ND PILGRIM   Sure, I think by none,
Only her brother's instigation.
1ST PILGRIM What was it with such violence he took
Off from her finger?
2ND PILGRIM   'Twas her wedding-ring;   625
Which he vow'd shortly he would sacrifice
To his revenge.
1ST PILGRIM   Alas, Antonio!
If that a man be thrust into a well,
No matter who sets hands to 't, his own weight   630
Will bring him sooner to th' bottom. Come, let's hence.
Fortune makes this conclusion general,
All things do help th' unhappy man to fall. (*Exeunt*)

Scene 5

Near Loretto

        (*Enter* DUCHESS, ANTONIO, CHILDREN, CARIOLA, *and* SERVANTS)   635
DUCHESS Banish'd Ancona?
ANTONIO   Yes, you see what power
Lightens in great men's breath.
DUCHESS   Is all our train
Shrunk to this poor remainder?   640
ANTONIO   These poor men,
Which have got little in your service, vow
To take your fortune: but your wiser buntings,*
Now they are fledg'd, are gone.
DUCHESS   They have done wisely.   645
This puts me in mind of death: physicians thus,
With their hands full of money, use to give o'er
Their patients.

---

643 Small birds.

ANTONIO   Right the fashion of the world:
  From decayed fortunes every flatterer shrinks;   650
  Men cease to build where the foundation sinks.

DUCHESS   I had a very strange dream to-night.

ANTONIO   What was 't?

DUCHESS Methought I wore my coronet of state,
  And on a sudden all the diamonds   655
  Were chang'd to pearls.

ANTONIO   My interpretation
  Is, you'll weep shortly; for to me the pearls
  Do signify your tears.

DUCHESS   The birds that live   660
  I' th' field on the wild benefit of nature
  Live happier than we; for they may choose their mates,
  And carol their sweet pleasures to the spring.

                    (*Enter* BOSOLA *with a letter*)

BOSOLA You are happily o'erta'en.   665

DUCHESS   From my brother?

BOSOLA Yes, from the Lord Ferdinand your brother
  All love and safety.

DUCHESS   Thou dost blanch* mischief,
  Wouldst make it white. See, see, like to calm weather   670
  At sea before a tempest, false hearts speak fair
  To those they intend most mischief. (*Reads*)
    "Send Antonio to me; I want his head in a business."
  A politic equivocation!
  He doth not want your counsel, but your head;   675
  That is, he cannot sleep till you be dead.
  And here 's another pitfall that 's strew'd o'er
  With roses: mark it, 'tis a cunning one: (*Reads*)
    "I stand engaged for your husband for several debts at Naples: let not
  that trouble him; I had rather have his heart than his money:"—   680
  And I believe so too.

BOSOLA   What do you believe?

DUCHESS That he so much distrusts my husband's love,
  He will by no means believe his heart is with him
  Until he see it: the devil is not cunning   685
  Enough to circumvent us in riddles.

BOSOLA Will you reject that noble and free league
  Of amity and love which I present you?

DUCHESS Their league is like that of some politic kings,
  Only to make themselves of strength and power   690
  To be our after-ruin: tell them so.

BOSOLA And what from you?

ANTONIO   Thus tell him; I will not come.

---

669 Bleach.

BOSOLA And what of this? (*Pointing to the letter*)

ANTONIO   My brothers have dispers'd   695
    Blood-hounds abroad; which till I hear are muzzl'd,
    No truce, though hatch'd with ne'er such politic skill,
    Is safe, that hangs upon our enemies' will.
    I'll not come at them.

BOSOLA   This proclaims your breeding: 700
    Every small thing draws a base mind to fear,
    As the adamant draws iron. Fare you well, sir
    You shall shortly hear from 's. (*Exit*)

DUCHESS   I suspect some ambush:
    Therefore by all my love I do conjure you   705
    To take your eldest son, and fly towards Milan.
    Let us not venture all this poor remainder
    In one unlucky bottom.

ANTONIO   You counsel safely.
    Best of my life, farewell. Since we must part,   710
    Heaven hath a hand in 't; but no otherwise
    Than as some curious artist takes in sunder
    A clock or watch, when it is out of frame,
    To bring 't in better order.

DUCHESS   I know not   715
    Which is best, to see you dead, or part with you.
    —Farewell, boy:
    Thou art happy that thou hast not understanding
    To know thy misery; for all our wit
    And reading brings us to a truer sense   720
    Of sorrow.—In the eternal church, sir,
    I do hope we shall not part thus.

ANTONIO   Oh, be of comfort!
    Make patience a noble fortitude,
    And think not how unkindly we are used: 725
    Man, like to cassia, is prov'd best being bruised.

DUCHESS Must I, like to a slave-born Russian,
    Account it praise to suffer tyranny?
    And yet, O heaven, thy heaven hand is in 't!
    I have seen my little boy oft scourge his top,*   730
    And compar'd myself to 't: naught made me e'er
    Go right but heaven's scourge-stick.

ANTONIO   Do not weep:
    Heaven fashion'd us of nothing, and we strive
    To bring ourselves to nothing.—Farewell, Cariola,   735
    And thy sweet armful.—If I do never see thee more,
    Be a good mother to your little ones,
    And save them from the tiger: fare you well.

---

730 That is, whip his toy top to make it go.

DUCHESS   Let me look upon you once more; for that speech
    Came from a dying father.—Your kiss is colder   ₇₄₀
    Than that I have seen an holy anchorite
    Give to a dead man's skull.
ANTONIO   My heart is turn'd to a heavy lump of lead,
    With which I sound my danger: fare you well.
                (*Exeunt* ANTONIO *and his* SON)   745
DUCHESS   My laurel is all withered.
CARIOLA   Look, madam, what a troop of armed men
    Make toward us.
DUCHESS   Oh, they are very welcome:
    When Fortune's wheel is over-charg'd with princes,   750
    The weight makes it move swift: I would have my ruin
    Be sudden.
           (*Re-enter* BOSOLA *visarded, with a* GUARD)
         I am your adventure, am I not?
BOSOLA   You are: you must see your husband no more.   755
DUCHESS   What devil art thou that counterfeits heaven's thunder?
BOSOLA   Is that terrible? I would have you tell me whether
    Is that note worse that frights the silly birds
    Out of the corn, or that which doth allure them
    To the nets? You have hearkened to the last too much.   760
DUCHESS   Oh, misery! Like to a rusty o'ercharg'd cannon,
    Shall I never fly in pieces?—Come, to what prison?
BOSOLA   To none.
DUCHESS   Whither, then?
BOSOLA   To your palace.
DUCHESS   I have heard   765
    That Charon's boat serves to convey all o'er
    The dismal lake, but brings none back again.
BOSOLA   Your brothers mean you safety and pity.
DUCHESS   Pity!   770
    With such a pity men preserve alive
    Pheasants and quails, when they are not fat enough
    To be eaten.
BOSOLA   These are your children?
DUCHESS   Yes.
BOSOLA   Can they prattle?   775
DUCHESS   No;
    But I intend, since they were born accurs'd,
    Curses shall be their first language.
BOSOLA   Fie, madam!   780
    Forget this base, low fellow,—
DUCHESS   Were I a man,
    I'd beat that counterfeit face into thy other.
BOSOLA   One of no birth.

DUCHESS   Say that he was born mean, ⁷⁸⁵
   Man is most happy when 's own actions
   Be arguments and examples of his virtue.
BOSOLA   A barren, beggarly virtue!
DUCHESS   I prithee, who is greatest? Can you tell?
   Sad tales befit my woe: I'll tell you one. ⁷⁹⁰
   A salmon, as she swam unto the sea,
   Met with a dog-fish, who encounters her
   With this rough language: "Why art thou so bold
   To mix thyself with our high state of floods,
   Being no eminent courtier, but one ⁷⁹⁵
   That for the calmest and fresh time o' the year
   Dost live in shallow rivers, rank'st thyself
   With silly smelts and shrimps? And darest thou
   Pass by our dog-ship without reverence?"
   "Oh!" quoth the salmon, "sister, be at peace: ⁸⁰⁰
   Thank Jupiter we both have pass'd the net!
   Our value never can be truly known,
   Till in the fisher's basket we be shown:
   I' th' market then my price may be the higher,
   Even when I am nearest to the cook and fire." ⁸⁰⁵
   So to great men the moral may be stretchèd;
   Men oft are valued high, when they're most wretched.—
   But come, whither you please. I am arm'd 'gainst misery;
   Bent to all sways of the oppressor's will:
   There 's no deep valley but near some great hill. (*Exeunt*) ⁸¹⁰

Act Four

Scene 1

A Room in the Duchess's Palace at Malfi
(*Enter* FERDINAND *and* BOSOLA)

FERDINAND   How doth our sister duchess bear herself
   In her imprisonment?
BOSOLA   Nobly: I'll describe her. ⁵
   She 's sad as one long used to 't, and she seems
   Rather to welcome the end of misery
   Than shun it; a behaviour so noble
   As gives a majesty to adversity:
   You may discern the shape of loveliness ¹⁰
   More perfect in her tears than in her smiles:
   She will muse four hours together; and her silence,
   Methinks, expresseth more than if she spake.
FERDINAND   Her melancholy seems to be fortified
   With a strange disdain. ¹⁵
BOSOLA   'Tis so; and this restraint,

Like English mastiffs that grow fierce with tying,
Makes her too passionately apprehend
Those pleasures she 's kept from.

FERDINAND   Curse upon her! ⟨20⟩
I will no longer study in the book
Of another's heart. Inform her what I told you. (*Exit*)
                        (*Enter* DUCHESS)

BOSOLA   All comfort to your grace!

DUCHESS   I will have none. ⟨25⟩
Pray thee, why dost thou wrap thy poison'd pills
In gold and sugar?

BOSOLA   Your elder brother, the Lord Ferdinand,
Is come to visit you, and sends you word,
'Cause once he rashly made a solemn vow ⟨30⟩
Never to see you more, he comes i' th' night;
And prays you, gently, neither torch nor taper
Shine in your chamber: he will kiss your hand
And reconcile himself; but for his vow
He dares not see you. ⟨35⟩

DUCHESS   At his pleasure.—Take hence the lights.—
He's come. (*Exit* SERVANTS *with the lights*)
                        (*Enter* FERDINAND)

FERDINAND   Where are you?

DUCHESS   Here, sir.

FERDINAND   This darkness suits you well. ⟨40⟩

DUCHESS   I would ask you pardon.

FERDINAND   You have it; for I account it
The honorabl'st revenge, where I may kill
To pardon.—Where are your cubs?

DUCHESS   Whom? ⟨45⟩

FERDINAND   Call them your children;
For though our national law distinguish bastards
From true legitimate issue, compassionate nature
Makes them all equal. ⟨50⟩

DUCHESS   Do you visit me for this?
You violate a sacrament o' th' Church
Shall make you howl in hell for 't.

FERDINAND   It had been well
Could you have liv'd thus always; for, indeed,
You were too much i' th' light:—but no more; ⟨55⟩
I come to seal my peace with you. Here 's a hand (*Gives her a dead man's hand*)
To which you have vow'd much love; the ring upon 't
You gave.

DUCHESS   I affectionately kiss it.

FERDINAND   Pray, do, and bury the print of it in your heart. ⟨60⟩
I will leave this ring with you for a love-token;

And the hand as sure as the ring; and do not doubt
But you shall have the heart too: when you need a friend,
Send it to him that owned it; you shall see   65
Whether he can aid you.

DUCHESS   You are very cold:
I fear you are not well after your travel.—
Ha! lights!——Oh, horrible!

FERDINAND   Let her have lights enough. (*Exit*)   70
                    (*Re-enter* SERVANTS *with lights*)

DUCHESS What witchcraft doth he practise, that he hath left
A dead man's hand here?
(*Here is discovered, behind a traverse,* the artificial figures of Antonio and his
                    Children, appearing as if they were dead*)   75

BOSOLA Look you, here 's the piece from which 'twas ta'en.
He doth present you this sad spectacle,
That, now you know directly they are dead,
Hereafter you may wisely cease to grieve
For that which cannot be recovered.   80

DUCHESS There is not between heaven and earth one wish
I stay for after this: it wastes me more
Than were 't my picture, fashion'd out of wax,
Stuck with a magical needle, and then buried
In some foul dunghill;* and yond 's an excellent property   85
For a tyrant, which I would account mercy.

BOSOLA   What 's that?

DUCHESS If they would bind me to that lifeless trunk,
And let me freeze to death.

BOSOLA   Come, you must live.   90

DUCHESS That 's the greatest torture souls feel in hell,
In hell, that they must live, and cannot die.
Portia, I'll new kindle thy coals again,
And revive the rare and almost dead example
Of a loving wife.*   95

BOSOLA   Oh, fie! Despair? Remember
You are a Christian.

DUCHESS   The Church enjoins fasting:
I'll starve myself to death.

BOSOLA   Leave this vain sorrow.   100
Things being at the worst begin to mend: the bee
When he hath shot his sting into your hand, may then
Play with your eyelid.

DUCHESS   Good comfortable fellow,
Persuade a wretch that 's broke upon the wheel   105
To have all his bones new set; entreat him live

---

74 A curtain.

85 Practices by which witches destroyed their enemies.

95 Portia, Brutus' wife, killed herself by swallowing hot coals.

To be executed again. Who must dispatch me?
I account this world a tedious theatre,
For I do play a part in 't 'gainst my will.

BOSOLA   Come, be of comfort; I will save your life.   110

DUCHESS   Indeed,
I have not leisure to tend so small a business.

BOSOLA   Now, by my life, I pity you.

DUCHESS   Thou art a fool, then.
To waste thy pity on a thing so wretched   115
As cannot pity itself. I am full of daggers.
Puff, let me blow these vipers from me. (*She turns to a* SERVANT)
What are you?

SERVANT   One that wishes you long life.

DUCHESS   I would thou wert hang'd for the horrible curse   120
Thou hast given me: I shall shortly grow one
Of the miracles of pity. I'll go pray;—
No, I'll go curse.

BOSOLA   Oh, fie!

DUCHESS   I could curse the stars—   125

BOSOLA   Oh, fearful!

DUCHESS   And those three smiling seasons of the year
Into a Russian winter: nay, the world
To its first chaos.

BOSOLA   Look you, the stars shine still.   130

DUCHESS   Oh, but you must
Remember, my curse hath a great way to go.—
Plagues that make lanes through largest families
Consume them!—

BOSOLA   Fie, lady!   135

DUCHESS   Let them, like tyrants,
Never be remembered but for the ill they have done;
Let all the zealous prayers of mortified
Churchmen forget them!—

BOSOLA   Oh, uncharitable!   140

DUCHESS   Let Heaven a little while cease crowning martyrs
To punish them!—
Go, howl them this, and say, I long to bleed:
It is some mercy when men kill with speed. (*Exeunt* DUCHESS *and* SERVANT)
                    (*Re-enter* FERDINAND)   145

FERDINAND   Excellent, as I would wish; she 's plagued in art:
These presentations are but fram'd in wax
By the curious master in that quality,*
Vincentio Lauriola, and she takes them
For true substantial bodies.   150

BOSOLA   Why do you do this?

FERDINAND   To bring her to despair.

[148] Profession.

BOSOLA   'Faith, end here,
And go no farther in your cruelty:
Send her a penitential garment to put on   155
Next to her delicate skin, and furnish her
With beads and prayer-books.
FERDINAND   Damn her! That body of hers,
While that my blood ran pure in 't, was more worth
Than that which thou wouldst comfort, called a soul.   160
I will send her masks of common courtezans,
Have her meat serv'd up by bawds and ruffians,
And, 'cause she'll needs be mad, I am resolv'd
To remove forth the common hospital
All the mad-folk, and place them near her lodging;   165
There let them practise together, sing and dance,
And act their gambols to the full o' th' moon:
If she can sleep the better for it, let her.
Your work is almost ended.
BOSOLA   Must I see her again?   170
FERDINAND   Yes.
BOSOLA   Never.
FERDINAND   You must.
BOSOLA   Never in mine own shape;
That 's forfeited by my intelligence*   175
And this last cruel lie: when you send me next,
The business shall be comfort.
FERDINAND   Very likely;
Thy pity is nothing of kin to thee. Antonio
Lurks about Milan: thou shalt shortly thither   180
To feed a fire as great as my revenge,
Which ne'er will slack till it have spent his fuel:
Intemperate agues make physicians cruel. (*Exeunt*)

Scene 2

Another Room in the Duchess's Lodging
(*Enter* DUCHESS *and* CARIOLA)   185
DUCHESS   What hideous noise was that?
CARIOLA   'Tis the wild consort*
Of madmen, lady, which your tyrant brother
Hath plac'd about your lodging: this tyranny,
I think, was never practis'd till this hour.   190
DUCHESS   Indeed, I thank him: nothing but noise and folly
Can keep me in my right wits; whereas reason
And silence make me stark mad. Sit down;
Discourse to me some dismal tragedy.

175 Spying.
187 Band.

CARIOLA   Oh, 'twill increase your melancholy.   195
DUCHESS   Thou art deceived:
  To hear of greater grief would lessen mine.
  This is a prison?
CARIOLA   Yes, but you shall live
  To shake this durance off.   200
DUCHESS   Thou art a fool:
  The robin-redbreast and the nightingale
  Never live long in cages.
CARIOLA   Pray, dry your eyes.
  What think you of, madam?   205
DUCHESS   Of nothing; when I muse thus,
  I sleep.
CARIOLA   Like a madman, with your eyes open?
DUCHESS   Dost thou think we shall know one another in th' other
                                                    world?   210
CARIOLA   Yes, out of question.
DUCHESS   Oh, that it were possible
  We might but hold some two days' conference
  With the dead! From them I should learn somewhat, I am sure,
  I never shall know here. I'll tell thee a miracle;   215
  I am not mad yet, to my cause of sorrow:
  Th' heaven o'er my head seems made of molten brass,
  The earth of flaming sulphur, yet I am not mad.
  I am acquainted with sad misery
  As the tann'd galley-slave is with his oar;   220
  Necessity makes me suffer constantly,
  And custom makes it easy. Who do I look like now?
CARIOLA   Like to your picture in the gallery,
  A deal of life in show, but none in practice;
  Or rather like some reverend monument   225
  Whose ruins are even pitied.
DUCHESS   Very proper;
  And Fortune seems only to have her eyesight
  To behold my tragedy.—
  How now! what noise is that?   230
                    (*Enter* SERVANT)
SERVANT   I am come to tell you
  Your brother hath intended you some sport.
  A great physician, when the Pope was sick
  Of a deep melancholy, presented him   235
  With several sorts of madmen, which wild object,
  Being full of change and sport, forc'd him to laugh,
  And so the imposthume* broke: the self-same cure
  The duke intends on you.
DUCHESS   Let them come in.   240

    ²³⁷ Abscess.

SERVANT   There's a mad lawyer; and a secular priest;
          A doctor that hath forfeited his wits
          By jealousy; an astrologian
          That in his works said such a day o' th' month
          Should be the day of doom, and, failing of 't,   245
          Ran mad; an English tailor crazed i' th' brain
          With the study of new fashions; a gentleman-usher*
          Quite beside himself with care to keep in mind
          The number of his lady's salutations
          Or "How do you 's" she employ'd him in each morning;   250
          A farmer, too, an excellent knave in grain,
          Mad 'cause he was hindered transportation:
          And let one broker that 's mad loose to these,
          You'd think the devil were among them.
DUCHESS   Sit, Cariola.—Let them loose when you please,   255
          For I am chain'd to endure all your tyranny.
          (*Enter* MADMEN. *Here this Song is sung by a* MADMAN *to a dismal kind of
                                     music*)
MADMAN   Oh, let us howl some heavy note,
              Some deadly dogged howl,   260
          Sounding as from the threatening throat
              Of beasts and fatal fowl!
          As ravens, screech-owls, bulls, and bears,
              We'll bell,* and bawl our parts,
          Till irksome noise have cloy'd your ears   265
              And corrosived your hearts.
          At last, whenas our quire wants breath,
              Our bodies being blest,
          We'll sing, like swans, to welcome death,
              And die in love and rest.   270

1ST MADMAN (*Astrologer*)   Doom's-day not come yet? I'll draw it nearer by a
    perspective,* or make a glass that shall set all the world on fire upon an in-
    stant. I cannot sleep; my pillow is stuffed with a litter of porcupines.

2ND MADMAN (*Lawyer*)   Hell is a mere glass-house, where the devils are con-
    tinually blowing up women's souls on hollow irons, and the fire never   275
    goes out.

3RD MADMAN (*Priest*)   I will lie with every woman in my parish the tenth
    night; I will tithe them over like haycocks.*

4TH MADMAN (*Doctor*)   Shall my pothecary out-go me because I am a cuckold?
    I have found out his roguery; he makes alum of his wife's urine, and sells   280
    it to Puritans that have sore throats with overstraining.*

1ST MADMAN   I have skill in heraldry.

---

247 An attendant who preceded, or ushered, a nobleman.
264 Bellow.
272 Telescope.
278 That is, pay them over as haystacks are paid over as tax.
281 Overpreaching.

2ND MADMAN Hast?

1ST MADMAN You do give for your crest a woodcock's head* with the brains
picked out on 't; you are a very ancient gentleman. 285

3RD MADMAN Greek is turn'd Turk:* we are only to be sav'd by the Helvetian
translation.

1ST MADMAN Come on, sir, I will lay the law to you.

2ND MADMAN Oh, rather lay a corrosive: the law will eat to the bone.

3RD MADMAN He that drinks but to satisfy nature is damned. 290

4TH MADMAN If I had my glass here, I would show a sight should make all the
women here call me mad doctor.

1ST MADMAN What's he? A rope-maker? (*Pointing to the Priest*)

2ND MADMAN No, no, no, a snuffling knave* that, while he shows the tombs,
will have his hand in a wench's placket. 295

3RD MADMAN Woe to the caroche that brought home my wife from the masque
at three o'clock in the morning! It had a large feather-bed in it.

4TH MADMAN I have pared the devil's nails forty times, roasted them in raven's
eggs, and cur'd agues with them.

3RD MADMAN Get me three hundred milchbats, to make possets* to procure 300
sleep.

4TH MADMAN All the college may throw their caps* at me: I have made a soap-
boiler costive;* it was my masterpiece.

(*Here the dance, consisting of Eight* MADMEN, *with music answerable thereunto;
after which* BOSOLA, *like an Old Man, enters*) 305

DUCHESS Is he mad too?

SERVANT   Pray, question him. I'll leave you.
(*Exeunt* SERVANT *and* MADMEN)

BOSOLA I am come to make thy tomb.

DUCHESS   Ha! My tomb? 310
Thou speak'st as if I lay upon my death-bed,
Gasping for breath: dost thou perceive me sick?

BOSOLA Yes, and the more dangerously, since thy sickness
Is insensible.

DUCHESS   Thou art not mad, sure: dost know me? 315

BOSOLA Yes.

DUCHESS Who am I?

BOSOLA Thou art a box of worm-seed, at best but a salvatory of green mummy.*
What's this flesh? a little crudded* milk, fantastical puff-paste. Our bodies
are weaker than those paper-prisons boys use to keep flies in; more con- 320
temptible, since ours is to preserve earthworms. Didst thou ever see a lark
in a cage? Such is the soul in the body: this world is like her little turf of

---

284 Proverbially a stupid fowl.

286 That is, the Greek text of the Bible has been put in the service of the infidels.

294 An allusion to the whining, nasal speech of the Puritans.

300 Made of hot milk, wine or ale, and sugar and spice.

302 Congratulate me.

303 Suppository.

318 An ointment-box containing undried dead flesh such as was powdered and used in medicines.

319 Curdled.

grass, and the heaven o'er our heads, like her looking-glass, only gives us a miserable knowledge of the small compass of our prison.

DUCHESS   Am not I thy duchess?   325

BOSOLA   Thou art some great woman, sure, for riot begins to sit on thy forehead (clad in grey hairs) twenty years sooner than on a merry milk-maid's. Thou sleep'st worse than if a mouse should be forc'd to take up her lodging in a cat's ear: a little infant that breeds its teeth, should it lie with thee, would cry out, as if thou wert the more unquiet bed-fellow.   330

DUCHESS   I am Duchess of Malfi still.

BOSOLA   That makes thy sleeps so broken:
Glories, like glow-worms, afar off shine bright,
But looked to near, have neither heat nor light.

DUCHESS   Thou art very plain.   335

BOSOLA   My trade is to flatter the dead, not the living; I am a tomb-maker.

DUCHESS   And thou com'st to make my tomb?

BOSOLA   Yes.

DUCHESS   Let me be a little merry:—of what stuff wilt thou make it?

BOSOLA   Nay, resolve me first, of what fashion?   340

DUCHESS   Why, do we grow fantastical in our death-bed? Do we affect fashion in the grave?

BOSOLA   Most ambitiously. Princes' images on their tombs do not lie, as they were wont, seeming to pray up to heaven; but with their hands under their cheeks, as if they died of the toothache: they are not carved with their eyes 345 fix'd upon the stars; but as their minds were wholly bent upon the world, the self-same way they seem to turn their faces.

DUCHESS   Let me know fully therefore the effect
Of this thy dismal preparation,
This talk fit for a charnel.   350

BOSOLA   Now I shall:—
        (*Enter* EXECUTIONERS, *with a coffin, cords, and a bell*)
Here is a present from your princely brothers;
And may it arrive welcome, for it brings
Last benefit, last sorrow.   355

DUCHESS   Let me see it:
I have so much obedience in my blood,
I wish it in their veins to do them good.

BOSOLA   This is your last presence-chamber.

CARIOLA   O my sweet lady!   360

DUCHESS   Peace; it affrights not me.

BOSOLA   I am the common bellman.
                (*He takes up the bell*)
That usually is sent to condemn'd persons
The night before they suffer.   365

DUCHESS   Even now
Thou said'st thou wast a tomb-maker.

BOSOLA   'Twas to bring you
By degrees to mortification. Listen. (*Rings his bell*)

Hark, now every thing is still   370
The screech-owl and the whistler shrill
Call upon our dame aloud,
And bid her quickly don her shroud!
Much you had of land and rent:
Your length in clay's now competent:*   375
A long war disturb'd your mind;
Here your perfect peace is sign'd.
Of what is 't fools make such vain keeping?
Sin their conception, their birth weeping,
Their life a general mist of error,   380
Their death a hideous storm of terror.
Strew your hair with powders sweet,
Don clean linen, bathe your feet,
And (the foul fiend more to check)
A crucifix let bless your neck: 385
'Tis now full tide 'tween night and day;
End your groan, and come away.

CARIOLA   Hence, villains, tyrants, murderers! Alas!
     What will you do with my lady?—Call for help.
DUCHESS   To whom? To our next neighbours? They are madfolks.   390
BOSOLA   Remove that noise.
DUCHESS   Farewell, Cariola.
     In my last will I have not much to give:
     A many hungry guests have fed upon me;
     Thine will be a poor reversion.   395
CARIOLA   I will die with her.
DUCHESS   I pray thee, look thou giv'st my little boy
     Some syrup for his cold, and let the girl
     Say her prayers ere she sleep. (CARIOLA *is forced out by the* EXECUTIONERS)
                              Now what you please: 400
     What death?
BOSOLA   Strangling;
     Here are your executioners.
DUCHESS   I forgive them:
     The apoplexy, catarrh, or cough o' th' lungs,   405
     Would do as much as they do.
BOSOLA   Doth not death fright you?
DUCHESS   Who would be afraid on 't,
     Knowing to meet such excellent company
     In th' other world?   410
BOSOLA   Yet, methinks,
     The manner of your death should much afflict you:
     This cord should terrify you.
DUCHESS   Not a whit:

---

375 That is, all you require.

What would it pleasure me to have my throat cut   415
With diamonds? Or to be smothered
With cassia? Or to be shot to death with pearls?
I know death hath ten thousand several doors
For men to take their exits; and 'tis found
They go on such strange geometrical hinges,   420
You may open them both ways.—Any way, for heaven sake,
So I were out of your whispering. Tell my brothers
That I perceive death, now I am well awake,
Best gift is they can give or I can take.
I would fain put off my last woman's fault,   425
I'd not be tedious to you.

FIRST EXECUTIONER   We are ready.

DUCHESS   Dispose my breath how please you; but my body
Bestow upon my women, will you?

FIRST EXECUTIONER   Yes.   430

DUCHESS   Pull, and pull strongly, for your able strength
Must pull down heaven upon me:—
Yet stay: heaven-gates are not so highly arch'd
As princes' palaces; they that enter there
Must go upon their knees (*Kneels*).—Come, violent death.   435
Serve for mandragora to make me sleep!—
Go tell my brothers, when I am laid out,
They then may feed in quiet. (*They strangle her*)

BOSOLA   Where's the waiting woman? Fetch her: some other
Strangle the children.   440
        (*Exeunt* EXECUTIONERS, *some of whom return with* CARIOLA)
Look you, there sleeps your mistress.

CARIOLA   Oh, you are damn'd
Perpetually for this! My turn is next,
Is 't not so order'd?   445

BOSOLA   Yes, and I am glad
You are so well prepar'd for 't.

CARIOLA   You are deceiv'd, sir,
I m not prepar'd for 't, I will not die;
I will first come to my answer, and know   450
How I have offended.

BOSOLA   Come, dispatch her.—
You kept her counsel; now you shall keep ours.

CARIOLA   I will not die, I must not; I am contracted
To a young gentleman.   455

FIRST EXECUTIONER   Here's your wedding-ring.

CARIOLA   Let me but speak with the duke; I'll discover
Treason to his person.

BOSOLA   Delays:—throttle her.

FIRST EXECUTIONER   She bites and scratches.   460

CARIOLA   If you kill me now,
    I am damn'd; I have not been at confession
    This two years.
BOSOLA (*To* EXECUTIONERS)   When?
CARIOLA   I am quick with child.   465
BOSOLA   Why, then,
    Your credit's sav'd. (*They strangle* CARIOLA)
                Bear her into th' next room;
    Let this lie still. (*Exeunt the* EXECUTIONERS *with the body of* CARIOLA)
               (*Enter* FERDINAND)   470
FERDINAND   Is she dead?
BOSOLA   She is what
    You'd have her. But here begin your pity: (*Shows the* CHILDREN *strangled*)
    Alas, how have these offended?
FERDINAND   The death   475
    Of young wolves is never to be pitied.
BOSOLA   Fix
    Your eye here.
FERDINAND   Constantly.
BOSOLA   Do you not weep?   480
    Other sins only speak; murder shrieks out:
    The element of water moistens the earth,
    But blood flies upwards and bedews the heavens.
FERDINAND   Cover her face; mine eyes dazzle: she died young.
BOSOLA   I think not so; her infelicity   485
    Seem'd to have years too many.
FERDINAND   She and I were twins;
    And should I die this instant, I had liv'd
    Her time to a minute.
BOSOLA   It seems she was born first: 490
    You have bloodily approv'd the ancient truth,
    That kindred commonly do worse agree
    Than remote strangers.
FERDINAND   Let me see her face
    Again. Why didst not thou pity her? What   495
    An excellent honest man mightst thou have been,
    If thou hadst borne her to some sanctuary!
    Or, bold in a good cause, oppos'd thyself,
    With thy advancèd sword above thy head,
    Between her innocence and my revenge!   500
    I bade thee, when I was distracted of my wits,
    Go kill my dearest friend, and thou hast done 't.
    For let me but examine well the cause:
    What was the meanness of her match to me?
    Only I must confess I had a hope,   505
    Had she continu'd widow, to have gain'd

An infinite mass of treasure by her death:
And that was the main cause; her marriage,
That drew a stream of gall quite through my heart.
For thee, as we observe in tragedies   510
That a good actor many times is curs'd
For playing a villain's part, I hate thee for 't,
And, for my sake, say thou hast done much ill well.

BOSOLA   Let me quicken your memory, for I perceive
You are falling into ingratitude: I challenge   515
The reward due to my service.

FERDINAND   I'll tell thee
What I'll give thee.

BOSOLA   Do.

FERDINAND   I'll give thee a pardon   520
For this murder.

BOSOLA   Ha!

FERDINAND   Yes, and 'tis
The largest bounty I can study to do thee.
By what authority didst thou execute   525
This bloody sentence?

BOSOLA   By yours.

FERDINAND   Mine? Was I her judge?
Did any ceremonial form of law
Doom her to not-being? Did a complete jury   530
Deliver her conviction up i' th' court?
Where shalt thou find this judgement register'd,
Unless in hell? See, like a bloody fool,
Thou'st forfeited thy life, and thou shalt die for 't.

BOSOLA   The office of justice is perverted quite   535
When one thief hangs another. Who shall dare
To reveal this?

FERDINAND   Oh, I'll tell thee;
The wolf shall find her grave, and scrape it up,
Not to devour the corpse, but to discover   540
The horrid murder.

BOSOLA   You, not I, shall quake for 't.

FERDINAND   Leave me.

BOSOLA   I will first receive my pension.

FERDINAND   You are a villain.   545

BOSOLA   When your ingratitude
Is judge, I am so.

FERDINAND   Oh, horror, that not the fear
Of him which binds the devils can prescribe man
Obedience!—Never look upon me more.   550

BOSOLA   Why, fare thee well.
Your brother and yourself are worthy men:
You have a pair of hearts are hollow graves,

Rotten, and rotting others; and your vengeance,
Like two chain'd bullets, still goes arm in arm:
You may be brothers; for treason, like the plague,
Doth take much in a blood. I stand like one
That long hath ta'en a sweet and golden dream:
I am angry with myself, now that I wake.

FERDINAND　Get thee into some unknown part o' th' world,
That I may never see thee.

BOSOLA　　　　　　　　　Let me know
Wherefore I should be thus neglected. Sir,
I serv'd your tyranny, and rather strove
To satisfy yourself than all the world:
And though I loath'd the evil, yet I lov'd
You that did counsel it; and rather sought
To appear a true servant than an honest man.

FERDINAND　I'll go hunt the badger by owl-light:
'Tis a deed of darkness. (*Exit*)

BOSOLA　He's much distracted. Off, my painted honour!
While with vain hopes our faculties we tire,
We seem to sweat in ice and freeze in fire.
What would I do, were this to do again?
I would not change my peace of conscience
For all the wealth of Europe.—She stirs; here's life:—
Return, fair soul, from darkness, and lead mine
Out of this sensible hell:—she's warm, she breathes:—
Upon thy pale lips I will melt my heart,
To store them with fresh colour.—Who's there!
Some cordial drink!—Alas! I dare not call:
So pity would destroy pity.—Her eye opes,
And heaven in it seems to ope, that late was shut,
To take me up to mercy.

DUCHESS　Antonio!

BOSOLA　　　　　Yes, madam, he is living;
The dead bodies you saw were but feign'd statues:
He's reconcil'd to your brothers: the Pope hath wrought
The atonement.

DUCHESS　Mercy! (*Dies*)

BOSOLA　Oh, she's gone again! There the cords of life broke.
Oh, sacred innocence, that sweetly sleeps
On turtles' feathers, whilst a guilty conscience
Is a black register wherein is writ
All our good deeds and bad, a perspective
That shows us hell! That we cannot be suffer'd
To do good when we have a mind to it!
This is manly sorrow; these tears, I am very certain,
Never grew in my mother's milk. My estate
Is sunk below the degree of fear: where were

These penitent fountains while she was living?
Oh, they were frozen up! Here is a sight
As direful to my soul as is the sword
Unto a wretch hath slain his father. Come, I'll bear thee
Hence, and execute thy last will; that's deliver 605
Thy body to the reverend dispose
Of some good women: that the cruel tyrant
Shall not deny me. Then I'll post to Milan,
Where somewhat I will speedily enact
Worth my dejection. (*Exit with her body*) 610

Act Five

Scene 1

A Public Place in Milan
(*Enter* ANTONIO *and* DELIO)

ANTONIO   What think you of my hope of reconcilement
To the Arragonian brethren?

DELIO   I misdoubt it; 5
For though they have sent their letters of safe-conduct
For your repair to Milan, they appear
But nets to entrap you. The Marquis of Pescara,
Under whom you hold certain land in cheat,*
Much 'gainst his noble nature hath been mov'd 10
To seize those lands; and some of his dependents
Are at this instant making it their suit
To be invested in your revenues.
I cannot think they mean well to your life
That do deprive you of your means of life, 15
Your living.

ANTONIO   You are still an heretic
To any safety I can shape myself.

DELIO   Here comes the marquis: I will make myself
Petitioner for some part of your land, 20
To know whither it is flying.

ANTONIO   I pray do. (*Withdraws to back*)
(*Enter* PESCARA)

DELIO   Sir, I have a suit to you.

PESCARA   To me? 25

DELIO   An easy one:
There is the citadel of Saint Bennet,
With some demesnes, of late in the possession
Of Antonio Bologna,—please you bestow them on me.

PESCARA   You are my friend; but this is such a suit, 30
Nor fit for me to give, nor you to take.

⁹ Escheat, that is, in the absence of lawful heirs.

DELIO No, sir?

PESCARA   I will give you ample reason for 't
  Soon in private:—here's the Cardinal's mistress.
                    (*Enter* JULIA)

JULIA My lord, I am grown your poor petitioner,
  And should be an ill beggar, had I not
  A great man's letter here, the Cardinal's,
  To court you in my favour. (*Gives a letter*)

PESCARA   He entreats for you
  The citadel of Saint Bennet, that belong'd
  To the banish'd Bologna.

JULIA   Yes.

PESCARA   I could not
  Have thought of a friend I could rather pleasure with it:
  'Tis yours.

JULIA Sir, I thank you; and he shall know
  How doubly I am engag'd both in your gift,
  And speediness of giving, which makes your grant
  The greater. (*Exit*)

ANTONIO (*Aside*) How they fortify themselves
  With my ruin!

DELIO   Sir, I am little bound to you.

PESCARA   Why?

DELIO Because you denied this suit to me, and gave 't
  To such a creature.

PESCARA   Do you know what it was?
  It was Antonio's land; not forfeited
  By course of law, but ravish'd from his throat
  By the Cardinal's entreaty: it were not fit
  I should bestow so main a piece of wrong
  Upon my friend; 'tis a gratification
  Only due to a strumpet, for it is injustice.
  Shall I sprinkle the pure blood of innocents
  To make those followers I call my friends
  Look ruddier upon me? I am glad
  This land, ta'en from the owner by such wrong,
  Returns again unto so foul an use
  As salary for his lust. Learn, good Delio,
  To ask noble things of me, and you shall find
  I'll be a noble giver.

DELIO   You instruct me well.

ANTONIO (*Aside*) Why, here's a man who would fright impudence
  From sauciest beggars.

PESCARA   Prince Ferdinand's come to Milan,
  Sick, as they give out, of an apoplexy;
  But some say 'tis a frenzy: I am going
  To visit him. (*Exit*)

ANTONIO   'Tis a noble old fellow.

DELIO What course do you mean to take, Antonio? ⁸⁰

ANTONIO This night I mean to venture all my fortune,
Which is no more than a poor lingering life,
To the Cardinal's worst of malice: I have got
Private access to his chamber, and intend
To visit him about the mid of night, ⁸⁵
As once his brother did our noble duchess.
It may be that the sudden apprehension
Of danger,—for I'll go in mine own shape,—
When he shall see it fraught with love and duty,
May draw the poison out of him, and work ⁹⁰
A friendly reconcilement: if it fail,
Yet it shall rid me of this infamous calling;
For better fall once than be ever falling.

DELIO I'll second you in all danger; and, howe'er,
My life keeps rank with yours. ⁹⁵

ANTONIO   You are still my lov'd
And best friend. (*Exeunt*)

Scene 2

A Gallery in the Cardinal's Palace at Milan
(*Enter* PESCARA *and* DOCTOR)

PESCARA Now, doctor, may I visit your patient? ¹⁰⁰

DOCTOR If 't please your lordship: but he's instantly
To take the air here in the gallery
By my direction.

PESCARA   Pray thee, what's his disease?

DOCTOR A very pestilent disease, my lord, ¹⁰⁵
They call it lycanthropia.*

PESCARA   What's that?
I need a dictionary to 't.

DOCTOR   I'll tell you.
In those that are possess'd with 't there o'erflows ¹¹⁰
Such melancholy humour* they imagine
Themselves to be transformed into wolves;
Steal forth to churchyards in the dead of night,
And dig dead bodies up: as two nights since
One met the duke 'bout midnight in a lane ¹¹⁵
Behind Saint Mark's Church, with the leg of a man
Upon his shoulder; and he howl'd fearfully;
Said he was a wolf, only the difference
Was, a wolf's skin was hairy on the outside,
His on the inside; bade them take their swords, ¹²⁰

<hr>

106 A form of insanity in which the afflicted thinks he is a wolf.
111 One of the four fluids which were thought to determine a person's temperament.

Rip up his flesh, and try: straight I was sent for,
And, having minister'd to him, found his grace
Very well recovered.

PESCARA   I am glad on 't.

DOCTOR   Yet not without some fear   125
Of a relapse. If he grow to his fit again,
I'll go a nearer way to work with him
Than ever Paracelsus* dream'd of; if
They'll give me leave, I'll buffet his madness
Out of him. Stand aside; he comes.   130

(*Enter* FERDINAND, CARDINAL, MALATESTE, *and* BOSOLA)

FERDINAND   Leave me.

MALATESTE Why doth your lordship love this solitariness?

FERDINAND Eagles commonly fly alone: they are crows, daws, and starlings that
flock together. Look, what's that follows me?   135

MALATESTE Nothing, my lord.

FERDINAND Yes.

MALATESTE 'Tis your shadow.

FERDINAND Stay it; let it not haunt me.

MALATESTE Impossible, if you move, and the sun shine.   140

FERDINAND I will throttle it. (*Throws himself on the ground*)

MALATESTE O, my lord, you are angry with nothing.

FERDINAND You are a fool: how is 't possible I should catch my shadow, unless
I fall upon 't? When I go to hell, I mean to carry a bribe; for, look you,
good gifts evermore make way for the worst persons.   145

PESCARA Rise, good my lord.

FERDINAND I am studying the art of patience.

PESCARA 'Tis a noble virtue.

FERDINAND To drive six snails before me from this town to Moscow; neither
use goad nor whip to them, but let them take their own time;—the   150
patient'st man i' th' world match me for an experiment;—and I'll crawl
after like a sheep-biter.*

CARDINAL Force him up. (*They raise him*)

FERDINAND Use me well, you were best. What I have done, I have done:
I'll confess nothing.   155

DOCTOR Now let me come to him.—Are you mad, my lord? Are you out of
your princely wits?

FERDINAND What's he?

PESCARA Your doctor.

FERDINAND Let me have his beard saw'd off, and his eyebrows fil'd more   160
civil.

DOCTOR I must do mad tricks with him, for that's the only way on 't.—I have
brought your grace a salamander's skin to keep you from sunburning.

FERDINAND I have cruel sore eyes.

[128] A famous German physician (1493–1541), half-quack, half-scientist. Here an anachronism.
[152] A dog that worries sheep to keep them grouped.

DOCTOR   The white of a cockatrix's egg is present* remedy.   165

FERDINAND   Let it be a new laid one, you were best.—Hide me from him:
physicians are like kings,—they brook no contradiction.

DOCTOR   New he begins to fear me: now let me alone with him. (*He takes off
his gown*)

CARDINAL   How now? Put off your gown?   170

DOCTOR   Let me have some forty urinals fill'd with rosewater: he and I'll go
pelt one another with them.—Now he begins to fear me.—Can you fetch
a frisk,* sir?—Let him go, let him go, upon my peril: I find by his eye he
stands in awe of me; I'll make him as tame as a dormouse.

FERDINAND   Can you fetch your frisks, sir?—I will stamp him into a cullis,   175
flay off his skin, to cover one of the anatomies* this rogue hath set i' th' cold
yonder in Barber-Chirurgeon's-hall.—Hence, hence! You are all of you like
beasts for sacrifice: there's nothing left of you but tongue and belly, flattery
and lechery. (*Exit*)

PESCARA   Doctor, he did not fear you throughly.   180

DOCTOR   True;
I was somewhat too forward.

BOSOLA   Mercy upon me,
What a fatal judgement hath fall'n upon this Ferdinand!

PESCARA   Knows your grace what accident hath brought   185
Unto the prince this strange distraction?

CARDINAL (*Aside*)   I must feign somewhat.—Thus they say it grew.
You have heard it rumour'd, for these many years
None of our family dies but there is seen
The shape of an old woman, which is given   190
By tradition to us to have been murder'd
By her nephews for her riches. Such a figure
One night, as the prince sat up late at 's book,
Appear'd to him; when crying out for help,
The gentlemen of 's chamber found his grace   195
All on a cold sweat, alter'd much in face
And language: since which apparition,
He hath grown worse and worse, and I much fear
He cannot live.

BOSOLA   Sir, I would speak with you.   200

PESCARA   We'll leave your grace,
Wishing to the sick prince, our noble lord,
All health of mind and body.

CARDINAL   You are most welcome.
        (*Exeunt* PESCARA, MALATESTE, *and* DOCTOR)   205
Are you come? So.—(*Aside*) This fellow must not know
By any means I had intelligence
In our duchess' death; for, though I counsell'd it,

165 Immediate.
173 Cut a caper.
176 Skeletons.

The full of all th' engagement seem'd to grow
From Ferdinand.—Now, sir, how fares our sister?
I do not think but sorrow makes her look
Like to an oft-dyed garment: she shall now
Taste comfort from me. Why do you look so wildly?
Oh, the fortune of your master here the prince
Dejects you; but be you of happy comfort:
If you'll do one thing for me I'll entreat,
Though he had a cold tombstone o'er his bones,
I'd make you what you would be.

BOSOLA   Anything;
Give it me in a breath, and let me fly to 't:
They that think long small expedition win,
For musing much o' th' end cannot begin.

                    (*Enter* JULIA)

JULIA   Sir, will you come in to supper?

CARDINAL   I am busy;
Leave me.

JULIA (*Aside*)   What an excellent shape hath that fellow! (*Exit*)

CARDINAL   'Tis thus. Antonio lurks here in Milan:
Inquire him out, and kill him. While he lives,
Our sister cannot marry; and I have thought
Of an excellent match for her. Do this, and style me
Thy advancement.

BOSOLA   But by what means shall I find him out?

CARDINAL   There is a gentleman called Delio
Here in the camp, that hath been long approv'd
His loyal friend. Set eye upon that fellow;
Follow him to mass; maybe Antonio,
Although he do account religion
But a school-name, for fashion of the world
May accompany him; or else go inquire out
Delio's confessor, and see if you can bribe
Him to reveal it. There are a thousand ways
A man might find to trace him; as to know
What fellows haunt the Jews for taking up
Great sums of money, for sure he 's in want;
Or else to go to th' picture-makers, and learn
Who bought her picture lately: some of these
Happily may take.

BOSOLA   Well, I'll not freeze i' th' business:
I would see that wretched thing, Antonio,
Above all sights i' th' world.

CARDINAL   Do, and be happy. (*Exit*)

BOSOLA   This fellow doth breed basilisks in 's eyes,
He's nothing else but murder; yet he seems
Not to have notice of the duchess' death.

'Tis his cunning: I must follow his example;
There cannot be a surer way to trace
Than that of an old fox.

(*Re-enter* JULIA, *with a pistol*)

JULIA   So, sir, you are well met.   260

BOSOLA   How now?

JULIA   Nay, the doors are fast enough: Now, sir,
I will make you confess your treachery.

BOSOLA   Treachery?

JULIA   Yes,   265
Confess to me which of my women 'twas
You hired to put love-powder into my drink?

BOSOLA   Love-powder?

JULIA   Yes, when I was at Malfi.
Why should I fall in love with such a face else?   270
I have already suffer'd for thee so much pain,
The only remedy to do me good
Is to kill my longing.

BOSOLA   Sure, your pistol holds
Nothing but perfumes or kissing-comfits.*   275
Excellent lady! You have a pretty way on 't
To discover your longing. Come, come, I'll disarm you,
And arm you thus (*Embraces her*): yet this is wondrous strange.

JULIA   Compare thy form and my eyes together, you'll find
My love no such great miracle. Now you'll say   280
I am wanton: this nice modesty in ladies
Is but a troublesome familiar that haunts them.

BOSOLA   Know you me, I am a blunt soldier.

JULIA   The better.
Sure, there wants fire where there are no lively sparks   285
Of roughness.

BOSOLA   And I want compliment.

JULIA   Why, ignorance
In courtship cannot make you do amiss,
If you have a heart to do well.   290

BOSOLA   You are very fair.

JULIA   Nay, if you lay beauty to my charge,
I must plead unguilty.

BOSOLA   Your bright eyes carry
A quiver of darts in them sharper than sunbeams.   295

JULIA   You will mar me with commendation,
Put yourself to the charge of courting me,
Whereas now I woo you.

BOSOLA (*Aside*)   I have it, I will work upon this creature.—
Let us grow most amorously familiar: 300

275 Sweetmeats to scent the breath.

If the great Cardinal now should see me thus,
Would he not count me a villain?

JULIA   No; he might
Count me a wanton, not lay a scruple
Of offence on you; for if I see and steal   305
A diamond, the fault is not i' th' stone,
But in me the thief that purloins it. I am sudden
With you: we that are great women of pleasure
Use to cut off these uncertain wishes
And unquiet longings, and in an instant join   310
The sweet delight and the pretty excuse together.
Had you been i' th' street, under my chamber-window,
Even there I should have courted you.

BOSOLA   Oh, you are
An excellent lady!   315

JULIA   Bid me do somewhat for you
Presently to express I love you.

BOSOLA   I will;
And if you love me, fail not to effect it.
The Cardinal is grown wondrous melancholy;   320
Demand the cause, let him not put you off
With feign'd excuse; discover the main ground on 't.

JULIA Why would you know this?

BOSOLA   I have depended on him,
And I hear that he is fall'n in some disgrace   325
With the emperor: if he be, like the mice
That forsake falling houses, I would shift
To other dependence.

JULIA   You shall not need
Follow the wars: I'll be your maintenance.   330

BOSOLA And I your loyal servant: but I cannot
Leave my calling.

JULIA   Not leave an ungrateful
General for the love of a sweet lady?
You are like some cannot sleep in feather-beds,   335
But must have blocks for their pillows.

BOSOLA   Will you do this?

JULIA Cunningly.

BOSOLA To-morrow I'll expect th' intelligence.

JULIA To-morrow? Get you into my cabinet;   340
You shall have it with you. Do not delay me,
No more than I do you: I am like one
That is condemn'd; I have my pardon promis'd,
But I would see it seal'd. Go, get you in:
You shall see me wind my tongue about his heart   345
Like a skein of silk. (*Exit* BOSOLA)

(Re-enter CARDINAL)

CARDINAL   Where are you?

(Enter SERVANTS)

SERVANTS   Here.   350

CARDINAL   Let none, upon your lives, have conference
With the Prince Ferdinand, unless I know it.—
(Aside) In this distraction he may reveal
The murder. (Exeunt SERVANTS)
              Yond's my lingering consumption: 355
I am weary of her, and by any means
Would be quit of.

JULIA   How now, my lord? What ails you?

CARDINAL   Nothing.

JULIA   Oh, you are much alter'd: come, I must be   360
Your secretary,* and remove this lead
From off your bosom: what's the matter?

CARDINAL   I may not
Tell you.

JULIA   Are you so far in love with sorrow   365
You cannot part with part of it? Or think you
I cannot love your grace when you are sad
As well as merry? Or do you suspect
I, that have been a secret to your heart
These many winters, cannot be the same   370
Unto your tongue?

CARDINAL   Satisfy thy longing,—
The only way to make thee keep my counsel
Is, not to tell thee.

JULIA   Tell your echo this,   375
Or flatterers, that like echoes still report
What they hear though most imperfect, and not me;
For if that you be true unto yourself,
I'll know.

CARDINAL   Will you rack me?*   380

JULIA   No, judgement shall
Draw it from you: it is an equal fault,
To tell one's secrets unto all or none.

CARDINAL   The first argues folly.

JULIA   But the last tyranny.   385

CARDINAL   Very well: why, imagine I have committed
Some secret deed which I desire the world
May never hear of.

JULIA   Therefore may not I know it?
You have conceal'd for me as great a sin   390
As adultery. Sir, never was occasion

---

³⁶¹ Confidante.

³⁸⁰ Put me on the rack; torture me.

For perfect trial of my constancy
Till now: sir, I beseech you——

CARDINAL   You'll repent it.

JULIA Never.

CARDINAL It hurries thee to ruin: I'll not tell thee. 395
Be well advis'd, and think what danger 'tis
To receive a prince's secrets: they that do,
Had need have their breasts hoop'd with adamant
To contain them. I pray thee, yet be satisfi'd; 400
Examine thine own frailty; 'tis more easy
To tie knots than unloose them: 'tis a secret
That, like a lingering poison, may chance lie
Spread in thy veins, and kill thee seven year hence.

JULIA Now you dally with me. 405

CARDINAL   No more; thou shalt know it.
By my appointment the great Duchess of Malfi
And two of her young children, four nights since,
Were strangled.

JULIA   O Heaven! Sir, what have you done!

CARDINAL How now? How settles this? Think you your bosom 410
Will be a grave dark and obscure enough
For such a secret?

JULIA   You have undone yourself, sir.

CARDINAL Why?

JULIA   It lies not in me to conceal it. 415

CARDINAL   No?
Come, I will swear you to 't upon this book.

JULIA Most religiously.

CARDINAL   Kiss it. (*She kisses the book*) 420
Now you shall never utter it; thy curiosity
Hath undone thee: thou'rt poison'd with that book;
Because I knew thou couldst not keep my counsel,
I have bound thee to 't by death.

                    (*Re-enter* BOSOLA) 425

BOSOLA   For pity sake,
Hold!

CARDINAL Ha! Bosola?

JULIA   I forgive you
This equal piece of justice you have done;
For I betray'd your counsel to that fellow: 430
He overheard it; that was the cause I said
It lay not in me to conceal it.

BOSOLA   O foolish woman,
Couldst not thou have poison'd him?

JULIA   'Tis weakness, 435
Too much to think what should have been done. I go,
I know not whither. (*Dies*)

CARDINAL   Wherefore com'st thou hither?

BOSOLA   That I might find a great man like yourself,   440
    Not out of his wits as the Lord Ferdinand,
    To remember my service.

CARDINAL   I'll have thee hew'd in pieces.

BOSOLA   Make not yourself such a promise of that life
    Which is not yours to dispose of.   445

CARDINAL   Who plac'd thee here?

BOSOLA   Her lust, as she intended.

CARDINAL   Very well:
    Now you know me for your fellow-murderer.

BOSOLA   And wherefore should you lay fair marble colours   450
    Upon your rotten purposes to me?
    Unless you imitate some that do plot great treasons,
    And when they have done, go hide themselves i' th' graves
    Of those were actors in 't?

CARDINAL   No more; there is   455
    A fortune attends thee.

BOSOLA   Shall I go sue
    To Fortune any longer? 'Tis the fool's
    Pilgrimage.

CARDINAL   I have honours in store for thee.   460

BOSOLA   There are a many ways that conduct to seeming
    Honour, and some of them very dirty ones.

CARDINAL   Throw
    To the devil thy melancholy. The fire burns well:
    What need we keep a stirring of 't, and make   465
    A greater smother? Thou wilt kill Antonio?

BOSOLA   Yes.

CARDINAL   Take up that body.

BOSOLA   I think I shall
    Shortly grow the common bearer for churchyards.   470

CARDINAL   I will allow thee some dozen of attendants
    To aid thee in the murder.

BOSOLA   Oh, by no means. Physicians that apply horseleeches to any rank
    swelling use to cut off their tails, that the blood may run through them the
    faster: let me have no train when I go to shed blood, lest it make me have 475
    a greater when I ride to the gallows.

CARDINAL   Come to me after midnight, to help to remove
    That body to her own lodging: I'll give out
    She died o' th' plague; 'twill breed the less inquiry
    After her death.   480

BOSOLA   Where's Castruccio her husband?

CARDINAL   He's rode to Naples, to take possession
    Of Antonio's citadel.

BOSOLA   Believe me, you have done
    A very happy turn.   485

CARDINAL   Fail not to come:
   There is the master-key of our lodgings; and by that
   You may conceive what trust I plant in you.
BOSOLA   You shall find me ready. (*Exit* CARDINAL)
                              O poor Antonio,   490
   Though nothing be so needful to thy estate
   As pity, yet I find nothing so dangerous;
   I must look to my footing:
   In such slippery ice-pavements men had need
   To be frost-nailed well, they may break their necks else;   495
   The precedent's here afore me. How this man
   Bears up in blood!* Seems fearless! Why, 'tis well:
   Security some men call the suburbs of hell,
   Only a dead wall between. Well, good Antonio,
   I'll seek thee out; and all my care shall be   500
   To put thee into safety from the reach
   Of these most cruel biters that have got
   Some of thy blood already. It may be,
   I'll join with thee in a most just revenge:
   The weakest arm is strong enough that strikes   505
   With the sword of justice. Still methinks the duchess
   Haunts me.—There, there, 'tis nothing but my melancholy.
   O Penitence, let me truly taste thy cup,
   That throws men down only to raise them up! (*Exit*)

Scene 3

                    A Fortification at Milan   510
                  (*Enter* ANTONIO *and* DELIO)
DELIO   Yond's the Cardinal's window. This fortification
   Grew from the ruins of an ancient abbey;
   And to yond side o' th' river lies a wall,
   Piece of a cloister, which in my opinion   515
   Gives the best echo that you ever heard,
   So hollow and so dismal, and withal
   So plain in the distinction of our words,
   That many have suppos'd it is a spirit
   That answers.   520
ANTONIO   I do love these ancient ruins.
   We never tread upon them but we set
   Our foot upon some reverend history:
   And, questionless, here in this open court,
   Which now lies naked to the injuries   525
   Of stormy weather, some men lie interr'd
   Lov'd the church so well, and gave so largely to 't,
   They thought it should have canopied their bones

---

497 Keeps up his courage.

Till doomsday; but all things have their end:
Churches and cities, which have diseases   530
Like to men, must have like death that we have.

ECHO   "Like death that we have."

DELIO   Now the echo hath caught you.

ANTONIO   It groaned, methought, and gave
A very deadly accent.   535

ECHO   "Deadly accent."

DELIO   I told you 'twas a pretty one: you may make it
A huntsman, or a falconer, a musician,
Or a thing of sorrow.

ECHO   "A thing of sorrow."   540

ANTONIO   Aye, sure, that suits it best.

ECHO   "That suits it best."

ANTONIO   'Tis very like my wife's voice.

ECHO   "Aye, wife's voice."

DELIO   Come, let's walk further from 't. I would not have you   545
Go to th' Cardinal's to-night: do not.

ECHO   "Do not."

DELIO   Wisdom doth not more moderate wasting sorrow
Than time: take time for 't; be mindful of thy safety.

ECHO   "Be mindful of thy safety."   550

ANTONIO   Necessity compels me:
Make scrutiny throughout the passes of
Your own life, you'll find it impossible
To fly your fate.

ECHO   "Oh, fly your fate."   555

DELIO   Hark!
The dead stones seem to have pity on you, and give you
Good counsel.

ANTONIO   Echo, I will not talk with thee,
For thou art a dead thing.   560

ECHO   "Thou art a dead thing."

ANTONIO   My duchess is asleep now,
And her little ones, I hope sweetly: O Heaven,
Shall I never see her more?

ECHO   "Never see her more."   565

ANTONIO   I mark'd not one repetition of the echo
But that; and on the sudden a clear light
Presented me a face folded in sorrow.

DELIO   Your fancy merely.

ANTONIO   Come, I'll be out of this ague,   570
For to live thus is not indeed to live;
It is a mockery and abuse of life:
I will not henceforth save myself by halves;
Lose all, or nothing.

DELIO   Your own virtue save you!   575
I'll fetch your eldest son, and second you:
It may be that the sight of his own blood
Spread in so sweet a figure may beget
The more compassion. However, fare you well.
Though in our miseries Fortune have a part,   580
Yet in our noble sufferings she hath none:
Contempt of pain, that we may call our own. (*Exeunt*)

Scene 4

A Room in the Cardinal's Palace
(*Enter* CARDINAL, PESCARA, MALATESTE, RODERIGO, *and* GRISOLAN)
CARDINAL   You shall not watch to-night by the sick prince;
His grace is very well recover'd.   585
MALATESTE   Good my lord, suffer us.
CARDINAL   Oh, by no means;
The noise, and change of object in his eye,
Doth more distract him: I pray, all to bed;
And though you hear him in his violent fit,   590
Do not rise, I entreat you.
PESCARA   So, sir; we shall not.
CARDINAL   Nay, I must have you promise upon your honours,
For I was enjoin'd to 't by himself; and he seem'd
To urge it sensibly.   595
PESCARA   Let our honours bind
This trifle.
CARDINAL   Nor any of your followers.
MALATESTE   Neither.
600
CARDINAL   It may be, to make trial of your promise,
When he's asleep, myself will rise and feign
Some of his mad tricks, and cry out for help,
And feign myself in danger.
MALATESTE   If your throat were cutting,   605
I'd not come at you, now I have protested against it.
CARDINAL   Why, I thank you.
GRISOLAN   'Twas a foul storm to-night.
RODERIGO   The Lord Ferdinand's chamber shook like an osier.*
MALATESTE   'Twas nothing but pure kindness in the devil,   610
To rock his own child. (*Exeunt all except the* CARDINAL)
CARDINAL   The reason why I would not suffer these
About my brother is because at midnight
I may with better privacy convey
Julia's body to her own lodging. Oh, my conscience!   615
I would pray now; but the devil takes away my heart
For having any confidence in prayer.
609 A willow tree.

About this hour I appointed Bosola
To fetch the body: when he hath serv'd my turn,
He dies. (*Exit*)   620

(*Enter* BOSOLA)

BOSOLA   Ha! 'twas the Cardinal's voice; I heard him name
Bosola and my death. Listen; I hear
One's footing.

(*Enter* FERDINAND)   625

FERDINAND   Strangling is a very quiet death.

BOSOLA (*Aside*)   Nay, then, I see I must stand upon my guard.

FERDINAND   What say to that? Whisper softly; do you agree to 't? So; it must
be done i' th' dark: the Cardinal would not for a thousand pounds the doctor
should see it.   630

BOSOLA   My death is plotted; here 's the consequence of murder.
We value not desert nor Christian breath,
When we know black deeds must be cur'd with death.

(*Enter* ANTONIO *and* SERVANT)

SERVANT   Here stay, sir, and be confident, I pray: 635
I'll fetch you a dark lantern. (*Exit*)

ANTONIO   Could I take him
At his prayers, there were hope of pardon.

BOSOLA   Fall right, my sword!—(*Stabs him*)
I'll not give thee so much leisure as to pray.   640

ANTONIO   Oh, I am gone! Thou hast ended a long suit
In a minute.

BOSOLA   What art thou?

ANTONIO   A most wretched thing,
That only have thy benefit in death,   645
To appear myself.

(*Re-enter* SERVANT *with a lantern*)

SERVANT   Where are you, sir?

ANTONIO   Very near my home.—Bosola?

SERVANT   Oh, misfortune!   650

BOSOLA   Smother thy pity, thou art dead else.—Antonio?
The man I would have saved 'bove mine own life!
We are merely the stars' tennis-balls, struck and bandied
Which way please them.—O good Antonio,
I'll whisper one thing in thy dying ear   655
Shall make thy heart break quickly! Thy fair duchess
And two sweet children——

ANTONIO   Their very names

Kindle a little life in me.

BOSOLA   Are murder'd.   660

ANTONIO   Some men have wish'd to die
At the hearing of sad tidings; I am glad
That I shall do 't in sadness: I would not now

Wish my wounds balm'd nor heal'd, for I have no use
To put my life to. In all our quest of greatness, 665
Like wanton boys, whose pastime is their care,
We follow after bubbles blown in th' air.
Pleasure of life, what is 't? Only the good
Hours of an ague; merely a preparative
To rest, to endure vexation. I do not ask
The process of my death; only commend me 670
To Delio.

BOSOLA   Break, heart!
ANTONIO   And let my son
Fly the courts of princes. (*Dies*) 675
BOSOLA   Thou seem'st
To have lov'd Antonio?
SERVANT   I brought him hither,
To have reconcil'd him to the Cardinal.
BOSOLA   I do not ask thee that.
Take him up, if thou tender thine own life, 680
And bear him where the lady Julia
Was wont to lodge.—Oh, my fate moves swift;
I have this Cardinal in the forge already;
Now I'll bring him to th' hammer. O direful misprision!*
I will not imitate things glorious, 685
No more than base; I'll be mine own example.—
On, on, and look thou represent, for silence,
The thing thou bear'st. (*Exeunt*)

Scene 5

Another Room in the same
(*Enter* CARDINAL, *with a book*) 690
CARDINAL   I am puzzled in a question about hell:
He says, in hell there 's one material fire,
And yet it shall not burn all men alike.
Lay him by. How tedious is a guilty conscience!
When I look into the fish-ponds in my garden, 695
Methinks I see a thing arm'd with a rake,
That seems to strike at me.
                (*Enter* BOSOLA, *and* SERVANT *bearing* ANTONIO'S *body*)
                            Now, art thou come?
Thou look'st ghastly: 700
There sits in thy face some great determination
Mix'd with some fear.
BOSOLA   Thus it lightens into action:
I am come to kill thee.
705

685 Mistake.

CARDINAL   Ha!—Help! Our guard!

BOSOLA   Thou art deceived; they are out of thy howling.

CARDINAL   Hold; and I will faithfully divide
    Revenues with thee.

BOSOLA   Thy prayers and proffers   710
    Are both unseasonable.

CARDINAL   Raise the watch!
    We are betrayed!

BOSOLA   I have confin'd your flight:
    I'll suffer your retreat to Julia's chamber,   715
    But no further.

CARDINAL   Help! We are betrayed!
        (*Enter, above,* PESCARA, MALATESTE, RODERIGO, *and* GRISOLAN)

MALATESTE   Listen.

CARDINAL   My dukedom for rescue!   720

RODERIGO   Fie upon
    His counterfeiting!

MALATESTE   Why, 'tis not the Cardinal.

RODERIGO   Yes, yes, 'tis he: but I'll see him hang'd
    Ere I'll go down to him.   725

CARDINAL   Here 's a plot upon me;
    I am assaulted! I am lost, unless some rescue.

GRISOLAN   He doth this pretty well; but it will not serve
    To laugh me out of mine honour.

CARDINAL   The sword 's at my throat!   730

RODERIGO   You would not bawl so loud then.

MALATESTE   Come, come,
    Let 's go to bed: he told us thus much aforehand.

PESCARA   He wish'd you should not come at him; but, believe 't,
    The accent of the voice sounds not in jest: 735
    I'll down to him, howsoever, and with engines*
    Force ope the doors. (*Exit above*)

RODERIGO   Let 's follow him aloof,
    And note how the Cardinal will laugh at him.
        (*Exeunt, above,* MALATESTE, RODERIGO, *and* GRISOLAN)   740

BOSOLA   There's for first, (*Kills the* SERVANT)
    'Cause you shall not unbarricade the door
    To let in rescue.

CARDINAL   What cause hast thou to pursue my life?

BOSOLA   Look there.   745

CARDINAL   Antonio?

BOSOLA   Slain by my hand unwittingly.
    Pray, and be sudden: when thou killed'st thy sister,
    Thou took'st from Justice her most equal balance,
    And left her naught but her sword.   750

736 Tools.

276   WEBSTER

CARDINAL   Oh, mercy!

BOSOLA   Now, it seems thy greatness was only outward;
   For thou fall'st faster of thyself than calamity
   Can drive thee. I'll not waste longer time; there! (*Stabs him*)

CARDINAL   Thou hast hurt me.

BOSOLA   Again! (*Stabs him again*)

CARDINAL   Shall I die like a leveret,*
   Without any resistance?—Help, help, help!
   I am slain!

             (*Enter* FERDINAND)

FERDINAND   Th' alarum? Give me a fresh horse;
   Rally the vaunt-guard, or the day is lost.
   Yield, yield! I give you the honour of arms,*
   Shake my sword over you; will you yield?

CARDINAL   Help me;
   I am your brother!

FERDINAND   The devil! My brother fight
   Upon the adverse party? (*He wounds the* CARDINAL, *and, in the scuffle,*
          gives BOSOLA *his deathwound*)
          There flies your ransom.*

CARDINAL   O justice!
   I suffer now for what hath former been:
   Sorrow is held the eldest child of sin.

FERDINAND   Now you 're brave fellows. Caesar's fortune was harder than Pompey's; Caesar died in the arms of prosperity, Pompey at the feet of disgrace. You both died in the field. The pain 's nothing: pain many times is taken away with the apprehension of greater, as the toothache with the sight of a barber that comes to pull it out: there's philosophy for you.

BOSOLA   Now my revenge is perfect.—Sink, thou main cause (*Kills* FERDINAND)
   Of my undoing!—The last part of my life
   Hath done me best service.

FERDINAND   Give me some wet hay; I am broken-winded.* I do account this world but a dog-kennel: I will vault credit* and affect high pleasures beyond death.

BOSOLA   He seems to come to himself, now he 's so near
   The bottom.

FERDINAND   My sister, O my sister! There 's the cause on 't.
   Whether we fall by ambition, blood, or lust,
   Like diamonds we are cut with our own dust. (*Dies*)

CARDINAL   Thou hast thy payment too.

BOSOLA   Yes, I hold my weary soul in my teeth.

755

760

765

770

775

780

785

790

[757] Rabbit.

[763] Fair terms of surrender.

[770] Being dead, he cannot ask for ransom.

[782] A cure for a horse with the heaves, a respiratory ailment.

[783] Disregard probability.

'Tis ready to part from me. I do glory
That thou, which stood'st like a huge pyramid
Begun upon a large and ample base,
Shalt end in a little point, a kind of nothing.   795
    (*Enter, below,* PESCARA, MALATESTE, RODERIGO, *and* GRISOLAN)

PESCARA How now, my lord?
MALATESTE   O sad disaster!
RODERIGO   How
Comes this?   800
BOSOLA   Revenge for the Duchess of Malfi murdered
By th' Arragonian brethren; for Antonio
Slain by this hand; for lustful Julia
Poison'd by this man; and lastly for myself,
That was an actor in the main of all,   805
Much 'gainst mine own good nature, yet i' th' end
Neglected.
PESCARA How now, my lord?
CARDINAL   Look to my brother: he gave us these large
                            wounds   810

As we were struggling here i' the rushes. And now,
I pray, let me be laid by and never thought of. (*Dies*)
PESCARA How fatally, it seems, he did withstand
His own rescue!
MALATESTE Thou wretched thing of blood,   815
How came Antonio by his death?
BOSOLA   In a mist;
I know not how: such a mistake as I
Have often seen in a play. Oh, I am gone!
We are only like dead walls or vaulted graves,   820
That, ruin'd, yield no echo. Fare you well.
It may be pain, but no harm to me to die
In so good a quarrel. Oh, this gloomy world!
In what a shadow, or deep pit of darkness,
Doth, womanish and fearful, mankind live!   825
Let worthy minds ne'er stagger in distrust
To suffer death or shame for what is just:
Mine is another voyage. (*Dies*)
PESCARA The noble Delio, as I came to the palace,
Told me of Antonio's being here, and show'd me   830
A pretty gentleman, his son and heir.
          (*Enter* DELIO *and* ANTONIO'S *Son*)

MALATESTE O sir,
You come too late!
DELIO   I heard so, and was arm'd for 't   835
Ere I came. Let us make noble use
Of this great ruin; and join all our force
To establish this young hopeful gentleman

In 's mother's right. These wretched eminent things
Leave no more fame behind 'em, than should one   840
Fall in a frost, and leave his print in snow;
As soon as the sun shines, it ever melts,
Both form and matter. I have ever thought
Nature doth nothing so great for great men
As when she 's pleas'd to make them lords of truth: 845
Integrity of life is fame's best friend,
Which nobly, beyond death, shall crown the end. (*Exeunt*)

Francis Beaumont *and* John Fletcher

*Francis Beaumont (c.1584–1616) and John Fletcher (1579–1625)
combined to produce the most successful collaboration of the
Elizabethan Age. Although both men wrote some plays alone
or with other playwrights, they did their most important work
jointly in the period from 1607–1614, first with a group of
lively comedies and then a group of tragedies.* THE KNIGHT
OF THE BURNING PESTLE *began a vigorous tradition of satiric,
mock-heroic comedy, though the collaborators gained their most
immediate success and influence with the type of play represented by*
PHILASTER, *the tragicomic serious drama with a happy ending.
Urbane and highly skillful both at constructing plots and writing
verse, Beaumont and Fletcher brought to English drama standards
of professional expertise and sentimental elegance that were long
admired and influential.*

Chronology

*c.*1584 **Francis Beaumont** born, third
son of Francis Beaumont, Justice
of the Common Pleas in Leicester.

1597 Entered Broadgates Hall (now
Pembroke College), Oxford.

1600 Admitted to study law at the
Inner Temple, London.

1602 Published, anonymously, *Salmacis and Hermaphroditus.*

1607 Contributed commendatory
verses to *Volpone* (his affection and
admiration for Jonson continued
throughout his life). His first play,
The Woman Hater, was published.
This was also the probable year of
The Knight of The Burning Pestle.
The collaboration with John
Fletcher was probably already
underway, but whether he wrote
Knight with Fletcher or alone is
uncertain. The play was not a success with the public.

1607–10 Period of the early plays in
collaboration with Fletcher, including, *Love's Cure, The Noble
Gentleman, The Coxcomb,* and *Love's
Pilgrimage.*

1610–14 Second period of plays, including *Philaster, The Maid's
Tragedy, A King and No King,* and
The Scornful Lady.

*c.*1614 Married and retired from the
theater and London.

1616 Died; buried in Westminster
Abbey.

1579 **John Fletcher** born at Rye,
Sussex, son of a Protestant minister who successively became
Bishop of Bristol, Worcester, and
London.

1591 Perhaps entered Corpus Christi
College, Cambridge.

1607 Probably already launched on a
theatrical career when he assisted
Francis Beaumont with *The
Woman Hater.*

1607–14 Period of his collaboration
with Beaumont.

c.1608 Wrote *The Faithful Shepherdess* alone.

1613 Collaborated with Shakespeare on *Two Noble Kinsmen* and *Henry VIII*.

1615–25 Period of plays written alone or in collaboration with a variety of hands. The most important are: *The Wild Goose Chase* (1621), *The Island Princess* (1621), *Rule a Wife and Have a Wife* (1624)—all of which he wrote alone.

1625 Died.

Selected Bibliography

Appleton, W. W., *Beaumont and Fletcher, A Critical Study*, London, 1956.

Gayley, Charles Mills, *Beaumont the Dramatist*, New York, 1914.

Hatcher, Orie Latham, *John Fletcher, A Study in Dramatic Method*, Chicago, 1905.

Lindsey, E. S., "The Original Music for Beaumont's Play, *The Knight of The Burning Pestle*," *Studies in Philology*, XXVI (1929), 425–443.

Macauley, George Campbell, *Francis Beaumont, A Critical Study*, London, 1883.

Maxwell, Baldwin, *Studies in Beaumont, Fletcher, and Massinger*, Chapel Hill, N.C., 1939.

Oliphant, E. H. C., *The Plays of Beaumont and Fletcher*, New Haven, Conn., 1927.

Waith, Eugene M., *The Pattern of Tragicomedy in Beaumont and Fletcher*, New Haven, Conn., 1952.

Wallis, L. B., *Fletcher, Beaumont and Company, Entertainers to the Jacobean Gentry*, New York, 1947.

Frontispiece to *The Wits* (1672) by Francis Kirkman,
showing an improvised Commonwealth stage for burlesque
performances of drolls. Under the Commonwealth (1653–1658),
the Puritans had closed the theaters. *Folger Library*

THE KNIGHT
OF
THE BURNING PESTLE

by Francis Beaumont and John Fletcher

Characters

THE PROLOGUE

A CITIZEN

THE CITIZEN'S WIFE   *sitting below amidst the spectators*

RAFE *her man*

VENTUREWELL, *a rich merchant*

JASPER, *his apprentice*

MASTER HUMPHREY, *a friend to the merchant*

LUCE, *merchant's daughter*

MISTRESS MERRYTHOUGHT, *Jasper's mother*

MICHAEL, *a second son of Mistress Merrythought*

OLD MASTER MERRYTHOUGHT, *Jasper's father*

TIM, *a squire*
GEORGE, *a dwarf*   *apprentices to the* CITIZEN

A TAPSTER

A BOY *that danceth and singeth*

AN HOST

A BARBER

TWO MEN *as captive knights*

A MAN *and* A WOMAN, *captives*

A CAPTAIN

A SERGEANT

SOLDIERS

BOYS

POMPIONA, *daughter of the King of Moldavia*

Various parts of London, Waltham Forest, etc.

(*Enter the* PROLOGUE)

PROLOGUE   Where the bee can suck no honey, she leaves her sting behind; and, where the bear cannot find origanum* to heal his grief, he blasteth all other leaves with his breath. We fear it is like to fare so with us—that, seeing you cannot draw from our labors sweet content, you leave behind you a sour

---

[2] Marjoram, a wild herb.

mislike, and with open reproach blame our good meanings, because you 5 cannot reap the wonted* mirth. Our intent was at this time to move inward delight, not outward lightness, and to breed (if it might be) soft smiling, not loud laughing, knowing it to the wise to be a great pleasure to hear counsel mixed with wit, as to the foolish to have sport mingled with rudeness. They were banished the theater of Athens, and from Rome hissed, that 10 brought parasites on the stage with apish actions, or fools with uncivil habits, or courtesans with immodest words. We have endeavored to be as far from unseemly speeches to make your ears glow as we hope you will be free from unkind reports or mistaking the author's intention (who never aimed at any any one particular in this play) to make our cheeks blush. And thus I leave 15 it, and thee to thine own censure, to like or dislike.—*Vale.** (*Exit*)

Induction

Several GENTLEMEN *sitting on stools on the stage; the* CITIZEN, *his* WIFE,
and RAFE *standing below among the audience*
(*Re-enter* PROLOGUE)

PROLOGUE   From all that's near the court, from all that's great,
Within the compass of the city* walls,   5
We now have brought our scene—
(*Enter* CITIZEN, *climbing onto the stage*)

CITIZEN   Hold your peace, Goodman* Boy!

PROLOGUE   What do you mean, sir?

CITIZEN   That you have no good meaning. This seven years there hath been 10 plays at this house,* I have observed it, you have still girds* at citizens; and now you call your play *The London Merchant*. Down with your title, boy! Down with your title!

PROLOGUE   Are you a member of the noble city?

CITIZEN   I am.   15

PROLOGUE   And a freeman?*

CITIZEN   Yea, and a grocer.

PROLOGUE   So, grocer, then, by your sweet favor, we intend no abuse to the city.

CITIZEN   No, sir! Yes, sir! If you were not resolved to play the Jacks,* what need you study for new subjects, purposely to abuse your betters? Why 20 could not you be contented, as well as others, with the legend of Whittington, or the life and death of Sir Thomas Gresham, with the building of the Royal Exchange, or the story of Queen Eleanor, with the rearing of London Bridge upon woolsacks?*

6 Usual.
16 Farewell.
5 To, that is, the business district of London.
8 Master.
11 (a) Probably Whitefriars, a private theater.   (b) Sneers.
16 A member of one of the craft guilds.
19 That is, play the knave or rascal.
24 An allusion to popular plays of the day.

PROLOGUE You seem to be an understanding man. What would you have us do, sir? 25

CITIZEN Why, present something notably in honor of the commons of the city.

PROLOGUE Why, what do you say to *The Life and Death of Fat Drake,** or *The Repairing of Fleet Privies?*

CITIZEN I do not like that; but I will have a citizen, and he shall be of my own trade. 30

PROLOGUE O, you should have told us your mind a month since; our play is ready to begin now.

CITIZEN 'Tis all one for that; I will have a grocer, and he shall do admirable things.
                                                                                            35

PROLOGUE What will you have him do?

CITIZEN Marry, I will have him—

WIFE (*Below**) Husband, husband!

RAFE (*Below*) Peace, mistress!

WIFE Hold thy peace, Rafe; I know what I do, I warrant tee.*—Husband, husband! 40

CITIZEN What sayst thou, cunny*?

WIFE Let him kill a lion with a pestle,* husband! Let him kill a lion with a pestle!

CITIZEN So he shall.—I'll have him kill a lion with a pestle. 45

WIFE Husband! Shall I come up, husband?

CITIZEN Ay, cunny.—Rafe, help your mistress this way.—Pray, gentlemen, make her a little room.—I pray you, sir, lend me your hand to help up my wife. I thank you, sir.—So. (WIFE *is pulled onto the stage*)

WIFE By your leave, gentlemen all; I'm something troublesome. I'm a 50 stranger here; I was ne'er at one of these plays, as they say, before; but I should have seen Jane Shore* once; and my husband hath promised me, any time this twelvemonth, to carry me to *The Bold Beauchamps,** but in truth he did not. I pray you, bear with me.

CITIZEN Boy, let my wife and I have a couple stools and then begin; and let 55 the grocer do rare things. (*Stools are brought*)

PROLOGUE But, sir, we have never a boy* to play him; everyone hath a part already.

WIFE Husband, husband, for God's sake, let Rafe play him! Beshrew me, if I do not think he will go beyond them all. 60

CITIZEN Well remembered, wife.—Come up, Rafe.—I'll tell you, gentlemen; let them but lend him a suit of reparel* and necessaries, and, by Gad, if any

---

[28] This Drake has not been identified, but he may have been a scavenger.
[38] That is, from the "pit" or orchestra.
[40] Thee.
[42] Rabbit or pet.
[43] Perhaps an allusion to Thomas Heywood's *Four Prentices of London,* in which one of the heroes kills a lion singlehanded.
[52] Thought to be an allusion to Thomas Heywood's *Edward IV.*
[53] Nothing is known of this play.
[57] A children's company, the Children of Her Majesty's Revels, was performing at Whitefriars.
[62] Malapropism for "apparel."

of them all blow wind in the tail on him,* I'll be hanged. (RAFE *leaps onto the stage*)

WIFE I pray you, youth, let him have a suit of reparel—I'll be sworn, gentle- 65
men, my husband tells you true. He will act you sometimes at our house
that all the neighbors cry out on him; he will fetch you up a couraging* part
so in the garret that we are all as feared, I warrant you, that we quake again.
We'll fear* our children with him; if they be never so unruly, do but cry,
"Rafe comes, Rafe comes!" to them, and they'll be as quiet as lambs.— 70
Holy up thy head, Rafe; show the gentlemen what thou canst do. Speak
a huffing* part; I warrant you, the gentlemen will accept of it.

CITIZEN Do, Rafe, do.

RAFE "By heaven, methinks, it were an easy leap
　　To pluck bright honor from the palefaced moon, 75
　　Or dive into the bottom of the sea,
　　Where never fathom line touched any ground,
　　And pluck up drownéd honor from the lake of hell."*

CITIZEN How say you, gentlemen, is it not as I told you?

WIFE Nay, gentlemen, he hath played before, my husband says, *Mucedorus,* 80
before the wardens of our Company.

CITIZEN Ay, and he should have played Jeronimo* with a shoemaker for a
wager.

PROLOGUE He shall have a suit of apparel, if he will go in.

CITIZEN In, Rafe, in, Rafe, and set out the grocery in their kind,* if thou 85
lov'st me. (*Exit* RAFE)

WIFE I warrant, our Rafe will look finely when he's dressed.

PROLOGUE But what will you have it called?

CITIZEN *The Grocer's Honor.*

PROLOGUE Methinks *The Knight of the Burning Pestle* were better. 90

WIFE I'll be sworn, husband, that's as good a name as can be.

CITIZEN Let it be so.—Begin, begin; my wife and I will sit down.

PROLOGUE I pray you, do.

CITIZEN What stately music have you? You have shawms?*

PROLOGUE Shawms? No. 95

CITIZEN No? I'm a thief if my mind did not give me so.* Rafe plays a stately
part, and he must needs have shawms. I'll be at the charge of them myself
rather than we'll be without them.

PROLOGUE So you are like to be.

CITIZEN Why, and so I will be; there's two shillings. (*Gives money*) Let's 100

---

63 That is, approach him in excellence.
67 Violent.
69 Frighten.
72 Blustering.
78 From Shakespeare's *Henry IV, i* (slightly inaccurate).
80 A popular old play.
82 An allusion to Kyd's *The Spanish Tragedy,* another popular old play.
85 That is, portray grocers as they really are.
94 Woodwind instruments.
96 That is, I was afraid of that.

have the waits* of Southwark; they are as rare fellows as any are in England; and that will fetch them all o'er the water* with a vengeance, as if they were mad.

PROLOGUE   You shall have them. Will you sit down then?

CITIZEN   Ay.—Come, wife.   105

WIFE   Sit you merry all, gentlemen; I'm bold to sit amongst you for my ease.

(CITIZEN *and* WIFE *sit down*)

PROLOGUE   From all that's near the court, from all that's great,
   Within the compass of the city walls,
   We now have brought our scene. Fly far from hence   110
   All private taxes,* immodest phrases,
   Whatever may but show like vicious!
   For wicked mirth never true pleasure brings,
   But honest minds are pleased with honest things.—
   Thus much for that we do; but for Rafe's part you must answer for   115
                                                          yourself.

CITIZEN   Take you no care for Rafe; he'll discharge himself, I warrant you.

(*Exit* PROLOGUE)

WIFE   I' faith, gentlemen, I'll give my word for Rafe.

Act One

Scene 1

A room in Venturewell's house
(*Enter* MERCHANT VENTUREWELL *and* JASPER, *his prentice*)

MERCHANT   Sirrah, I'll make you know you are my prentice,
   And whom my charitable love redeemed
   Even from the fall of fortune; gave thee heat   5
   And growth, to be what now thou art; new-cast* thee,
   Adding the trust of all I have at home,
   In foreign staples,* or upon the sea,
   To thy direction; tied the good opinions
   Both of myself and friends to thy endeavors.   10
   So fair were thy beginnings. But with these,
   As I remember, you had never charge
   To love your master's daughter, and even then
   When I had found a wealthy husband for her.
   I take it, sir, you had not. But, however,   15
   I'll break the neck of that commission,*
   And make you know you are but a merchant's factor.*

---

101 Musicians.
102 Over the Thames.
111 Personal attacks.
6 Re-made.
8 Trading posts.
16 Charge.
17 Agent or deputy.

JASPER Sir, I do liberally confess I am yours,
　　　Bound both by love and duty to your service,
　　　In which my labor hath been all my profit.　　　　　　　　20
　　　I have not lost in bargain, nor delighted
　　　To wear your honest gains upon my back;
　　　Nor have I given a pension to my blood,*
　　　Or lavishly in play consumed your stock.
　　　These, and the miseries that do attend them,　　　　　　25
　　　I dare with innocence proclaim are strangers
　　　To all my temperate actions. For your daughter,
　　　If there be any love to my deservings
　　　Borne by her virtuous self, I cannot stop it;
　　　Nor am I able to refrain* her wishes.　　　　　　　　　30
　　　She's private to herself and best of knowledge*
　　　Whom she'll make so happy as to sigh for;
　　　Besides, I cannot think you mean to match her
　　　Unto a fellow of so lame a presence,*
　　　One that hath little left of nature in him.　　　　　　　35
MERCHANT 'Tis very well, sir; I can tell your wisdom
　　　How all this shall be cured.
JASPER 　　　　　　　　　　Your care becomes you.
MERCHANT And thus it must be, sir: I here discharge you
　　　My house and service; take your liberty;　　　　　　　40
　　　And, when I want a son, I'll send for you. (*Exit*)
JASPER These be the fair rewards of them that love!
　　　O, you that live in freedom, never prove
　　　The travail of a mind led by desire!
　　　　　　　　　　　(*Enter* LUCE)　　　　　　　　45
LUCE Why, how now, friend? Struck with my father's thunder?
JASPER Struck, and struck dead, unless the remedy
　　　Be full of speed and virtue. I am now,
　　　What I expected long, no more your father's.
LUCE But mine.　　　　　　　　　　　　　　　　50
JASPER 　　　　　But yours, and only yours, I am;
　　　That's all I have to keep me from the statute.*
　　　You dare be constant still?
LUCE 　　　　　　　　　O, fear me not!
　　　In this I dare be better than a woman.　　　　　　　55
　　　Nor shall his anger nor his offers move me,
　　　Were they both equal to a prince's power.
JASPER You know my rival?
LUCE 　　　　　　　　Yes, and love him dearly,

　　23 That is, allowed my passion to run riot.
　　30 Restrain.
　　31 That is, she is secretive and knows herself best.
　　34 Uncouth behavior.
　　52 That is, keep me from being arrested as a vagrant.

Even as I love an ague or foul weather.
I prithee, Jasper, fear him not.   60
JASPER   O, no!
I do not mean to do him so much kindness.
But to our own desires: you know the plot
We both agreed on?
LUCE   Yes, and will perform   65
My part exactly.
JASPER   I desire no more.
Farewell, and keep my heart; 'tis yours.
LUCE   I take it;   70
He must do miracles makes me forsake it. (*Exeunt*)

CITIZEN   Fie upon 'em, little infidels! What a matter's here now? Well, I'll be
hanged for a halfpenny, if there be not some abomination knavery in this
play. Well, let 'em look to 't; Rafe must come, and if there be any tricks
a-brewing—   75
WIFE   Let 'em brew, and bake too, husband, a* God's name; Rafe will find all
out, I warrant you, and* they were older than they are.—
                       (*Enter* BOY)
I pray, my pretty youth, is Rafe ready?
BOY   He will be presently.   80
WIFE   Now, I pray you, make my commendations unto him, and withal carry
him this stick of licorice. Tell him his mistress sent it him, and bid him
bite a piece; 'twill open his pipes the better, say. (*Exit* BOY)

Scene 2

                (*Enter* VENTUREWELL *and* MASTER HUMPHREY)
MERCHANT   Come, sir, she's yours; upon my faith, she's yours!   85
You have my hand. For other idle lets*
Between your hopes and her, thus with a wind
They are scattered and no more. My wanton prentice,
That like a bladder blew himself with love,
I have let out, and sent him to discover   90
New masters yet unknown.
HUMPHREY   I thank you, sir;
Indeed, I thank you, sir; and, ere I stir,
It shall be known, however you do deem,
I am of gentle blood and gentle seem.*   95
MERCHANT   Oh, sir, I know it certain.
HUMPHREY   Sir, my friend,
Although, as writers say, all things have end,

<hr>

76 In.
77 Even if.
86 Obstacles.
95 Appearance.

And that we call a pudding hath his two,*
O, let it not seem strange, I pray, to you,   100
If in this bloody simile I put
My love, more endless than frail things or gut!

WIFE   Husband, I prithee, sweet lamb, tell me one thing, but tell me truly.—
Stay, youths, I beseech you, till I question my husband.

CITIZEN   What is it, mouse?   105

WIFE   Sirrah, didst thou ever see a prettier child? How it behaves itself, I warrant
ye, and speaks and looks and perts up* the head!—I pray you, brother, with
your favor, were you never none of Master Monkester's* scholars?

CITIZEN   Chicken, I prithee heartily, contain thyself; the childer* are pretty
childer; but, when Rafe comes, lamb—   110

WIFE   Ay, when Rafe comes, conny!—Well, my youth, you may proceed.

MERCHANT   Well, sir, you know my love, and rest, I hope,
Assured of my consent; get but my daughter's,
And wed her when you please. You must be bold,
And clap in close unto her; come, I know   115
You have language good enough to win a wench.

WIFE   A whoreson* tyrant! H'as been an old stringer* in 's days, I warrant him.

HUMPHREY   I take your gentle offer, and withal
Yield love again for love reciprocal.

MERCHANT   What, Luce! Within there!   120

(*Enter* LUCE)

LUCE   Called you, sir?

MERCHANT   I did.
Give entertainment to this gentleman,
And see you be not froward.—To her, sir;   125
My presence will but be an eyesore to you. (*Exit*)

HUMPHREY   Fair, Mistress Luce, how do you do? Are you well?
Give me your hand, and then, I pray you, tell
How doth your little sister and your brother,
And whether you love me or any other.   130

LUCE   Sir, these are quickly answered.

HUMPHREY   So they are,
Where women are not cruel. But how far
Is it now distant from this place we are in,
Unto that blessed place, your father's warren?*   135

LUCE   What makes you think of that, sir?

99 That is, ends.
107 Tosses.
108 Richard Mulcaster, Headmaster of St. Paul's School.
109 Children.
117 (*a*) Rascally.   (*b*) Rake or libertine.
135 Place used for rabbit-breeding.

HUMPHREY   Even that face;
    For, stealing rabbits whilom* in that place,
    God Cupid, or the keeper, I know not whether,*
    Unto my cost and charges brought you thither,   140
    And there began—
LUCE   Your game, sir.
HUMPHREY   Let no game,
    Or anything that tendeth to the same,
    Be evermore remembered, thou fair killer,   145
    For whom I sat me down, and brake my tiller.*

WIFE There's a kind gentleman, I warrant you; when will you do as much for
me, George?

LUCE Beshrew* me, sir, I am sorry for your losses,
    But, as the proverb says, I cannot cry.
    I would you had not seen me!   150
HUMPHREY   So would I,
    Unless you had more maw* to do me good.
LUCE Why, cannot this strange passion be withstood?
    Send for a constable, and raise the town.
HUMPHREY O, no! My valiant love will batter down   155
    Millions of constables, and put to flight
    Even that great watch of Midsummer Day at night.*
LUCE Beshrew me, sir, 'twere good I yielded then;
    Weak women cannot hope, where valiant men   160
    Have no resistance.
HUMPHREY   Yield, then; I am full
    Of pity, though I say it, and can pull
    Out of my pocket thus a pair of gloves.
    Look, Lucy, look; the dog's tooth nor the dove's   165
    Are not so white as these; and sweet they be,
    And whipped* about with silk, as you may see.
    If you desire the price, shoot from your eye
    A beam to this place, and you shall espy
    "F S,"* which is to say, my sweetest honey,   170
    They cost me three and twopence, or no money.
LUCE Well, sir, I take them kindly, and I thank you.
    What would you more?
HUMPHREY   Nothing.

138 Formerly.
139 Which of the two.
146 Part of a crossbow.
149 A mild curse like "Devil take it."
153 Appetite or desire.
158 The annual assembly of the London militia.
167 Embroidered.
170 A dealer's trade mark or price mark.

LUCE   Why, then, farewell.

HUMPHREY   Nor so, nor so; for, lady, I must tell,
 Before we part, for what we met together.
 God grant me time and patience and fair weather!

LUCE   Speak, and declare your mind in terms so brief.

HUMPHREY   I shall. Then, first and foremost, for relief   180
 I call to you, if that you can afford it;
 I care not at what price, for, on my word, it
 Shall be repaid again, although it cost me
 More than I'll speak of now; for love hath tossed me
 In furious blanket like a tennis ball,   185
 And now I rise aloft, and now I fall.

LUCE   Alas, good gentleman, alas the day!

HUMPHREY   I thank you heartily; and, as I say,
 Thus do I still continue without rest,
 I' th' morning like a man, at night a beast,   190
 Roaring and bellowing mine own disquiet,
 That much I fear forsaking of my diet
 Will bring me presently to that quandary
 I shall bid all adieu.

LUCE   Now, by St. Mary,   195
 That were great pity!

HUMPHREY   So it were, beshrew me;
 Then, ease me, lusty* Luce, and pity show me.

LUCE   Why, sir, you know my will is nothing worth
 Without my father's grant; get his consent,   200
 And then you may with assurance try me.

HUMPHREY   The worshipful your sire will not deny me;
 For I have asked him, and he hath replied,
 "Sweet Master Humphrey, Luce shall be thy bride."

LUCE   Sweet Master Humphrey, then I am content.   205

HUMPHREY   And so am I, in truth.

LUCE   Yet take me with you;*
 There is another clause must be annexed,
 And this it is (I swore, and will perform it):
 No man shall ever joy* me as his wife   210
 But he that stole me hence. If you dare venter,*
 I am yours (you need not fear; my father loves you);
 If not, farewell forever!

HUMPHREY   Stay, nymph, stay.
 I have a double gelding, colored bay,   215
 Sprung by his father from Barbarian* kind;

198 Jolly.
207 Understand me fully.
210 Enjoy.
211 Venture.
216 Barbary.

Another for myself, though somewhat blind,
Yet true as trusty tree.
LUCE   I am satisfied;
And so I give my hand. Our course must lie   220
Through Waltham Forest,* where I have a friend
Will entertain us. So, farewell, Sir Humphrey,
And think upon your business. (*Exit* LUCE)
HUMPHREY   Though I die,
I am resolved to venter life and limb   225
For one so young, so fair, so kind, so trim. (*Exit* HUMPHREY)

WIFE   By my faith and troth, George, and as I am virtuous, it is e'en the kindest
young man that ever trod on shoe leather.—Well, go thy ways; if thou hast
her not, 'tis not thy fault, faith.
CITIZEN   I prithee, mouse, be patient; a* shall have her, or I'll make some   230
of 'em smoke* for 't.
WIFE   That's my good lamb, George.—Fie, this stinking tobacco kills me! Would
there were none in England!—Now, I pray, gentlemen, what good does this
stinking tobacco do you? Nothing, I warrant you. You make chimneys a*
your faces!—O, husband, husband, now, now! There's Rafe, there's Rafe.   235

Scene 3

(*Enter* RAFE, *like a grocer in 's shop with two Prentices,* TIM *and* GEORGE,
reading Palmerin of England)*

CITIZEN   Peace, fool! Let Rafe alone.—Hark you, Rafe; do not strain yourself
too much at the first.—Peace!—Begin, Rafe.

RAFE (*Reading*)   "Then Palmerin and Trineus, snatching their launces from   240
their dwarfs, and clasping their helmets, galloped amain* after the giant;
and Palmerin, having gotten a sight of him, came posting amain, saying,
'Stay traitorous thief! For thou mayst not so carry away her that is worth
the greatest lord in the world;' and with these words gave him a blow on
the shoulder that he stroke him besides* his elephant. And Trineus,   245
coming to the knight that had Agricola behind him, set him soon besides
his horse, with his neck broken in the fall, so that the princess, getting out
of the throng, between joy and grief, said, 'All happy knight, the mirror
of all such as follows arms, now may I be well assured of the love thou
bearest me.' "—I wonder why the kings do not raise an army of fourteen   250

221 North of London.
230 He.
231 Suffer.
234 Of.
237 A popular romance of knightly adventure. But the quotation comes from Anthony Munday's translation of *Palmerin de Oliva.*
241 At full speed.
245 That is, knocked him off.

or fifteen hundred thousand men, as big as the army that the Prince of Portigo brought against Rosicleer,* and destroy these giants; they do much hurt to wandering damsels that go in quest of their knights.

WIFE   Faith, husband, and Rafe says true; for they say the King of Portugal cannot sit at his meat but the giants and the ettins* will come and snatch 255 it from him.

CITIZEN   Hold thy tongue!—On, Rafe!

RAFE   And certainly those knights are much to be commended, who, neglecting their possessions, wander with a squire and a dwarf through the deserts to relieve poor ladies.   260

WIFE   Ay, by faith, are they, Rafe; let 'em say what they will, they are indeed. Our knights neglect their possessions well enough, but they do not the rest.

RAFE   There are no such courteous and fair well-spoken knights in this age. They will call one "the son of a whore" that Palmerin of England would have called "fair sir"; and one that Rosicleer would have called "right 265 beauteous damsel" they will call "damned bitch."

WIFE   I'll be sworn will they, Rafe; they have called me so an hundred times about a scurvy pipe of tobacco.

RAFE   But what brave spirit could be content to sit in his shop, with a flappet* of wood and a blue apron before him, selling mithridatum and dragon's- 270 water* to visited houses,* that might pursue feats of arms, and, through his noble achievements, procure such a famous history to be written of his heroic prowess?

CITIZEN   Well said, Rafe; some more of those words, Rafe!

WIFE   They go finely, by my troth.   275

RAFE   Why should not I then pursue this course, both for the credit of myself and our company? For, amongst all the worthy books of achievements, I do not call to mind that I yet read of a grocer-errant. I will be the said knight. —Have you heard of any that hath wandered unfurnished of his squire and dwarf? My elder prentice Tim shall be my trusty squire, and little George 280 my dwarf. Hence, my blue apron! Yet, in remembrance of my former trade, upon my shield shall be portrayed a burning pestle, and I will be called the Knight o' th' Burning Pestle.*

252 Characters from a Spanish romance, *The Mirror of Princely Deeds and Knighthood.*
255 A race of giants.
269 A flap of wood to keep away flies.
271 (*a*) Medicines used against the plague. (*b*) Houses visited by the plague.
283 "Burning" perhaps in the sense of burnished or golden.

WIFE Nay, I dare swear thou wilt not forget thy old trade; thou wert ever meek. 285

RAFE Tim!

TIM Anon.

RAFE My beloved squire, and George my dwarf, I charge you that from henceforth you never call me by any other name but "the right courteous and valiant Knight of the Burning Pestle," and that you never call any female 290 by the name of a woman or wench, but "fair lady," if she have her desires; if not, "distressed damsel"; that you call all forests and heaths "deserts," and all horses "palfreys."

WIFE This is very fine, faith.—Do the gentlemen like Rafe, think you, husband?

CITIZEN Ay, I warrant thee; the players would give all the shoes in their 295 shop for him.

RAFE My beloved squire Tim, stand out. Admit this were a desert, and over it a knight-errant pricking,* and I should bid you inquire of his intents, what would you say?

TIM Sir, my master sent me to know whither you are riding? 300

RAFE No, thus: "Fair sir, the right courteous and valiant Knight of the Burning Pestle commanded me to inquire upon what adventure you are bound, whether to relieve some distressed damsels, or otherwise."

CITIZEN Whoreson blockhead, cannot remember!

WIFE I' faith, and Rafe told him on 't before; all the gentlemen heard him. 305 —Did he not, gentlemen? Did not Rafe tell him on 't?

GEORGE Right courteous and valiant Knight of the Burning Pestle, here is a distressed damsel to have a halfpennyworth of pepper.

WIFE That's a good boy! See, the little boy can hit it; by my troth, it's a fine child. 310

RAFE Relieve her, with all courteous language. Now shut up shop; no more my prentice, but my trusty squire and dwarf. I must bespeak* my shield and arming* pestle. (*Exeunt* TIM *and* GEORGE)

CITIZEN Go thy ways, Rafe! As I'm a true man, thou art the best on 'em all.

WIFE Rafe, Rafe! 315

RAFE What say you, mistress?

WIFE I prithee, come again quickly, sweet Rafe.

RAFE By-and-by. (*Exit* RAFE)

298 Spurring.
312 Order.
313 Armorial.

Scene 4

A room in Merrythought's house

(*Enter* JASPER *and his mother,* MRS. MERRYTHOUGHT) 320

MRS. MERRYTHOUGHT Give thee my blessing? No, I'll ne'er give thee my blessing; I'll see thee hanged first; it shall ne'er be said I gave thee my blessing. Th' art thy father's own son, of the right blood of the Merrythoughts. I may curse the time that e'er I knew thy father; he hath spent all his own and mine too; and, when I tell him of it, he laughs, and 325 dances, and sings, and cries, "A merry heart lives long-a." And thou art a wastethrift,* and art run away from thy master that loved thee well, and art come to me; and I have laid up a little for my younger son Michael, and thou think'st to bezzle* that, but thou shalt never be able to do it.—Come hither, Michael! Come, Michael. 330

(*Enter* MICHAEL)

Down on thy knees; thou shalt have my blessing.

MICHAEL (*Kneeling*) I pray you, mother, pray to God to bless me.

MRS. MERRYTHOUGHT God bless thee! (MICHAEL *rises*) But Jasper shall never have my blessing; he shall be hanged first; shall he not, Michael? How 335 say'st thou?

MICHAEL Yes, forsooth, mother, and grace of God.

MRS. MERRYTHOUGHT That's a good boy!

WIFE Ay, faith, it's a fine-spoken child.

JASPER Mother, though you forget a parent's love, 340
    I must preserve the duty of a child.
    I ran not from my master, nor return
    To have your stock maintain my idleness.

WIFE Ungracious child, I warrant him; hark, how he chops logic with his mother!—Thou hadst best tell her she lies; do tell her she lies. 345

CITIZEN If he were my son, I would hang him up by the heels, and flay him, and salt him, whoreson haltersack.*

JASPER My coming only is to beg your love,
    Which I must ever, though I never gain it;
    And, howsoever you esteem of me, 350
    There is no drop of blood hid in these veins
    But, I remember well, belongs to you
    That brought me forth, and would be glad for you
    To rip them all again, and let it out.

MRS. MERRYTHOUGHT Ay, faith, I had sorrow enough for thee, God knows; 355 but I'll hamper thee well enough. Get thee in, thou vagabond, get thee in, and learn of thy brother Michael. (*Exeunt* JASPER *and* MICHAEL)

---

327 Spendthrift.

329 Embezzle, or, perhaps, squander.   347 Gallows bird.

OLD MERRYTHOUGHT (*Singing within*)   Nose, nose, jolly red nose,
And who gave thee this jolly red nose?

MRS. MERRYTHOUGHT   Hark, my husband! He's singing and hoiting,* and 360 I'm fain to cark* and care, and all little enough.—Husband! Charles! Charles Merrythought!

(*Enter* OLD MERRYTHOUGHT)

OLD MERRYTHOUGHT (*Singing*)   Nutmegs and ginger, cinnamon and cloves—
And they gave me this jolly red nose.   365

MRS. MERRYTHOUGHT   If you would consider your state, you would have little list* to sing, iwis.*

OLD MERRYTHOUGHT   It should never be considered, while it were an estate, if I thought it would spoil my singing.

MRS. MERRYTHOUGHT   But how wilt thou do, Charles? Thou art an old 370 man, and thou canst not work, and thou hast not forty shillings left, and thou eatest good meat, and drinkest good drink, and laughest.

OLD MERRYTHOUGHT   And will do.

MRS. MERRYTHOUGHT   But how wilt thou come by it, Charles?

OLD MERRYTHOUGHT   How? Why, how have I done hitherto this forty 375 years? I never came into my dining room but at eleven and six a-clock I found excellent meat and drink a th' table; my clothes were never worn out but next morning a tailor brought me a new suit; and without question it will be so ever; use makes perfectness. If all should fail, it is but a little straining myself extraordinary, and laugh myself to death.   380

WIFE   It's a foolish old man this, is not he, George?

CITIZEN   Yes, cunny.

WIFE   Give me a penny i' th' purse while I live, George.

CITIZEN   Ay, by Lady, cunny; hold thee there.*

MRS. MERRYTHOUGHT   Well, Charles, you promised to provide for Jasper, 385 and I have laid up for Michael. I pray you, pay Jasper his portion. He's come home, and he shall not consume Michael's stock; he says his master turned him away, but, I promise you truly, I think he ran away.

WIFE   No, indeed, Mrs. Merrythought; though he be a notable gallows,* yet I'll assure you his master did turn him away, even in this place. 'Twas, i' 390 faith, within this half hour, about his daughter; my husband was by.

CITIZEN   Hang him, rogue! He served him well enough. Love his master's daughter! By my troth, cunny, if there were a thousand boys, thou wouldst spoil them all with taking their parts. Let his mother alone with him.

WIFE   Ay, George; but yet truth is truth.   395

---

360 Making merry.
361 Anxiety.
367 (*a*) Desire.   (*b*) Certainly.
384 That is, stand by your belief.
389 Gallows bird.

OLD MERRYTHOUGHT Where is Jasper? He's welcome, however. Call him in; he shall have his portion. Is he merry?

(Enter JASPER and MICHAEL)

MRS. MERRYTHOUGHT Ay, foul chive* him, he is too merry!—Jasper! Michael!

OLD MERRYTHOUGHT Welcome, Jasper! Though thou runn'st away, wel- 400
come! God bless thee! 'Tis thy mother's mind thou shouldst receive thy portion. Thou hast been abroad, and I hope hast learned experience enough to govern it; thou art of sufficient years. Hold thy hand—one, two, three, four, five, six, seven, eight, nine, there's ten shillings for thee. (Gives money) Thrust thyself into the world with that, and take some settled course. If fortune 405
cross thee, thou hast a retiring place. Come home to me; I have twenty shillings left. Be a good husband,* that is, wear ordinary clothes, eat the best meat, and drink the best drink; be merry, and give to the poor; and, believe me, thou hast no end of thy goods.

JASPER Long may you live free from all thought of ill, 410
And long have cause to be thus merry still!
But, father—

OLD MERRYTHOUGHT No more words, Jasper; get thee gone. Thou hast my blessing; thy father's spirit upon thee! Farewell, Jasper!

(Sings) But yet, or ere you part (O, cruel!), 415
        Kiss me, kiss me, sweeting, mine own dear jewel!
So, now begone; no words. (Exit JASPER)

MRS. MERRYTHOUGHT So, Michael, now get thee gone too.

MICHAEL Yes, forsooth, mother; but I'll have my father's blessing first.

MRS. MERRYTHOUGHT No, Michael; 'tis no matter for his blessing. Thou 420
hast my blessing; begone. I'll fetch my money and jewels, and follow thee; I'll stay no longer with him, I warrant thee.—(Exit MICHAEL) Truly, Charles, I'll be gone too.

OLD MERRYTHOUGHT What, you will not?

MRS. MERRYTHOUGHT Yes, indeed will I. 425

OLD MERRYTHOUGHT (Singing) Heigh-ho, farewell, Nan!
        I'll never trust wench more again, if I can.

MRS. MERRYTHOUGHT You shall not think, when all your own is gone, to spend that I have been scraping up for Michael.

OLD MERRYTHOUGHT Farewell, good wife; I expect it not. All I have to do 430
in this world is to be merry, which I shall, if the ground be not taken from me; and, if it be,
(Sings) When earth and seas from me are reft,*
        The skies aloft for me are left. (Exeunt)

(BOY danceth. Music) 435

WIFE I'll be sworn he's a merry old gentleman for all that. Hark, hark, husband, hark! Fiddles, fiddles! Now surely they go finely. They say 'tis present* death

399 That is, ill befall.
407 Manager.
433 Robbed.
437 Immediate.

for these fiddlers to tune their rebecks* before the great Turk's grace,* is 't
not, George? But look, look! Here's a youth dances!—Now, good youth, do a
turn a th' toe.—Sweetheart, i' faith, I'll have Rafe come and do some of his 440
gambols.—He'll ride the wild mare,* gentlemen, 'twould do your hearts good
to see him.—I thank you, kind youth; pray, bid Rafe come.

CITIZEN   Peace, cunny!— Sirrah, you scurvy boy, bid the players send Rafe; or,
by God's——, and they do not, I'll tear some of their periwigs beside their
heads; this is all riffraff. (*Exit* BOY)   445

Act Two

Scene 1

A room in VENTUREWELL'S house
(Enter MERCHANT and HUMPHREY)

MERCHANT   And how, faith, how goes it now, son Humphrey?

HUMPHREY   Right worshipful, and my beloved friend
And father dear, this matter's at an end.

MERCHANT   'Tis well; it should be so. I'm glad the girl   5
Is found so tractable.

HUMPHREY   Nay, she must whirl
From hence (and you must wink, for so, I say,
The story tells*) tomorrow before day.   10

WIFE   George, dost thou think in thy conscience now 'twill be a match? Tell
me but what thou think'st, sweet rogue. Thou seest the poor gentleman, dear
heart, how it labors and throbs, I warrant you, to be at rest! I'll go move the
father for 't.

CITIZEN   No, no; I prithee, sit still, honeysuckle; thou'lt spoil all. If he deny 15
him, I'll bring half a dozen good fellows myself, and in the shutting of an
evening* knock 't up, and there's an end.

WIFE   I'll buss thee for that, i' faith, boy. Well, George, well, you have been a
wag* in your days, I warrant you; but God forgive you, and I do with all my
heart.   20

MERCHANT   How was it, son? You told me that tomorrow
Before daybreak you must convey her hence.

HUMPHREY   I must, I must; and thus it is agreed:
Your daughter rides upon a brown-bay steed,
I on a sorrel, which I bought of Brian,   25
The honest host of the red roaring Lion,

---

438 (*a*) Medieval string instrument.   (*b*) The Sultan of Turkey.
441 Seesaw.
10 That is, the plan for eloping goes.
17 At twilight.
19 Joker or mischief-maker.

In Waltham situate. Then, if you may,
Consent in seemly sort, lest, by delay,
The Fatal Sisters* come, and do the office,
And then you'll sing another song. 30
MERCHANT   Alas,
Why should you be thus full of grief to me,
That do as willing as yourself agree
To anything, so it be good and fair?
Then, steal her when you will, if such a pleasure 35
Content you both; I'll sleep and never see it,
To make your joys more full. But tell me why
You may not here perform your marriage?

WIFE   God's blessing a thy soul, old man! I' faith, thou art loath to part true
hearts. I see a has her, George; and I'm as glad on 't!—Well, go thy ways, 40
Humphrey; for a fair-spoken man, I believe thou hast not thy fellow within
the walls of London; and I should say the suburbs too, I should not lie.—
Why dost not rejoice with me, George?
CITIZEN   If I could but see Rafe again, I were as merry as mine host, i' faith.

HUMPHREY   The cause you seem to ask, I thus declare— 45
Help me, O Muses nine! Your daughter swore
A foolish oath, and more it was the pity;
Yet none but myself within this city
Shall dare to say so, but a bold defiance
Shall meet him, were he of the noble science;* 50
And yet she swore, and yet why did she swear?
Truly, I cannot tell, unless it were
For her own ease; for, sure, sometimes an oath,
Being sworn thereafter, is like cordial broth.
And thus it was she swore, never to marry 55
But such a one whose mighty arm could carry
(As meaning me, for I am such a one)
Her bodily away, through stick and stone,
Till both of us arrive, at her request,
Some ten miles off, in the wild Waltham Forest. 60
MERCHANT   If this be all, you shall not need to fear
Any denial in your love. Proceed;
I'll neither follow, nor repent the deed.
HUMPHREY   Good night, twenty good nights, and twenty more,
And twenty more good nights—that makes threescore! (*Exeunt*) 65

---

29 The Three Fates.
50 A fencer.

Scene 2

Waltham Forest

(*Enter* MRS. MERRYTHOUGHT *and her son* MICHAEL)

MRS. MERRYTHOUGHT   Come, Michael; art thou not weary, boy?

MICHAEL   No, forsooth, mother, not I.

MRS. MERRYTHOUGHT   Where be we now, child?   70

MICHAEL   Indeed, forsooth, mother, I cannot tell, unless we be at Mile End.* Is not all the world Mile End, mother?

MRS. MERRYTHOUGHT   No, Michael, not all the world, boy; but I can assure thee, Michael, Mile End is a goodly matter. There has been a pitchfield,* my child, between the naughty Spaniels* and the Englishmen; and the Span- 75 iels ran away, Michael, and the Englishmen followed. My neighbor Cox-stone was there, boy, and killed them all with a birding piece.*

MICHAEL   Mother, forsooth—

MRS. MERRYTHOUGHT   What says my white* boy?

MICHAEL   Shall not my father go with us too?   80

MRS. MERRYTHOUGHT   No, Michael, let thy father go snick up;* he shall never come between a pair of sheets with me again while he lives. Let him stay at home, and sing for his supper, boy. Come, child, sit down, and I'll show my boy fine knacks, indeed. (*They sit down; and she opens a casket*) Look here, Michael; here's a ring, and here's a brooch, and here's a bracelet, and here's 85 two rings more, and here's money and gold by th' eye,* my boy.

MICHAEL   Shall I have all this, mother?

MRS. MERRYTHOUGHT   Ay, Michael, thou shalt have all, Michael.

CITIZEN   How lik'st thou this, wench?

WIFE   I cannot tell; I would have Rafe, George; I'll see no more else, indeed- 90 law;* and, I pray you, let the youths understand so much by word of mouth; for, I tell you truly, I'm afraid a my boy. Come, come, George, let's be merry and wise; the child's a fatherless child; and say they should put him into a strait pair of gaskins,* 'twere worse than knotgrass;* he would never grow after it.   95

(*Enter* RAFE, SQUIRE [*Tim*], *and* DWARF [*George*])

CITIZEN   Here's Rafe, here's Rafe!

WIFE   How do you do, Rafe? You are welcome, Rafe, as I may say. It's a good boy, hold up thy head, and be not afraid. We are thy friends, Rafe; the gentle-men will praise thee, Rafe, if thou play'st thy part with audacity. Begin, 100 Rafe, a God's name!

71 A drill and maneuver ground east of London.

74 Field of sham battles.

75 Spaniards.

77 Bird-gun.

79 Sweet.

81 Go hang.

86 In great quantities.

91 An exclamation of annoyance.

94 (*a*) Tight breeches.   (*b*) A herb that was supposed to retard growth.

RAFE My trusty squire, unlace my helm; give me my hat. Where are we, or what desert may this be?

DWARF Mirror of knighthood, this is, as I take it, the perilous Waltham Down, in whose bottom stands the enchanted valley. [105]

MRS. MERRYTHOUGHT O, Michael, we are betrayed, we are betrayed! Here be giants! Fly, boy! Fly, boy, fly!

(*Exeunt* MOTHER *and* MICHAEL, *leaving the casket*)

RAFE Lace on my helm again. What noise is this?
A gentle lady, flying the embrace [110]
Of some uncourteous knight! I will relieve her.
Go, squire, and say the knight that wears this pestle
In honor of all ladies swears revenge
Upon that recreant* coward that pursues her.
Go, comfort her, and that same gentle squire [115]
That bears her company.

SQUIRE   I go, brave knight. (*Exit*)

RAFE My trusty dwarf and friend, reach me my shield,
And hold it while I swear. First, by my knighthood;
Then by the soul of Amadis de Gaul,* [120]
My famous ancestor; then by my sword
The beauteous Brionella* girt about me;
By this bright burning pestle, of mine honor
The living trophy; and by all respect
Due to distressed damsels, here I vow [125]
Never to end the quest of this fair lady
And that forsaken squire till by my valor
I gain their liberty!

DWARF   Heaven bless the knight
That thus relieves poor errant gentlewomen! (*Exit with* RAFE) [130]

WIFE Ay, marry, Rafe, this has some savor in 't; I would see the proudest of them all offer to carry his books after him. But, George, I will not have him go away so soon; I shall be sick if he go away, that I shall. Call Rafe again, George, call Rafe again; I prithee, sweetheart, let him come fight before me, and let's ha' some drums and some trumpets, and let him kill all that [135] comes near him, and thou lov'st me, George!

CITIZEN Peace a little, bird; he shall kill them all, and they were twenty more on 'em than there are.

(*Enter* JASPER)

JASPER Now, Fortune, if thou beest not only ill, [140]
Show me thy better face, and bring about
Thy desperate wheel,* that I may climb at length,
And stand. This is our place of meeting,

---

114 Craven or cowardly, hence a redundancy.

120 Hero of a famous romance of knight-errantry.

122 A lady in *Palmerin de Oliva*.

142 Fortune was often represented with a wheel which raised up and cast down its victims whimsically.

If love have any constancy. O age
Where only wealthy men are counted happy!
How shall I please thee, how deserve thy smiles,   145
When I am only rich in misery?
My father's blessing and this little coin
Is my inheritance—a strong revenue!
From earth thou art, and to the earth I give thee. (*Throws away the money*) 150
There grow and multiply, whilst fresher air
Breeds me a fresher fortune.—(*Spies the casket*) How! Illusion?
What, hath the devil coined himself before me?
'Tis metal good; it rings well. I am waking,
And taking too, I hope. Now, God's dear blessing   155
Upon his heart that left it here! 'Tis mine;
These pearls, I take it, were not left for swine. (*Exit with the casket*)

WIFE I do not like that this unthrifty youth should embezzle away the money;
the poor gentlewoman his mother will have a heavy heart for it, God knows.
CITIZEN And reason good, sweetheart.   160
WIFE But let him go; I'll tell Rafe a tale in 's ear shall fetch him again with a
wanion,* I warrant him, if he be above ground; and besides, George, here
are a number of sufficient gentlemen can witness, and myself, and yourself,
and the musicians, if we be called in question. But here comes Rafe, George;
thou shalt hear him speak as he were an emperal.*   165

Scene 3

Another part of the forest
(*Enter* RAFE *and* DWARF)

RAFE Comes not Sir Squire again?
DWARF   Right courteous knight,
Your squire doth come, and with him comes the lady,   170
(*Enter* MRS. MERRYTHOUGHT *and* MICHAEL *and* SQUIRE)
For and* the Squire of Damsels,* as I take it.
RAFE Madam, if any service or devoir*
Of a poor errant knight may right your wrongs,
Command it; I am prest* to give you succor,   175
For to that holy end I bear my armor.
MRS. MERRYTHOUGHT Alas, sir, I am a poor gentlewoman, and I have lost my
money in this forest!
RAFE Desert, you would say, lady; and not lost
Whilst I have sword and lance. Dry up your tears,   180
Which ill befits the beauty of that face,

162 Vengeance.
165 Emperor.
172 (a) And also. (b) Perhaps an allusion to Spenser's "Squire of Dames," from the *Faerie Queene*, III,
vii, 51.
173 Duty.
175 Ready.

And tell the story, if I may request it,
Of your disastrous fortune.

MRS. MERRYTHOUGHT   Out, alas! I left a thousand pound, a thousand pound,
    e'en all the money I had laid up for this youth, upon the sight of your 185
    mastership—you looked so grim, and, as I may say it, saving your presence,
    more like a giant than a mortal man.

RAFE   I am as you are, lady; so are they
    All mortal. But why weeps this gentle squire?

MRS. MERRYTHOUGHT   Has he not cause to weep, do you think, when he 190
    hath lost his inheritance?

RAFE   Young hope of valor, weep not; I am here
    That will confound thy foe, and pay it dear
    Upon his coward head that dares deny
    Distressed squires and ladies equity.*   195
    I have but one horse, on which shall ride
    This lady fair behind me, and, before,
    This courteous squire. Fortune will give us more
    Upon our next adventure. Fairly speed
    Beside us, squire and dwarf, to do us need! (*Exeunt*)   200

CITIZEN   Did not I tell you, Nell, what your man would do? By the faith of my
    body, wench, for clean action and good delivery they may all cast their caps
    at him.*

WIFE   And so they may, i' faith; for, I dare speak it boldly, the twelve companies
    of London* cannot match him, timber for timber.* Well, George, and he 205
    be not inveigled by some of these paltry players, I ha' much marvel. But,
    George, we ha' done our parts, if the boy have any grace to be thankful.

CITIZEN   Yes, I warrant thee, duckling.

Scene 4

Another part of the forest
(*Enter* HUMPHREY *and* LUCE)   210

HUMPHREY   Good Mistress Luce, however I in fault am
    For your lame horse, you're welcome unto Waltham;
    But which way now to go, or what to say,
    I know not truly, till it be broad day.

LUCE   O, fear not, Master Humphrey; I am guide   215
    For this place good enough.

HUMPHREY   Then up and ride;
    Or, if it please you, walk, for your repose;
    Or sit, or, if you will, go pluck a rose*—
    Either of which shall be indifferent   220

---

195 Fair treatment.
203 That is, take off their caps to him.
205 (*a*) The 12 major guilds.   (*b*) Man for man.
219 Relieve yourself.

To your good friend and Humphrey, whose consent
Is so entangled ever to your will
As the poor harmless horse is to the mill.
LUCE Faith, and you say the word, we'll e'en sit down,
And take a nap.
HUMPHREY   'Tis better in the town, ²²⁵
Where we may nap together, for, believe me,
To sleep without a snatch* would mickle* grieve me.
LUCE You're merry, Master Humphrey.
HUMPHREY   So I am, ²³⁰
And have been ever merry from my dam.
LUCE Your nurse had the less labor.
HUMPHREY   Faith, it may be,
Unless it were by chance I did beray* me.

(Enter JASPER) ²³⁵

JASPER Luce! Dear friend Luce!
LUCE   Here, Jasper.
JASPER   You are mine.
HUMPHREY If it be so, my friend, you use me fine.
What do you think I am?
JASPER   An arrant noddy.* ²⁴⁰
HUMPHREY A word of obloquy! Now, by God's body,
I'll tell thy master, for I know thee well.
JASPER Nay, and you be so forward for to tell,
Take that, and that! *(Beats him)* And tell him, sir, I gave it,
And say I paid you well. ²⁴⁵
HUMPHREY   O, sir, I have it,
And do confess the payment! Pray, be quiet.
JASPER Go, get you to your nightcap and the diet
To cure your beaten bones. ²⁵⁰
LUCE   Alas, poor Humphrey!
Get thee some wholesome broth, with sage and comfrey,*
A little oil of roses and a feather
To noint* thy back withal.
HUMPHREY   When I came hither, ²⁵⁵
Would I had gone to Paris with John Dory!*
LUCE Farewell, my pretty nump;* I am very sorry
I cannot bear thee company.
HUMPHREY   Farewell!
The devil's dam was ne'er so banged in hell. *(Exeunt.* HUMPHREY *remains)* ²⁶⁰

---

²²⁸ (a) Snack. (b) Greatly.
²³⁴ Befoul.
²⁴¹ Fool.
²⁵² A herb used for wounds.
²⁵⁴ Anoint.
²⁵⁶ The hero of a popular song.
²⁵⁷ Blockhead, or perhaps a pet name for Humphrey.

WIFE This young Jasper will prove me anotherthings,* a my conscience, and he may be suffered. George, dost not see, George, how a swaggers, and flies at the very heads a folks, as he were a dragon? Well, if I do not do his lesson* for wronging the poor gentleman, I am no true woman. His friends that brought him up might have been better occupied, iwis, than ha' taught 265 him these fegaries;* he's e'en in the high way to the gallows, God bless him!

CITIZEN You're too bitter, cunny; the young man may do well enough for all this.

WIFE Come hither, Master Humphrey; has he hurt you? Now, beshrew his fingers for 't! Here, sweetheart, here's some green ginger for thee. Now, 270 beshrew my heart, but a has peppernel* in 's head as big as a pullet's egg! Alas, sweet lamb, how thy temples beat! Take the peace on him,* sweetheart, take the peace on him.

(Enter a BOY)

CITIZEN No, no; you talk like a foolish woman. I'll ha' Rafe fight with him, 275 and swinge him up well-favoredly.*—Sirrah Boy, come hither. Let Rafe come in and fight with Jasper.

WIFE Ay, and beat him well; he's an unhappy* boy.

BOY Sir, you must pardon us; the plot of our play lies contrary, and 'twill hazard the spoiling of our play.   280

CITIZEN Plot me no plots! I'll ha' Rafe come out; I'll make your house too hot for you else.

BOY Why, sir, he shall; but, if anything fall out of order, the gentlemen must pardon us.

CITIZEN Go your ways, Goodman Boy!—*(Exit Boy)* I'll hold* him a penny 285 he shall have his bellyful of fighting now. Ho, here comes Rafe! No more!*

(Enter RAFE, MRS. MERRYTHOUGHT, MICHAEL, SQUIRE, *and* DWARF)

RAFE What knight is that, squire? Ask him if he keep
The passage, bound by love of lady fair,
Or else but prickant.*   290

HUMPHREY   Sir, I am no knight,
But a poor gentleman, that this same night
Had stolen from me, on yonder green,
My lovely wife, and suffered (to be seen
Yet extant on my shoulders) such a greeting   295
That whilst I live I shall think of that meeting.

---

261 Otherwise.
263 That is, teach him.
266 Pranks.
271 A lump.
272 That is, have him bound to keep the peace.
276 That is, beat him soundly.
278 Mischievous.
285 Bet.
286 Silence.
290 Riding by.

WIFE Ay, Rafe, he beat him unmercifully, Rafe; and thou spar'st him, Rafe, I
would thou wert hanged.

CITIZEN No more, wife, no more.

RAFE Where is the caitiff* wretch hath done this deed?   300
Lady, your pardon, that I may proceed
Upon the quest of this injurious knight.—
And thou, fair squire, repute me not the worse
In leaving the great venture of the purse
And the rich casket, till some better leisure.   305
                    (*Enter* JASPER *and* LUCE)

HUMPHREY Here comes the broker hath purloined my treasure.

RAFE Go, squire, and tell him I am here,
An errant knight-at-arms, to crave delivery
Of that fair lady to her own knight's arms.   310
If he deny, bid him take choice of ground,*
And so defy him.

SQUIRE   From the knight that bears
The golden pestle, I defy thee, knight,
Unless thou make fair restitution   315
Of that bright lady.

JASPER   Tell the knight that sent thee
He is an ass; and I will keep the wench,
And knock his headpiece.

RAFE   Knight, thou art but dead,   320
If thou recall not thy uncourteous terms.

WIFE Break 's pate, Rafe; break 's pate, Rafe, soundly!

JASPER Come, knight; I am ready for you. Now your pestle
                    (*Snatches away his pestle*)
Shall try what temper, sir, your mortar 's of.   325
"With that he stood upright in his stirrups,
And gave the Knight of the Calfskin such a knock (*Knocks* RAFE *down*)
That he forsook his horse and down he fell;
And then he leaped upon him, and, plucking off his helmet—"

HUMPHREY Nay, and my noble knight be down so soon,   330
Though I can scarcely go,* I needs must run. (*Exeunt* HUMPHREY *and* RAFE)

WIFE Run, Rafe; run, Rafe! Run for thy life, boy! Jasper comes, Jasper comes!

JASPER Come, Luce, we must have other arms for you;
Humphrey and golden pestle, both adieu! (*Exeunt*)

300 Evil or cowardly.
311 That is, choose his ground for battle.
331 Walk.

WIFE Sure the devil (God bless us!) is in this springald!* Why, George, didst 335
ever see such a firedrake?* I am afraid my boy's miscarried;* if he be, though
he were Master Merrythought's son a thousand times, if there be any law
in England, I'll make some of them smart for 't.

CITIZEN No, no; I have found out the matter, sweetheart. Jasper is enchanted;
as sure as we are here, he is enchanted. He could no more have stood in 340
Rafe's hands than I can stand in my lord mayor's. I'll have a ring to discover
all enchantments, and Rafe shall beat him yet. Be no more vexed, for it
shall be so.

Scene 5

Before the Bell Inn at Waltham

(*Enter* RAFE, SQUIRE, DWARF, MRS. MERRYTHOUGHT, *and* MICHAEL)   345

WIFE O, husband, here's Rafe again!—Stay, Rafe, let me speak with thee. How
dost thou, Rafe? Art thou not shrowdly* hurt?—The foul great lungis* laid
unmercifully on thee; there's some sugar candy for thee. Proceed; thou shalt
have another bout with him.

CITIZEN If Rafe had him at the fencing school, if he did not make a puppy 350
of him, and drive him up and down the school, he should ne'er come in my
shop more.

MRS. MERRYTHOUGHT Truly, Master Knight of the Burning Pestle, I am
weary.

MICHAEL Indeed-law, mother, and I am very hungry.   355

RAFE Take comfort, gentle dame, and you, fair squire;
For in this desert there must needs be placed
Many strong castles held by courteous knights;
And, till I bring you safe to one of those,
I swear by this my order ne'er to leave you.   360

WIFE Well said, Rafe!—George, Rafe was ever comfortable,* was he not?

CITIZEN Yes, duck.

WIFE I shall ne'er forget him. When we had lost our child (you know it was
strayed almost, alone, to Puddle Wharf, and the criers were abroad for it,
and there it had drowned itself but for a sculler),* Rafe was the most 365
comfortablest to me. "Peace, mistress," says he, "let it go; I'll get you
another as good." Did he not, George, did he not say so?

CITIZEN Yes, indeed did he, mouse.

DWARF I would we had a mess of pottage and a pot of drink, squire, and were
going to bed!   370

---

335 Young man.
336 (*a*) Fiery dragon. (*b*) Ruined.
347 (*a*) Severely. (*b*) Lout.
361 Comforting.
365 Row-boat, or oarsman.

SQUIRE   Why, we are at Waltham town's end, and that's the Bell Inn.
DWARF   Take courage, valiant knight, damsel, and squire!
    I have discovered, not a stonecast off,
    An ancient castle, held by the old knight
    Of the most holy Order of the Bell,   375
    Who gives to all knights-errant entertain.*
    There plenty is of food, and all prepared
    By the white hands of his own lady dear.
    He hath three squires that welcome all his guests:
    The first, hight* Chamberlino, who will see   380
    Our beds prepared, and bring us snowy sheets,
    Where never footman stretched his buttered hams;*
    The second, hight Tapstero, who will see
    Our pots full filled, and no froth therein;
    The third, a gentle squire, Ostlero hight,   385
    Who will our palfreys slick with wisps of straw,
    And in the manger put them oats enough,
    And never grease their teeth with candle snuff.*

WIFE   That same dwarf's a pretty boy, but the squire's a groutnole.*

RAFE   Knock at the gates, my squire, with stately lance. (SQUIRE *knocks*) 390
                    (*Enter* TAPSTER)
TAPSTER   Who's there?—You're welcome, gentlemen. Will you see a room?
DWARF   Right courteous and valiant Knight of the Burning Pestle, this is the
    Squire Tapstero.
RAFE   Fair Squire Tapstero, I a wandering knight,   395
    Hight of the Burning Pestle, in the quest
    Of this fair lady's casket and wrought purse,
    Losing myself in this vast wilderness,
    Am to this castle well by fortune brought,
    Where, hearing of the goodly entertain   400
    Your knight of holy Order of the Bell
    Gives to all damsels and all errant knights,
    I thought to knock, and now am bold to enter.
TAPSTER   An 't please you see a chamber, you are very welcome. (*Exeunt*)

WIFE   George, I would have something done, and I cannot tell what it is. 405
CITIZEN   What is it, Nell?
WIFE   Why, George, shall Rafe beat nobody again? Prithee, sweetheart, let him.
CITIZEN   So he shall, Nell; and, if I join with him, we'll knock them all.

---

376 Reception.
380 Called.
382 The calves of grooms were often greased to prevent cramps.
388 An inn-keeper's trick to keep horses from eating their feed.
389 Blockhead.

Scene 6

WIFE O, George, here's Master Humphrey again now, that lost Mistress Luce, and Mistress Lucy's father. Master Humphrey will do somebody's errand, I'll warrant him.

HUMPHREY Father, it's true, in arms I ne'er shall clasp her,
For she is stol'n away by your man Jasper.   415

WIFE I thought he would tell him.

MERCHANT Unhappy that I am, to lose my child!
Now I begin to think on Jasper's words,
Who oft hath urged to me thy foolishness.
Why didst thou let her go? Thou lov'st her not,   420
That wouldst bring home thy life, and not bring her.
HUMPHREY Father, forgive me. Shall I tell you true?
Look on my shoulders; they are black and blue.
Whilst to and fro fair Luce and I were winding,
He came and basted me with a hedge binding.*   425
MERCHANT Get men and horses straight; we will be there
Within this hour. You know the place again?
HUMPHREY I know the place where he my loins did swaddle;*
I'll get six horses, and to each a saddle.
MERCHANT Meantime I'll go talk with Jasper's father. (*Exeunt*)   430

WIFE George, what wilt thou lay with* me now, that Master Humphrey has not Mistress Luce yet? Speak, George, what wilt thou lay with me?
CITIZEN No, Nell; I warrant thee Jasper is at Puckeridge* with her by this.
WIFE Nay, George, you must consider Mistress Lucy's feet are tender; and besides 'tis dark; and, I promise you truly, I do not see how he should 435 get out of Waltham Forest with her yet.
CITIZEN Nay, cunny, what wilt thou lay with me that Rafe has her not yet?
WIFE I will not lay against Rafe, honey, because I have not spoken with him. But look, George, peace! Here comes the merry old gentleman again.

Scene 7

OLD MERRYTHOUGHT (*Singing*) When it was grown to dark midnight,
                                                  And all were fast asleep,

---

425 That is, beat me with a cane.
428 Beat soundly.
431 Wager.
433 A village 25 miles north of London.

> In came Margaret's grimely* ghost,
> And stood at William's feet. 445

I have money, and meat and drink beforehand, till tomorrow at noon; why should I be sad? Methinks I have half a dozen jovial spirits within me! (*Sings*) I am three merry men, and three merry men! To what end should any man be sad in this world? Give me a man that, when he goes to hanging, cries, "Troll* the black bowl to me!"—and 450 a woman that will sing a catch in her travail! I have seen a man come by my door with a serious face, in a black cloak, without a hatband, carrying his head as if he looked for pins in the street; I have looked out of my window half a year after, and have spied that man's head upon London Bridge.* 'Tis vile. Never trust a tailor that does not sing at his work; his mind is 455 of nothing but filching.

WIFE Mark this, George; 'tis worth noting: Godfrey, my tailor, you know, never sings, and he had fourteen yards to make this gown; and, I'll be sworn, Mistress Pennistone the draper's wife had one made with twelve.

OLD MERRYTHOUGHT (*Singing*) 'Tis mirth that fills the veins with blood, 460
> More than wine, or sleep, or food.
> Let each man keep his heart at ease;
> No man dies of that disease.
> He that would his body keep
> From diseases, must not weep; 465
> But whoever laughs and sings,
> Never he his body brings
> Into fevers, gouts, or rheums,
> Or ling'ringly his lungs consumes,
> Or meets with aches in the bone, 470
> Or catarrhs or griping stone,
> But contended lives for aye.
> The more he laughs, the more he may.

WIFE Look, George; how say'st thou by this, George? Is 't not a fine old man? —Now, God's blessing a thy sweet lips!—When wilt thou be so merry, 475 George? Faith, thou art the frowning'st little thing, when thou art angry, in a country.

(*Enter* MERCHANT)

CITIZEN Peace, cony; thou shalt see him taken down too, I warrant thee. Here's Luce's father come now. 480

OLD MERRYTHOUGHT (*Singing*) As you came from Walsingham,
> From that holy land,

---

444 Grim-looking.
450 Pass.
454 The heads of executed traitors and heretics were thus displayed.

There met you not with my true love
By the way as you came?

MERCHANT O, Master Merrythought, my daughter's gone! 485
This mirth becomes you not; my daughter's gone!

OLD MERRYTHOUGHT (*Singing*) Why, an if she be, what care I?
Or let her come, or go, or tarry.

MERCHANT Mock not my misery; it is your son
(Whom I have made my own, when all forsook him) 490
Has stol'n my only joy, my child, away.

OLD MERRYTHOUGHT (*Singing*) He set her on a milk-white steed,
And himself upon a gray;
He never turned his face again,
But he bore her quite away. 495

MERCHANT Unworthy of the kindness I have shown
To thee and thine! Too late I well perceive
Thou art consenting to my daughter's loss.

OLD MERRYTHOUGHT Your daughter! What a stir 's here wi' your daughter?
Let her go, think no more on her, but sing loud. If both my sons were 500
on the gallows, I would sing,
Down, down, down—they fall
Down, and arise they never shall.

MERCHANT O, might I behold her once again,
And she once more embrace her aged sire! 505

OLD MERRYTHOUGHT Fie, how scurvily this goes! "And she once more embrace
her aged sire"? You'll make a dog on* her, will ye? She cares much for her
aged sire, I warrant you.
(*Sings*) She cares not for her daddy,
Nor she cares not for her mammy, 510
For she is, she is, she is, she is
My Lord of Lowgave's lassy.

MERCHANT For this thy scorn I will pursue
That son of thine to death.

OLD MERRYTHOUGHT Do; and when you ha' killed him, 515
(*Sings*) Give him flowers enow, palmer,* give him flowers enow;
Give him red and white, and blue, green, and yellow.

MERCHANT I'll fetch my daughter—

OLD MERRYTHOUGHT I'll hear no more a your daughter; it spoils my mirth.

MERCHANT I say, I'll fetch my daughter. 520

OLD MERRYTHOUGHT (*Singing*) Was never man for lady's sake—
Down, down—
Tormented as I, poor Sir Guy—
De derry down—
For Lucy's sake, that lady bright— 525
Down, down—

---

507 Of.

516 "Enow" means enough; a palmer is a pilgrim to the Holy Land who brings back a palm symbolic of
his journey.

As ever men beheld with eye—
De derry down.

MERCHANT   I'll be revenged, by heaven! (*Exeunt*)
(*Music*)   530

WIFE   How dost thou like this, George?

CITIZEN   Why, this is well, cony; but, if Rafe were hot once, thou shouldst see more.

WIFE   The fiddlers go again, husband.

CITIZEN   Ay, Nell; but this is scurvy music. I gave the whoreson gallows* 535
money, and I think he has not got me the waits of Southwark. If I hear 'em
not anon, I'll twinge him by the ears.—You musicians, play *Baloo!**

WIFE   No, good George, let's ha' *Lachrymæ!*

CITIZEN   Why, this is it, cony.

WIFE   It's all the better, George. Now, sweet lamb, what story is that painted 540
upon the cloth? The Confutation* of St. Paul?

CITIZEN   No, lamb; that's Rafe and Lucrece.

WIFE   Rafe and Lucrece! Which Rafe? Our Rafe?

CITIZEN   No, mouse; that was a Tartarian.*

WIFE   A Tartarian? Well, I would the fiddlers had done, that we might see 545
our Rafe again!

Act Three

Scene 1

Waltham Forest
(*Enter* JASPER *and* LUCE)

JASPER   Come, my dear dear; though we have lost our way,
We have not lost ourselves. Are you not weary
With this night's wand'ring broken from your rest,
And frighted with the terror that attends   5
The darkness of this wild unpeopled place?

LUCE   No, my best friend; I cannot either fear,
Or entertain a weary thought, whilst you
(The end of all my full desires) stand by me.
Let them that lose their hopes, and live to languish   10
Amongst the number of forsaken lovers,
Tell* the long, weary steps, and number time,
Start at a shadow, and shrink up their blood,
Whilst I (possessed with all content and quiet)   15
Thus take my pretty love, and thus embrace him. (*Embraces him*)

JASPER   You have caught me, Luce, so fast that, whilst I live,

535 Rogue.
537 A ballad tune, as are the following.
541 His blunder for "conversion."
544 His blunder for "Tarquin." The Wife intended *The Rape of Lucrece.*
13 Count.

THE KNIGHT OF THE BURNING PESTLE   313

I shall become your faithful prisoner,
And wear these chains forever. Come, sit down,
And rest your body, too-too delicate   20
For these disturbances. (*They sit down*) So, will you sleep?
Come, do not be more able* than you are;
I know you are not skillful in these watches,
For women are no soldiers. Be not nice,*
But take it;* sleep, I say.   25

LUCE   I cannot sleep;
        Indeed, I cannot, friend.

JASPER   Why, then we'll sing,
        And try how that will work upon our senses.

LUCE   I'll sing, or say, or anything but sleep.   30

JASPER Come, little mermaid, rob me of my heart
        With that enchanting voice.

LUCE   You mock me, Jasper.
                        (*Song*)

JASPER   Tell me, dearest, what is love?   35
LUCE   'Tis a lightning from above;
            'Tis an arrow; 'tis a fire;
            'Tis a boy they call Desire;
                'Tis a smile
                Doth beguile   40
JASPER   The poor hearts of men that prove.

            Tell me more, are women true?
LUCE   Some love change, and so do you.
JASPER   Are they fair and never kind?
LUCE   Yes, when men turn with the wind.   45
JASPER   Are they froward?
LUCE   Ever toward,*
            Those that love, to love anew.

JASPER Dissemble it no more; I see the god
        Of heavy sleep lay on his heavy mace   50
        Upon your eyelids.

LUCE   I am very heavy. (*Sleeps*)

JASPER Sleep, sleep; and quiet rest crown thy sweet thoughts!
        Keep from her fair blood distempers,* startings,
        Horrors, and fearful shapes! Let all her dreams   55
        Be joys, and chaste delights, embraces, wishes,
        And such new pleasures as the ravished soul

22 Active.
24 Foolish.
25 Give in, acquiesce.
47 Apt.
54 Ill health or disorders.

Gives to the senses!—So; my charms have took.—
Keep her, you powers divine, whilst I contemplate
Upon the wealth and beauty of her mind!
She is only fair and constant, only kind,
And only to thee, Jasper. O, my joys!
Whither will you transport me? Let not fullness
Of my poor buried hopes come up together
And overcharge my spirits! I am weak.
Some say (however ill) the sea and women
Are governed by the moon; both ebb and flow,
Both full of changes; yet to them that know,
And truly judge, these but opinions are,
And heresies, to bring on pleasing war
Between our tempers, that without these were
Both void of after-love and present fear,
Which are the best of Cupid. O, thou child
Bred from despair, I dare not entertain thee,
Having a love without the faults of women,
And greater in her perfect goods than men!
Which to make good, and please myself the stronger,
Though certainly I am certain of her love,
I'll try her, that the world and memory
May sing to aftertimes her constancy.—(*Draws his sword*)
Luce! Luce! Awake!

LUCE   Why do you fright me, friend,
With those distempered looks? What makes* your sword
Drawn in your hand? Who hath offended you?
I prithee, Jasper, sleep; thou art wild with watching.

JASPER   Come, make your way to heaven, and bid the world,
With all the villainies that stick upon it,
Farewell; you're for another life.

LUCE   O, Jasper,
How have my tender years committed evil,
Especially against the man I love,
Thus to be cropped untimely?*

JASPER   Foolish girl,
Canst thou imagine I could love his daughter
That flung me from my fortune into nothing,
Dischargéd me his service, shut the doors
Upon my poverty, and scorned my prayers,
Sending me, like a boat without a mast,
To sink or swim? Come; by this hand you die.
I must have life and blood to satisfy
Your father's wrongs.

60

65

70

75

80

85

90

95

100

83 Does.
92 Prematurely.

WIFE Away, George, away! Raise the watch at Ludgate,* and bring a mittimus* from the justice for this desperate villain!—Now, I charge you, gentlemen, see the king's peace kept!—O, my heart, what a varlet's this to offer man-slaughter upon the harmless gentlewoman!   105

CITIZEN I warrant thee, sweetheart, we'll have him hampered.

LUCE O, Jasper, be not cruel!
    If thou wilt kill me, smile, and do it quickly,
    And let not many deaths appear before me.
    I am a woman, made of fear and love,   110
    A weak, weak woman; kill not with thy eyes;
    They shoot me through and through. Strike, I am ready;
    And, dying, still I love thee.

(Enter MERCHANT, HUMPHREY, and his Men)

MERCHANT   Whereabouts?   115

JASPER (*Aside*) No more of this; now to myself again.

HUMPHREY There, there he stands, with sword, like martial knight,
    Drawn in his hand; therefore beware the fight,
    You that be wise; for, were I good Sir Bevis,*
    I would not stay his coming, by your leaves.   120

MERCHANT Sirrah, restore my daughter!

JASPER   Sirrah, no!

MERCHANT Upon him, then! (*They set upon* JASPER *and take* LUCE *from him*)

WIFE So; down with him, down with him, down with him! Cut him i' th' leg, boys, cut him i' th' leg!   125

MERCHANT Come your ways, minion;* I'll provide a cage
    For you, you're grown so tame.—Horse her away.

HUMPHREY Truly, I'm glad your forces have the day. (*Exeunt.* JASPER *remains*)

JASPER They are gone, and I am hurt; my love is lost,
    Never to get again. O, me unhappy!   130
    Bleed, bleed and die! I cannot. O, my folly,
    Thou hast betrayed me! Hope, where art thou fled?
    Tell me, if thou beest anywhere remaining,
    Shall I but see my love again? O, no!
    She will not deign to look upon her butcher,   135
    Nor is it fit she should; yet I must venter.
    O, Chance, or Fortune, or whate'er thou art
    That men adore for powerful, hear my cry,
    And let me loving live, or losing die! (*Exit*)

WIFE Is a gone, George?   140

CITIZEN Ay, cony.

---

102 (*a*) Like Newgate, a gate-house used as a prison or police-station. (*b*) A warrant for arrest.
119 Bevis of Hampton, another hero of romance.
126 Hussy.

WIFE   Marry, and let him go, sweetheart. By the faith a my body, a has put me into such a fright that I tremble (as they say) as 'twere an aspine leaf. Look a my little finger, George, how it shakes. Now, i' truth, every member of my body is the worse for 't.   145

CITIZEN   Come, hug in mine arms, sweet mouse; he shall not fright thee any more. Alas, mine own dear heart, how it quivers!

Scene 2

Before the Bell Inn at Waltham

(*Enter* MRS. MERRYTHOUGHT, RAFE, MICHAEL, SQUIRE, DWARF, HOST, *and a* TAPSTER)   150

WIFE   O, Rafe! How dost thou, Rafe? How hast thou slept tonight?* Has the knight used thee well?

CITIZEN   Peace, Nell; let Rafe alone.

TAPSTER   Master, the reckoning is not paid.

RAFE   Right courteous knight, who, for the order's sake   155
      Which thou hast ta'en, hang'st out the holy Bell,
      As I this flaming pestle bear about,
      We render thanks to your puissant* self,
      Your beauteous lady, and your gentle squires
      For thus refreshing of our wearied limbs,   160
      Stiffened with hard achievements in wild desert.

TAPSTER   Sir, there is twelve shillings to pay.

RAFE   Thou merry Squire Tapstero, thanks to thee
      For comforting our souls with double jug;*
      And, if advent'rous fortune prick thee forth,   165
      Thou jovial squire, to follow feats of arms,
      Take heed thou tender* every lady's cause,
      Every true knight, and every damsel fair;
      But spill the blood of treacherous Saracens,
      And false enchanters that with magic spells   170
      Have done to death full many a noble knight.

HOST   Thou valiant Knight of the Burning Pestle, give ear to me. There is twelve shillings to pay, and, as I am a true knight, I will not bate* a penny.

WIFE   George, I pray thee, tell me, must Rafe pay twelve shillings now?

CITIZEN   No, Nell, no; nothing but the old knight is merry with Rafe.   175

WIFE   O, is 't nothing else? Rafe will be as merry as he.

RAFE   Sir Knight, this mirth of yours becomes you well;
      But, to requite this liberal courtesy,

151 Last night.
158 Mighty.
164 Strong beer.
167 Treat with care.
173 Subtract or reduce.

If any of your squires will follow arms,
He shall receive from my heroic hand   180
A knighthood, by the virtue of this pestle.
HOST   Fair knight, I thank you for your noble offer;
Therefore, gentle knight,
Twelve shillings you must pay, or I must cap* you.

WIFE   Look, George! Did not I tell thee as much? The Knight of the Bell is 185
in earnest. Rafe shall not be beholding to him; give him his money, George,
and let him go snick up.
CITIZEN   Cap Rafe? No.—Hold your hand, Sir Knight of the Bell; there's your
money. (*Gives money*) Have you anything to say to Rafe now? Cap Rafe!
WIFE   I would you should know it, Rafe has friends that will not suffer him 190
to be capped for ten times so much, and ten times to the end of that.—Now
take thy course, Rafe.

MRS. MERRYTHOUGHT   Come, Michael; thou and I will go home to thy father.
He hath enough left to keep us a day or two, and we'll set fellows abroad
to cry* our purse and our casket. Shall we, Michael?   195
MICHAEL   Ay, I pray, mother; in truth my feet are full of chilblains* with
traveling.

WIFE   Faith, and those chilblains are a foul trouble. Mrs. Merrythought, when
your youth comes home, let him rub all the soles of his feet, and the heels,
and his ankles, with a mouse skin; or, if none of your people can catch a 200
mouse, when he goes to bed, let him roll his feet in the warm embers, and,
I warrant you, he shall be well; and you may make him put his fingers
between his toes, and smell to them; it's very sovereign for his head, if he
be costive.*

MRS. MERRYTHOUGHT   Master Knight of the Burning Pestle, my son Michael 205
and I bid you farewell. I thank your worship heartily for your kindness.
RAFE   Farewell, fair lady, and your tender squire.
If, pricking through these deserts, I do hear
Of any traitorous knight, who through his guile
Hath light upon your casket and your purse,   210
I will despoil him of them, and restore them.
MRS. MERRYTHOUGHT   I thank your worship. (*Exit with* MICHAEL)
RAFE   Dwarf, bear my shield; squire, elevate my lance.
And now farewell, you Knight of Holy Bell.

CITIZEN   Ay, ay, Rafe, all is paid.   215

RAFE   But yet, before I go, speak, worthy knight,

184 Arrest.
195 That is, have public criers announce the loss of.
196 Swelling.   204 Constipated.

If aught you do of sad adventures know,
Where errant knight may through his prowess win
Eternal fame, and free some gentle souls
From endless bonds of steel and ling'ring pain.   220

HOST   Sirrah, go to Nick the barber, and bid him prepare himself, as I told you
before, quickly.

TAPSTER   I am gone, sir. (*Exit* TAPSTER)

HOST   Sir Knight, this wilderness affordeth none
But the great venter, where full many a knight   225
Hath tried his prowess, and come off with shame,
And where I would not have you lose your life
Against no man, but furious fiend of hell.

RAFE   Speak on, Sir Knight; tell what he is and where,
For here I vow, upon my blazing badge,   230
Never to blaze* a day in quietness,
But bread and water will I only eat,
And the green herb and rock shall be my couch,
Till I have quelled* that man, or beast, or fiend
That works such damage to all errant knights.   235

HOST   Not far from hence, near to a craggy cliff,
At the north end of this distressed town,
There doth stand a lowly house,
Ruggedly builded, and in it a cave
In which an ugly giant now doth wone,*   240
Ycleped* Barbaroso; in his hand
He shakes a naked lance of purest steel,
With sleeves turned up; and him before he wears
A motley garment,* to preserve his clothes
From blood of those knights which he massacres,   245
And ladies gent;* without his door doth hang
A copper basin on a prickant spear,*
At which no sooner gentle knights can knock
But the shrill sound fierce Barbaroso hears,
And, rushing forth, brings in the errant knight   250
And sets him down in an enchanted chair;
Then with an engine, which he hath prepared
With forty teeth, he claws his courtly crown,
Next makes him wink,* and underneath his chin
He plants a brazen piece of mighty bord,*   255

---

231 Celebrate.
234 Killed.
240 Dwell.
241 Called.
244 A many-colored garment such as jesters wore.
246 Gentle or noble.
247 That is, a spear pointed upwards. The basin and spear advertized a barber-surgeon.
254 Close his eyes to anoint them with perfume.
255 The barber's basin, which fitted about the customer's neck.

And knocks his bullets* round about his cheeks,
Whilst with his fingers and an instrument
With which he snaps his hair off, he doth fill
The wretch's ears with a most hideous noise.
Thus every knight adventurer he doth trim,   260
And now no creature dares encounter him.

RAFE   In God's name, I will fight him. Kind sir,
Go but before me to this dismal cave,
Where this huge giant Barbaroso dwells,
And, by that virtue that* brave Rosicleer   265
That damned brood of ugly giants slew,
And Palmerin Frannarco* overthrew,
I doubt not but to curb this traitor foul,
And to the devil send his guilty soul.

HOST   Brave-sprighted* knight, thus far I will perform   270
This your request: I'll bring you within sight
Of this most loathsome place, inhabited
By a more loathsome man; but dare not stay,
For his main force soops* all he sees away.

RAFE   Saint George, set on before! March, squire and page! (*Exeunt*)   275

WIFE   George, dost think Rafe will confound the giant?

CITIZEN   I hold my cap to a farthing* he does. Why, Nell, I saw him wrestle
with the great Dutchman, and hurl him.

WIFE   Faith, and that Dutchman was a goodly man, if all things were answerable to his bigness. And yet they say there was a Scotchman higher than   280
he, and that they two and a knight met, and saw one another for nothing.
But of all the sights that ever were in London, since I was married, methinks
the little child that was so fair grown about the members was the prettiest;
that and the hermaphrodite.

CITIZEN   Nay, by our leave, Nell, Ninivy* was better.   285

WIFE   Ninivy! O, that was the story of Jone and the wall,* was it not, George?

CITIZEN   Yes, lamb.

Scene 3

Before MERRYTHOUGHT'S *house*
(*Enter* MRS. MERRYTHOUGHT)

WIFE   Look, George, here comes Mrs. Merrythought again! And I would have   290
Rafe come and fight with the giant; I tell you true, I long to see 't.

---

256 Soap pellets.
265 That is, by which.
267 A giant killed by Palmerin de Oliva.
270 Brave-spirited.
274 Sweeps.
277 That is, bet my cap for a farthing.
285 A popular puppet show about Nineveh.
286 Jonah and the whale.

CITIZEN   Good Mrs. Merrythought, begone, I pray you, for my sake; I pray you, forbear a little; you shall have audience presently. I have a little business.

WIFE   Mrs. Merrythought, if it please you to refrain* your passion a little, till Rafe have dispatched the giant out of the way, we shall think ourselves 295 much bound to you. I thank you, good Mrs. Merrythought. (*Exit* MRS. MERRYTHOUGHT)

(*Enter a* BOY)

CITIZEN   Boy, come hither. Send away Rafe and this whoreson giant quickly.

BOY   In good faith, sir, we cannot; you'll utterly spoil our play, and make it to 300 be hissed; and it cost money; you will not suffer us to go on with our plot.— I pray, gentlemen, rule him.

CITIZEN   Let him come now and dispatch this, and I'll trouble you no more.

BOY   Will you give me your hand of that?

WIFE   Give him thy hand, George, do; and I'll kiss him. I warrant thee, the 305 youth means plainly.*

BOY   I'll send him to you presently.

WIFE   (*Kissing him*)   I thank you, little youth.—(*Exit* BOY) Faith, the child hath a sweet breath, George; but I think it be troubled with the worms. *Carduus Benedictus** and mare's milk were the only thing in the world for 't.—O, 310 Rafe's here, George!—God send thee good luck, Rafe!

Scene 4

Before a barber's shop
(*Enter* RAFE, HOST, SQUIRE, *and* DWARF)

HOST   Puissant knight, yonder his mansion is.
   Lo, where the spear and copper basin are!
   Behold that string, on which hangs many a tooth,   315
   Drawn from the gentle jaw of wand'ring knights!
   I dare not stay to sound;* he will appear. (*Exit* HOST)

RAFE   O, faint not, heart! Susan, my lady dear,
   The cobbler's maid in Milk Street, for whose sake
   I take these arms, O, let the thought of thee   320
   Carry thy knight through all adventerous deeds;
   And, in the honor of thy beauteous self,
   May I destroy this monster Barbaroso!—
   Knock, squire, upon the basin till it break   325
   With the shrill* strokes, or till the giant speak. (SQUIRE *knocks upon the basin*)
                                    (*Enter* BARBER)

WIFE   O, George, the giant, the giant!—
   Now, Rafe, for thy life!

BARBER   What fond unknowing wight* is this, that dares   330

---

294 Restrain.
306 Honestly.
310 A species of thistle used medicinally.
318 Blow a trumpet.
326 Keen or sharp.   330 That is, foolish, ignorant creature.

So rudely knock at Barbaroso's cell,
Where no man comes but leaves his fleece behind?

RAFE   I, traitorous caitiff, who am sent by fate
    To punish all the sad enormities
    Thou hast committed against ladies gent   335
    And errant knights. Traitor to God and men,
    Prepare thyself! This is the dismal hour
    Appointed for thee to give strict account
    Of all thy beastly, treacherous villainies.

BARBER   Foolhardy knight, full soon thou shalt aby*   340
    This fond reproach; thy body will I bang; (*He takes down his pole*)
    And lo, upon that string thy teeth shall hang!
    Prepare thyself, for dead soon shalt thou be.

RAFE   Saint George for me! (*They fight*)
BARBER   Gargantua* for me!   345

WIFE   To him, Rafe, to him! Hold up the giant! Set out thy leg before, Rafe!
CITIZEN   Falsify* a blow, Rafe, falsify a blow! The giant lies open on the left
    side.
WIFE   Bear 't off, bear 't off still! There, boy!—O, Rafe's almost down, Rafe's
    almost down!   350

RAFE   Susan, inspire me! Now have up again.

WIFE   Up, up, up, up, up! So, Rafe! Down with him, down with him, Rafe!
CITIZEN   Fetch him o'er the hip, boy! (RAFE *knocks the* BARBER *down*)
WIFE   There, boy! Kill, kill, kill, kill, kill, Rafe!
CITIZEN   No, Rafe; get all out of him first.   355

RAFE   Presumptuous man, see to what desperate end
    Thy treachery hath brought thee! The just gods,
    Who never prosper those that do despise them,
    For all the villainies which thou hast done
    To knights and ladies, now have paid thee home   360
    By my stiff arm, a knight adventurous.
    But say, vile wretch, before I send thy soul
    To sad Avernus* (whither it must go),
    What captives hold'st thou in thy sable cave?

BARBER   Go in, and free them all; thou hast the day.   365
RAFE   Go, squire and dwarf, search in this dreadful cave,
    And free the wretched prisoners from their bonds.
            (*Exeunt* SQUIRE *and* DWARF)
BARBER   I crave for mercy, as thou art a knight,

---

340 Pay for.
345 Father of Pantagruel; both are heroes in Rabelais' satiric romance.
347 Feint.
363 Hades.

And scorn'st to spill the blood of those that beg.   370

RAFE Thou showed'st no mercy, nor shalt thou have any;
      Prepare thyself, for thou shalt surely die.
      (*Enter* SQUIRE, *leading* [*1st Man*] *winking, with a basin under his chin*)

SQUIRE Behold, brave knight, here is one prisoner,
      Whom this wild man hath used as you see.   375

WIFE This is the first wise word I heard the squire speak.

RAFE Speak what thou art, and how thou hast been used,
      That I may give him condign* punishment.

1ST KNIGHT I am a knight that took my journey post*
      Northward from London; and in courteous wise   380
      This giant trained* me to his loathsome den
      Under pretense of killing of the itch;
      And all my body with a powder strewed,
      That smarts and stings, and cut away my beard,
      And my curled locks wherein were ribands tied,   385
      And with a water washed my tender eyes
      (Whilst up and down about me still he skipped),
      Whose virtue is that, till my eyes be wiped
      With a dry cloth, for this my foul disgrace,
      I shall not dare to look a dog i' th' face.   390

WIFE Alas, poor knight!—Relieve him, Rafe; relieve poor knights, whilst you
      live.

RAFE My trusty squire, convey him to the town,
      Where he may find relief.—Adieu, fair knight. (*Exit* 1ST KNIGHT)
          (*Enter* DWARF, *leading* [*2nd Man*] *with a patch o'er his nose*)   395

DWARF Puissant knight, of the Burning Pestle hight,
      See here another wretch, whom this foul beast
      Hath scorched* and scored in this inhuman wise.

RAFE Speak me thy name, and eke thy place of birth,
      And what hath been thy usage in this cave.   400

2ND KNIGHT I am a knight, Sir Pockhole is my name,
      And by my birth I am a Londoner,
      Free by my copy,* but my ancestors
      Were Frenchmen* all; and, riding hard this way
      Upon a trotting horse, my bones did ache,
      And I, faint knight, to ease my weary limbs,   405
      Light at this cave, when straight this furious fiend,

378 Deserved.
379 With speed.
381 Led.
398 Cut.
403 Officially enrolled as a free citizen.
404 An allusion to the "French disease," the pox or syphilis.

With sharpest instrument of purest steel,
Did cut the gristle of my nose away,
And in the place this velvet plaster stands.   410
Relieve me, gentle knight, out of his hands!

WIFE Good Rafe, relieve Sir Pockhole, and send him away; for in truth his
breath stinks.

RAFE Convey him straight after the other knight.—
Sir Pockhole, fare you well.   415
2ND KNIGHT   Kind sir, good night. (*Exit. Cries within*)
MAN Deliver us!
WOMAN Deliver us!

WIFE Hark, George, what a woeful cry there is! I think some woman lies-in
there.   420

MAN Deliver us!
WOMAN Deliver us!
RAFE What ghastly noise is this? Speak, Barbaroso,
Or, by this blazing steel, thy head goes off!
BARBER Prisoners of mine, whom I in diet keep.   425
Send lower down into the cave,
And in a tub that's heated smoking hot*
There may they find them, and deliver them.
RAFE Run, squire and dwarf; deliver them with speed.
(*Exeunt* SQUIRE *and* DWARF)   430
WIFE But will not Rafe kill this giant? Surely I am afeard, if he let him go, he
will do as much hurt as ever he did.
CITIZEN Not so, mouse, neither, if he could convert him.
WIFE Ay, George, if he could convert him; but a giant is not so soon converted
as one of us ordinary people. There's a pretty tale of a witch that had the 435
devil's mark about her (God bless us!), that had a giant to her son, that was
called Lob-lie-by-the-fire; didst never hear it, George?
(*Enter* SQUIRE, *leading a* MAN, *with a glass of lotion in his hand, and the*
DWARF, *leading a* WOMAN, *with diet bread and drink*)
CITIZEN Peace, Nell, here comes the prisoners.   440

DWARF Here be these pined wretches, manful knight,
That for these six weeks have not seen a wight.
RAFE Deliver what you are, and how you came
To this sad cave, and what your usage was.
MAN I am an errant knight that followed arms   445
With spear and shield; and in my tender years
I stricken was with Cupid's fiery shaft,
And fell in love with this my lady dear,

427 A treatment for venereal disease.

And stole her from her friends in Turnbull Street,*
And bore her up and down from town to town,   450
Where we did eat and drink, and music hear,
Till at the length at this unhappy town
We did arrive, and, coming to this cave,
This beast us caught and put us in a tub,
Where we this two months sweat, and should have done   455
Another month, if you had not relieved us.
WOMAN   This bread and water hath our diet been,
Together with a rib cut from a neck
Of burned mutton; hard hath been our fare.
Release us from this ugly giant's snare!   460
MAN   This hath been all the food we have received;
But only twice a day, for novelty,
He gave a spoonful of this hearty broth (*Pulls out a syringe*)
To each of us, through this same slender quill.
RAFE   From this infernal monster you shall go,   465
That useth knights and gentle ladies so!—
Convey them hence. (*Exeunt* MAN *and* WOMAN)

CITIZEN   Cony, I can tell thee, the gentlemen like Rafe.
WIFE   Ay, George, I see it well enough.—Gentlemen, I thank you all heartily
for gracing my man Rafe; and, I promise you, you shall see him oft'ner. 470

BARBER   Mercy, great knight! I do recant my ill,
And henceforth never gentle blood will spill.
RAFE   I give thee mercy; but yet shalt thou swear
Upon my burning pestle, to perform
Thy promise uttered.   475
BARBER   I swear and kiss. (*Kisses the pestle*)
RAFE   Depart then, and amend.—(*Exit* BARBER)
Come, squire and dwarf, the sun grows towards his set,
And we have many more adventures yet. (*Exeunt*)

CITIZEN   Now Rafe is in this humor, I know he would ha' beaten all the boys 480
in the house, if they had been set on him.
WIFE   Ay, George, but it is well as it is. I warrant you, the gentlemen do consider
what it is to overthrow a giant. But look, George; here comes Mrs. Merrythought and her son Michael.—Now you are welcome, Mrs. Merrythought;
now Rafe has done, you may go on.   485

Scene 5

Before MERRYTHOUGHT'S *house*
(*Enter* MRS. MERRYTHOUGHT *and* MICHAEL)
MRS. MERRYTHOUGHT   Mick, my boy—
MICHAEL   Ay, forsooth, mother.

449 A street famous for its brothels.

MRS. MERRYTHOUGHT Be merry, Mick; we are at home now, where, I war- 490
rant you, you shall find the house flung out at the windows. (*Music within*)
Hark! Hey, dogs, hey! This is the old world.* i' faith, with my husband.
If I get in among 'em, I'll play 'em such a lesson that they shall have little
list* to come scraping hither again.—Why, Master Merrythought! Husband!
Charles Merrythought!   495

OLD MERRYTHOUGHT (*Singing within*) If you will sing, and dance, and laugh,
                                         And hollo, and laugh again,
                                     And then cry, "There, boys, there!"
                                         why, then,
                                       One, two, three, and four,   500
                                       We shall be merry within this hour.

MRS. MERRYTHOUGHT Why, Charles, do you not know your own natural wife?
I say, open the door, and turn me out those mangy companions; 'tis more
than time that they were fellow and fellowlike with you. You are a gentleman, Charles, and an old man, and father of two children; and I myself 505
(though I say it) by my mother's side niece to a worshipful gentleman and a
conductor;* he has been three times in his majesty's service at Chester, and
is now the fourth time, God bless him and his charge, upon his journey.

OLD MERRYTHOUGHT (*Singing*)   Go from my window, love, go;
                                       Go from my window, my dear!   510
                                    The wind and the rain will drive you back
                                       again;
                                    You cannot be lodgéd here.

Hark you, Mrs. Merrythought, you that walk upon adventures, and forsake
your husband, because he sings with never a penny in his purse, what shall 515
I think myself the worse? Faith, no; I'll be merry.
   You come not here; here's none but lads of mettle, lives of a hundred years
and upwards; care never drunk their bloods, nor want made 'em warble,
"Heigh-ho, my heart is heavy."

MRS. MERRYTHOUGHT Why, Master Merrythought, what am I that you 520
should laugh me to scorn* thus abruptly? Am I not your fellow-feeler, as we
may say, in all our miseries? Your comforter in health and sickness? Have I
not brought you children? Are they not like you, Charles? Look upon thine
own image, hard-hearted man! And yet for all this—

OLD MERRYTHOUGHT (*Within*)   Begone, begone, my juggy,* my puggy,* 525
                                       Begone, my love, my dear!
                                    The weather is warm, 'twill do thee no harm;
                                       Thou canst not be lodgéd here.—

Be merry, boys! Some light music, and more wine!

WIFE He's not in earnest, I hope, George, is he?   530
CITIZEN What if he be, sweetheart?

---

492 Way.   494 Desire.
507 Military officer.
521 That is, ridicule me.
525 (*a*) Diminutive of Joan.   (*b*) A term of endearment.

WIFE Marry, if he be, George, I'll make bold to tell him he's an ingrant* old man to use his bedfellow so scurvily.

CITIZEN What! How does he use her, honey?

WIFE Marry, come up, Sir Saucebox! I think you'll take his part, will you not? 535 Lord, how hot you are grown! You are a fine man, an you had a fine dog;* it becomes you sweetly!

CITIZEN Nay, prithee, Nell, chide not, for, as I am an honest man and a true Christian grocer, I do not like his doings.

WIFE I cry you mercy, then, George! You know we are all frail and full of 540 infirmities.—D'ye hear, Mr. Merrythought? May I crave a word with you?

OLD MERRYTHOUGHT (*Within*) Strike up lively, lads!

WIFE I had not thought, in truth, Mr. Merrythought, that a man of your age and discretion (as I may say), being a gentleman, and therefore known by your gentle conditions,* could have used so little respect to the weakness 545 of his wife, for your wife is your own flesh, the staff of your age, your yoke-fellow, with whose help you draw through the mire of this transitory world; nay, she's your own rib! And again—

OLD MERRYTHOUGHT (*Singing*) I come not hither for thee to teach;
I have no pulpit for thee to preach; 550
I would thou hadst kissed me under the breech,
As thou art a lady gay.

WIFE Marry, with a vengeance! I am heartily sorry for the poor gentlewoman, but, if I were thy wife, i' faith, graybeard, i' faith—

CITIZEN I prithee, sweet honeysuckle, be content.

WIFE Give me such words, that am a gentlewoman born! Hang him, hoary 555 rascal! Get me some drink, George; I am almost molten with fretting. Now, beshrew his knave's heart for it! (*Exit* CITIZEN)

OLD MERRYTHOUGHT Play me a light lavolta.* Come, be frolic. Fill the good fellows' wine.

MRS. MERRYTHOUGHT Why, Mr. Merrythought, are you disposed to make me 560 wait here? You'll open, I hope; I'll fetch them that shall open else.

OLD MERRYTHOUGHT Good woman, if you will sing, I'll give you something; if not—

(*Song*) 565
You are no love for me, Margret;
I am no love for you.—
Come aloft,* boys, aloft!

---

532 Ignorant, or ingrate.
536 A mark of gentility.
545 Qualities.
559 A lively dance.
568 Be merry.

MRS. MERRYTHOUGHT Now a churl's fart in your teeth, sir!—Come, Mick, we'll not trouble him; a shall not ding us i' th' teeth* with his bread and his broth, that he shall not. Come, boy; I'll provide for thee, I warrant thee. We'll go to Master Venturewell's, the merchant; I'll get his letter to mine host of the Bell in Waltham; there I'll place thee with the tapster. Will not that do well for thee, Mick? And let me alone for that old cuckoldly knave your father; I'll use him in his kind,* I warrant ye. (*Exeunt*) 575

(*Enter* CITIZEN *with beer*)

WIFE Come, George, where's the beer?

CITIZEN Here, love.

WIFE This old fornicating fellow will not out of my mind yet.—Gentlemen, I'll begin to you all; and I desire more of your acquaintance with all my heart.—(*Drinks*) Fill the gentlemen some beer, George. 580

(*Music*)

Act Four

Scene 1

(*A Street.* BOY *danceth*)

WIFE Look, George, the little boy 's come again; methinks he looks something like the Prince of Orange in his long stocking, if he had a little harness* about his neck. George, I will have him dance *Fading.—Fading* is a fine jig,* I'll assure you, gentlemen.—Begin, brother.—Now a capers, sweetheart!— 5 Now a turn a th' toe, and then tumble! Cannot you tumble, youth?

BOY No, indeed, forsooth.

WIFE Nor eat fire?

BOY Neither.

WIFE Why, then, I thank you heartily; there's twopence to buy you points* 10 withal. (*Exit* BOY)

(*Enter* JASPER *and* BOY)

JASPER There, boy, deliver this. (*Gives a letter*) But do it well.
Hast thou provided me four lusty fellows,
Able to carry me? And art thou perfect 15
In all thy business?

BOY   Sir, you need not fear;
I have my lesson here, and cannot miss it.
The men are ready for you and what else
Pertains to this employment. 20

JASPER   There, my boy. (*Gives money*)
Take it, but buy no land.

BOY   Faith, sir, 'twere rare

---

570 That is, reproach us.
575 That is, according to his nature.
3 Armor.
4 A combination of dance and song.
10 Laces for fastening breeches.

To see so young a purchaser. I fly,
And on my wings carry your destiny. (*Exit*)
JASPER Go and be happy!—Now, my latest hope, ²⁵
Forsake me not, but fling thy anchor out,
And let it hold! Stand fixed, thou rolling stone,
Till I enjoy my dearest! Hear me, all
You powers, that rule in men, celestial! (*Exit*)
³⁰

WIFE Go thy ways; thou art as crooked a sprig as ever grew in London. I warrant
him, he'll come to some naughty end or other, for his looks say no less.
Besides, his father (you know, George) is none of the best; you heard him
take me up like a flirt-gill,* and sing bawdy songs upon me; but, i' faith, if I
live, George— ³⁵
CITIZEN Let me alone, sweetheart; I have a trick in my head shall lodge him in
the Arches* for one year, and make him sing *peccavi** ere I leave him; and yet
he shall never know who hurt him neither.
WIFE Do, my good George, do!
CITIZEN What shall we have Rafe do now, boy?
BOY You shall have what you will, sir. ⁴⁰
CITIZEN Why, so, sir, go and fetch me him then, and let the Sophy of Persia
come and christen him a child.*
BOY Believe me, sir, that will not do so well; 'tis stale; it has been had before
at the Red Bull.*
⁴⁵
WIFE George, let Rafe travel over great hills, and let him be very weary, and
come to the King of Cracovia's* house, covered with velvet; and there let
the king's daughter stand in her window, all in beaten gold, combing her
golden locks with a comb of ivory; and let her spy Rafe, and fall in love with
him, and come down to him, and carry him into her father's house; and ⁵⁰
then let Rafe talk with her.
CITIZEN Well said, Nell; it shall be so.—Boy, let's ha't done quickly.
BOY Sir, if you will imagine all this to be done already, you shall hear them talk
together; but we cannot present a house covered with black velvet, and a lady
in beaten gold.
⁵⁵
CITIZEN Sir Boy, let's ha't as you can, then.
BOY Besides, it will show ill-favoredly to have a grocer's prentice to court a
king's daughter.
CITIZEN Will it so, sir? You are well read in histories!* I pray you, what was Sir
Dagonet?* Was not he prentice to a grocer in London? Read the play of ⁶⁰
The Four Prentices of London,* where they toss their pikes so. I pray you, fetch
him in, sir, fetch him in.

³⁴ Loose woman.
³⁷ (*a*) An ecclesiastical court. (*b*) "I have sinned."
⁴³ That is, christen a child for him. This alludes to another play, *The Travels of the Three English Brothers.*
⁴⁵ A rival public theater which catered to popular audiences.
⁴⁷ Poland. Perhaps an allusion to an unknown romance.
⁵⁹ Fiction.
⁶⁰ The jester at the court of King Arthur.
⁶¹ By Thomas Heywood.

BOY It shall be done.—(*To audience*) It is not our fault, gentlemen. (*Exit*)

WIFE Now we shall see fine doings, I warrant tee, George.

Scene 2

A hall in the palace of the King of Moldavia 65
(*Enter* RAFE *and the* LADY, SQUIRE, *and* DWARF)

WIFE O, here they come; see how prettily the King of Cracovia's daughter is dressed!

CITIZEN Ay, Nell, it is the fashion of that country, I warrant tee.

LADY Welcome, Sir Knight, unto my father's court, 70
    King of Moldavia,* unto me, Pompiona,
    His daughter dear! But, sure, you do not like
    Your entertainment, that will stay with us
    No longer but a night.

RAFE   Damsel right fair, 75
    I am on many sad adventures bound,
    That call me forth into the wilderness.
    Besides, my horse's back is something galled,
    Which will enforce me ride a sober pace.
    But many thanks, fair lady, be to you 80
    For using errant knight with courtesy!

LADY But say, brave knight, what is your name and birth?

RAFE My name is Rafe; I am an Englishman,
    As true as steel, a hearty Englishman,
    And prentice to a grocer in the Strand 85
    By deed indent,* of which I have one part;
    But, Fortune calling me to follow arms,
    On me this holy order I did take
    Of Burning Pestle, which in all men's eyes
    I bear, confounding ladies' enemies. 90

LADY Oft have I heard of your brave countrymen,
    And fertile soil, and store of wholesome food;
    My father oft will tell me of a drink
    In England found, and nippitato* called,
    Which driveth all the sorrow from your hearts. 95

RAFE Lady, 'tis true; you need not lay your lips
    To better nippitato than there is.

LADY And of a wild fowl he will often speak,
    Which powdered*-beef-and-mustard called is;
    For there have been great wars twixt us and you. 100
    But truly, Rafe, it was not long* of me.
    Tell me then, Rafe, could you contented be

71 A province in Rumania.
86 Indenture. It was drawn up in two copies, of which the signer kept one.
94 Strong liquor.
99 Salted. 101 Because.

BEAUMONT AND FLETCHER

To wear lady's favor in your shield?

RAFE I am a knight of religious order,
And will not wear a favor of a lady's
That trusts in Antichrist and false traditions.   105

CITIZEN Well said, Rafe! Convert her, if thou canst.

RAFE Besides, I have a lady of my own
In merry England, for whose virtuous sake
I took these arms; and Susan is her name,   110
A cobbler's maid in Milk Street, whom I vow
Ne'er to forsake whilst life and pestle last.

LADY Happy that cobbling dame, whoe'er she be,
That for her own, dear Rafe, hath gotten thee!
Unhappy I, that ne'er shall see the day   115
To see thee more, that bear'st my heart away!

RAFE Lady, farewell; I needs must take my leave.

LADY Hard-hearted Rafe, that ladies dost deceive!

CITIZEN Hark thee, Rafe; there's money for thee. (*Gives money*) Give something
in the King of Cracovia's house; be not beholding to him.   120

RAFE Lady, before I go, I must remember
Your father's officers, who, truth to tell,
Have been about me very diligent.
Hold up thy snowy hand, thou princely maid!
There's twelvepence for your father's chamberlain;   125
And another shilling for his cook,
For, by my troth, the goose was roasted well;
And twelvepence for your father's horse keeper,
For nointing my horse' back, and for his butter*
There is another shilling; to the maid   130
That washed my boothose* there's an English groat,
And twopence to the boy that wiped my boots;
And last, fair lady, there is for yourself
Threepence to buy you pins at Bumbo Fair.

LADY Full many thanks; and I will keep them safe   135
Till all the heads be off, for thy sake, Rafe.

RAFE Advance, my squire and dwarf! I cannot stay.

LADY Thou kill'st my heart in parting thus away. (*Exeunt*)

WIFE I commend Rafe yet, that he will not stoop to a Cracovian; there's
properer* women in London than any are there, iwis. But here comes 140
Master Humphrey and his love again now, George.

CITIZEN Ay, cony; peace.

129 Used to rub a horse's back.
131 Leggings.   140 Handsomer.

Scene 3

A room in VENTUREWELL'S *house*

(*Enter* MERCHANT, HUMPHREY, LUCE, *and a* BOY)

MERCHANT Go, get you up;* I will not be entreated;   145
    And, gossip* mine, I'll keep you sure hereafter
    From gadding out again with boys and unthrifts.
    Come, they are women's tears; I know your fashion.—
    Go, sirrah, lock her in, and keep the key
    Safe as you love your life.—(*Exeunt* LUCE *and* BOY)   150
                    Now, my son Humphrey,
    You may both rest assured of my love
    In this, and reap your own desire.

HUMPHREY I see this love you speak of, through your daughter,
    Although the hole be little; and hereafter   155
    Will yield the like in all I may or can,
    Fitting a Christian and a gentleman.

MERCHANT I do believe you, my good son, and thank you,
    For 'twere an impudence to think you flattered.

HUMPHREY It were, indeed; but shall I tell you why?   160
    I have been beaten twice about the lie.

MERCHANT Well, son, no more of compliment. My daughter
    Is yours again; appoint the time and take her.
    We'll have no stealing for it; I myself
    And some few of our friends will see you married.   165

HUMPHREY I would you would, i' faith, for, be it known,
    I ever was afraid to lie alone.

MERCHANT Some three days hence, then.

HUMPHREY   Three days! Let me see;
    'Tis somewhat of the most;* yet I agree,   170
    Because I mean against* the appointed day
    To visit all my friends in new array.

(*Enter* SERVANT)

SERVANT Sir, there's a gentlewoman without would speak with your worship.

MERCHANT What is she?   175

SERVANT Sir, I asked her not.

MERCHANT Bid her come in. (*Exit* SERVANT)

(*Enter* MRS. MERRYTHOUGHT *and* MICHAEL)

MRS. MERRYTHOUGHT Peace be to your worship! I come as a poor suitor to
    you, sir, in the behalf of this child.   180

MERCHANT Are you not wife to Merrythought?

MRS. MERRYTHOUGHT Yes, truly. Would I had ne'er seen his eyes! Ha has
    undone me and himself and his children; and there he lives at home, and
    sings and hoits and revels among his drunken companions! But, I warrant

¹⁴⁵ Upstairs.
¹⁴⁶ Relative.
¹⁷⁰ Rather long.
¹⁷¹ In preparation for.

you, where to get a penny to put bread in his mouth he knows not; and 185
therefore, if it like your worship, I would entreat your letter to the honest
host of the Bell in Waltham that I may place my child under the protection
of his tapster, in some settled course of life.

MERCHANT   I'm glad the heavens have heard my prayers. Thy husband,
When I was ripe in sorrows, laughed at me;   190
Thy son, like an unthankful wretch, I having
Redeemed him from his fall, and made him mine,
To show his love again first stole my daughter,
Then wronged this gentleman, and, last of all,
Gave me that grief had almost brought me down   195
Unto my grave, had not a stronger hand
Relieved my sorrows. Go, and weep as I did,
And be unpitied, for I here profess
An everlasting hate to all thy name.

MRS. MERRYTHOUGHT   Will you so, sir? How say you by that?—Come, 200
Mick; let him keep his wind to cool his porridge. We'll go to thy nurse's,
Mick; she knits silk stockings, boy; and we'll knit too, boy, and be behold-
ing to none of them all. (*Exeunt* MICHAEL *and* MOTHER)

(*Enter a* BOY *with a letter*)

BOY   Sir, I take it you are the master of this house.   205
MERCHANT   How then, boy?
BOY   Then to yourself, sir, comes this letter.
MERCHANT   From whom, my pretty boy?
BOY   From him that was your servant; but no more
Shall that name ever be, for he is dead.   210
Grief of your purchased anger* broke his heart.
I saw him die, and from his hand received
This paper, with a charge to bring it hither.
Read it, and satisfy yourself in all.

(*Letter*)   215

MERCHANT   "Sir, that I have wronged your love I must confess, in which I have
purchased to myself, besides mine own undoing, the ill opinion of my friends.
Let not your anger, good sir, outlive me, but suffer me to rest in peace with
your forgiveness. Let my body (if a dying man may so much prevail with you)
be brought to your daughter, that she may truly know my hot flames are 220
now buried, and withal receive a testimony of the zeal I bore her virtue. Farewell forever, and be ever happy!   JASPER."
God's hand is great in this. I do forgive him;
Yet I am glad he's quiet,* where I hope
He will not bite again.—Boy, bring the body,   225
And let him have his will, if that be all.

BOY   'Tis here without, sir.
MERCHANT   So, sir; if you please,
You may conduct it in; I do not fear it.

211 That is, the anger learned from you.
224 Dead.

HUMPHREY I'll be your usher, boy, for, though I say it,   230
    He owed me something once, and well did pay it. (*Exeunt*)
                    (*Enter* LUCE, *alone*)

LUCE If there be any punishment inflicted
    Upon the miserable more than yet I feel,
    Let it together seize me; and at once   235
    Press down my soul! I cannot bear the pain
    Of these delaying tortures.—Thou that art
    The end of all, and the sweet rest of all,
    Come, come, O Death! Bring me to thy peace,
    And blot out all the memory I nourish   240
    Both of my father and my cruel friend!—
    O, wretched maid, still living to be wretched,
    To be a say* to Fortune in her changes,
    And grow to number times and woes together,
    How happy had I been, if, being born,   245
    My grave had been my cradle!
                (*Enter* SERVANT)

SERVANT   By your leave,
    Young mistress, here's a boy hath brought a coffin.
    What a would say, I know not; but your father   250
    Charged me to give you notice. Here they come. (*Exit*)
          (*Enter Two bearing a coffin,* JASPER *in it*)

LUCE For me I hope 'tis come, and 'tis most welcome.

BOY Fair mistress, let me not add greater grief
    To that great store you have already. Jasper   255
    (That whilst he lived was yours, now dead
    And here enclosed) commanded me to bring
    His body hither, and to crave a tear
    From those fair eyes (though he deserved not pity)
    To deck his funeral; for so he bid me   260
    Tell her for whom he died.

LUCE   He shall have many.—
    Good friends, depart a little, whilst I take
    My leave of this dead man that once I loved.
          (*Exeunt* COFFIN CARRIER *and* BOY)   265
    Hold yet a little, life, and then I give thee
    To thy first heavenly being. O, my friend!
    Hast thou deceived me thus, and got before me?
    I shall not long be after. But, believe me,
    Thou wert too cruel, Jasper, gainst thyself,   270
    In punishing the fault I could have pardoned,
    With so untimely death. Thou didst not wrong me,
    But ever wert most kind, most true, most loving;
    And I the most unkind, most false, most cruel!
    Didst thou but ask a tear? I'll give thee all,   275

243 Subject for experiment.

Even all my eyes can pour down, all my sighs,
And all myself, before thou goest from me.
These are but sparing rites; but, if thy soul
Be yet about this place, and can behold
And see what I prepare to deck thee with,   280
It shall go up, borne on the wings of peace,
And satisfied. First will I sing thy dirge,
Then kiss thy pale lips, and then die myself,
And fill one coffin and one grave together.
                            (*Song*)   285

   Come, you whose loves are dead,
     And, whiles I sing,
     Weep and wring
   Every hand, and every head
   Bind with cypress and sad yew;   290
   Ribands black and candles blue
   For him that was of men most true!

   Come with heavy moaning,
     And on his grave
     Let him have   295
   Sacrifice of sighs and groaning;
   Let him have fair flowers enow,
   White and purple, green and yellow,
   For him that was of men most true!

Thou sable cloth, sad cover of my joys,   300
I lift thee up, and thus I meet with death.
    (*Removes the cloth, and* JASPER *rises out of the coffin*)
JASPER And thus you meet the living!
LUCE   Save me, heaven!
JASPER Nay, do not fly me, fair; I am no spirit.   305
Look better on me; do you know me yet?
LUCE O, thou dear shadow* of my friend!
JASPER   Dear substance,
I swear I am no shadow. Feel my hand;
It is the same it was. I am your Jasper,
Your Jasper that's yet living, and yet loving.   310
Pardon my rash attempt, my foolish proof
I put in practice of your constancy;
For sooner should my sword have drunk my blood,
And set my soul at liberty, than drawn
The least drop from that body, for which boldness   315
Doom me to anything; if death, I take it,
And willingly.
LUCE   This death I'll give you for it. (*Kisses him*)
   ³⁰⁷ Ghost.

So, now I am satisfied you are no spirit,   320
But my own truest, truest, truest friend.
Why do you come thus to me?
JASPER   First, to see you;
    Then to convey you hence.
LUCE   It cannot be;   325
    For I am locked up here, and watched at all hours,
    That 'tis impossible for me to scape.
JASPER Nothing more possible. Within this coffin
    Do you convey yourself. Let me alone;
    I have the wits of twenty men about me;   330
    Only I crave the shelter of your closet*
    A little, and then fear me* not. Creep in,
    That they may presently convey you hence.
    Fear nothing, dearest love; I'll be your second.
            (LUCE *places herself in the coffin and* JASPER *puts the cloth over her*)   335
    Lie close. So; all goes well yet.—Boy!
                    (*Enter* COFFIN CARRIER *and* BOY)
BOY   At hand, sir.
JASPER Convey away the coffin, and be wary.
BOY 'Tis done already. (*Exeunt* COFFIN CARRIER *and* BOY *with the coffin*)   340
JASPER   Now must I go conjure. (*Exit*)
                    (*Enter* MERCHANT)
MERCHANT Boy, boy!
                    (*Enter* BOY)
BOY Your servant, sir.   345
MERCHANT Do me this kindness, boy. Hold, here's a crown. Before thou bury
    the body of this fellow, carry it to his old merry father, and salute him from
    me, and bid him sing; he hath cause.
BOY I will, sir.
MERCHANT And then bring me word what tune he is in, and have another   350
    crown; but do it truly. I have fitted him a bargain now will vex him.
BOY God bless your worship's health, sir!
MERCHANT Farewell, boy. (*Exeunt*)

Scene 4

                    Before MERRYTHOUGHT'S *house*
                    (*Enter* MASTER MERRYTHOUGHT)   355
WIFE Ah, old Merrythought, art thou there again? Let's hear some of thy songs.

OLD MERRYTHOUGHT (*Singing*)   Who can sing a merrier note
                        Than he that cannot change a groat?
    Not a denier* left, and yet my heart leaps! I do wonder yet, as old as I am,
    that any man will follow a trade, or serve, that may sing and laugh, and   360

331 Private room.
332 That is, fear not for me.
359 Penny.

walk the streets. My wife and both my sons are I know not where; I have nothing left, nor know I how to come by meat to supper; yet am I merry still, for I know I shall find it upon the table at six a-clock; therefore, hang thought!

(*Sings*) I would not be a serving-man 365
      To carry the cloak bag still,
    Nor would I be a falconer
      The greedy hawks to fill;
    But I would be in a good house,
      And have a good master too; 370
    But I would eat and drink of the best,
      And no work would I do.

This is it that keeps life and soul together—mirth; this is the philosophers' stone that they write so much on, that keeps a man ever young.

(*Enter a* BOY) 375

BOY Sir, they say they know all your money is gone, and they will trust you for no more drink.

OLD MERRYTHOUGHT Will they not? Let 'em choose! The best is, I have mirth at home, and need not send abroad for that. Let them keep their drink to themselves. 380

(*Sings*) For Jillian of Berry, she dwells on a hill,
    And she hath good beer and ale to sell,
    And of good fellows she thinks no ill;
      And thither will we go now, now, now, now,
      And thither will we go now. 385

    And, when you have made a little stay,
    You need not ask what is to pay,
    But kiss your hostess, and go your way;
      And thither, etc.

(*Enter another* BOY) 390

2ND BOY Sir, I can get no bread for supper.

OLD MERRYTHOUGHT Hang bread and supper! Let's preserve our mirth, and we shall never feel hunger, I'll warrant you. Let's have a catch. Boy, follow me; come, sing this catch.

      Ho, ho, nobody at home! 395
    Meat, nor drink, nor money ha' we none.
      Fill the pot, Eedy,
      Never more need I.

So, boys, enough. Follow me. Let's change our place, and we shall laugh afresh.

(*Exeunt*) 400

WIFE Let him go, George; a shall not have any countenance from us, nor a good word from any i' th' company, if I may strike stroke in 't.*

CITIZEN No more a sha' not, love. But, Nell, I will have Rafe do a very notable

---

402 That is, have anything to do with it.

matter now, to the eternal honor and glory of all grocers.—Sirrah! You there, boy! Can none of you hear? 405

(Enter BOY)

BOY Sir, your pleasure?

CITIZEN Let Rafe come out on May Day in the morning, and speak upon a conduit,* with all his scarfs about him, and his feathers, and his rings, and his knacks. 410

BOY Why, sir, you do not think of our plot; what will become of that, then?

CITIZEN Why, sir, I care not what become on 't. I'll have him come out, or I'll fetch him out myself; I'll have something done in honor of the city. Besides, he hath been long enough upon adventures. Bring him out quickly; or, if I come in amongst you— 415

BOY Well, sir, he shall come out, but if our play miscarry, sir, you are like to pay for 't. (*Exit* BOY)

CITIZEN Bring him away then!

WIFE This will be brave, i' faith! George, shall not he dance the morris* too, for the credit of the Strand? 420

CITIZEN No, sweetheart, it will be too much for the boy. O, there he is, Nell! He's reasonable well in reparel; but he has not rings enough.

(*Enter* RAFE *dressed as the Lord of the May*)

RAFE London, to thee I do present the merry month of May;
Let each true subject be content to hear me what I say. 425
For from the top of conduit head, as plainly may appear,
I will both tell my name to you, and wherefore I came here.
My name is Rafe, by due descent though not ignoble I,
Yet far inferior to the flock of gracious grocery;
And by the common counsel of my fellows in the Strand, 430
With gilded staff and crossed scarf, the May Lord here I stand.
Rejoice, O English hearts, rejoice! Rejoice, O lovers dear!
Rejoice, O city, town, and country! Rejoice, eke every shire!
For now the fragrant flowers do spring and sprout in seemly sort,
The little birds do sit and sing, the lambs do make fine sport; 435
And now the birchen tree doth bud, that makes the schoolboy cry;
The morris rings, while hobbyhorse* doth foot it featously;*
The lords and ladies now abroad, for their disport and play,
Do kiss sometimes upon the grass, and sometimes in the hay;
Now butter with a leaf of sage is good to purge the blood; 440
Fly Venus and phlebotomy,* for they are neither good;
Now little fish on tender stone begin to cast their bellies,*
And sluggish snails, that erst were mewed,* do creep out of their shellies;
The rumbling rivers now do warm, for little boys to paddle;
The sturdy steed now goes to grass, and up they hang his saddle; 445

409 Actually, a conduit-head, one of the cisterns at which water was drawn in the city.
419 A grotesque dance using fancy costumes.
437 (*a*) A horse-figure strapped to a morris-performer. (*b*) Expertly.
441 Blood-letting.
442 Spawn.
443 Shut up.

The heavy hart, the bellowing buck, the rascal, and the pricket*
Are now among the yeoman's peas, and leave the fearful thicket.
And be like them, O you, I say, of this same noble town,
And lift aloft your velvet heads, and, slipping off your gown,
With bells on legs, and napkins* clean unto your shoulders tied,   450
With scarfs and garters as you please, and "Hey for our town!"* cried,
March out, and show your willing minds, by twenty and by twenty,
To Hogsdon or to Newington,* where ale and cakes are plenty;
And let it ne'er be said for shame that we, the youths of London,
Lay thrumming of our caps* at home, and left our custom undone.   455
Up, then, I say, both young and old, both man and maid a-maying,
With drums and guns that bounce* aloud, and merry tabor playing!
Which to prolong, God save our king, and send his country peace,
And root out treason from the land! And so, my friends, I cease. (*Exit*)

Act Five

Scene 1

A room in VENTUREWELL'S house
(*Enter* MERCHANT, *alone*)

MERCHANT   I will have no great store of company at the wedding—a couple of
neighbors and their wives; and we will have a capon in stewed broth, with
marrow, and a good piece of beef stuck with rosemary.   5

(*Enter* JASPER, *his face mealed**)

JASPER   Forbear thy pains, fond man! It is too late.

MERCHANT   Heaven bless me! Jasper?

JASPER   Ay, I am his ghost,
Whom thou hast injured for his constant love;
Fond worldly wretch, who dost not understand   10
In death that true hearts cannot parted be!
First, know thy daughter is quite borne away
On wings of angels, through the liquid air,
To far out of thy reach, and never more
Shalt thou behold her face; but she and I   15
Will in another world enjoy our loves,
Where neither father's anger, poverty,
Nor any cross that troubles earthly men
Shall make us sever our united hearts.
And never shalt thou sit or be alone   20
In any place, but I will visit thee

446 The inferior deer of the herd and the young buck.
450 Handkerchiefs.
451 A cry in the morris dance.
453 Villages north of London.
455 That is, trifling.
457 Boom.
6 That is, whitened with flour in the fashion of stage-ghosts.

With ghastly looks, and put into thy mind
The great offenses which thou didst to me.
When thou art at thy table with thy friends, 25
Merry in heart, and filled with swelling wine,
I'll come in midst of all thy pride and mirth,
Invisible to all men but thyself,
And whisper such a sad tale in thine ear
Shall make thee let the cup fall from thy hand, 30
And stand as mute and pale as Death itself.

MERCHANT Forgive me, Jasper! O, what might I do,
Tell me, to satisfy thy troubled ghost?

JASPER There is no means; too late thou think'st of this.

MERCHANT But tell me what were best for me to do? 35

JASPER Repent thy deed, and satisfy my father,
And beat fond Humphrey out of thy doors. (*Exit* JASPER)
(*Enter* HUMPHREY)

WIFE Look, George; his very ghost would have folks beaten.

HUMPHREY Father, my bride is gone, fair Mistress Luce; 40
My soul's the fount of vengeance, mischief's sluice.*

MERCHANT Hence, fool, out of my sight; with thy fond passion
Thou hast undone me. (*Beats him*)

HUMPHREY   Hold, my father dear,
For Luce thy daughter's sake, that had no peer! 45

MERCHANT Thy father, fool? There's some blows more; begone.—(*Beats him*)
Jasper, I hope thy ghost be well appeased
To see thy will performed. Now will I go
To satisfy thy father for thy wrongs. (*Exit*)

HUMPHREY What shall I do? I have been beaten twice, 50
And Mistress Luce is gone. Help me, device!
Since my true love is gone, I never more,
Whilst I do live, upon the sky will pore,
But in the dark will wear out my shoe soles
In passion in Saint Faith's Church under Paul's.* (*Exit*) 55

WIFE George, call Rafe hither; if you love me, call Rafe hither. I have the
bravest* thing for him to do, George; prithee, call him quickly.

CITIZEN Rafe! Why, Rafe, boy!
(*Enter* RAFE)

RAFE Here, sir. 60

CITIZEN Come hither, Rafe; come to thy mistress, boy.

WIFE Rafe, I would have thee call all the youths together in battle ray,* with
drums, and guns, and flags, and march to Mile End in pompous fashion, and

41 Channel or drain.
55 That is, near St. Paul's Cathedral.
57 Finest.
62 Array.

there exhort your soldiers to be merry and wise, and to keep their beards from
burning, Rafe; and then skirmish, and let your flags fly, and cry, "Kill, kill, 65
kill!" My husband shall lend you his jerkin,* Rafe, and there's a scarf; for the
rest, the house shall furnish you, and we'll pay for 't. Do it bravely, Rafe;
and think before whom you perform, and what person you represent.

RAFE   I warrant you, mistress; if I do it not for the honor of the city and the
credit of my master, let me never hope for freedom!*   70

WIFE   'Tis well spoken, i' faith. Go thy ways; thou art a spark* indeed.

CITIZEN   Rafe, Rafe, double your files bravely, Rafe!

RAFE   I warrant you, sir. (*Exit* RAFE)

CITIZEN   Let him look narrowly to his service;* I shall take him else. I was there
myself a pikeman once, in the hottest of the day, wench, had my feather 75
shot sheer away, the fringe of my pike burnt off with powder, my pate broken
with a scouring stick,* and yet, I thank God, I am here. (*Drum within*)

WIFE   Hark, George, the drums!

CITIZEN   Ran, tan, tan, tan: ran, tan! O, wench, an thou hadst but seen little Ned
of Algate, Drum* Ned, how he made it roar again, and laid on like a 80
tyrant, and then stroke softly till the ward* came up, and then thundered
again, and together we go! "Sa, sa, sa, bounce!" quoth the guns; "Courage,
my hearts!" quoth the captains; "Saint George!" quoth the pikemen; and
withal, here they lay, and there they lay. And yet for all this I am here, wench.

WIFE   Be thankful for it, George, for indeed 'tis wonderful.   85

Scene 2

(*Enter* RAFE *and his Company with drums and colors*)

RAFE   March fair, my hearts! Lieutenant, beat the rear up.—Ancient,* let your
colors fly; but have a great care of the butchers' hooks at Whitechapel; they
have been the death of many a fair ancient.—Open your files that I may take
a view both of your persons and munition.—Sergeant, call a muster.   90

SERGEANT   A stand!*—William Hammerton, pewterer?

HAMMERTON   Here, captain.

RAFE   A corselet and a Spanish pike; 'tis well. Can you shake it with a terror?

HAMMERTON   I hope so, captain.

RAFE   Charge upon me. (*He charges on* RAFE) 'Tis with the weakest; put more 95
strength, William Hammerton, more strength. As you were, again!—Proceed, sergeant.

SERGEANT   George Greengoose, poulterer?

GREENGOOSE   Here.

RAFE   Let me see your piece,* Neighbor Greengoose. When was she shot in? 100

66 Close-fitting jacket.
70 That is, full membership in the Grocers' Company.
71 Elegant young man.
74 Drill.   77 Ramrod.
80 Drummer.
81 The troops from his ward.
87 Ensign or standard-bearer.
91 Halt!   100 Musket.

GREENGOOSE And 't like you, Master Captain, I made a shot even now, partly to scour her, and partly for audacity.

RAFE It should seem so certainly, for her breath is yet inflamed; besides, there is a main* fault in the touchhole—it runs and stinketh; and I tell you, moreover, and believe it, ten such touchholes would breed the pox in the army. 105 Get you a feather,* neighbor, get you a feather, sweet oil, and paper, and your piece may do well enough yet. Where's your powder?

GREENGOOSE Here.

RAFE What, in a paper? As I am a soldier and a gentleman, it craves a martial court!* You ought to die for 't. Where's your horn? Answer me to that. 110

GREENGOOSE An 't like you, sir, I was oblivious.

RAFE It likes me not you should be so; 'tis a shame for you, and a scandal to all our neighbors, being a man of worth and estimation, to leave your horn behind you; I am afraid 'twill breed example. But let me tell you no more on 't.—Stand, till I view you all. What's become o' th' nose of your flask? 115

1ST SOLDIER Indeed-law, captain, 'twas blown away with powder.

RAFE Put on a new one at the city's charge.—Where's the stone* of this piece?

2ND SOLDIER The drummer took it out to light tobacco.

RAFE 'Tis a fault, my friend; put it in again.—You want a nose, and you a stone. —Sergeant, take a note on 't, for I mean to stop it in the pay—Remove, 120 and march! (*They march*) Soft and fair, gentlemen, soft and fair! Double your files! As you were! Faces about! Now, you with the sodden* face, keep in there! Look to your match, sirrah; it will be in your fellow's flask anon! So; make a crescent now! Advance your pikes! Stand and give ear!—Gentlemen, countrymen, friends, and my fellow soldiers, I have brought you this day 125 from the shops of security and the counters of content to measure out in these furious fields honor by the ell* and prowess by the pound. Let it not, O, let it not, I say, be told hereafter, the noble issue of this city fainted; but bear yourselves in this fair action like men, valiant men, and free men! Fear not the face of the enemy, nor the noise of the guns, for, believe me, brethren, 130 the rude rumbling of a brewer's car is far more terrible, of which you have a daily experience; neither let the stink of powder offend you, since a more valiant stink is nightly with you. To a resolved mind his home is everywhere. I speak not this to take away the hope of your return, for you shall see (I do not doubt it), and that very shortly, your loving wives again and your 135 sweet children, whose care doth bear you company in baskets.* Remember, then, whose cause you have in hand, and, like a sort* of true-born scavengers, scour me this famous realm of enemies. I have no more to say but this: stand to your tacklings,* lads, and show to the world you can as well brandish a sword as shake an apron. Saint George, and on, my hearts! 140

---

104 Serious.

106 A shaft for cleaning a musket bore.

110 Deserves a courtmartial.

117 Flint.

122 Soaked with intoxicants.

127 A measure of length.

136 Perhaps lunch baskets.

137 Company.   139 That is, hold your ground.

OMNES   St. George, St. George! (*Exeunt*)

WIFE   'Twas well done, Rafe! I'll send thee a cold capon afield and a bottle of March beer, and, it may be, come myself to see thee.

CITIZEN   Nell, the boy has deceived me much; I did not think it had been in him. He has performed such a matter, wench, that, if I live, next year I'll have 145 him captain of the galley foist* or I'll want my will.

Scene 3

A room in MERRYTHOUGHT'S *house*
(*Enter* OLD MERRYTHOUGHT)

OLD MERRYTHOUGHT   Yet, I thank God, I break not a wrinkle more than I had, not a stoop, boys! Care, live with cats; I defy thee! My heart is as sound 150 as an oak; and, though I want drink to wet my whistle, I can sing.

(*Sings*)   Come no more there, boys, come no more there,
            For we shall never whilst we live come any more there.

(*Enter a* BOY *and a* COFFIN CARRIER *with a coffin*)

BOY   God save you, sir!   155

OLD MERRYTHOUGHT   It's a brave boy. Canst thou sing?

BOY   Yes, sir, I can sing; but 'tis not so necessary at this time.

OLD MERRYTHOUGHT (*Singing*)   Sing we, and chant it,
                                    Whilst love doth grant it.

BOY   Sir, sir, if you knew what I have brought you, you would have little list 160 to sing.

OLD MERRYTHOUGHT (*Singing*)   O, the Mimon round,
                              Full long, long I have thee sought,
                              And now I have thee found,
                              And what hast thou here brought?   165

BOY   A coffin, sir, and your dead son Jasper in it. (*Exit with* COFFIN CARRIER)

OLD MERRYTHOUGHT   Dead? Why, farewell he!
   (*Sings*)   Thou wast a bonny boy, and I did love thee.

(*Enter* JASPER)

JASPER   Then, I pray you, sir, do so still.

OLD MERRYTHOUGHT   Jasper's ghost?   170
   (*Sings*)   Thou art welcome from Stygian lake so soon;
              Declare to me what wondrous things in Pluto's court are done.

JASPER   By my troth, sir, I ne'er came there; 'tis too hot for me, sir.

OLD MERRYTHOUGHT   A merry ghost, a very merry ghost!   175
   (*Sings*)   And where is your true love? O, where is yours?

JASPER   Marry, look you, sir! (*Heaves up the coffin, and* LUCE *steps forth*)

OLD MERRYTHOUGHT   Ah, ha! Art thou good at that, i' faith?
   (*Sings*)   With hey, trixy, terlery-whiskin,
              The world it runs on wheels;
              When the young man's——,   180
              Up goes the maiden's heels.

---

146 Barge used in the Lord Mayor's procession.

(MRS. MERRYTHOUGHT *and* MICHAEL *within*)

MRS. MERRYTHOUGHT   What, Mr. Merrythought, will you not let 's in? What do you think shall become of us?   185

OLD MERRYTHOUGHT (*Singing*)   What voice is that, that calleth at our door?

MRS. MERRYTHOUGHT   You know me well enough; I am sure I have not been such a stranger to you.

OLD MERRYTHOUGHT (*Singing*)   And some they whistled, and some they sung,
    "Hey, down, down!"   190
    And some did loudly say,
Ever as the Lord Barnet's horn blew,
    "Away, Musgrave, away!"

MRS. MERRYTHOUGHT   You will not have us starve here, will you, Mr. Merry-thought?   195

JASPER   Nay, good sir, be persuaded; she is my mother. If her offenses have been great against you, let your own love remember she is yours, and so forgive her.

LUCE   Good Mr. Merrythought, let me entreat you; I will not be denied.

MRS. MERRYTHOUGHT   Why, Mr. Merrythought, will you be a vexed thing   200 still?

OLD MERRYTHOUGHT   Woman, I take you to my love again; but you shall sing before you enter; therefore despatch your song and so come in.

MRS. MERRYTHOUGHT   Well, you must have your will, when all's done.—Mick, what song canst thou sing, boy?   205

MICHAEL   I can sing none, forsooth, but "A lady's daughter of Paris properly."
                        (*Song*)

MRS. MERRYTHOUGHT *and* MICHAEL   It was a lady's daughter, etc.

    (MERRYTHOUGHT *opens the door and* MRS. MERRYTHOUGHT *and* MICHAEL
                        enter)   210

OLD MERRYTHOUGHT   Come, you're welcome home again.
    (*Sings*)   If such danger be in playing,
            And jest must to earnest turn,
        You shall go no more a-maying—

MERCHANT (*Within*)   Are you within, sir, Master Merrythought?   215

JASPER   It is my master's voice! Good sir, go hold him in talk, whilst we convey ourselves into some inward room. (*Exit with* LUCE)

OLD MERRYTHOUGHT   What are you? Are you merry? You must be very merry, if you enter.

MERCHANT   I am, sir.   220

OLD MERRYTHOUGHT   Sing, then.

MERCHANT   Nay, good sir, open to me.

OLD MERRYTHOUGHT   Sing, I say, or, by the merry heart, you come not in!

MERCHANT   Well, sir, I'll sing.
    (*Sings*)   Fortune, my foe, etc.   225
        (MERRYTHOUGHT *opens the door and* VENTUREWELL *enters*)

OLD MERRYTHOUGHT   You are welcome, sir; you are welcome. You see your entertainment; pray you, be merry.

MERCHANT   O, Mr. Merrythought, I'm come to ask you
    Forgiveness for the wrongs I offered you
    And your most virtuous son! They're infinite;   230
    Yet my contrition shall be more than they.
    I do confess my hardness broke his heart,
    For which just heaven hath given me punishment
    More than my age can carry. His wand'ring spirit,   235
    Not yet at rest, pursues me everywhere,
    Crying, "I'll haunt thee for thy cruelty."
    My daugther, she is gone, I know not how,
    Taken invisible, and whether living
    Or in grave, 'tis yet uncertain to me.   240
    O, Master Merrythought, these are the weights
    Will sink me to my grave! Forgive me, sir.
OLD MERRYTHOUGHT   Why, sir, I do forgive you; and be merry.
    And, if the wag in 's lifetime played the knave,
    Can you forgive him too?   245
MERCHANT   With all my heart, sir.
OLD MERRYTHOUGHT   Speak it again, and heartly.
MERCHANT   I do, sir.
    Now, by my soul, I do.
OLD MERRYTHOUGHT (*Singing*)   With that came out his paramour;   250
                                    She was as white as the lily flower.
                                        Hey, troll, trolly, lolly!
                            (*Enter* LUCE *and* JASPER)
                                    With that came out her own dear knight;
                                    He was as true as ever did fight, etc.   255
    Sir, if you will forgive him, clap their hands together; there's no more to be
    said i' th' matter.
MERCHANT   I do, I do.

CITIZEN   I do not like this! Peace, boys! Hear me, one of you! Everybody's part
    is come to an end but Rafe's, and he's left out.   260
BOY   'Tis long of yourself, sir; we have nothing to do with his part.
CITIZEN   Rafe, come away!—Make on him, as you have done of the rest; boys,
    come.
WIFE   Now, good husband, let him come out and die.
CITIZEN   He shall, Nell.—Rafe, come away quickly, and die, boy!   265
BOY   'Twill be very unfit he should die, sir, upon no occasion—and in a comedy
    too.
CITIZEN   Take you no care of that, Sir Boy; is not his part at an end, think you,
    when he's dead?—Come away, Rafe!
            (*Enter* RAFE, *with a forked arrow through his head*)   270
RAFE*   When I was mortal, this my costive corpse
    Did lap up figs and raisins in the Strand,

---

[271] Much of the following speech is a parody of the opening speech of Andrea's ghost in *The Spanish Tragedy*.

Where, sitting, I espied a lovely dame,
Whose master wrought with lingel* and with awl,*
And underground he vampied* many a boot.   275
Straight did her love prick forth me, tender sprig,
To follow feats of arms in warlike wise
Through Waltham Desert, where I did perform
Many achievements, and did lay on ground
Huge Barbaroso, that insulting giant,   280
And all his captives soon set at liberty.
Then honor pricked me from my native soil
Into Moldavia, where I gained the love
Of Pompiona, his beloved daughter;
But yet proved constant to the black-thumbed maid,   285
Susan, and scorned Pompiona's love;
Yet liberal I was, and gave her pins,
And money for her father's officers.
I then returned home, and thrust myself
In action, and by all men chosen was   290
Lord of the May, where I did flourish it,
With scarfs and rings, and posy in my hand.
After this action I preferred was,
And chosen city captain at Mile End,
With hat and feather, and with leading staff,   295
And trained my men, and brought them all off clear,
Save one man that berayed* him with the noise.
But all these things I, Rafe, did undertake
Only for my beloved Susan's sake.
Then coming home, and sitting in my shop   300
With apron blue, Death came into my stall
To cheapen* *aqua vitæ;* but ere I
Could take the bottle down and fill a taste,
Death caught a pound of pepper in his hand,
And sprinkled all my face and body o'er,   305
And in an instant vanished away.

CITIZEN   'Tis a pretty fiction, i' faith.

RAFE   Then took I up my bow and shaft in hand,
And walked into Moorfields* to cool myself;
But there grim cruel Death met me again,   310
And shot this forked arrow through my head.
And now I faint. Therefore be warned by me,

274 (a) Shoemaker's waxed thread.   (b) A sharp piercing instrument.
275 Patched.
297 Befouled.
302 Bargain for.
309 A marsh south of London.

My fellows every one, of forked heads!
Farewell, all you good boys in merry London!
Ne'er shall we more upon Shrove Tuesday* meet, 315
And pluck down houses of iniquity.—
My pain increaseth—I shall never more
Hold open, whilst another pumps both legs,
Nor daub a satin gown with rotten eggs;
Set up a stake,* O, never more I shall! 320
I die! Fly, fly, my soul, to Grocers' Hall!
O, O, O, etc.

WIFE Well said, Rafe! Do your obeisance to the gentlemen, and go your ways. Well said, Rafe! (*Exit* RAFE)

OLD MERRYTHOUGHT Methinks all we, thus kindly and unexpectedly recon- 325 ciled, should not depart without a song.
MERCHANT A good motion.
OLD MERRYTHOUGHT Strike up, then!

(*Song*)

Better music ne'er was known 330
Than a choir of hearts in one.
Let each other that hath been
Troubled with the gall or spleen
Learn of us to keep his brow
Smooth and plain, as ours are now. 335
Sing, though before the hour of dying;
He shall rise, and then be crying,
"Hey, ho, 'tis naught but mirth
That keeps the body from the earth!" (*Exeunt omnes*)

Epilogus

CITIZEN Come, Nell, shall we go? The play's done.
WIFE Nay, by my faith, George, I have more manners than so; I'll speak to these gentlemen first.—I thank you all, gentlemen, for your patience and countenance to Rafe, a poor fatherless child; and, if I might see you at my house, it should go hard but I would have a pottle* of wine and a pipe of tabacco for 5 you; for, truly, I hope you do like the youth, but I would be glad to know the truth. I refer it to your own discretions, whether you will applaud him or no, for I will wink, and whilst* you shall do what you will. I thank you with all my heart. God give you good night!—Come, George. (*Exeunt*)

---

315 On Shrove Tuesday the apprentices used to celebrate by looting the brothels.
320 To which cocks were tied for target practice.
5 Bottle.
8 In the meantime.

Lope Felix de Vega Carpio

Lope Felix de Vega Carpio (1562–1635), *Spain's greatest dramatist, wrote more than 1000, perhaps more than 1500 plays in the course of his prolific career. A writer of prodigious energy and facile brilliance, he tried his hand at all the dramatic forms known to his age and excelled at all. His best known plays, however, consist of a reasonably small group of* comedias, *the term used to describe the three-act structure which, depending on subject matter and emphasis, might be a tragedy, a comedy, or a melodrama. At a typical theatrical performance in Spain during the Golden Age, the* comedia *was the principal offering of the afternoon; Lope's* FUENTE OVEJUNA, *a social drama;* JUSTICE WITHOUT REVENGE, *an "honor" play; and* THE IDIOT LADY, *a comedy, rank with the best. In addition to his genius for contriving plots, Lope's skill with the intricate verse forms of Spanish drama established him as a major poet of his age.*

Chronology

1562 Born in Madrid.

1575–81 Studied at the Theatine College in Madrid; sent to the University of Alcala by his patron, the Bishop of Avila.

1582 Took part in the Azores expedition.

1583–87 Secretary to the Marquis de las Navas.

1588 Banished for circulating libels against his mistress Elena Osorio. The same year he returned to Madrid, defying the law, and eloped with Isabel de Urbina. Later that year, he sailed with the Armada.

c.1590–95 Joined the household of the Duke of Alva. His wife died.

1596 Prosecuted for criminal conversation; became secretary to the Marquis de Malpica.

1598 Married a second time and had two children by his second wife.

1605 The Duke of Sessa became his patron.

1613 Death of his second wife; de Vega ordained; wrote *The Idiot Lady.*

1614 Wrote *Peribañez;* the probable year of *Fuente Ovejuna.*

1615–26 Period of *The Knight from Olmedo,* among many others.

1620–23 Period of *The King, The Greatest Alcade.*

1627 Pope Urban VIII awarded him the diploma of Doctor of Theology and the Cross of the Order of St. John of Jerusalem.

1631 Wrote *Justice Without Revenge.*

1635 Died.

Selected Bibliography

Casalduero, Joaquin, "*Fuenteovejuna:* Form and Meaning," *Tulane Drama Review,* IV (1959), 83–107.

Flores, Angel, *Lope de Vega, Monster of Nature,* New York, 1930.

McCrary, William C., "*Fuenteovejuna:* Its Platonic Vision and Execution," *Studies in Philology,* LVIII (1961), 179–192.

Pring-Mill, R. D. F., "Sententiousness in *Fuente Ovejuna*," *Tulane Drama Review,* VII (1962), 5–37.

Rennert, H. A. *The Life of Lope de Vega,* Philadelphia, 1904.

Schevill, Rudolph, *The Dramatic Art of Lope de Vega,* Berkeley, Calif., 1918.

A Spanish *corral* theater,
in the courtyard (*corral*)
formed by adjoining houses.

FUENTE OVEJUNA

by Lope de Vega

English Version by Roy Campbell

Characters

QUEEN ISABEL (ISABELA) OF CASTILE

HER HUSBAND, KING FERNANDO (FERDINAND) OF ARAGÓN

RODRIGO TÉLLEZ GIRÓN, *Master of the Order of Calatrava**

FERNÁN (ERNANDO) GÓMEZ DE GUZMÁN, *Comendador of the Order of Calatrava*

ORTUÑO
FLORES *his servants*

DON MANRIQUE, *Master of the Order of Santiago*

A JUDGE

TWO ALDERMEN OF CIUDAD REAL*

AN ALDERMAN OF FUENTE OVEJUNA*

ESTEBAN
ALONSO *mayors of Fuente Ovejuna*

LAURENCIA
JACINTA *peasant women*
PASCUALA

JUAN ROJO
FRONDOSO
BARRILDO *peasants*
MENGO

LEONELO, *a student of law*

CIMBRANOS, *a soldier*

MUSICIANS

ATTENDANTS

PEASANTS AND PEASANT WOMEN

SOLDIERS

* *Order of Calatrava:* Much that is noblest in Spanish history traces to the great military and religious orders organized in the latter part of the twelfth century on the model of the monastic orders established during the crusades, and chief among these were the Orders of Calatrava, Santiago, and Alcantara. The headquarters for the Order of Calatrava was a fortress in southern Castile, or south-central Spain; after 1400 its insignia was the Red Cross of St. George. The headquarters for the Order of Santiago was Santiago in the northwestern corner of Spain; its insignia was the badge of St. James, a red cross "carved like a lily" on a white mantle.

* *Ciudad Real:* The "Royal City"; located in south-central Castile, roughly between Toledo and Cordoba. At the time of the action of the play the Iberian peninsula consisted of three main strips of territory: Portugal in the west, Castile running the length of the peninsula in the center, and Aragon in the east. Granada was located on a strip of territory in the south along the Mediterranean and was still under Moorish rule.

* *Fuente:* Means fountain or well; *ovejuna* means pertaining to sheep. The town is located in southern Castile, northwest of Cordoba.

Act One

The house of the Master of Calatrava in Almagro
(*Enter the* COMENDADOR, FLORES, ORTUÑO)

COMENDADOR   The Master knows I'm here in town?

FLORES   He knows
Already.

ORTUÑO   He gets more serious, as he grows.

COMENDADOR   But does he know that it is I, Fernán   5
Gómez de Guzmán?

FLORES   He's not yet a man.
Do not be shocked.

COMENDADOR   My name he may ignore
But not my rank of Grand Comendador!   10

ORTUÑO   He has advisers who abet his pride
In setting common courtesy aside.

COMENDADOR   Then he will win but little love, for still
Courtesy is the key to men's good will.
Stupid discourtesy's the key to naught   15
But hate.

ORTUÑO   If a discourteous man but thought
How all must come to hate him in the end
Although to kiss his shoe they now contend—
He would prefer to die than be like this.   20

FLORES   How sickening and importunate it is
To suffer such discourtesy! In men
Of equal rank, it's foolishness, but when
Their rank's unequal, it becomes a curse,
And smacks of arrant tyranny or worse.   25
But you can well ignore a slight like this
From one too young even to've known the kiss
Of women.

COMENDADOR   But the sword he buckled on
The day the cross of Calatrava shone   30
First on his breast conferred the obligation
Of courtesy.

FLORES   If in his estimation
You have been slandered, you will soon find out.

ORTUÑO   You still can go, if you are still in doubt.   35

COMENDADOR   It is a question I would fain decide.
(*Enter the* MASTER OF CALATRAVA *with his train of* ATTENDANTS)

MASTER   Your pardon, on my life! Fernando Gómez!
I've only just been told you were in town.

COMENDADOR   With much good reason I had cause to frown   40
Thinking you slighted me, since mutual love
And noble birth should raise us both above
Such wrangling thoughts. You're Master of the Order.

                                          I, Gómez, am your Grand Comendador
                                          And very faithful servant ever more.   45

MASTER I little guessed; I had no news of you.
                                          Welcome! Embrace me!

COMENDADOR   It is but my due
                                          That you should honour me: I risked my life
                                          On your behalf so often in the strife   50
                                          Ere the Pope raised you to this lofty rank,
                                          Waiving your youth.

MASTER   It's you I have to thank,
                                          That's true; and by the holy sign across
                                          Our breasts, I shall repay your toil and loss   55
                                          With my esteem, and as a father, too,
                                          Shall honour you.

COMENDADOR   I'm now content with you.

MASTER What tidings of the war?

COMENDADOR   Hear what I say   60
                                          And learn how much you owe me.

MASTER   Tell me, pray.

COMENDADOR Grand Master of the cross of Calatrava,
                                          Raised by the valour of a famous father
                                          To that high station! He, eight years ago,   65
                                          In favour of yourself renounced his Mastership.*
                                          This was confirmed and sworn by kings and captains
                                          For greater surety. The most Holy Pontiff,
                                          Pius the Second, sent some Bulls, and others
                                          Were sent thereafter by Pope Paul, appointing   70
                                          That Juan Pacheco, Master of the Order
                                          Of Santiago, should share equal rank
                                          As your coadjutor. He died; and you,
                                          Despite your tender years, were given sole
                                          Dominion. You must realise your honour   75
                                          Depends in such a case on serving truly
                                          The cause of your great House. Hear how things stand:
                                          Upon the death of Henry of Castile,*
                                          Alfonso, King of Portugal, laid claim
                                          To Henry's title—Joan, Alfonso's wife,   80
                                          Is Henry's daughter. A like claim is made,
                                          Though with less obvious right to your allegiance,
                                          By Ferdinand of Aragón who cites
                                          His marriage to Castilian Isabel.
                                          Your House, great sir, supports Alfonso's claim.   85

---

66 Rodrigo's father was Pedro Girón II, and in the story of his transfer of the mastership of the Order of
   Calatrava to Rodrigo which follows the Popes mentioned are Pius II (1458–64) and Paul II (1467–71).
78 This is Henry IV of Castile (1454–74) and Alfonso V of Portugal (1438–81). Ferdinand of Aragon
   (1452–1504) bases his claim to Castile on the fact that his wife, Isabela (1474–1504), was Henry IV's
   sister.

Your cousin, as it happens, holds this Joan
Fast in his power . . . My advice is this:
To summon all the Knights of Calatrava
With those here of Almagro, and to capture
Ciudad Real, the city on the frontier   90
Dividing Andalusia from Castile.
Few forces will be needed. As their soldiers
They only have the natives of the place
And some few gentry who support the cause
Of Isabela and King Ferdinand.   95
It steads you now to make the whole world ring
And stun the misbelief of all beholders
Who deem your cross too broad for the slim shoulders
Of such a child as you are. Think of them—
Urueña's mighty counts* from whom you stem   100
And how from forth their tombs, to urge your quarrel,
They show the garlands of unwithering laurel
They won in life! Think of Villena's lords*
And other captains famous for their swords,
Too many for the wings of Fame to bear!   105
Remember them. Your pure, white blade make bare,
Which you must stain the colour of the sign
That spans with crimson cross your chest and mine—
Since Master of the red cross or its knight
No man can be while yet his sword is white!   110
Both cross and sword in scarlet must be dyed
One on your breast, the other at your side,
And you, the sovereign of your deathless line,
Must as the dome upon their temple shine!

MASTER Fernando Gómez, rest assured, I'll fight   115
This quarrel for my lineage and my right,
And, when the city to my conquest falls,
Like forked, red lightning, scorch its battered walls.
So, though my uncle's dead,* the world may know
That in my veins his deeds of valour flow,   120
And, when I draw my sword, its silver flare
Shall flush as crimson as the cross I wear!
But tell me how you're settled now, and where,
And have you any soldiers quartered there?

COMENDADOR But few; yet trained by me. Inured to battle,   125
They'll fight like lions. But, as for the village,
Fuente Ovejuna's folk think more of tillage,
And care more for their humble crops and cattle

---

[100] Urueña is a small town in north-central Castile.

[103] Villena was the seat of the Pacheco family, which furnished many important figures during this period, including Juan Pacheco, Marquis of Villena, one of Alfonso's allies.

[119] Juan Pacheco; he and Pedro Girón were brothers.

Than about martial glories. They know naught
Of war.

MASTER   You live there?

COMENDADOR   Yes, I've sought
A haven there in these rough times. But, mind,
Let not a single vassal stay behind!

MASTER   No fear of that! My horse I'll mount today,
Couching my lance, and eager for the fray! (*They go out*)

135

Village square in Fuente Ovejuna
(*Enter* PASCUALA *and* LAURENCIA)

LAURENCIA   Never may he return!

PASCUALA   Why so?
I thought, when you had heard the news
Of his departure, you would show
More sorrow.

LAURENCIA   May heaven still refuse
To let him come back here!

PASCUALA   I've heard
Oaths angrier far than those you utter,
But when it came to test the word
The hearts have proved as soft as butter.

LAURENCIA   D'you think, you'll find a holm-oak drier
Than I am?

PASCUALA   Get along with you!
It is the driest cork takes fire.
Yet when one's talking of desire,
And when the gentry come to woo,
What girl can say, and prove no liar,
"I shall not go the same way too"?

LAURENCIA   By this bright sun, I swear it's true,
Though the whole world would say I lie!
Why should I love Fernando who
Pursues me? Here's the reason why:
D'you think he'd marry me?

PASCUALA   Why, no!

LAURENCIA   His infamy I then condemn.
How many girls have suffered for
The ruin that was made of them
All by this same Comendador!

PASCUALA   I'll hold it as a marvel, though,
If from his clutches you go free.

LAURENCIA   It's nonsense—all that you foresee!
For ever since a month ago,
In vain, he has been after me.
Ortuño, that sly cur, and Flores,

140

145

150

155

160

165

170

356 DE VEGA

His pandar, showed me silks and pearls
And costly headgear for my curls,
And tried to frighten me with stories   175
About his power to do me harm.
Yet, though they filled me with alarm,
They could not bait me with their hook.

PASCUALA   Where did they tempt you?   180

LAURENCIA   Last weekend,
While washing linen by the brook.

PASCUALA   I fear they'll trick you in the end.

LAURENCIA   What? Me?

PASCUALA   Or, if not you, the priest.   185

LAURENCIA   Though toothsome, I am just too tough
To serve His Reverence for a feast.
But of this "love" I've had enough.
I am more interested far
In any slice of roasted bacon   190
That from the embers I have taken
And placed between the bread I've kneaded;
Or from my mother's favorite jar
To steal a cup of wine unheeded;
Or watch at noon the simmering broth   195
Where beef chunks in the humming froth
Of greens are somersaulting round;
Or, if I've come in tired from walking,
To splice an *aubergine** well-browned
With a ham-slice; or else be caulking   200
The crannies of my appetite
With a grape-bunch from my own vine
(Which God preserve from hail or blight)
Till we on salmagundi* dine
With oil and pepper seasoned fine;   205
And then to bed—to my oration
Of "Lead me not into temptation"—
And sleep contented with my prayer.
These are the things for which I care
And prize a hundred times above   210
The foolish, foxy wiles of love
With which these villains weave their snare.
For if you wish to take their measure
Their only aim's to work us harm,
To make us go to bed with pleasure,   215
Then to awake in dire alarm.

PASCUALA   You're right, Laurencia, and when

---

199 Eggplant.

204 A dish of chopped meat, eggs, etc., flavored with onions, anchovies, and vinegar, as well as salt and pepper.

They leave off loving us, the men
Deal with us as the thankless sparrows
Deal with the peasant in the winter: 220
For when the days begin to narrow
And the fields with frosts to splinter,
Then down, as fast as they are able,
They flit from chimney, cave, and gable
With melting voice to croon and coo   225
"Tweenie-tweenie-tweenie-twoo"
While with the crumbs swept from his table
The fool regales the faithless crew.
But when the cold has ceased to freeze them
And the fields their flowers reveal,   230
Past delights no longer please them,
Thanklessness is all they feel.
For all the largesse of his table
They miscall the friend they knew
For an unbelieving Jew   235
Flitting up to cave and gable
No longer chirping "tweeny-tweeny"
But cursing "Sheeny-sheeny-sheeny!"
Such are men with every maiden:
When they need us, then we are   240
The wealth with which their hearts are laden,
Their life, their soul, their guiding star,
But when their flames die down to embers,
They chirrup, bill, and coo no more:
All the names their faith remembers   245
Are the names of "bitch" and "whore"!

LAURENCIA Trust no man that comes to woo!

PASCUALA So say I, Laurencia, too!

(Enter MENGO, BARRILDO, FRONDOSO)

FRONDOSO Your arguments have got lopsided,   250
Barrildo.

BARRILDO Look! Here's one at hand
By whose decision we may stand.

MENGO But ere the point has been decided,
You both must swear to pay the cost   255
You've wagered if the verdict's mine.

BARRILDO I swear we shall! But, if you've lost,
What prize, in turn, have you provided?

MENGO I'll bet you, then, my flute of box*
Worth a lot more than barns or flocks   260
Were you to value it as I did.

BARRILDO I'm satisfied.

---

259 In the Renaissance, flutes were more frequently made of boxwood than of any other materials. Boxwood
flutes were usually ornamented with ivory bands.

MENGO	Then let's proceed.

FRONDOSO Ladies! Good day!

LAURENCIA   "Ladies" indeed!

FRONDOSO   Yes, it's the fashion and the law
    Which euphemises every flaw.
    The fat man's "well-set-up"; the lean
    Is "slim" and "graceful in his mien";
    The fledgling scholar, still at college,
    Is called "a doctor" for his knowledge;
    The stone-blind has a "visual failing";
    The squint-eyed has a "roving glance";
    The cripple "does not like to dance";
    The big-mouthed churl who's always railing
    Is "fearless"; the potato-eyed
    Old blinkard is called "shrewd and sharp";
    The ignorant is magnified
    For "wisdom"; he who loves to carp
    And cavil, why, he's "persevering";
    The busybody's "most endearing";
    The gasbag's "deep" and "wise"; the shameless
    Is "daring"; and the coward's blameless,
    Though "falling short"; the domineering,
    Insulting ruffian is miscalled
    "A martial figure"; he who's bald
    For "grave authority's" extolled;
    The grudging sulk is praised for "gravity";
    There's "wit" in ignorant depravity;
    The insolent is "brave and bold";
    The madman goes for "free and easy,"
    For "humourous" the tout who's broke;
    "Companionable, bright, and breezy"
    They call the brandy-gozzled soak;
    The snuffler and the bulbous-snouted
    Are only "suffering from a cold";
    Arrogance for "reserve" is doubted,
    And grumpiness for "shyness" goes;
    The hunchback passes for "well-loaded" . . .
    And so, lest I should be outmoded,
    I call you "Ladies" I suppose.
    But that's enough, for in this way
    I could talk nonsense all the day.

LAURENCIA   Up in the cities, those in fashion
    Use gentler words to be polite.
    But, by my faith, the terms they ration
    For human faults, appear more right
    Than the rough terms that can be flung
    At random by a spiteful tongue.

FRONDOSO   Well, could you let us have a sample?
LAURENCIA   I'll take the opposite example
    To each of yours. The man who's serious
    Is "grumpy." One who speaks the truth
    They call "self-righteous" and "uncouth."
    They call the grave man "sad"; "imperious"   315
    And "tiresome"—one who reprehends;
    "Importunate"—who counsels youth;
    "Officious"—one who helps his friends;
    "Cruel" they call the man who's just,
    Impartially though he should try us;   320
    "Listless and tame"—the humbly pious;
    And one who's constant in his trust
    They take for "simple, dull, and dense";
    Courtesy is to "cringe and flatter";
    Christian behaviour's "all pretence";   325
    Merit that earns is no such matter,
    But "merely luck"; misfortune's "shame"—
    For which the sufferer is to blame;
    A girl who's virtuous is "a fool";
    A wife who does not break the rule   330
    Is merely "dull" . . . But that should be
    More than enough to bring me level
    In answering your philosophy.
MENGO   By heavens, she is the very devil!
    The priest who functioned at your christening   335
    Laid on the salt, in handfuls too!*
LAURENCIA   But what's your strife (if I've been listening
    Correctly)?
FRONDOSO   Hark, Laurencia, do!
LAURENCIA   Well, what is it you want?   340
FRONDOSO   Laurencia,
    Lend me your hearing.
LAURENCIA   Only lend?
    To give it you for keeps, I'll venture,
    From this day onwards.   345
FRONDOSO   I depend
    On your discretion.
LAURENCIA   What's your bet?
FRONDOSO   I and Barrildo both have set
    A wager against Mengo here.   350
LAURENCIA   What does he say?
BARRILDO   —Denies a fact
    That's certain, absolute, and clear.

---

336 In the Roman Catholic baptismal service the placing of the symbolic salt of wisdom on the tongue of
    the subject is a ritual step.

MENGO   To put it plainly, I've come here
        To floor them with the truth exact.

LAURENCIA   What's that?

BARRILDO   That love does not exist
            Is what *he* holds.

LAURENCIA   But who can doubt it?
            Surely there's love.

BARRILDO   Of course. Without it
            How on this earth could life persist?

MENGO   Philosophy is all a mist
        To me. I know nothing about it.
        The written word is Greek to me.
        But can you watch, and dare to scout it,
        The strife between each element,
        The endless war they represent?
        And it's from them our bodies borrow
        Their nourishment, their wrath and sorrow,
        Their phlegm and blood—you must agree.

FRONDOSO   The worlds around us and above,
           Mengo, are harmony entire.
           Harmony is pure love, and love
           Is harmony.

MENGO   I state the worth
        Of self-love, native to this earth:
        That is the love which governs all things.
        Affinities in great and small things
        Must regulate all that we see:
        I don't deny *that*. I agree
        That everything is truly fond
        Of what to it may correspond
        In keeping its integrity:
        My hand against a coming blow
        Leaps up to guard my face, and so
        My feet, by running off, forestall
        A danger that might else befall
        My body. My eyes, blinking tight,
        Avoid whatever harms their sight.
        Such love is natural.

PASCUALA   Then why
         Object? What is it you deny?

MENGO   That anyone in love can fall
        (Except with his own self) at all.

PASCUALA   Your pardon, Mengo, but you're lying,
           Since is it any good denying
           That force is not material
           By which men love their womenkind,

Or animals their mates?   400
MENGO   It's blind,
  Sheer *amour-propre,* self-satisfaction,
  Not love. What's love, then? I'll enquire.
LAURENCIA Why, love is a divine desire
  Of beauty.   405
MENGO   Why does love pursue
  Beauty? Why? Surely, to acquire
  It for one's own good self.
LAURENCIA   That's true.
MENGO To love one's own self, one must woo   410
  The thing that self does most require.
LAURENCIA That's so.
MENGO   Well, there's no love
  Except what for one's own delight
  One hunts, to feed one's appetite,   415
  For one's own self the prize to grapple,
  To be of one's own eye the apple,
  And the sole eye of one's potato!
BARRILDO The preacher in his recent sermons
  Mentioned a certain man called Plato   420
  Who, speaking about love, determines
  That we should selflessly admire
  The soul and virtue of the one
  We love—to set our hearts on fire.
PASCUALA Right off the beaten track you've run 425
  And bogged your axle in the mire
  Where only doctors from the colleges
  Find foothold.
LAURENCIA   You are right: our knowledge is
  Too shallow. Do not grind too hard   430
  And fine, but thank the heavens above,
  Mengo, that you're so lucky-starred
  As to be ignorant of love.
MENGO Are you in love?
LAURENCIA   With my good name.   435
FRONDOSO May God chastise you for the same
  With jealous pangs!
PASCUALA   The wisest plan
  Is to consult the sacristan.
  He, or the priest, could answer best . . .   440
  Laurencia's never loved a man
  And I have scarcely stood the test.
  Our judgment would be all in vain.
FRONDOSO A curse upon your cold disdain!
                    (*Enter* FLORES)   445

FLORES God be with you, good people!

PASCUALA   Look!
  The page of the Comendador.

LAURENCIA Rather his carrion-kite and rook.
  What news abroad, friend?   450

FLORES   From the war
  I've just returned, as you may see.

LAURENCIA And what of Don Fernán? Is he
  Expected back?

FLORES   The war at last   455
  Has ended. Though it cost some lives,
  Our cause victoriously thrives.

FRONDOSO Well, señor, tell us how it passed.

FLORES Why, yes. Although myself I say it,
  There's no man better could portray it,   460
  Since I was there from first to last,
  And with my own eyes saw it all.
  Against that city which we call
  The Royal City, our young Master
  Of Calatrava raised his troop,   465
  Two thousand infantry, to swoop,
  And carry slaughter and disaster
  Together with three hundred horse
  Of seculars and monks and friars—
  For even priests must join the force   470
  When our great Order so requires
  (Though that is chiefly with the Moors)
  To take up arms and fight in wars.
  The youthful Master of our Order,
  In doublet green with gilded border,   475
  Slit at the sleeve-ends to unfold
  The bracelets held with links of gold,
  On a huge dapple horse was seen
  With grey hairs shot with hairs of silver,
  Whose underlip the Guadalquivir*   480
  Had bathed, and who had grazed its green.
  Its tail with deerskin plaits behind,
  Its mane, in front, was deftly twined
  With many a ribbon, lace, and bow
  Whose flattering whiteness, row by row,   485
  Vied with the dots and dancing speckles
  That starred his flanks with fiery freckles
  And showered his stalwart croup with snow.
  Our own Fernando Gómez rode
  With him. The horse that he bestrode   490

480 A river in southern Castile.

Was of the honey-coloured hue
But mane and tail and fetlock, too,
Were jetty-black at each extreme;
The muzzle was as black to view,
Save that it turned as white as cream   495
From snorting, slavering, and drinking
The froth that from its snaffle clinking
And champing jaws, flaked sud by sud,
The foam of its aspiring blood,
And smoke to which its wrath was flame.   500
In glittering scales his chain-mail bound him;
Bright plates of armour spanned his frame
And clipped his shoulders. In wide swirls
His orange tunic-fringe around him
Sparkled with gold and orient pearls.   505
Over his helmet, wreathed in curls,
The cream-white ostrich-plumes were towering
As if 'twere orange-blossom flowering
Out of his orange-coloured lace—
Slung on a white and scarlet brace,   510
An ash-tree, lifted on his arm,
To threaten all the Moorish race
And fill Granada with alarm!
The city rose in the King's name
Since for the Crown they all proclaim   515
Their loyalty to the King's succession.
They made resistance worthy fame.
But in the end, their strength to tame,
The Master entered in procession,
And those who had denied his right   520
He had beheaded upon sight.
As for the common people there,
He had each snaffled with a bit,
And, having stripped their bodies bare,
He flogged them in the public square   525
Till they could neither stand nor sit.
He made himself so roundly feared,
So popular and so revered,
Who in so short a time could win,
Chastise, and rule, though adolescent!   530
They augured that the pale blue crescent
Of Islam in eclipse would spin
To ignominy, shame, and loss,
Before the sun of his red cross.
After he'd lightened, struck, and thundered,   535
Out of the city's wreck, he plundered

Such vast largesse and wealth for all
(But chiefly the Comendador)
It seemed he had flung wide the door
Of his own house and dining-hall
And bade them ransack all the store. 540
But now I hear the band approaching.
Rejoice! Forget your cares and quarrels!
To win all hearts, with none reproaching,
Is worth a forest full of laurels. 545
(*Enter the* COMENDADOR *with* ORTUÑO, JUAN ROJO, *and the mayor and
deputy mayor,* ESTEBAN, *and* ALONSO)

MUSICIANS (*Singing*) You're welcome in our village,
Comendador, to stop!
Battlefields are his tillage 550
And lives of men his crop!

Long live the Guzmán faction
And the Girones line
Invincible in action
In peace the most benign. 555

Who stronger than the oak
Against the Moors did sally
And quelled the sturdy folk
Of Ciudad Reále.*

Fuente Ovejuna greets him 560
The village where his home is
Shout, everyone who meets him:
Long live Fernando Gómez!

COMENDADOR Dear village, let me thank you from my heart,
For all these signs of love that you have shown. 565
ALONSO Of what we feel we've only shown a part
Of all the love you merit as your own.
ESTEBAN Fuente Ovejuna's mayors and corporation
(Whom you've so graced), along with this ovation,
Beg that you will accept, as from our hearts, 570
The humble gifts that pile these rustic carts.
You'll find as much good will and homely thanks
Borne in the cradle of their creaking planks
As in more wealthy gifts. Here, two glazed jars
Brim with preserves. Here, from the wooden bars 575
A flock of geese poke forth their heads to cackle
Your valiant fame. Ten fattened hogs, to crackle
Upon your fire, here offer up their loves,

---

559 Mispronounce "Re/álly" as in original [trans. note].

And their smooth hides, as soft as scented gloves.
A hundred pairs of chanticleers* and chickens 580
For whom full many a widow sighs and sickens
And many an orphaned fledgling joins the mourners
Round dunghills, village-greens, and farmyard corners.
We bring no coats of arms nor gold-trapped steeds
But all from rustic loyalty proceeds 585
Offered by loyal vassals—men who hold
That love's more lasting and more pure than gold.
And (talking about purity) here's wine—
Twelve skins of it! which could defend a breach
In January, if it did but line 590
Your warriors' skins inside. It's common speech—
For furbishing clean steel, to make it shine
And cut like lightning, there is naught like wine.
Armour without, I say, but wine within,
Against all comers, they will always win! 595
I will not speak of cheeses and the rest:
Our house is yours, and you, most honoured guest,
Have won your own deserts from every heart.

COMENDADOR Thanks, councillors, in peace may you depart.

ALONSO Now rest, thrice welcome to our countryside! 600
  If these poor rushes that we strew before you
  Were pearls and rubies which we could provide,
  Even then, they would be insufficient for you.

COMENDADOR I well believe you. Thank you all. Good-bye.

ESTEBAN Now, singers, raise your voices up on high. 605

MUSICIANS (*Singing*) You're welcome in our village,
                Comendador, to stop!
                Battlefields are your tillage,
                And slaughtered men your crop! (*They all go off*)

  (*Reenter* COMENDADOR, LAURENCIA, PASCUALA, ORTUÑO, FLORES) 610

COMENDADOR Here! Wait, you two!

LAURENCIA   What does Your Lordship wish?

COMENDADOR You turned me down the other day. Yes! Me!
  What does this mean?

LAURENCIA   Pascuala, is he talking 615
  To you?

PASCUALA No! Leave me out of it! Not me!

COMENDADOR It is to you I'm talking, cruel beauty,
  And to this other wench. Are you not mine?

PASCUALA Your servants, yes. But not for other use. 620

COMENDADOR Go in, get in this doorway here. Come on!
  There are a lot of men here. Don't be frightened.

LAURENCIA I'll go in if the councillors go too
  (One of them is my father) not unless . . .

580 Roosters.

366   DE VEGA

COMENDADOR   Flores . . .   625
FLORES   My lord!
COMENDADOR   What do they mean not to obey my orders?
FLORES   In with you!
LAURENCIA   Here, don't claw us!
FLORES   Don't be foolish!   630
        Go in!
PASCUALA   No! If we do, you'll bolt us in.
FLORES   Go in! He only wants to let you see
        The trophies he's brought back.
COMENDADOR   Once they're inside,   635
        Ortuño, bolt the door. (*Exit*)
LAURENCIA   Flores, please let us pass.
ORTUÑO   What! Don't you know
        That you're included with the other presents?
PASCUALA   Out of my way, or I shall scream for help!   640
FLORES   That's taking things too far.
LAURENCIA   Cannot your master
        Be satisfied with all the meat they've brought him?
ORTUÑO   Yours is the sort of meat he likes the best.
LAURENCIA   Well, may it choke his throat and burst his innards! (*The women* 645
                                                            leave)
FLORES   And now we're in a fix! Think what he'll say! (FLORES *and* ORTUÑO
                                                            leave)

    In the palace of the Catholic kings at Medina del Campo
    (*Enter* KING FERDINAND, QUEEN ISABEL, DON MANRIQUE, *Master of*   650
                    Santiago, and ATTENDANTS)
QUEEN   My lord, we must be wary in this matter.
        The King of Portugal has got his army
        Ready to march. So we must pounce at once
        And win outright, or else we'll court defeat.   655
KING   Aragón and Navarre are sending help
        And I can soon reorganise Castile
        To bring us swift success.
QUEEN   Your Majesty,
        Our victory is ensured by that, believe me.   660
DON MANRIQUE   Two aldermen from Ciudad Real
        Beg leave of audience. Shall I bid them enter?
KING   Do not deny our presence. Let them in.
                (*Enter* TWO ALDERMEN *from Ciudad Real*)
FIRST ALDERMAN   Great Catholic King Ferdinand,* whom heaven
        Sent to Castile from Aragón to bless   665
        And shelter us. From Ciudad Real

---

⁶⁶⁵ Ferdinand and Isabela were known as "the Catholics"; it is to them that the peasants later appeal as to a
    Supreme Court.

We've humbly come to sue for the protection
Of your unrivalled valour. In the past
We have been happy as your subjects; now   670
Our adverse fate has brought us down from that
High honour. For the famous Don Rodrigo
Téllez Girón (though young to be the Master
Of Calatrava) that fierce thunderbolt
Of reckless valour, both for his own glory   675
And to extend the frontiers of his rule,
Laid close siege to our city. Though we fought,
Opposing bravery to violent force,
Till the blood ran in streams, we lost the war.
So then he took possession of the town,   680
Which he could not have done, save for the help,
Tactics, and counsels of Fernando Gómez.
So he remains our ruler, we his vassals,
Against our will, unless some remedy
Is soon applied.   685
KING   Where is Fernando Gómez?
FIRST ALDERMAN   He's in Fuente Ovejuna, I believe,
Since that's his fief. He has a house and land there,
And there, more freely than we dare to tell it,
He tyrannises over his poor vassals   690
Keeping them alien from content and peace.
KING   Have you a captain left among you?
SECOND ALDERMAN   Sire,
No one of noble blood escaped from death,
Capture, or wounds.   695
QUEEN   This case brooks no delay.
We must strike quickly without losing strength
Before our daring enemy can act.
The King of Portugal, advancing through
Estremadura,* finds a sure, safe gateway   700
And may cause far more harm if he's not checked.
KING   Now, Don Manrique, Master of Santiago,
Go! Take two regiments! Repair these harms
And grant no respite to the foe! The Count
Of Cabra can go with you: Córdova   705
Can claim in him a captain of world fame.
This is the most that I can send you now.
DON MANRIQUE   Yes, I think this solution is the best.
I'll stamp out his disorders, or I'll die.
QUEEN   Since it is you we send, victory's certain! (*They go off*)   710

---

700 The province in western Castile along the Portuguese border.

The countryside near Fuente Ovejuna
(*Enter* LAURENCIA *and* FRONDOSO)

LAURENCIA   I had come back from the river
    Although my washing's hardly wrung
    Lest we should be on every tongue   715
    Because, Frondoso, you're so reckless
    In what you say, that old and young
    Are spreading rumours through the village
    That I on you and you on me
    Are casting looks for all to see.   720
    They know that of the farmer people
    You are most bold, and proud, and free
    And wear the finest clothes, and so,
    In all the village, there's no man
    Or girl that does not claim to know   725
    That you and I will soon be one
    And that the village sacristan
    Will leave off playing his bassoon
    To see us from the vestry soon.
    For my own part I wish them thrift,   730
    Full barns in August, with the gift
    Of brimming must in every jar.
    Their tittle-tattle's very far
    From getting on my nerves. A lot
    Of sleep I'll lose on that account!   735
    I do not care one tiny jot.
FRONDOSO   Lovely Laurencia, this disdain
    Causes my soul such dreadful pain.
    It breaks my heart to see and hear you
    And makes me frightened to come near you.   740
    If you but realise that I
    For you alone would live and die
    Your faithful husband—my reward
    Is poor!
LAURENCIA   It's all I can afford.   745
FRONDOSO   But can you really feel no ruth
    To see the pain you cause? Mere thinking
    Of you prevents me eating, drinking
    Or sleeping, in my prime of youth.
    Can savagery so uncouth   750
    And cruelty so fierce, be hid
    Behind an angel's face? In truth
    I fear I shall go raving mad.
LAURENCIA   Try magic spells, if you feel bad.
FRONDOSO   No! I am begging for my life!   755
    My dear Laurencia, be my wife

And let us both, like turtledoves,
With beaks and hearts in amorous strife
Solemnly consummate our loves
When we come from the church together   760
To bill and coo through life forever.

LAURENCIA   You ask my uncle, old Juan Rojo!
Even if I'm not mad about you
And very well could do without you—
Yet I could care for you.   765

FRONDOSO   Confound!
Here comes the Grand Comendador.

LAURENCIA   He's hunting roebuck, I'll be bound.
Hide in this bush.

FRONDOSO   I'll hide, but where   770
Can I escape my jealous care? (*He hides*)
                (*Enter the* COMENDADOR *with a crossbow*)

COMENDADOR   It's not so bad when hunting buck
To fall in with such damned good luck
In place of *buck* to find a *dear*—   775
A deer so timorous and shy
And so precisely now and here!

LAURENCIA   I am just resting while I dry
Some linen, and, with your good will,
I shall return now to the rill.   780

COMENDADOR   This ugly kind of frown and fret
Insults my rank which you forget,
And does great havoc to the grace
Both of the figure and the face
Which heaven gave you. Though chance gave   785
You, other times, a way to save
Your virtue, now good fortune yields
These hushed, conniving, lonely fields
And you alone cannot deny
Your Master's rights, nor hope to fly   790
From one who holds you in control
And owns your house, your body, and your soul—
One whom, moreover, you insult by this.
Pedro Redondo's wife granted me bliss,
Sebastiania, too—they never parried   795
The strong urge of my love, though newly married.
Martin del Pozo's wife, two days a bride,
Gave herself up, and laid her by my side.

LAURENCIA   My lord, those women long were at the game
Before their husbands or Your Lordship came!   800
Follow your roebuck, sir, by God be blessed!
But for that Christian cross upon your chest

I'd say you were the fiend—

COMENDADOR   I will not stand it:
I'll fling my bow aside, and like a bandit
Will plunder you with my brute-strength alone,
For you are a mere chattel that I own!

LAURENCIA   What? Are you mad?

COMENDADOR   Don't struggle!

(FRONDOSO *steals out and takes the crossbow*)

FRONDOSO   Now I've got
The crossbow. Heaven help us all! If not,
I'll have to shoulder it and shoot.

LAURENCIA   Heaven be my aid!

COMENDADOR   Look, we are all alone. Don't be afraid!

FRONDOSO   Most generous Comendador, let go
Of this poor girl, or else with your own bow
I shall transfix your body without sparing.
Although I tremble at the cross you're wearing!

COMENDADOR   Villainous dog!

FRONDOSO   No dog, sir!

LAURENCIA   Have a care,
Frondoso, what you're doing.

FRONDOSO   (*To* LAURENCIA)   Run away! (*Exit* LAURENCIA)

COMENDADOR   Oh, what a fool I was to leave my sword,
Thinking that it would frighten her.

FRONDOSO   My lord,
I've but to press this trigger and you die.

COMENDADOR   She's gone, you lowborn villain. Leave that bow!
I tell you, put it down, quick!

FRONDOSO   How can I
Leave it, when you will kill me if I do?
True love is deaf to reason or to rhyme
When he is on his throne for the first time:
So take good warning.

COMENDADOR   Shoot me villain, do!
Rather than that upon a clod like you
One nobly born should turn his back and flee,
Shoot me, and see what it will lead you to!
Shoot, dog! I break the laws of chivalry
By speaking to you.

FRONDOSO   I'll not shoot you. No.
But as I'm forced to save my life, I'll go,
Taking your crossbow. (*He goes and takes the bow off with him*)

COMENDADOR   How could I foresee
This danger? But by heaven I shall be
Revenged for this rebellion and attack.
God give me patience till I've paid it back! (*He leaves*)

Act Two

(Enter ESTEBAN *and the* FIRST ALDERMAN)

ESTEBAN My view is this, good sir: let no more grain
    Be taken from the public granary.
    The year wears on. The harvest augurs badly.   5
    Let us store up reserves in case of need,
    Whatever voices murmur other views.

FIRST ALDERMAN That's always been my own idea in ruling
    The village peacefully in its best interests.

ESTEBAN We must present a plea to Fernán Gómez.   10
    We don't want these astrologers to make
    Long speeches about things they do not know
    Concerning secrets known to God alone.
    What right have they presumptuously to claim
    Deep theologic knowledge and to find   15
    The future corresponding with the past?
    The present is the time that counts; the wisest
    Of them is ignorant of all but that.
    You'd think they had the clouds on tap at home!
    You'd think the stars were at their beck and call!   20
    How can they know the goings-on in heaven
    Which fill us with such anxious hopes and fears?
    They think that they can regulate the seedtime
    And deal out laws to barley, wheat, peas, beans,
    Cucumbers, calabashes, pumpkins, and mustard!   25
    They are the pumpkin-heads! They prophesy
    A beast will die, and then they say it's happened
    Not here but somewhere else—in Transylvania!
    They say there'll be a shortage in our wine,
    But plenty of good beer in Germany.   30
    In Gascony the cherries will be frozen
    And there'll be lots of tigers in Hircania,
    But after all, whether we sow or not,
    The year is always ended in December!

(Enter LEONELO *the student, and* BARRILDO)   35

LEONELO We're not the first to get here for a gossip.

BARRILDO What's Salamanca like?

LEONELO   That's a long story.

BARRILDO You'll be a learnèd doctor.

LEONELO   Not so learnèd.   40
    There's not much future in my faculty.

BARRILDO Then some are cleverer than you?

LEONELO   Of course.

BARRILDO I'm sure that they must think you a fine scholar.

LEONELO   I've done my best to learn what mattered most.   45
BARRILDO   Now that the printing press has been invented
    Everyone seems to pride himself on knowledge.
LEONELO   In spite of that I think they know far less:
    There is a strange confusion in excess
    Which always must defeat its own intention   50
    And that is one result of that invention.
    Not that I would deny the printing art
    Finds genius out, and lifts it far apart
    From the base throng, where it would lie neglected,
    Raising it up by time to be respected.   55
    We owe the press to Gutenberg, a clever
    And worthy man from Mainz whose fame forever
    Will fill the world. But some deserve the curse
    Of the whole world for printing their own verse.
    Some people, till their works were printed, had   60
    Been much revered—but now we find them bad.
    Others, in envy, signed an honoured name
    To their own works, and brought it evil fame.
BARRILDO   Come, come, I can't think that.
LEONELO   Oh yes, it's true!   65
    Illiterates still grudge scholarship its due.
BARRILDO   But printing is important all the same.
LEONELO   Long centuries had passed before it came
    And yet it has not given us a second
    Augustine or Jerome who could be reckoned   70
    As due to it.
BARRILDO   Don't let us get so heated,
    Calm yourself down, and let us both be seated.
              (*Enter* JUAN ROJO *and another* PEASANT)
JUAN ROJO   Four farms are not sufficient for a dowry   75
    If gifts be reckoned in the modern way:
    Take heed, all you who have enquiring minds,
    Opinion in this town has gone astray!
PEASANT   Don't lose your temper. The Comendador—
    What news of him?   80
JUAN ROJO   He has ill-used Laurencia.
PEASANT   No brute is so lascivious as he.
    Would he were hanged upon that olive tree!
              (*Enter the* COMENDADOR, ORTUÑO, FLORES)
COMENDADOR   God save you all, good people.   85
ALDERMAN   Oh! My lord!
COMENDADOR   Please remain seated everyone.
ESTEBAN   Your Lordship
    Be seated. We are quite contented standing.
COMENDADOR   I say you must sit down.   90

ESTEBAN   All decent people
    Delight in honouring rank. One can't pay honour
    To any one, unless one has it.
COMENDADOR   Come.
    We'll have a talk. Sit down there, all of you.   95
ESTEBAN You've seen the greyhound, sir.
COMENDADOR   Yes, my good mayor,
    My servants are enchanted with its speed.
ESTEBAN It's a rare dog. I think it could keep up
    With any gaolbird on the run from justice   100
    Or any coward confessing on the rack.
COMENDADOR I only wish that you could send it after
    A certain bit of game that always beats me
    By giving me the slip.
ESTEBAN   Of course I'll send it.   105
COMENDADOR I mean your daughter.
ESTEBAN   What! My daughter!
COMENDADOR   Yes!
ESTEBAN What! Is she worthy to be wooed by you?
COMENDADOR She's very difficult, my worthy mayor.   110
ESTEBAN How do you mean?
COMENDADOR   She's causing me annoyance!
    Why, there are women of high class, and married
    To some I see around me in the square,
    Who, at the first advance, gave themselves to me.   115
ESTEBAN Well, they did wrong, my lord, and you yourself
    Are doing wrong in talking thus so freely.
COMENDADOR Oh, what an eloquent old country bumpkin!
    Flores, you ought to give him Aristotle's
    Treatise on *Politics*.   120
ESTEBAN   My lord, this village
    Would fain live peacefully beneath your rule.
    And surely they include some worthy people.
LEONELO His shamelessness is surely without equal!
COMENDADOR Alderman, have I said something to hurt you?   125
ALDERMAN Yes. What you say is most unjust. Unsay it,
    And do not try to rob us of our honour.
COMENDADOR *Honour?* Do such as *you* pretend to *honour?*
    You should be called the Calatrava Friars!
ALDERMAN And some there are boast of the cross you gave them   130
    Whose blood, for all that, is not all it might be!
COMENDADOR Do I pollute your blood then if I join
    My blood with it?
ALDERMAN   Yes! When it's fouled with lust,
    Your blood's unclean.   135
COMENDADOR   But surely you'll admit

I do your wives great honour when I woo them?

ESTEBAN Your words dishonour you. We can't believe them:
And what you said at first—forget that too!

COMENDADOR How dull and stupid is the country peasant! 140
It's only in the city life is pleasant,
Where husbands thank you to attend their wives
And men of wit can lead amusing lives.

ESTEBAN That's false. You cannot fob us off with that.
God lives in cities, too, and there are people 145
Quicker to punish crime than you'll find here.

COMENDADOR Clear out!

ESTEBAN Is that from you to me alone?

COMENDADOR Clear out, the lot of you, let none remain!

ESTEBAN We'll go, then. 150

COMENDADOR Not in that way, in one bunch!

FLORES My lord, contain yourself, beware!

COMENDADOR They've banded
Together in my absence to defy me.

ORTUÑO My lord, for God's sake, have some patience! 155

COMENDADOR Patience?
I marvel at the patience I have shown.
Go, separately, each to his own home!

LEONELO Heavens, do you permit this?

ESTEBAN I'll go this way. 160
(PEASANTS *go slowly and sullenly*)

COMENDADOR What do you make of them?

ORTUÑO They do not know
How to dissimulate; and you refuse
To take the measure of their discontent.

COMENDADOR What! Would they rank themselves, as equals, with me? 165

FLORES It's not exactly ranking as your equals . . .

COMENDADOR And that base boor that ran off with my crossbow—
Must he remain unpunished?

FLORES Last night I thought 170
I'd caught him by Laurencia's door. I hit
Him hard. But it was someone else.

COMENDADOR Where is he?

FLORES Frondoso? Oh, he's slinking round about.

COMENDADOR What! Does he dare to show himself round here— 175
A man who wished to kill me?—

FLORES Yes, like an unsuspecting bird, or else
A fish that glides towards the baited hook.

COMENDADOR A man that makes Córdoba and Granada
Tremble on their foundations—to be dared 180
And daunted by a yokel! Really, Flores,
I think this world is coming to an end!

FLORES The course of love was never smooth.

ORTUÑO   He must
  Be a good friend of yours to be still living.   185

COMENDADOR Ortuño, I have used dissimulation.
  Otherwise in two short hours, I'd have put
  The whole town to the sword. You wait and see,
  The moment that they give me the occasion,
  How I shall be revenged. Have you no news   190
  Of Pascuala?

FLORES   She's getting married soon
  She tells me.

COMENDADOR And till then she asks for credit?

FLORES As far as I can see, it won't be long   195
  Till the whole debt is paid.

COMENDADOR What of Olalla?

ORTUÑO   Why, she showed some humour
  In answering.

COMENDADOR She is a lively wench!   200
  What did she say?

ORTUÑO   Her bridegroom's getting jealous,
  To see the many messages you send
  And how you pay her visits with your servants.
  But when he's off his guard, you'll still be welcome.   205

COMENDADOR I swear upon my knighthood she's a fine one!
  But as for that young whippersnapping husband
  Let him beware!

ORTUÑO   He's scared enough already.

COMENDADOR What news of Inés?   210

FLORES   Which one?

COMENDADOR   Antón's wife.

FLORES She's game at any time with all her charms,
  I spoke to her outside her stableyard
  By which she bids you enter when you like.   215

COMENDADOR These easy women I like very well
  And yet I pay them poorly. They don't know
  The value of a decent reputation.

FLORES You do not get the necessary setbacks
  To contrast with their favours. Quick surrender   220
  Undoes the interest and excitement of
  Crowning a hope deferred. But there are women
  (So the philosopher relates) who need
  Men, just as abstract forms require a substance.
  That men become mere habit with such women   225
  Is not so strange.

COMENDADOR When a man's mad with love
  He's pleased with quick surrender, but he values

The woman less, tires quickly, and forgets her.
For even the most grateful man esteems
At a low value that which cost him least.   230
                    (*Enter* CIMBRANOS, *a soldier*)
CIMBRANOS   Where's the Comendador?
FLORES   You're in his presence.
CIMBRANOS   Valiant Fernando Gómez, change that green   235
    Cap of a hunter for your shining morion*
    And change this tunic for your bright new arms.
    The Master of the Knights of Santiago,
    Joined with the Count of Cabra, has laid siege
    In Ciudad Real to Don Rodrigo   240
    Girón—and in the name of Isabela
    Queen of Castile. And so we are in danger
    Of losing that which cost us so much blood
    As well you know. At early dawn were sighted,
    From the high battlements, the crests and colours,   245
    The lions and the castles of Castile
    And the bright bars of Aragón. Although
    The King of Portugal would aid Girón,
    The best that he can hope for, at this pass,
    Is to escape, alive, home to Almagro.   250
    So mount your horse. The sight of you alone
    Should send them limping back into Castile.
COMENDADOR   Stop! Say no more! Ortuño, in the square
    Get them to sound the trumpet. Say, how many
    Soldiers are quartered here?   255
ORTUÑO   Fifty, I think.
COMENDADOR   Get them all mounted.
CIMBRANOS   If you are not quick,
    Ciudad Real will be the King's and Queen's.
COMENDADOR   Oh, never fear that such a thing could happen! (*They go*)   260

Countryside round Fuente Ovejuna
            (*Enter* MENGO, PASCUALA, *and* LAURENCIA, *fleeing*)
PASCUALA   Don't go away from us!
MENGO   Whom do you fear?
LAURENCIA   Mengo, let's all return to town together   265
    In case we meet with him.
MENGO   The cruel devil—
    Where will he end?
LAURENCIA   He never lets us rest
    Either in sun or shade.   270

---

²³⁶ A military helmet.

MENGO   Would heaven could send
     A thunderbolt to finish with this madman!
LAURENCIA   A foul bloodthirsty beast, I'd rather call him—
     The pestilence and arsenic of the place!
MENGO   They tell me that in this same very meadow   275
     Frondoso threatened him with his own arrow
     To rescue you, Laurencia, from his lust.
LAURENCIA   Before that day I hated all men, Mengo.
     But now I see them in another light.
     Frondoso was so valiant! Now, I fear   280
     That it will cost his life.
MENGO   That man must leave
     The village.
LAURENCIA   Though I've come to love him dearly
     That is what I advised him, too. But he   285
     Receives my loving counsels with disdain
     And rage, though the Comendador has sworn
     To have him hanged head downward by the feet.
PASCUALA   May he be throttled!
MENGO   Stoning would be better.   290
     I wish I had the sling I used when herding—
     To lodge one in the cracked shell of his noodle!
     Galabalo, the Roman emperor,
     Was not so wicked.
LAURENCIA   Heliogabalus,   295
     You mean, who was a foul inhuman beast.
MENGO   "Pelly, oh, gaballer"? I don't care how
     You say it. History's not my strong point!
     But his revolting memory is outstunk,
     In this Fernando Gómez, by a mile!   300
     Is any man in nature quite so evil?
PASCUALA   No: for he is a tiger in his harshness!
                    (*Enter* JACINTA)
JACINTA   Help me, for God's sake, if you are my friends!
LAURENCIA   What's wrong, Jacinta dear?   305
PASCUALA   We are yours.
JACINTA   The pimps of the Comendador, more strongly
     Armed with their native infamy than with
     Their weapons, are about to drag me with them
     To Ciudad Real, whither they're bound.   310
LAURENCIA   If that is so, Jacinta, I must flee
     Since if with you he takes such liberty
     What would he do with me? May God protect you. (*She goes*)
PASCUALA   Jacinta dear, since I am not a man
     I can be of no use. (*She goes*)   315
MENGO   It seems that I'm

Forced now to be a man, bearing the gender
And name of one. Jacinta, come with me!

JACINTA But have you arms?

MENGO   The first in all the world.   320

JACINTA Oh! if you only had.

MENGO   Why, here are stones,
Jacinta. Yes, and plenty of them too!

(Enter FLORES *and* ORTUÑO)

FLORES You thought you could escape from us on foot!   325

JACINTA Oh, Mengo, I am lost.

MENGO   Why, gentlemen . . .
You surely don't molest poor countryfolk?

ORTUÑO Can I believe my eyes? You have the cheek
To try to save this woman?   330

MENGO   With my pleadings,
Yes, as a near relation, I would save her!

FLORES Kill him at once.

MENGO   I swear by this bright gun
If you get in such tantrums, I shall loosen   335
This hempen sling—to make it life for life.

(Enter COMENDADOR *and* CIMBRANOS)

COMENDADOR What's this? You two have caused me to dismount.
For such a vile and trivial cause.

FLORES   The vile   340
And common folk of this place are defying
Our arms—it's time you had them massacred—
In nothing do they seem disposed to please you.

MENGO My lord, if pity lives within your breast to see
This unjust act, chastise these soldiers here   345
Who have misused your name to rob this woman
From her own husband and her honest parents
And give me leave to take her to her people.

COMENDADOR I'll give them leave to punish you, vile dog!
Let go that sling!   350

MENGO   My lord . . . !

COMENDADOR   Flores! Ortuño!
Cimbranos! Tie his hands up with that thing!

MENGO Is that how you protect a woman's honour?

COMENDADOR What do Fuente Ovejuna and its peasants   355
Say about me?

MENGO   Sir, how have we offended
You in the slightest thing?

FLORES   Shall he be killed?

COMENDADOR No, do not foul your swords upon such dirt,   360
Since you must houour them in nobler work.

ORTUÑO Your orders then?

COMENDADOR	To flog him. Strip him naked,

COMENDADOR   To flog him. Strip him naked,
   And tie him to that oak, then with the reins . . .

MENGO   Have pity, since you are a noble! Please!   365

COMENDADOR   And do not cease from flogging him until
   The buckles and the studs jump from the thongs
   And leave the leather naked . . .

MENGO   Oh, you heavens!
   How long until such evil deeds are punished?   370

       (FLORES, ORTUÑO, *and* CIMBRANOS *carry off* MENGO)

COMENDADOR   Why do you run away, you countrywoman,
   Am I not better than a sweaty peasant?

JACINTA   Is that the way that you restore the honour
   My name has lost by being chased out here   375
   By your paid bloodhounds?

COMENDADOR   How can it have harmed you?

JACINTA   I have an honourable father, sir,
   Who though he's lower in his rank than you
   Is nobler in his dealings, yes, by far!   380

COMENDADOR   The troubles and the insolence I get
   From such as you will not appease my anger.
   Come on, this way!

JACINTA   With whom?

COMENDADOR   With me!   385

JACINTA   Take care!

COMENDADOR   Of course I'll take good care. You're now
   A woman of the commissariat,
   The baggage train, and brothels for the army
   At large, but for myself, no more! Away!   390

JACINTA   I will not live to let them outrage me!

COMENDADOR   Gee up! You dirty slut! Get on the march!

JACINTA   Have pity on me, sir!

COMENDADOR   Pity, be damned!

JACINTA   I solemnly appeal to the divine   395
   Justice of God against your cruelty! (JACINTA *is dragged off*)

       ESTEBAN'S *house*
    (*Enter* LAURENCIA *and* FRONDOSO)

LAURENCIA   How do you dare to come here, risking death?

FRONDOSO   Only to show how deeply I adore you.   400
   I saw, from that far slope, the bloody squadron
   Of the Comendador go marching out—
   So trusting in your faith, I lost all fear.
   May he have left us, never to return!

LAURENCIA   Don't curse him, for the ones men curse the most   405
   Always appear to go on living longest.

FRONDOSO   If that's so, may he live a thousand years!
That ought to settle him, if wishing well
Can do him any harm. Laurencia, listen!
I want to know if my deep loyalty   410
Has found the harbour it deserves. All round
The people think we are already one.
And that we're not united yet they wonder.
Leave off your coyness. Tell me yes or no.
LAURENCIA   To you, and all the village, I'll say yes.   415
FRONDOSO   Then let me kiss your feet for this great mercy
It's like receiving a new life, I swear.
LAURENCIA   Enough of compliments. Talk to my father,
That's the important part. He's coming here
Now with my uncle. And I'm sure that I shall be   420
Your wife. Good luck.
FRONDOSO   I trust it all to God!
                    (*Exit* LAURENCIA. FRONDOSO *hides*)
                    (*Enter* ESTEBAN *and the* ALDERMAN)
ESTEBAN   It finished up like this. In the town square   425
There was almost a riot. His behaviour
Passed all belief or toleration. All
Are stunned by his excesses. Poor Jacinta
Has had to pay the cost of his last madness.
ALDERMAN   All Spain will soon be for the Catholic Princes   430
(As now they call Queen Isabela and
King Ferdinand) and their just laws obey.
The Master of the Knights of Santiago,
Now as the captain general of their armies,
Sweeps on his way to Ciudad Real   435
Where still Rodrigo Girón holds the town.
But I am sick to think of poor Jacinta;
She was a well-bred girl, so good and honest.
ESTEBAN   The way they flogged poor Mengo too!
ALDERMAN   His skin   440
Was black with weals as ink or pitch or tar!
ESTEBAN   Don't speak about it. Why, it burns me up
To see and suffer this most fiendish treatment
And live beneath the stench of his bad name.
I'd like to know what use is this damned bauble,   445
A mayor's staff of office? It's a mockery!
ALDERMAN   These dastard crimes were done by his own men,
Not yours. Why should you feel so sore at it?
ESTEBAN   And there's another thing. Redondo's wife—
After he'd finished with her in the valley,   450
He gave her to his flunkeys after him!
ALDERMAN   But someone's lurking here. Who can it be?

FRONDOSO   It's only I. I hope you do not mind.

ESTEBAN   Frondoso, to my house you're always welcome.
You owe your father one life, but to me   455
You owe another since I reared you up
And loved you as a son.

FRONDOSO   Trusting in that
I'll ask a favour. Sir, you know full well
Whose son I am.   460

ESTEBAN   Has ·mad Fernando Gómez
Done you some foul injustice?

FRONDOSO   Yes. A great one.

ESTEBAN   The heart within me warned me that was so!

FRONDOSO   Well sir, taking advantage of your kindness,   465
I came to beg the hand of your Laurencia,
With whom I am in love. Forgive my haste
If I have spoken it too soon, for others
There are who would opine that I'm too daring.

ESTEBAN   Frondoso, from your words I draw new life   470
Because great dread was growing in my soul.
Thank heaven, my dear son, that for the honour
Of me and mine, you venture this. I thank
Your love, and bless the dear, fine zeal you show.
First now, consult your father, since I'd like   475
To know how it strikes him. As for myself
I could not have been happier about it.

ALDERMAN   But you should know the girl's opinion first.

ESTEBAN   Don't worry about that. The bargain's made.
I'll bet they had it settled long ago.   480
As for the dowry, we can deal with that
Now, on the spot. I've got a little hoard
Which I'll be pleased to settle on you both.

FRONDOSO   I don't want any dowry, sir, at all:
Don't let's get saddened about such affairs.   485

ALDERMAN   You should be glad he doesn't ask for her
Stark naked.

ESTEBAN   Well, we'll ask *her* what she thinks
If you don't mind.

FRONDOSO   Yes, that is just. You ask her.   490
Opinions should be studied, not ignored.

ESTEBAN   (*calling*) Daughter! Laurencia!
                    (LAURENCIA, *entering to them*)

LAURENCIA   Yes, my lord and father?

ESTEBAN (*To the* ALDERMAN)   See if I told you right! You see how quickly   495
She answered me.
(*To* LAURENCIA)   Laurencia, my darling,
I've sent to know your mind about this question,
Come over here. D'you think that your friend, Gila,

Should be the wife of young Frondoso? He 500
Seems to be quite as upright a young man
As in any village.
LAURENCIA   Gila's marrying?
ESTEBAN If any one deserves him, she's his equal.
LAURENCIA I say so too. 505
ESTEBAN   Yes, but I say she's ugly
And that Frondoso would be better mated
With you.
LAURENCIA Why, Father, haven't you forgotten
In your old age this scurvy jesting habit? 510
ESTEBAN Well, do you love him?
LAURENCIA   Yes, I am his. He's mine
But there is this affair . . .
ESTEBAN   Shall I agree?
LAURENCIA You say the word for me. 515
ESTEBAN   The keys are mine
And it is done. (*To the* ALDERMAN) Let's go and find his father
Down in the village square.
ALDERMAN   Yes, come, let's go.
ESTEBAN (*To* FRONDOSO) What shall I say to him about the dowry? 520
I can well spare for you a cool four thousand
Maravedis.
FRONDOSO Why, sir, discuss it now?
It's wounding to my honour.
ESTEBAN   Don't talk nonsense. 525
That is a thing you will get over quickly.
To lose a dowry, why, you'll miss a lot. (*Exeunt* ESTEBAN *and* ALDERMAN)
LAURENCIA Frondoso, are you glad?
FRONDOSO   What! Am I glad?
I think I shall go mad with all the joy 530
And the good feeling in my heart. Laurencia,
My heart seems darting laughter from my eyes
To see you at long last in my possession. (*They go*)

The country near Ciudad Real
(*Enter the* MASTER OF CALATRAVA, *the* COMENDADOR, FLORES, 535
and ORTUÑO)

COMENDADOR Fly, Master, now there is no other way!
MASTER It was the weakness of the rampart caused it
And the great strength of the invading army.
COMENDADOR It cost them blood and many thousand lives. 540
MASTER But they can never boast it to their glory
The flag of Calatrava graced their spoils
With other captured standards.
COMENDADOR   None the less,

Girón, your proudest hopes are in the dust. ₅₄₅

MASTER It's not my fault if fortune blindly heaves me
Aloft today, and then tomorrow leaves me.

VOICES (*Within*) Victory for the monarchs of Castile!

MASTER The battlements are crowned with lights, the windows
Of all the highest towers are hung with banners ₅₅₀
And with victorious flags.

COMENDADOR   It cost them dear,
Rather a funeral than a feast, I fear
For them today.

MASTER   I'll home to Calatrava, ₅₅₅
Fernando Gómez.

COMENDADOR   I to Fuente Ovejuna
While you continue following your cause
Or yield yourself up to the Catholic King.

MASTER I'll write to you what I intend to do. ₅₆₀

COMENDADOR Yes, time will teach you.

MASTER   Though so young, yet time
With his deceitful rigour proves my master. (*They leave*)

The country near Fuente Ovejuna
(*Enter, in a crowd,* MUSICIANS, MENGO, FRONDOSO, LAURENCIA, ₅₆₅
PASCUALA, BARRILDO, ESTEBAN, *and* JUAN ROJO)

MUSICIANS (*Singing*) Long live the bridegroom
Long live the bride.

MENGO Your singing must be difficult.

BARRILDO D'you think that music made by you ₅₇₀
Would have a happier result?

FRONDOSO Poor Mengo, you're so black and blue,
You know far more of blows and curses
Than notes and tremolos and verses.

MENGO There is one in this place knows how ₅₇₅
To stop your junketing I vow,
And that's the grim Comendador!

BARRILDO That's enough, Mengo! Say no more!
That foul, barbarian, murderous stot
Has of our honour robbed the lot. ₅₈₀

MENGO He had me beaten by a hundred
Men in turn. Is it to be wondered,
When I had nothing but a sling,
That I submitted to this thing?
It was both heathen and herètic ₅₈₅
To force so powerful an emetic
Upon a man of such good fame
Though modesty conceals his name . . .
How can you bear with it? For shame!

BARRILDO   Why, for a joke!
MENGO   There is no laughter
   In such a dose. It feels like flame,
   And makes you wish to die thereafter.
FRONDOSO   I ask you if your rhyme's in season—
   Too coarse either for rhyme or reason!   595
MENGO   Well, listen. "May the bride together
   With her bridegroom make good weather,
   Nor ever feel the need to quarrel,
   Nor jealousy at things immoral,
   And may they in this way behave   600
   Till, tired of living, to the grave
   They're trundled off in the same hearse!
   Long live the pair!"
FRONDOSO   May heaven curse
   The poet who spawns such a verse.   605
BARRILDO   He made it quickly on the spot.
MENGO   Talking of poets, have you not
   Seen doughnut-bakers at their toil
   Chuck chunks of dough into the oil
   To fill their cauldron on the boil?   610
   Some come out cooked, some come out charred,
   Some come out soft, some come out hard.
   Well, that's how poets (I suppose)
   Deal with the poems they compose.
   Choosing one's matter, just like duff,   615
   In different shapes one kneads the stuff
   Then flings it in his paper pot
   Hoping to make a lucky shot
   And smother up with treacle thick
   Such thoughts as might make people sick.   620
   But when he touts the things for sale
   On nobody can he prevail.
   At last then (without praise or pelf)
   He must digest them by himself.
BARRILDO   Hush! let the lovers speak, quit fooling, Mengo.   625
LAURENCIA   Give us your hands to kiss.
JUAN ROJO   Yes, my dear niece,
   After you and Frondoso kiss your father's.
ESTEBAN   Rojo, to her and her good man, may heaven
   Grant deepest blessings!   630
FRONDOSO   You two, bless us both.
JUAN ROJO   Now all together sing, since they are one!
MUSICIANS (Singing)   Through Fuente Ovejuna's valleys
                      A long-haired girl goes light of foot
                      A knight of Calatrava sallies,   635
                      With his red cross, in her pursuit.

So she hides in bushes green
To conceal her wrath and shame,
Feigning that she has not seen
That running on her tracks he came.   640
    O why do you hide there
    My lovely girl, alone?
    For my desires can fare
    Through walls and see through stone.

The nobleman comes near her now   645
And, she confused and frightened, tries
Closer to pull each sheltering bough
To hide her beauty from his eyes.
But since, for one who is in love,
No obstacle was ever met   650
On seas beneath or peaks above,
He goes on singing to her yet:
    O why do you hide there,
    My lovely girl, alone?
    For my desires can fare   655
    Through walls and see through stone.

(*Enter the* COMENDADOR, FLORES, ORTUÑO, CIMBRANOS)

COMENDADOR   On with the wedding! Don't let *me* disturb you.

JUAN ROJO   This is no game, my lord; we're glad to take
    Your orders. May we find a seat for you?   660
    What tidings of your warlike enterprise?
    I'll wager that you conquered.

FRONDOSO   I am lost!
    May heaven save me!

LAURENCIA   Fly from here, Frondoso!   665

COMENDADOR   Don't let him go. Arrest him. Tie him up.

JUAN ROJO   Obey, my lad.

FRONDOSO   You want them, then, to kill me?

COMENDADOR   I'm not the sort of man to kill a fellow
    Who's guiltless. If I were, these soldiers here   670
    Would have already riddled you clean through.
    I order him to gaol where his own father
    Will have to judge and sentence him, as mayor.

PASCUALA   Why, sir, he's getting married.

COMENDADOR   Getting married?   675
    What's that to me? Are there no more young men?

PASCUALA   If he offended you, you should forgive him
    Being who you are.

COMENDADOR   Pascuala, I don't count
    For anything in this affair at all.   680
    It was that he insulted the Grand Master,

Téllez Girón, whom God preserve; he raised
His arm against the Order; aimed a crossbow
At its most holy symbol; and must suffer
Due punishment to stand as an example   685
Because it touches on the Master's honour.
Some others might rebel against his rule
Elsewhere, and raise their standards in the field.
It would not do to pardon one who threatened
The Master's Grand Comendador with death   690
As you all know he did the other day.
What loyal subjects!

ESTEBAN   As his father-in-law
I'll plead for him. Surely it is not much
That a young man in love should lose control   695
With you since you were ravishing his bride!
Surely he might defend her! That's no crime!

COMENDADOR   Mayor! You are an interfering fool!

ESTEBAN   It's for your virtue's sake, my lord.

COMENDADOR   I never   700
Annoyed his bride—since she was not his bride then!

ESTEBAN   Yes, you molested her. Let this suffice you.
There are a pair of monarchs in Castile
Who are giving out new laws and making havoc
Of old abuses. They would do great wrong,   705
When resting from their victories, to permit
That lords and barons in the villages
Should be allowed to tyrannise and murder
Because they wear big crosses on their breasts!
Let great King Ferdinand put on the cross,   710
For such a symbol is for true-born princes!

COMENDADOR   Hey! Take away his staff of office from him!

ESTEBAN   Take it! You're welcome to the useless bauble.

COMENDADOR   And now I'm going to batter him with it
As I would any horse that gets too frisky!   715
                (Breaks the staff on ESTEBAN's head)

ESTEBAN   Being a vassal, I must suffer this.

PASCUALA   How dare you strike an aged man like that?

LAURENCIA   If you thrash him because he is my father—
What is it in me you would take revenge on?   720

COMENDADOR   Take her and guard her for me with ten soldiers!
        (Exeunt COMENDADOR and his followers, dragging LAURENCIA and
                                FRONDOSO)

ESTEBAN   May justice come down from on high! (He goes)

PASCUALA   The wedding   725
Has turned into a day of bitter mourning. (She goes)

BARRILDO   Will no man raise his voice?

MENGO	I've had my flogging

MENGO   I've had my flogging
    Already, just for raising it a little.
    I've got the seven cardinal colours striped   730
    Upon my hide, and yet I never went
    To Rome to fetch them.
JUAN ROJO   All shall raise our voices!
MENGO Well, sirs, it seems to me all should be silent.
    My buttocks are like slices of raw salmon. (*They all leave*)   735

Act Three

Council chamber in Fuente Ovejuna
(*Enter* ESTEBAN, ALONSO, BARRILDO)

ESTEBAN Have they not come yet to the council?
BARRILDO   No.
ESTEBAN Unless they're quick, we run a mortal danger.   5
BARRILDO Most of the people have been warned already.
    Frondoso is in shackles in the tower.
    Laurencia, my girl's in such a plight
    That unless God comes quickly to our aid . . .
            (*Enter* JUAN ROJO *and the* ALDERMAN. MENGO *after them*)   10
JUAN ROJO Why are you shouting, when our enterprise
    Depends on secrecy, Esteban?
ESTEBAN That I'm so silent should surprise you more
    Considering my wrongs.
MENGO   I've also come   15
    To sit on this great council.
ESTEBAN   An old man
    Whose snow-white beard is watered by his eyes,
    You honourable farmers, asks of you
    What funeral oration should be made   20
    For our lost country and its trampled honour?
    Yet of what use to mourn our honours now,
    Since which of you has not been vilely injured
    By this barbarian? Answer! Is there one
    Among you who does not feel that his honour   25
    And life have not been utterly destroyed?
    Are all of you not sick of mere lamenting?
    Then, since you have lost all that is worth while,
    What are you waiting for? What worse misfortune?
JUAN ROJO We've suffered that already—the world's worst!   30
    But since it now is manifest and public
    The King and Queen have pacified Castile,
    And now, from Córdoba, are on the way.
    Let's send two councillors to beg their mercy
    And ask them to deliver us from woe.   35

BARRILDO   While Ferdinand is humbling to the earth
    So many stronger enemies far off,
    The greater wars absorb his time and strength:
    Some other swifter method should be found.
ALDERMAN   If you would hear my voice, my vote should be   40
    That we desert this village, one and all.
JUAN ROJO   There is not time enough for such a move.
MENGO   If anyone should hear this noisy meeting
    It would cost several lives amongst the council.
ALDERMAN   But now the mast of patience has been splintered   45
    Our ship drives on beyond the scope of fear
    To that of desperation. From her wedding
    They take the daughter of an honoured mayor,
    Breaking his staff upon his own white head.
    What slave has ever suffered such injustice?   50
JUAN ROJO   What do you think the people should attempt?
    Die, or else perish in the bold attempt
    Since they are few and we are many.
BARRILDO   How!
    To arm ourselves against our rightful lord?   55
ESTEBAN   The King alone, after our God in heaven,
    Is our true lord. All right of mastership
    Is forfeited by inhumanity.
    With God to help our zeal, why fear the cost?
MENGO   Look, sirs, be very cautious in such projects.   60
    I came here on the part of simple peasants
    Who suffer the worst injuries of all—
    And I must also represent their fears.
JUAN ROJO   If what we've suffered far outweighs the loss
    Of life that's scarce worth living—why hold back?   65
    They burn our barns, our vineyards, and our farms.
    Tyrants they are. To vengeance let us go!
                (Enter LAURENCIA, *dishevelled and torn*)
LAURENCIA   Let me inside! For well I have the right
    To enter into council with the men   70
    Since if I cannot vote, at least I can
    Scream out aloud. Do any of you know me?
ESTEBAN   Great God in heaven! Can this be my daughter?
JUAN ROJO   Do you not know Laurencia?
LAURENCIA   I have come   75
    In such condition, that you well may wonder
    Who this is here.
ESTEBAN   My daughter!
LAURENCIA   Do not call me
    Your daughter!   80
ESTEBAN   Why, my dear one, tell me why?
LAURENCIA   For many reasons and of these the weightiest

Is that you neither rescued me from traitors
Nor yet took vengeance on those bestial tyrants
Whom you let kidnap me! I was not yet   85
Frondoso's, so you can't fob off on him
The duty of avenging me. On you
The duty lies as well. Until the night
When marriage is fulfilled and consummated,
It is the father's duty, not the husband's.   90
When one has bought a gem, till it's delivered
The buyer does not pay. It is not he
Who has to guard it from the hands of robbers
Till it's been handed over. I was taken
Under your eyes to Fernán Gómez' house   95
While you looked on like coward shepherds, letting
The wolf escape uninjured with the sheep.
They set their daggers to my breasts! The vileness
And filth of what they said to me! The threats
They made to tear me limb from limb! The foul   100
And bestial tricks by which they tried to have me!
Do you not see my hair torn out? These cuts
And bruises and the bleeding flesh that shows
Through my torn rags? You call yourselves true men?
Are you my parents and relations, you   105
Whose entrails do not burst with grief to see me
Reduced to this despair? You're all tame sheep!
Fuente Ovejuna means the fount where sheep drink—
And now I see the reason! Cowards, give
Me weapons! You are stones and bronze and marble   110
And tigers—tigers? no! for tigers follow
The stealers of their cubs, and kill the hunters
Before they can escape back to their ships.
No, you are craven rabbits, mice, and hares!
You are not Spaniards but barbarian slaves!   115
Yes, you are hens to suffer that your women
By brutal force should be enjoyed by others.
Put spindles in your belts. Why wear those swords?
As God lives now, I shall make sure that women
Alone redeem our honour from these tyrants,   120
And make these traitors bleed! And as for you,
You chickenhearted nancy-boys and sissies,
Spinning-wheel gossips and effeminate cowards,
We will throw stones at you and have you dressed
In petticoats and crinolines and bonnets,   125
With rouge and powder on your pansy faces!
Now the Comendador's about to hang
Frondoso up alive, to starve and die,

Head downwards from the castle's battlements,
And so he'll soon be doing with you all! 130
But I am glad of it, you half-men, since
The town will thus be ridded of its women,
And thus become a town of Amazons
Like me, to be the wonder of the age.
ESTEBAN   I am not one who suffers such vile titles. 135
I shall rebel, though it should be alone
And all the world against me.
JUAN ROJO   So will I!
Though frightened by the greatness of our foe.
ALDERMAN   Let us all die, rather than cringe! 140
BARRILDO   Unfurl
A cloth upon a pole to be our banner!
Death and destruction to this breed of monsters!
JUAN ROJO   What order shall we march in?
MENGO   Without order! 145
Let's kill him straight! One cry will join the people
Since they are all agreed upon his death!
ESTEBAN   Then arm yourselves! Grab swords and pikes and cudgels,
Crossbows and slings and anything you can!
MENGO   Long live the Catholic Kings, our rightful masters! 150
ALL   Long live the Kings!
MENGO   Death to the bloody tyrants!
ALL   Death to the traitor-tyrants one and all! (*Exeunt all the men*)
LAURENCIA   March on! And may the heavens hear your cry!
(*Shouting very loudly*)   All women of the village, join the ranks! 155
The time has come now to retrieve our honour!
          (*Enter* PASCUALA, JACINTA, *and other women to* LAURENCIA)
PASCUALA   What's this? What are you shouting for so loudly?
LAURENCIA   Can't you see how they've all gone off to kill
Fernando Gómez—dotards, boys, and men, 160
All furiously rushing to the fray?
And we, the women, must we yield the honour
Of such a noble action to the men,
Since we have suffered far more harm than them?
JACINTA   Well, what do you propose to do? 165
LAURENCIA   Line up!
In order! For we'll show the world today
A deed which centuries will hear with awe
When we are dead and gone. Jacinta, here,
Your greater wrongs earn you the higher rank 170
So you will be the corporal of the band.
JACINTA   Your own wrongs are not less than mine.
LAURENCIA   Pascuala,
You will be the ensign.

PASCUALA   Give me the flag
To hoist upon a lance, and you will see
Whether I merited the rank or not.

LAURENCIA   There is no time. Strike while the iron's hot!
Let kerchiefs, shawls, and bonnets be our standards!

PASCUALA   Now we'll elect our captain.

LAURENCIA   There's no need.

PASCUALA   Why?

LAURENCIA   Because, when I go into action—watch me!
You will not need the Cid or Rodomont!* (*They go*)

The hall in the Comendador's castle
(*Enter* FRONDOSO *with his hands tied,* FLORES, ORTUÑO, CIMBRANOS,
and the COMENDADOR)

COMENDADOR   Whatever rope's left over from his hands
Will do to hang him from and hurt the worse.

FRONDOSO   Oh, what an evil name your birth retrieves!

COMENDADOR   Now hang him from that nearest battlement.

FRONDOSO   My lord, I never did intend the deed
When shouldering the crossbow. (*A great noise is heard*)

FLORES   What's the uproar?

COMENDADOR   What does it mean?

FLORES   Like thunder from the highest
It breaks in on our judgment. (*More noise*)

ORTUÑO   All the doors
Are being crashed and splintered into dust! (*A tremendous noise*)

COMENDADOR   What? Breaking in the doors of my own house?
And the headquarters of the Order?

FLORES   Yes!
The whole town has arrived in force together.

JUAN ROJO (*Within*)   Kill, destroy, burn, crush, and smash them all!

ORTUÑO   These mob revolts are nasty to control!

COMENDADOR   You mean they've risen against me?

FLORES   Not only risen.
Your gates are sprawling headlong to their fury
And they are here on top of you!

COMENDADOR (*Pointing to* FRONDOSO)   Untie him.
And humour this poor bumpkin of a mayor,
Frondoso, if you can.

FRONDOSO   I'll go: it's only
Through love they have committed this offence.

              (*He goes out. The voice of* MENGO *is heard from within*)

MENGO (*Within*)   Long live King Ferdinand and Isabel!
Death to the traitors here!

------

[184] The Cid, Rodrigo de Vivar (*c.*1043–99), led Castile in its effort to drive the Moors out and became a
great national hero. Rodomont was his Saracen counterpart, a fierce King of Algiers.

FLORES   Don't be found here,
My lord, for God's sake!

COMENDADOR   Let them try to force it!   220
This central hall is very strongly walled
And guarded. Soon enough they will slink home.

FLORES   When a whole people which has been outraged
Makes up its mind, it never goes back home
Without its freight of vengeance and red blood.   225

COMENDADOR   In this great door, as if at a portcullis,
We can defend ourselves against them all.

FRONDOSO (*Within*)   Long live Fuente Ovejuna!

COMENDADOR (*Derisively*)   What a captain!
Set on them, and you'll see their fury fade!   230

FLORES   By your own fury, sir, I'm more dismayed!

     (*Enter* ESTEBAN, FRONDOSO, JUAN ROJO, MENGO, BARRILDO, *and other*
                   PEASANTS, *all armed*)

ESTEBAN   Now we confront the tyrant and his flunkeys!
Fuente Ovejuna, let those tyrants die!   235

COMENDADOR   Wait, my good people.

ALL   Insults cannot wait!

COMENDADOR   Tell me your injuries, and I'll repair them,
I swear upon my knighthood and my faith.

ALL   Fuente Ovejuna! Long live the Catholic Kings!   240
And death to all bad Christians and to traitors!

COMENDADOR   Will you not listen to me? I'm your master!

ALL   The Catholic King and Queen are now our masters!

COMENDADOR   Here, wait a minute!

ALL   Die, Fernando Gómez!   245
Long live Fuente Ovejuna! (*Exeunt fighting, the* COMENDADOR *driven*
                back by the insurgents)
             (*Enter the women, armed*)

LAURENCIA   Halt at this door. You are no longer women
But desperate legionnaires.   250

PASCUALA   Those poor old pansies
We once called men, it seems, are men once more
And letting out his blood!

JACINTA   Throw down his body
And we'll impale the carcass on our spears.   255

ESTEBAN (*Within*)   Die, foul Comendador!

COMENDADOR (*Within*)   I'm dying
And may the Lord have mercy on my soul
And pity for my monstrous sins.

BARRILDO (*Within*)   Here's Flores!   260

MENGO (*Within*)   Have at him! He's the very man that sliced me
Across my back two thousand fiery lashes.

FRONDOSO (*Within*)   I would not be avenged were I to spare him.

LAURENCIA   We'll enter now.

PASCUALA	Wait! Let us guard the door!	265

BARRILDO (*Within*) What! soften us with tears? You scurvy cowards
Who were the lords and masters of us all?

LAURENCIA I can't wait, Pascuala, I must enter.
My sword is sick of loafing in its sheath. (*She goes in*)

BARRILDO (*Within*) Ortuño too! Ortuño! 270

FRONDOSO (*Within*)   Slash his face!
        (*Suddenly enter* FLORES *from within,* MENGO *pursuing him*)

FLORES Have mercy, Mengo, it was not my fault:
I was obeying orders.

MENGO   If you don't 275
Deserve it 'cause you are a filthy pimp
You more than merit it for flogging me!

PASCUALA You give him to us women, Mengo, now.
Stop flogging him. Just hand him over. Lovely!

MENGO I've given him enough to pay my stripes. 280

PASCUALA I shall avenge you more.

MENGO   Well, fire ahead!

JACINTA Die, dirty rat!

FLORES   What, to be killed by women?

JACINTA Weren't women in your line? 285

PASCUALA   What tears are those?

JACINTA Die, traitor, and the pandar to his vices!

LAURENCIA (*Within*) Die, you dirty devil!

FLORES   Have pity on me, ladies!
        (*Enter* ORTUÑO *fleeing,* LAURENCIA *after him*) 290

ORTUÑO Look, but I am not him you mean!

LAURENCIA   I know
The creature that you are. (*To the women*) Go in, you women,
Kill! Finish off these villains once for all!

PASCUALA I shall die killing. 295

ALL THE WOMEN   Live the Catholic Kings!
Long live Fuente Ovejuna! Tyrants, die! (*They all go*)

King's palace in Toro
(*Enter* KING FERDINAND, QUEEN ISABEL, *and* DON MANRIQUE,
Master of Santiago) 300

DON MANRIQUE Having foreseen and calculated well
We carried out our plans with few obstructions.
There wasn't much resistance. If there had been
It would have fizzled out. Cabra is busy
And well-prepared against a chance attack. 305

KING He has done well. The way to help him best
Is to reorganise our force and send
Covering troops. The King of Portugal
Can be checkmated thus. The Count of Cabra

Is in the key position where he is.   310
That's to the good. He's one who knows his work.

(Enter FLORES, *wounded)*

FLORES   Great Catholic King Ferdinand, to whom
God grants, as worthiest of His knights, to wear
The diadem of Castile, I come to tell you   315
Of the worst cruelty the sun has seen,
From rise to set, among the whole world's peoples!

KING   Come, come, contain yourself.

FLORES   My sovereign lord,
My wounds prevent me from more lengthy detail,   320
Since I am near my death and bleeding fast.
I've come from Fuente Ovejuna where
The village people slew their rightful lord
Fernando Gómez who lies mangled by
Disloyal vassals for a trivial cause.   325
The countryfolk proclaimed him as a "tyrant"
And worked themselves to frenzy with this cry.
They burst his doors in though he made the promise,
Upon his knightly faith, of reparation
To all whom he had injured. Deaf to prayers,   330
With ruthless fury, they all fell on him
And, with a thousand cruel wounds, destroyed
A breast that bore the cross of Calatrava.
Then, from the topmost windows, down they hurled him
To fall upon the serried pikes and swords   335
The women held upright to catch his body.
The clawed out all his beard and half his hair
And hacked his face about with fearful gashes
As his poor corpse was carried to the channel.
Their brutal fury raged to such a height,   340
His very ears were bargained for, as trophies,
And fetched high prices. After this was done
They chipped away with pikes the coat-of-arms
Over his gateway, saying they were hateful,
And that they would supplant them with your own.   345
They sacked his palace, and they shared the plunder
As though he'd been a foe in open war.
I saw all this from where I hid, for fate
Would not permit my miserable life
To end just then but thus I lay till night   350
Permitted my escape to tell of it.
Great lord, since you are just, punish the villains
With a just sentence for their barbarous crimes.
Fernando's blood cries out to you for vengeance
And rigorous justice.   355

KING   You may rest assured

They'll not remain unpunished. This sad thing
Amazes me. A judge must go forthwith
To verify this case and make examples
Of those who're guilty. Let him take a captain   360
For his protection. Such barefaced rebellion
As this requires exemplary chastisement.
Attend that soldier's wounds. (*They go out*)

Town square in Fuente Ovejuna
(*The village people and their women come in with the head of* FERNANDO   365
GÓMEZ *on a lance*)

MUSICIANS (*Singing*)   Long life to Ferdinand our King
       And to Queen Isabel
       But death to all the tyrants
       That on this earth may dwell!   370
BARRILDO   Now it's Frondoso's turn, to say
His piece of verse.
FRONDOSO   I have no art.
Although my lines may limp astray
Forgive them, coming from my heart: 375
Long live the lovely Isabel
And Ferdinand of Aragón,
In one and other's arms to dwell,
Each with each, and both as one!
Then may the great Archangel Michael   380
Raise them in glory to the sky!
Long live the Kings for many a cycle
But let all tyrants quickly die!
LAURENCIA   Your turn, Barrildo!
BARRILDO   I don't mind.   385
I've thought mine out with studious care.
PASCUALA   Say it with care, too; then you'll find
It will sound even yet more rare!
BARRILDO   Long live the famous Kings, since they
     Have been so many times victorious,   390
     And may they come to reign, some day,
     As our own masters, great and glorious!
     In triumph, over dwarfs and giants,
     We wish them power to rise on high
     But to all tyrants shout defiance!   395
     Forever may they burst and die!
MUSICIANS (*Singing*)   Long life to Ferdinand our King
       And to Queen Isabel
       But death to all the tyrants
       That on this earth may dwell!   400
LAURENCIA   Now, Mengo, you recite.

FRONDOSO	Yes, you!

MENGO I am no "true-blue" as to verse.

PASCUALA Rather you mean, and it's quite true,
    You're black and blue on your *reverse!* 405

MENGO Well, here goes, without more verbosity:
    That fellow, on a Sunday morning
    Had my back thrashed with such ferocity
    It put my hide in hues of mourning
    But now I feel no animosity. 410
    Long live the Kings of Christianosity
    And perish thus all Tyrannosity!

MUSICIANS (*Singing*) Long life to Ferdinand our King
                And to Queen Isabel
                But death to all the tyrants 415
                That on this earth may dwell!

ESTEBAN Take out that head.

MENGO   How horribly it grins!
    (*Enter* JUAN ROJO *carrying the Royal Arms on a shield*)

ALDERMAN The new Arms have arrived. 420

ESTEBAN   Let's look at them!

JUAN ROJO Where shall we place them?

ALDERMAN   Here, on the Town Hall.

ESTEBAN A splendid shield!

BARRILDO   What happiness it means! 425

FRONDOSO With this new sun, our day begins to break.

ESTEBAN Long live Castile, León, and Aragón!
    Die, tyranny, forever! But now heed me,
    Fuente Ovejuna! Hear an old man's words,
    Whose counsel never harmed a soul among you. 430
    The King will wish to clarify this case
    And, since the town lies in his journey's route,
    You should agree on what you'll have to say
    When they examine you, as well they may.

FRONDOSO What's your advice? 435

ESTEBAN   If they ask who is guilty,
    Die saying "Fuente Ovejuna" only.
    Not one word more.

FRONDOSO   Nothing could be more straight!
    Fuente Ovejuna did it. 440

ESTEBAN   Will you all
    Answer thus?

ALL   Yes.

ESTEBAN   Now let me just pretend
    I'm the examiner, and we'll rehearse 445
    The better, thus, what we must say and do.
    Say Mengo, here, is being put to torture.

MENGO Can you find no one thinner to stretch out?

ESTEBAN Come, don't be foolish, Mengo! Were you thinking
   This was in earnest?   450
MENGO   Well, say on, then! Do!
ESTEBAN Who was it murdered the Comendador?
MENGO Fuente Ovejuna did it.
ESTEBAN   Now, you dog!
   Do you want to be racked in half?   455
MENGO   My lord!
   Although I die . . .
ESTEBAN   Confess, you knave!
MENGO   I do.
ESTEBAN Well, who was it?   460
MENGO   It was Fuente Ovejuna.
ESTEBAN Give him an extra turn!
MENGO   Why, that is nothing!
ESTEBAN A fig, then, for the worst the judge can do!
                   (*Another* ALDERMAN *enters*)   465
SECOND ALDERMAN What's going on here?
FRONDOSO   Why, what is the matter,
   Cuadrado?
SECOND ALDERMAN The examining judge has come.
ESTEBAN Then scatter round the town.   470
SECOND ALDERMAN   He is attended,
   Too, by a captain and his troops.
ESTEBAN   Although
   The devil came himself, we'll not be daunted.
   You know now the one word we all must answer.   475
SECOND ALDERMAN They are arresting everyone on sight.
ESTEBAN Don't fear. Who murdered the Comendador,
   Eh, Mengo?
MENGO   Who? Why, Fuente Ovejuna! (*They go out*)

          Palace of the Master of Calatrava in Almagro   480
              (*Enter the* MASTER *and a soldier*)
MASTER That such a thing could happen! What a fate!
   I almost feel like putting you to death
   For bringing such black news.
SOLDIER   I only brought it   485
   As messenger, not to arouse your anger.
MASTER To think an angry mob could dare so much!
   I'll take five hundred men to raze the village
   That not one person's name shall be remembered!
SOLDIER Contain your rage, my lord. They have declared   490
   Their loyalty to the King. Your one last hope
   Is not to anger him more than you've done.

MASTER   How can they give their village to the King
    Since they are of my Order?
SOLDIER   That will be   495
    A legal matter to discuss with him.
MASTER   No legal powers affect the papal tenure,
    Yet I must recognise the King and Queen
    And pay them homage; so I'll curb my rage
    Till I have come to some accommodation.   500
    For though they hold me heavily to blame,
    My youth will plead for me. I go with shame—
    Compelled to go that I may save my honour,
    For one must not be careless in that cause. (*They go*)

The square in Fuente Ovejuna   505
(*Enter* LAURENCIA, *alone*)
LAURENCIA   Loving, to know the loved one is in danger
    Doubles the pangs of love; foreseeing harms
    Adds fears to fears and multiplies alarms.
    The firm untroubled mind, to tears a stranger,   510
    Melts at the touch of fear. The steadfast faith,
    If fear comes near it, flickers like a wraith,
    Imagining the dear one snatched away.
    I love my husband. Yet when he is near,
    Fearing his harm, I am a prey to fear;   515
    And when he's absent, I am in worse dismay.
                (*Enter* FRONDOSO)
FRONDOSO   Laurencia!
LAURENCIA   My beloved husband, how
    Dare you be seen round here?   520
FRONDOSO   Is this the way
    You welcome my most loving care?
LAURENCIA   My dearest,
    Seek safety. You're in deadly peril here!
FRONDOSO   May heaven forbid that you're not glad to see me!   525
LAURENCIA   Do you not fear the cruelty of the judge?
    And how he's treated others? Save your life
    And do not court worse danger!
FRONDOSO   Save a life
    So ill-received? Should I desert my friends   530
    And lose the sight of you in this great danger?
    Do not tell *me* to fly. It is unthinkable
    That I should make an alien of my blood
    On such a terrible occasion. (*Cries within*) Listen
    I can hear cries—of someone being tortured,   535
    If my ears tell me truly. Listen hard.

(The voice of the JUDGE *can now be heard from within with the replies of the*
PEASANTS)

JUDGE (*Within*) Now, good old man, speak nothing but the truth!
FRONDOSO It's an old man they're putting on the rack.   540
LAURENCIA How dastardly!
ESTEBAN (*Within*)   Can they leave off?
JUDGE (*Within*)   Relax him.
    Now speak! Who was it killed Fernando Gómez?
ESTEBAN (*Within*) Fuente Ovejuna did it.   545
LAURENCIA   Oh, my father!
    Your name be praised forever to the skies!
FRONDOSO Oh, grand example!
JUDGE (*Within*)   Now let's rack that boy there.
    You, puppy! Yes, I know you've got the answer!   550
    Who was it? Are you silent? Give more turns,
    You bungling torturer!
BOY (*Within*)   Fuente Ovejuna!
JUDGE (*Within*) I'd have you hanged, you riffraff, were I able.
    Now on the King's life, tell me who it was!   555
    Who murdered the Comendador?
FRONDOSO   That they
    Could torture a child thus, and he resist them!
LAURENCIA Oh, valiant people!
FRONDOSO   Very brave and strong!   560
JUDGE (*Within*) Let's have that woman on the rack at once.
    (*To torturer*) And get that lever working there, come on!
LAURENCIA He's blind with rage!
JUDGE (*Within*)   I'll kill the lot of you
    Upon this rack here, on my word, you wretches!   565
    Who murdered him?
PASCUALA (*Within*)   My lord, Fuente Ovejuna!
JUDGE (*Within, to torturer*) Tighter!
FRONDOSO   In vain!
LAURENCIA   Pascuala lasted out.   570
FRONDOSO When children last, how can you be surprised?
JUDGE (*Within, to torturer*) Give her some more. It seems that you enchant
                                        them.
PASCUALA (*Within*) Oh, pitying heaven!
JUDGE (*Within, to torturer*) You swine, can you be deaf?   575
    Stretch her, I said!
PASCUALA (*Within*) Fuente Ovejuna did it!
JUDGE (*Within, to torturer*) Now let's have that half-naked bag of guts,
    That fattest one of all, him, over there!
LAURENCIA Mengo, no doubt!   580
FRONDOSO   He will break down, I fear.
MENGO (*Within*) Ay! Ay!

JUDGE (*Within*) Now turn the lever of the screw!

MENGO (*Within*) Ay!

JUDGE (*Within, to torturer*) Turn! More! Are you in need of help? 585

MENGO (*Within*)   Ay! Ay!

JUDGE (*Within*) Who murdered the Comendador, base villain?

MENGO (*Within*) Ay! Ay! I'll tell Your Lordship.

JUDGE (*Within, to torturer*)   Now relax it.

FRONDOSO He will confess! (*A pause—no answer from* MENGO) 590

JUDGE (*Within, to torturer*) Put your shoulder this time
    Against the lever!

MENGO (*Within*)   Wait! I've had enough.
    I'll tell you all, if you'll but let me free.

JUDGE (*Within*) Who was it? 595

MENGO (*Within*)   Why, my lord, to tell the truth . . .
    Little old Fuente Ovejunita did it!

JUDGE (*Within*) Was ever such a stubborn villainy?
    They seem to make a jest of agony,
    And he from whom I hoped the most results 600
    ·Was far more strongly stubborn than the rest.
    Leave them. I am exhausted. Let them go!

FRONDOSO Oh, Mengo, may God bless your honest soul!
    With fear enough for two I trembled here
    But fear for you had quite effaced that fear! 605

              (*Enter* MENGO, BARRILDO, *and the* ALDERMAN)

BARRILDO Mengo has conquered!

ALDERMAN   As you see!

BARRILDO Mengo's the victor!

FRONDOSO   I agree! 610

MENGO Ay! Ay! Ay! Ay!

BARRILDO   Come drink and eat!
    Here, take this bowl, this stuff's a treat!

MENGO Ay! Ay!

FRONDOSO   Pour him another jug! 615

BARRILDO The way it gurgles down his mug!

FRONDOSO It does him good. He soaks it neat.

LAURENCIA Now give him something more to eat.

MENGO Ay! Ay!

BARRILDO   This other is with me! 620

LAURENCIA Just look how solemnly he's drinking.

FRONDOSO One who defies the rack, I'm thinking,
    Needs a good drink!

ALDERMAN   The next, with me?

MENGO Ay! Ay! Yes! Yes! 625

FRONDOSO   Drink! You deserve it!

LAURENCIA He soaks as fast as one can serve it.

FRONDOSO Arrange his clothes: he's getting frozen.

BARRILDO   Some more to drink?

MENGO   Yes, three rounds more!

FRONDOSO   He needs more wine.

BARRILDO   There's lots in store.
    Come drink, man, drink! for you're our chosen!
    To be so brave a rack-defier
    Must give a thirst like raging fire.   635
    What's wrong?

MENGO   It has a tang of rosin,
    And also I've a cold in store.

FRONDOSO   Why, here's some sweet wine, if you'd sooner.
    But: who killed the Comendador?   640

MENGO   Why! little old Fuente Ovenjunita!

        (*Exeunt all but* FRONDOSO *and* LAURENCIA)

FRONDOSO   It's right that they should do him greatest honour
    But who killed the Comendador, my darling?

LAURENCIA   Fuente Ovejuna killed him, dearest love.   645

FRONDOSO   Who really killed him? Between you and me?

LAURENCIA   Fuente Ovejuna! Do not terrify me!

FRONDOSO   And how did *I* kill *you,* then? Tell me that.

LAURENCIA   You made me die of loving you so much! (*They go*)

       Palace of the King at Tordesillas   650
    (*Enter* KING FERDINAND *and* QUEEN ISABEL)

QUEEN   I did not know I'd meet with the good fortune
    To find you here, my lord.

KING   The sight of you
    Brings me new glory. I was on the way   655
    To Portugal, and had to come past here.

QUEEN   Your Majesty did well indeed to come
    Since it was convenient.

KING   What of Castile?

QUEEN   All peaceful, quiet, and smooth.   660

KING   Since it was you
    Who did the smoothing, I don't marvel at it.

    (*Enter* DON MANRIQUE, *Master of Santiago*)

DON MANRIQUE   Seeking an audience with Your Majesties
    The Master of the Calatrava Order   665
    Has just arrived.

QUEEN   I've always longed to see him.

DON MANRIQUE   I swear it by my faith, Your Majesty,
    Though very young, he is a valiant soldier. (*He goes*)

    (*Enter the* MASTER OF CALATRAVA)   670

MASTER   Rodrigo Téllez Girón is my name,
    Grand Master of the cross of Calatrava,
    Who never stints your praises. I have come

To sue your royal pardons. Ill-advised
By those around me, I broke all just bounds,   675
In rash excess to brave your royal wills.
It was Fernando's counsel that deceived me,
And then my own self-interest. I was wrong.
So humbly now I beg forgiveness of you,
Which, if my supplication can deserve,   680
Amidst the foremost of your ranks I'll serve
And, in your next crusade against Granada,
No man shall draw his sword with fiercer verve,
For I shall plant my crimson crosses farther
Than any, on the topmost battlements!   685
Five hundred men I'll bring to join your tents
And I shall sign and seal a solemn oath—
Never to discontent you—to you both!

KING   Rise up then, Master, from the ground, for since
You've come to me, you shall be well received.   690

MASTER   You are the comforter of the afflicted.

QUEEN   You're quite as good at talking as at fighting.

MASTER   You are the lovely Esther of our age;*
And you its godlike Xerxes, Majesty.

               (*Re-enter* DON MANRIQUE)   695

DON MANRIQUE   My lord, the judge examiner is here,
The one who went to Fuente Ovejuna.

KING (*To the* QUEEN)   Now you must judge these riotous aggressors.

MASTER (*Thinking erroneously the* KING *addressed him*)   Had I not learned the
                                  lesson of your mercy,   700
I would have served them all a bloody lesson
In how to kill Comendadors.

KING (*To the* MASTER)   Not you.
The days when you gave judgments are no more. (MASTER *falls back re-*
buked)   705

QUEEN (*To the* KING)   Would but to God this military might
Were subject to your orders or put down.

               (*Enter the* JUDGE)

JUDGE   I went to Fuente Ovejuna, sire,
As I was bid. With all my diligence   710
And special care, your orders were obeyed.
But as to finding out who did the crime,
No scrap of writing can I bring in proof
Because, with one accord and single valour,
When to the question racked, they all reply: 715
"Fuente Ovejuna did it" and no more.
Three hundred of them, tortured on the rack
With terrible severity, replied

---

693 A Jewess, sometimes called Hadassah, who saved her people, then refugees in Persia, by marrying the
Persian monarch King Ahasuerus, also known as Xerxes.

No other answer. Little boys of ten
Were stretched yet it was useless. Quite as vain
Were flatteries and promises and tricks.
It is so hard to verify the truth
That you must either hang the whole mad village
Or pardon every man-jack of them all.
All of them now are coming here before you
To certify the truth of all I say.

KING   Let them come in, then.

(*Enter the* TWO MAYORS, FRONDOSO, *all the* WOMEN *and the rest of the villagers*)

LAURENCIA   Are these two the Kings?

FRONDOSO   And very powerful ones!

LAURENCIA   How beautiful
They are, by my faith! Saint Anthony bless them!

QUEEN   Are these the fierce aggressors we were told of?

ESTEBAN   Fuente Ovejuna greets you here, my lady,
Wishing to serve you. The dire cruelty
And most unsufferable tyranny
Of the Comendador caused all these troubles.
A thousand vile insults were showered upon us.
Our farms were robbed, our daughters forced and raped,
Because he was a man who had no pity.

FRONDOSO   So much was this the case that this young farm girl,
By heaven granted for my wife, with whom
I am by far the happiest man on earth,
Even at our wedding feast, on the first night,
Was forced into his house for his own pleasure
And if she hadn't fought with desperation . . .
There is no need to tell you any more.

MENGO   Is it not time I also had a word
If you will give me leave. You'll be astounded
At how they treated me for once defending
A girl of ours. Seeing his pimp and pandar
About to do her violence, I protested—
When that perverted Nero ordered them
To thrash my back into red salmon slices!
My bum still trembles to remember it
And I have had to spend more cash on balm
Than on my farm.

ESTEBAN   All that we wish, my lord,
Is to become your own, whom we acknowledge
As our most natural sovereign. And your arms
Are hoisted on our village hall. Before you
We sue for mercy and yield up ourselves
As pledges of our innocence. Have mercy!

720

725

730

735

740

745

750

755

760

KING Since what has happened is not verified   765
      In writing (and it was a dreadful crime
      Worthy of direst punishment), you're pardoned.
      As to the town I'll keep it in my name
      Until, or if, we find a rightful heir.
FRONDOSO The king spoke grandly as one would expect   770
      From one who such great wonders could effect.
      Good night, discreet spectators, all be friends!
      And with this line FUENTE OVEJUNA ends. (*They all go out*)

1   2   3   4   5   6   7   8   9